Germany

at its best

BY **ROBERT S. KANE**

The World at Its Best Travel Series
BRITAIN AT ITS BEST
FRANCE AT ITS BEST
GERMANY AT ITS BEST
HAWAII AT ITS BEST
ITALY AT ITS BEST
MEXICO AT ITS BEST (in preparation)
SPAIN AT ITS BEST

A to Z World Travel Guides
PARIS A TO Z
LONDON A TO Z
GRAND TOUR A TO Z: THE CAPITALS OF EUROPE
EASTERN EUROPE A TO Z
SOUTH PACIFIC A TO Z
CANADA A TO Z
ASIA A TO Z
SOUTH AMERICA A TO Z
AFRICA A TO Z

Robert S. Kane

Germany
at its best

PASSPORT BOOKS
Trade Imprint of National Textbook Company
Lincolnwood, Illinois U.S.A.

For Anita Diamant Berke

1986 Printing

Published by Passport Books, Trade Imprint of National Textbook Company, 4255 West Touhy Avenue, Lincolnwood, Illinois 60646-1975.

Manufactured in the United States of America. Library of Congress Catalog Card Number: 84-62718

6 7 8 9 0 ML 9 8 7 6 5 4

N
NORTH SEA
DENMARK
BALTIC SEA
NETHERLANDS
BELGIUM
LUXEMBOURG
FRANCE
SWITZERLAND
AUSTRIA
ITALY
YUGOSLAVIA
CZECHOSLOVAKIA
POLAND
GERMANY
WEST GERMANY
EAST GERMANY
Travemünde
Lübeck
Hamburg
Bremen
Hannover
BERLIN
Potsdam
Rhine River
Düsseldorf
Kassel
Aachen
Cologne
Leipzig
Bonn
Marburg
Dresden
Koblenz
Moselle R.
Wiesbaden
Frankfurt
Mainz
Trier
Main River
Bayreuth
Würzburg
Bamberg
Heidelberg
Nuremberg
Dinkelsbühl
Regensburg
Baden-Baden
Stuttgart
BLACK FOREST
Ulm
Augsburg
Freiburg
Munich
GERMAN ALPS
Meersburg
Lindau
Konstanz
Lake Constance
Füssen
Berchtesgaden
Garmisch-Partenkirchen

Contents

Foreword

Germany's New-Found Popularity

Become a hot item in the international travel-destination sweepstakes—and there's no stopping you. I refer to the positively giant strides Germany has made in this respect. The Germany of the early eighties is anything but stereotype-ridden; hardly a case of, say, plump, blond ladies in dirndls, chunky gents in *Lederhosen,* and schmaltzy performances of *The Student Prince.*

The second half of the eighties sees Germany as the second most popular destination of transatlantic air travelers bound for Europe (Britain is No. 1, if you had any doubts) and the sixth most popular destination of American air travelers, worldwide. Not bad for the country that started World War II in Europe—and lost. But it took time.

What happened in the decades since the Federal Republic of Germany began rebuilding after the war is that it initially neglected image in favor of industry. Anxious for approbation—and understandably so—the Germans have wanted us to know that they work hard, maintain a high standard of living, govern themselves democratically, and are ever so well organized.

But no country is visited by holidaymakers because it obeys the Boy Scout law. Today's tourist wants more in a host than thrift, bravery, cleanliness, and reverence. We cross oceans for new—or at least novel—dimensions. And we have come to realize that contemporary Germany stimulates and excites any visitor with at least a modicum of sensitivity. This is a nation of imaginative, creative people. Indeed, no land rebuilt, after World War II damage, with more skill, daring, and taste. The Germans rank near the top—up there with the French, Swiss, and yes the innovative Americans—when it comes to finesse in operating hotels, small and large, country and city. Diversity? This book takes one from the Baltic Sea resort of Travemünde to tiny Mittenwald, tucked below peaks of the German Alps. After-dark diversion? All of the prosaic entertainments, but also superb symphony orchestras, even in the smaller cities, and opera, which is at least as widespread and high-caliber as in Italy.

Architecturally, Germany is the planet's wonder-country. No land of which I am aware has rebuilt monuments of past epochs—Rococo, Baroque, Renaissance, Gothic, and even earlier Romanesque—with more fidelity to the originals. And in no land save Italy are there so many splendid relics of the ancient Roman Empire.

As for art treasures, none of its European neighbors can best Germany when it comes to caches of Old Master paintings and engravings, porcelain and pottery, furniture and furnishings. Nor are the settings for collections—desanctified churches, onetime monasteries, moated castles, and elegant townhouses—in any country more evocative or atmospheric.

Then there are the Germans themselves. They are not, to be sure, as informal as Americans, or as quick to make new friends on first-time bases. We need to give them a little more chance to get to know us than is the case with our countrymen. But that is rarely difficult, given the Teutonic gift for foreign languages, English most especially.

Here, then, are my evaluations of some 40 selected West German destinations, North Sea to the Alps, Lake Constance to the Czech frontier, with a trio from East Germany, as well, to add a bit of spice. (In addition, there is a chapter that treats Berlin, its eastern as well as its western sector.) The order is alphabetical, for ease of use. The content is a consequence, as it has been in my earlier books, of personal involvement—sleeping in (or at least thoroughly inspecting) the hotels, dining in the restaurants, attending the operas, checking out the cafés, wandering through the museums and churches and streets, absorbing vistas from tops of mountains, and shores of lakes. *Gute reise!*

ROBERT S. KANE

1

Germany

A Mini A to Z

ADDRESSES: German National Tourist Office branches in North America are at 747 Third Avenue, New York, New York 10017; 444 South Flower Street, Los Angeles, California 90071; and 47 Fundy, Place Bonaventure, Montreal, Quebec, Canada. Head office: Deutsche Zentrale für Tourismus, Beethovenstrasse 69, Frankfurt, Bundesrepublik Deutschland. Local tourist offices—for help on the spot—are indicated, chapter by chapter.

BALLET: Not to be underestimated; companies are adjuncts of opera troupes in cities, both major and medium-sized. Best are the Stuttgart, Hamburg, Frankfurt, and Munich, along with that of the Komische Oper in East Berlin.

BEER: If our American beer is good—and of course it is—we can thank German brewmasters who came over and founded our breweries. Every German city has its *Brauerei;* from the small enterprises operating out of taverns, to the giants we know from their thriving export trade to our shores. Germans drink beer at the slightest provocation—at any time of the day, even breakfast, by the glass or stein. If you're already a beer-drinker, you'll enjoy sampling German brews; if you're not, chances are you'll become one. Most beers come from Munich and other cities of southern Bavaria, from points throughout the north as well. Most common type, *lager,* is not dissimilar to the beer we drink in America, and it is served chilled. Generally, light-hued species are *helle* and dark beers *dunkel,* with perhaps the best known (it is shipped transatlantic) *Bock* beer, available in the spring.

BREAD: Dark pumpernickel, lighter rye, firm-textured white, rolls both poppy seed and just plain crusty are primarily a breakfast proposition in German hotels and restaurants. Generally, except in the most expensive places, if you want bread at lunch or dinner, you must order it specifically and pay extra. In some simpler places there's an honor system for the basket you may find at your table; at meal's end the waiter or waitress will ask how many pieces you've consumed and charge accordingly.

BREAKFAST: As a rule, a Continental breakfast—bread and rolls, butter and jam, coffee or tea, occasionally fruit juice—is included in room rates, except in luxury-category hotels. Often, this meal is buffet-style, when it may also include cheeses, sausages, even boiled eggs. Room-service breakfasts are available in even the simplest hotels. My favorite spots for the morning meal served in the room: Hotel Vier Jahreszeiten in Hamburg and Brenner's Park Hotel in Baden-Baden. My favorite breakfast buffets: the groaning boards at the Hotel Inter-Continental Hannover and at the Inselhotel in Konstanz overlooking Lake Constance. My favorite hotel coffee shop: that of the Hotel Hilton International Düsseldorf.

CASTLES: In many places throughout the countryside castles have been converted to inns and are frequently but not always good bets. (Inquire about amenities like private baths.) Urban historic houses, many grouped in the "Romantik" chain, along with some venerable restaurants, also have a special flavor. Here, too, quality varies considerably.

CLIMATE: Rarely uncomfortably cold, seldom ever sizzling hot, very often very moist—and, in the north, fogs can be heavier than London's pea soup. Winter average is about the freezing point, 32°F, half that in the Alps; summer averages about 70°F. Frankfurt, as an example, averages mid-30s in winter, mid-50s in spring, mid-60s to low 70s in summer, high 40s to low 50s in fall. Spring and autumn are invariably lovely, with the turning fall leaves quite as brilliant as in, say, Vermont.

CLOTHES: Dress as you would at home in this temperate-zone land where seasonal variations are like those of much of the U.S. Be as informal as you like during the day, unless of course you're a business person meeting with German colleagues. Be dressier—especially for opera, concerts, and better restaurants—in the evening. Take a raincoat and collapsible umbrella with you, regardless of season.

CURRENCY: The Deutschmark (DM), divided into a hundred pfennig (Pf). Your American-dollar travelers checks are exchangeable everywhere. You receive better rates at banks (take your passport along) than from hotel cashiers. Notes come in DM500, 100, 50, 20, 10, and 5; coins in DM5, 2, and 1, and in Pf50, 10, 5, 2, and 1. I find major credit cards—American Express, Diners Club, Visa, MasterCard—valuable to have along: they are widely accepted. As in every country, the trick is to get small change from unsmiling bank and hotel cashiers; persevere.

CUSTOMS: Entering West Gemany—Generally, quick, polite, and easy, with a verbal declaration invariably acceptable. Besides the usual personal gear, you may take in $100 worth of gifts, 400 cigarettes or 100 cigars, as much as half a gallon of spirits or wine.

Returning to the United States—Each individual may bring back $400 worth of purchases, duty-free. That is allowable once every 30 days, provided you've been out of the country at least 48 hours. If you've spent more than $400, you'll be charged a flat 10-percent duty on the next $1000 worth of purchases. Remember, too, that antiques duly certified to be at least 100 years old are admitted duty-free, and do not count as part of your $400 quota; neither do paintings, sculptures, and other works of art of any date, if certified as original: it's advisable to have certification of their authenticity from the seller or some other authority. Also exempt from duty, but as a part of the $400 quota; one quart of liquor. And—this is important—there is no restriction on how much one may bring in beyond the $400 limit, as long as the duty is paid.

DRIVING: Take your own car, rent one in advance of your arrival, or buy one on the scene. Roads—especially the justifiably celebrated *Autobahnen*—are excellent, with restaurants, restrooms, and—at scenic points—observation lookouts, generously provided. Rental firms familiar at home—Avis, Hertz, National—are commonplace in Germany, along with others including Autobansa, Auto Sixt, and Severin. You'll need international car and driver's licenses and insurance; your local travel agent and auto club have details.

ELECTRIC CURRENT: 220 volts, which means that you will need an adapter as well as a set of plugs to fit in German hotel-room walls, so that you can use your American hairblower/dryer and other appliances.

ENGLISH is spoken by many Germans. By and large a visitor will have no trouble communicating with the overwhelming majority of the people in larger hotels, air terminals, better restaurants, and popular cafés. But Germany still is not Holland or Scandinavia where everyone above the age of, say four, is bilingual in English. In smaller restaurants, cafés, bars, hotels, railway station ticket windows, and even on trains (except the crack international ones), foreign languages are not always spoken. Take a little dictionary and phrase book along; I travel with *Just Enough German* published by Passport Books. Your French will occasionally—but only occasionally—help; Spanish even less so.

FRIGOBARS, or mini-bars as they are sometimes called, are found in many hotel rooms, especially first-class and luxury. They're convenient—filled with alcoholic and soft drinks, and sometimes peanuts and crackers. You will be charged for whatever you consume. Such food and drink are very expensive. Better to buy your own while out exploring.

GEOGRAPHY: The Federal Republic of Germany—what we call West Germany—while small in area compared to the United States or Canada, is not, say, Switzerland or Belgium. It runs 560 miles north to south, about half that west to east. And it is packed with variety, with the coasts of two seas (North and Baltic) in the north, a great inland sea (Lake Constance) in the southwest, and the magnificent German Alps on the southern frontier. The river valleys—Rhine (west central) and neighboring Moselle and Main—are beautifully verdant. Bordering countries? Well, there are Denmark to the north; the Netherlands, Belgium, Luxembourg, and France, all on the west; Switzerland and Austria to the south; and Czechoslovakia and East Germany, on the east. The last-mentioned—properly the German Democratic Republic—is much smaller than West Germany; it embraces under 42,000 square miles, compared with the Federal Republic's nearly 96,000 square miles, and has a population hovering at 17 million, compared with West Germany's 62 million. East Germany's touristic ace-in-the-hole is Berlin, located within its territory. In this book you'll find a single chapter on Berlin—covering both western and eastern sectors—and still another chapter on three additional East German cities of interest to visitors.

GEDECK is a word worth knowing when you're in restaurants. It's the German for table d'hôte—a full-course meal, generally a good value.

HAUPTBAHNHOF, which translates as main railway station (*haupt* meaning main and *Bahnhof* railway station), is often more than a point of departure or arrival. Services can include currency exchange, accommodation listings and other tourist information, shops, and restaurants.

HISTORY: Capsulized within the chapters on each city, sufficiently, I hope, to give you a bit of perspective on the area.

ITINERARIES: For an introductory trip, concentrate on the basics—major cities like Frankfurt (where most air travelers arrive), Munich, Hamburg, Cologne, and Berlin. Stay longer and take in enchanting Romantic Road towns like Würzburg, Bamberg, Rothenburg, and Augsburg. Not to mention classics like Heidelberg and Garmisch in the Alps. And why not, on an extended tour or repeat visit, lesser-appreciated but worthy destinations like Düsseldorf, Nuremberg, Regensburg, and Kassel? From all of the major—and many lesser—centers, day-long excursions can be effortless and fun. There's a lot to be seen if you're headquartered in Munich, for example, or Hamburg, or Frankfurt. Package tours? Why not? They're often excellent value. Among the many tour operators with a variety of German packages—and this is but a partial group—are American Express, Brendan Tours, Cortell Holidays, Inc., Cosmos Tours, Europabus, Hapag-Lloyd Travel, Osborne Travel, and TWA Getaway Tours. Sit down and plan it all with a travel agent, making sure the one you select has the experience to qualify him or her for affiliation with the estimable American Society of Travel Agents (ASTA).

KONDITOREI-CAFÉS are good friends to the ambulatory traveler. First, they're handy spots to rest the feet, and second, sources of sustenance—invariably delicious pastries, snacks, sandwiches, and drinks. With easy-to-take tabs.

KARSTADT AND KAUFHOF are not a TV comedy team, but rather the names of two distinct and ubiquitous chains of department stores, with one or the other—more often both—usually part of the core (often a delightful pedestrian shopping zone) of every German city. Prices are generally as good as one finds—often better than in boutiques and smaller specialty shops—for groceries and snacks, wine, candy, clothes, tableware (German porcelains are famous, albeit costly), and kitchen equipment and gadgets. Upon entering, look for information counters with multilingual personnel ready to help foreign visitors. The department stores' full-service restaurants, casual cafés, and lunch counters are good bets for meals and pick-me-ups. And their while-you-wait shoe-repair services can be invaluable.

LÄNDER of Bundesrepublik Deutschland are the states of the Federal Republic of Germany. (The singular is *Land*.) Not counting West Berlin (which has special status vis-à-vis the Federal Republic), there are 10, with their capitals, to wit: *Baden-Württemberg* (Stuttgart), *Bavaria* (*Bayern* in German; Munich), *Bremen* (a city-state), *Hamburg* (also a city-state), *Hessen* (Wiesbaden), *Lower Saxony* (*Niedersachsen* in German; Hannover), *North Rhine-Westphalia* (*Nordrhein-Westfalen* in German; Dusseldorf), *Rhineland-Palatinate* (*Rheinland-Pfalz* in German; Mainz), *Saarland* (Saarbrücken), and *Schleswig-Holstein* (Kiel). For a brief discussion of the operation of the federal government, see the chapter on Bonn, the federal capital.

LUFTHANSA is Germany aloft—an extraordinary global carrier that happily reflects all of the nicest German characteristics; brains, efficiency, good looks, and a sense of style. Lufthansa became long-range soon after it began flying, in 1926— throughout Germany, then Europe, and ere long, Asia. By 1929, it was the first airline to operate a transatlantic service by catapulting flying boats from steamships as they crossed the ocean. The planes were carried aboard ship until they were within flying range of their destination. They were then released into the air to fly ahead with cargoes of airmail. An understandable World War II hiatus preceded accelerated postwar development, with current routes to the South Pacific, South America, and Africa as well as to the Orient and North America. The fleet—of about 100 aircraft—flies some 14 million passengers a year to more than 120 points in 70-plus countries. When I last counted, there were 16 North American gateway cities—majors like New York, Chicago, and Los Angeles, and others, from Anchorage to Mexico City—for transatlantic flights to Frankfurt, Munich, Hamburg, and Düsseldorf in West Germany. I've flown virtually all the score-plus carriers over the Atlantic. None does better with service than Lufthansa. (I am a fan not only of the delicious first-class lunches, dinners, and snacks, but of those eastbound breakfasts that include made-to-order boiled eggs.) Nor is Lufthansa bested by any carrier in the operation of economy class, or for that matter, its increasingly popular Business Class. Lufthansa has transatlantic company; other carriers flying North

America to Germany include Capitol, Delta, Northwest Orient, Pakistan International, TWA, and Pan American. Air France, British Airways, and Pan American are the three Allied Powers' carriers allowed to fly into and out of West Berlin.

MONTAGS GESCHLOSSEN means Closed Mondays, and it applies almost universally to German museums, historic houses, palaces, and the like. Plan accordingly. Check locally.

OPEN HOURS: Generally sensible, with two major exceptions: not even big department stores have even a single open-evening, and Saturday afternoons are pretty much out for shopping. Shops are mostly open Monday through Friday, 9 a.m. to 6 or 6:30 p.m., and Saturdays until noon or 2 p.m. However, expect many to be closed for lunch, as late as 3 p.m., in small towns and villages. Banks are open 9 a.m. until noon and 2-4 p.m., Monday through Friday, but their branches at airports, along with *Wechselstuben* (private change-making companies) keep later hours, usually daily until 10 p.m.

OPERA is as much a national pastime in Germany as in Italy—which is saying a lot. And not only the major cities—like Munich and Hamburg (the top two), Berlin (East as well as West), and Frankfurt—have companies. Virtually every medium-sized city does, too. The government gives generous subsidies, so that sets, costumes, musical accompaniment, and—very often—singers are high-caliber. Almost always, foreign-language operas are translated into—and sung in—German.

PASSPORTS: Necessary for admission into Germany and for presentation to United States Immigration, upon your return. Apply at United States Department of State Passport Offices in a dozen-plus major cities (look under U.S. Government in the telephone directory) or—in smaller cities—at the office of the clerk of a federal court; and, so long as the practice continues, at certain post offices. Allow three to four weeks, especially for a first passport (valid ten years). You'll need a pair of two-inch-square photos, and a birth certificate.

There's a $42 fee for first passports; renewals—are cheaper. If you're in a hurry when you apply, say so; Uncle Sam will usually try to expedite. Upon receipt of this valuable document, sign your name where indicated, fill in the address of next of kin, and keep it with you—*not packed in a suitcase*—as you travel. In case of loss, contact local police, nearest U.S. Embassy or Consulate, or Passport Office, Department of State, Washington, D.C.

RATES: On the pages following, carefully selected hotels (which I've actually stayed in or have thoroughly inspected) and restaurants (where I've eaten) are categorized as *Luxury, First Class,* and *Moderate.* These terms translate pretty much into what they would mean in the U.S. The value judgments are my own; I've listed them in an order that reflects my own degree of enthusiasm—favorite spots first.

RESTAURANTS run a wide gamut. Those I've chosen (all of which are ones I like) are listed in *Luxury, First Class,* and *Moderate* price ranges. For top-rank places it's advisable to book in advance; do it yourself or ask your hotel concierge to do it for you. Less elaborate eateries are often casual to the point where strangers are expected to share tables with strangers—something foreign visitors often find not especially to their liking. As in England, the best meal is invariably breakfast (one of the alphabetical listings in this chapter). Afternoon cake and coffee replace the Britons' afternoon tea, and for many Germans this—quite sensibly—is the only time of day when sweets are consumed. (Desserts, more often than not, are skipped by the natives at restaurant lunches and dinners.) Best things to eat, aside from breakfasts and baked goods (including bread) are sausages (see below), soups, fresh and simply grilled fish (especially sole), one-dish casserole-type or stew specialties *(Pichelsteiner Fleisch* — a Bavarian favorite; *Hühnereintopf mit Mehlklössen*—chicken-and-dumpling variations on the theme of Hungarian goulash), and for meat dishes: pork *(Kasseler Rippchen*—smoked pork loin—is delicious), ham, schnitzels—veal breaded in various ways. Lamb is served in a variety of ways; beef is at best when it appears as the pot-roast masterwork, *Sauerbraten.* Transatlantic visitors tend to miss U.S.-type steaks. (Not that hamburgers are scarce; McDonald's outlets are everywhere.) Potatoes and cabbage (especially red and, of course, sauerkraut) are the most successfully cooked vegetables, and so is white asparagus, when in season, usually served with melted butter or hollandaise sauce, as a separate course. Salads tend to be concoctions of all manner of things, often—and disconcertingly—including beets. They tend to be dressed in sweetish sauces unless one firmly specifies oil and vinegar, begging—usually without luck—for a plain, simple, unencumbered green. No, the German cuisine is not a great cuisine. One has only to look about and observe the astonishing popularity of fast-food operations, in contrast with their relative sparsity in, say, France or Italy to realize why they've taken hold so quickly.

Still, there is no denying that the very good restaurants are very good indeed. Cities of any size have Italian restaurants—and often pizza stands—operated by real live Italians—and I've yet to find a poor one. The same goes for French restaurants, though they are not always entirely French-staffed. Spaniards are on scene as restauranteurs, too—invariably skilled. Chinese restaurants are frequently come across—and reliable. Yugoslavs have opened up restaurants throughout the country, but they're infinitely better on their own home ground. Hotels operated by American chains, like Hilton International and Inter-Continental, often import beef from the United States and prepare it Yank-style, as much for devoted German as for visiting U. S. clientele. Railway-station shops, supermarkets, and the excellent self-service grocery sections of department stores are good places to pick up snack foods for consumption in the course of train journeys, or with cocktails in one's hotel room. For details on beverages, look at the entries on *BEER* and *WINE*. As for coffee, it's mostly excellent.

RHINE AND MOSELLE RIVER CRUISES: A joy. An utter joy. Book at least a few days aboard one of the eight steamers of the Köln-Düsseldorfer German Rhine Line (KD for short) through your travel agent. The ships are quite as modern and luxurious—if smaller—as those on which you've cruised the Caribbean and Mediterranean. Cabins all have private baths and picture windows. Restaurants are luxury-category, with perfectly delicious food and wide choices, bar-lounges with dancing and entertainment, crews smiling and multilingual. You've a wide choice in cruise lengths, from four countries (Holland, Germany, France, Switzerland) in five days, to a couple of days within Germany, going, say, from Cologne to Mainz, to relive the schmaltzy operettas as you view the legendary castles, vineyards, and villages on the Rhine's handsomest stretch. Worth noting, too, are KD Line's newest itineraries, out of Koblenz (at the junction of the Rhine and the Moselle rivers, and the subject of Chapter 22, in this book) enroute along the Moselle to Trier (Chapter 37) and vice-versa, on two- and three-day cruises. KD Line's U.S. headquarters are at 170 Hamilton Avenue, White Plains, NY 10601.

ROMANTIC ROAD TOURS: The route from Würzburg to Munich is known as the Romantic Road. Buses make this trip with stops at such historic treasure-towns as Rothenburg, Bamberg, and Dinkelsbühl—April through October—with English-speaking guides aboard. But you may, of course, cover this area by train or car—your own or rented. You'll love going at your own speed. Principal towns along the route are covered in individual chapters.

SAUSAGES: Wurst stands are a familiar sight on principal squares of German towns. Happiness in Germany is a grilled wurst with a bun and dab of mustard. There are several hundred species; every region has its own variations. To get an idea of the variety, take time out to have a look inside when you pass a *wurstladen,* or sausage store. For snacking as you travel, concentrate on *weisswurst,* or white sausage, mostly of veal; *knockwurst* and *bauernwurst,* or farmer's sausage—both variations of the Frankfurt-origin *frankfurter,* usually skinnier in Germany than is the case with U.S. descendants. Which brings us to what has to be the universal favorite—*bratwurst,* born and bred in Nuremburg, but to be found Germany-wide, made mostly of deliciously spiced and seasoned pork—and positively habit-forming.

SWIMMING POOLS are an agreeable surprise in many *First Class* and *Luxury* hotels. Don't be surprised to see German fellow guests, clad in terry robes, going to and from the *Schwimmbad* as you're en route to breakfast. If you like, pack a swimsuit and plunge in, too; the facilities usually include saunas and gyms.

SYMPHONY ORCHESTRAS are a commonplace in cities from major (like Berlin) to relatively minor (like Bamberg), with quality usually extraordinary, and halls handsome (some boldly modern, others old and mellow). Still additional symphonies are sponsored by broadcasting networks.

TIPS: Except for the leech-like women who stand guard over public washrooms, happily not as ubiquitous as in the past, service personnel are not generally tip-happy. In restaurants and cafes, service is usually included in the bill; you need only round out the amount you pay the waiter, unless you're in a luxury place where you've had exceptional treatment, in which case tip more. Tip not at all when sitting directly at a bar. Tip taxi drivers, beauticians, and barbers 10 percent, hotel baggage porters Pf50 to a Mark per bag, theater-opera-concert ushers not at all (save the cost of the program, which is usually exorbitant), hotel concierges and chambermaids only if they've rendered special service.

VISAS: None for the Federal Republic (West Germany, including West Berlin), but necessary for East Germany, as I explain in the chapter on that country.

WINES: The most difficult to understand of the world's wines. They're mostly white (with a minority of this group *trocken*, or dry), and from two principal areas—Rhine (in tall brown bottles) and Moselle (in tall green bottles). All told, they're produced in 11 regions; *Baden* (the most southerly), *Mittelrhein* (below the crags of the Rhine River's castles), *Rheinpfalz* (west of the Rhine and north of France's Strasbourg), *Württemberg* (in—and I mean heart-of-town—and about Stuttgart), *Franken* (Franconia, in English—south of the Main River near Würzburg, with the highest proportion of dry whites, and always in squat, jug-shaped bottles), *Rheinhessen* (centered around Mainz), *Mosel-Saar-Ruwer* (with those from the Moselle Valley most familiar), *Rheingau* (Riesling from north of the Rhine around Wiesbaden), *Hessische Bergstrasse* (the tiniest region, around Bensheim), *Nahe* (named for a Rhine tributary flowing south from Mainz), and *Ahr* (on still another Rhine tributary, southeast of Bonn, and with good dry reds).

To remember when looking at labels: there are three categories of German wine, regardless of district; *Tafelwein*—table, the most ordinary; *Qualitätswein*—a better category; and *Qualitätswein mit Prädikat,* the very top rung. This last category has five *additional* grades, each connoting a distinct quality, in part determined by the time at which the grapes are harvested, and, therefore, their natural sugar content, or sweetness. In ascending order of sweetness, these are *Kabinett, Spätlese, Auslese, Beerenauslese,* and—the sweetest— *Trockenbeerenauslese.* German white wines, among the world's greatest, require study and orientation. Their sweetness cannot be lightly dismissed. Hugh Johnson puts it succinctly and well in his authoritative *Pocket Encyclopedia of Wine* (Simon & Schuster, 1977): "The secret . . . is the balance of sweetness against fruity acidity. A great vintage in Germany is one in which the autumn weather allows the late-ripening Riesling—the grape which makes virtually all the great German wines—to develop a high sugar content. What is so special about the Riesling is that as it ripens it also develops a concentration of fragrant acids and essences to balance the increasing sweetness. The resulting wine is tense and thrilling with this sugar/acid balance."

Infinitely less complicated are the German Champagne-type wines—*sekt* is the term for this category in the German language. And don't neglect them, by any means. When they are *trocken,* or dry, they can be delicious. The two top brands are Deinhard, out of Koblenz, and Henkell, with headquarters in Wiesbaden.

ZIMMER FREI translates as "Room Available." You'll see signs with this legend hanging from private homes, Germany-wide; they're the German counterparts of France's pensions and

Britain's bed-and-breakfast places. *Quality varies,* but can be very good—even to rooms with their own baths. Breakfast is invariably included in room rates—which are reasonable, and a sensible means to keep travel costs down. Local tourist offices—their addresses are at the end of each chapter following—can make specific recommendations and help with booking.

ZUG is the German for train. And no European country has an easier-to-use, better-equipped rail system. You can go virtually everywhere and anywhere in Germany by train; I speak from experience. This extraordinary network embraces 18,000 miles of track, with trains connecting the major cities—the Inter-City network—the most luxurious, the crack *Rheingold* most especially. Regardless of run, there are always two classes, First and Second, with even the latter spotless and comfortable, albeit less spacious. Trains of any substantial size carry full-service restaurant cars; in addition, there are ambultory vendors of snacks and beverages. If you're going to be traveling about for more than a week, buy—from your North American travel agent at a real bargain rate—or at a German Federal Railroad office on this side of the Atlantic—a Germanrail Card. (If you'll be traveling by train elsewhere in Europe, consider another excellent bargain—Eurailpass—which allows for limitless travel in 16 countries, including Germany, of course, for periods of 9 days upward, in first class.) *Further Information:* The German Federal Railroad (in German, *Deutsche Bundesbahn,* abbreviated "DB"), has these North American offices: 747 Third Avenue, New York, NY 10017; 625 Statler Office Building, Boston, MA 02116; 104 South Michigan Avenue, Chicago, IL 60603; 800 East Girard Avenue, Denver, CO 80231; 1121 Walker Street, Houston, TX 77002; 1 Hallidie Plaza, San Francisco, CA 94102; 520 Broadway, Santa Monica, CA 90401; and 1290 Bay Street, Toronto, Ontario, Canada M5R 2C3. *Tote note:* Station porters are an extinct species; supermarket-type baggage carts take, their place, so keep your eyes peeled for them en route to and from your train, and when you see one not in use, make a beeline for it—or someone else will beat you to it!

2

Aachen

A Celebration of Charlemagne

BACKGROUND BRIEFING

Aachen is oddball.

Very, very old. Located where three highly developed nations—Belgium, the Netherlands, and Germany—converge. Usually, when a town has a couple of thousand years behind it and the benefit of cultural crosscurrents of not one but a pair of next-door-neighbor countries, it achieves not only sophistication but a light touch.

Not so, Aachen. Still, if its heavy hand and apparent lack of ease with strangers disappoints—there is nothing like the conviviality of, say, Belgium's Liège, to name but one nearby city—it more than fulfills the promise of its past.

This is, after all, Charlemagne's town. Romans settled it as *Aquae Grani*—the basis of the present name—at the time of Christ, drawn by the same thermal springs that feed its still-used curative spa. The Romans were succeeded by native peoples, precursors of today's Germans, and the town developed to the point that—by the birth of Charlemagne (presumably in Aachen) in the mid-eighth century—its name began to appear in written records. And none too soon. Charlemagne—*Karl der Grosse* in German—was to put it on the map. Succeeding his father, Pippin the Short, as king of the Carolingian Empire, he made Aachen his northern base, building its extant cathedral, and otherwise enriching it. All the while, this multitalented man—he lived centuries before the highly touted men of the Renaissance were to master a gamut of disciplines—went about his business as soldier-conqueror. He expanded his realm beyond what is now France into Spain; he vanquished the Saxons (their land is now a part of East Germany), the Slavs, and the Bavarians. He came to the defense of Pope Leo III, defending the pontiff from hostile Romans.

As a reward he was crowned Emperor by Pope Leo. The year was 800 and the coronation was the first official act in the formal creation of what was to be styled—after Charlemagne's death—the Holy Roman Empire, which lasted all the way into the early nineteenth century.

But Charlemagne did more. He refined and sophisticated the machinery of administration and government. He fostered a well-educated clergy. He recognized the value of morale, and kept in touch—through personal travel—with lesser officials. He met with legislative councils whose formation he had encouraged. He appreciated the economics of foreign trade and worked to enlarge it. He made of his Aachen palace a stunning cultural center and there he himself crowned his son Ludwig I as his co-ruler and successor.

Charlemagne—although polygamous—was beatified after his death, and Aachen was the coronation site for most German emperors and kings well into the mid-sixteenth century. With the eminence gained during Charlemagne's reign, Aachen could not help but thrive. (The Coronations were renowned enough, in their own time, to draw Albrecht Dürer all the way from Nuremberg to Karl V's ceremonies in 1520; the artist not only sketched the event, he wrote enthusiastically about it, as well.)

Aachen remained a Free Imperial City—virtually self-governing—until the French occupied it at the end of the eighteenth century, later annexing it before an 1815 transfer to Prussia. Still another occupation followed World War I—the Allies remained from 1918 through 1930. Aachen fared even worse in World War II; it sustained 75 air raids that destroyed some two-thirds of its territory, on which two of the war's battles were fought, with compulsory civilian evacuation a consequence. It was the first major German city to fall. But rebuilding and recovery were achieved with fortitude and skill. Enough of the old remains in this largely rebuilt, essentially somber city for it to be taken almost as seriously as it takes itself.

ON SCENE

Lay of the Land: The historic core is not overly large. The Hauptbahnhof is on the southern fringe, facing Römerstrasse. By means of that thoroughfare, and Franzstrasse, into which it leads, one approaches the cathedral, the adjacent pedestrians-only shopping streets—especially Kramerstrasse—and, to the north, Marktplatz, with the town hall. Much—but by no means all—of what one wants to see is in this vicinity. The Stadtgarten-Kurgarten park with a casino and a thermal-bath resort is a 10-minute drive to the northeast. Additional thermal baths—Heilbad Aachen and Kaiserbad—are south of the center, as is the opera, and a major museum is to the east.

Dom (Münsterplatz): At first glance, the cathedral is neither as large nor as grand as one had expected. But stay a bit. There are facets of true beauty, not to mention historical fascination. Charlemagne himself had the central section of the interior built. It is a kind of church-within-a-church, a three-tier octagon under its own dome, which is a Romanesque masterwork. The high altar is newer—richly detailed Gothic with elongated windows lighting it from the rear. There are half a dozen art-filled chapels. You must take a guided tour (choose the first available, even if it's not in a language you know, if you're pressed for time). Upstairs, you'll find Aachen at its most thrilling: Charlemagne's very own marble throne.

Domschatz—the Cathedral treasury—is outstanding enough as a museum to rate this designation of its own. There are mostly medieval objects here—a golden bust of Charlemagne from the mid-fourteenth century, sculpted Apostles, jeweled crosses, fragments of sumptuous clerical vestments, chalices and reliquaries, works in ivory and enamel, paintings, and illuminated manuscripts.

Suermondt Museum (Wilhelmstrasse) houses what may well be the finest concentration of medieval sculpture in any German museum, with the exceptions of the Bayerisches National-museum in Munich and the fine Germanisches National-museum in Nuremberg. You walk through room after room filled with utterly beautiful painted-wood Madonnas, altars, and carved saints, not to mention likenesses of Jesus as child and adult. Here, too, there are tapestries, stained glass, and paintings. These last fall into three groups, basically—German medieval and early Renaissance with some Flemish greats like Dierick Bouts and Joos van Cleve; a cluster of baroque masters (Dutchmen like Cuyp, Brouwer, Vermeer, Snyders, van Ruysdael, Hals); and Flemings like Rubens and Van Dyck. But there are moderns too—Germans such as Max Beckmann, through Picasso on to Roy Lichtenstein of the New York school.

Couven Museum (Hühnermarkt) is a lovely Aachen surprise: a rococo monument that has absolutely nothing to do with Charlemagne. This is a beautifully restored furnished-in-period house. (The Couven of the title was an eighteenth-century designer-architect, not the occupant.) The showplace room—candlelit Chamber-music concerts take place in it—is the chandelier-hung Grosser Saal. But it's only one of many rooms full of eighteenth-century furniture, textiles, paintings, and china-filled cabinets. A bonus is a spectacular tile-decorated kitchen.

Rathaus (Marktplatz): Aachen's Town Hall—on the site of Charlemagne's palace—is at its best from without. The carved-stone fourteenth-century façade is more visually exciting than the ceremonial spaces within, especially the rather corny Imperial Hall, where the big attraction is replicas of guess who's crown jewels.

Spielcasino Bad Aachen (Kurpark) is still another colonnaded building out of the last century, but with an interior so remarkable—it is radically contemporary in style—that you should pop in some evening. Make sure you have your passport for presentation to the surly admissions-inspectors who have all of the charm of prison guards in the course of their interrogation, as they skillfully size up your honesty. The cafe and restaurant are no friendlier; nor is the fare, in my opinion, especially commendable. It's the fuchsia-and-white decor—with ingenious stalactite-like lighting fixtures—that you want to see.

SETTLING IN

Parkhotel Quellenhof (Monheimsallee in the Kurpark) is every inch the grand hotel—traditional-style, well appointed, with a thermal pool (gratis for house guests), and a complete thermal spa as well. Location is away from the center in the Kurpark next to the Casino. The 140 rooms and suites are attractive, and the restaurant is this house at its best. (More about it later.) Still, the Quellenhof doesn't really work—too somber, too unsmiling, with a staff attitude toward guests bordering on the suspicious. A Steigenberger hotel. *Luxury.*

Aquis Grana Hotel (Büchel-Buchkremerstrasse) is relatively recent, full-facility, even to an indoor pool, with 90 functional rooms, and the advantage of a central situation. *First Class.*

Novotel (Joseph-von-Görres Strasse) is the farthest away of the majors from the core of town, in its own garden near Europaplatz, due east of the Spielcasino complex. There are 121 well-equipped rooms, restaurant and bar-lounge. *First Class.*

Central Hotel (Römerstrasse 7) is just opposite the Hauptbahnhof and though unprepossessing from without, it brightens up within. Most of the 40 nicely updated rooms have private baths. Small restaurant, bar. *Moderate.*

Hotel Drei Könige (Marktplatz, corner of Büchel) is a welcome bit of Aachen cheer and perfectly central, in the shadow of the Rathaus. There are less than 20 rooms, but most have private baths, and they've all been recently refurbished, the walls having been finished in tasteful papers. Convenient restaurant. *Moderate.*

Hotel Danica (Franzstrasse 36) has the advantage of a good situation—on a street connecting the Hauptbahnhof with the heart of town. Smallish—26 rooms, a good number with bath—and functional. Breakfast only. *Moderate.*

Hotel Günther Krott (Wirichsbongardstrasse 16)—after you negotiate its multisyllabic street location—comes through as intimate and agreeable with a score of cheery rooms, most equipped with private facilities; restaurant. *Moderate.*

DAILY BREAD

Ratskeller (Rathaus, Marktplatz): If you're going to have one festive Aachen meal, select this smartly brick-walled Town Hall restaurant; specialties are stick-to-the-ribs roast goose, venison, ham steak—with especially good desserts. A distinguished wine list. Terrace. *First Class.*

Parkhotel Quellenhof Restaurant (Monheimsallee in the Kurpark) is a good choice for a fairly pricey meal in a handsome traditional setting on an evening when you might want to try your luck at the next-door Casino, over whose own restaurants I much prefer it. The fare is a compromise between German and international—interesting appetizers, a trolley full of tasty sweets, with the entrees, in between, ranging from schnitzels to steaks. Park-view terrace. *Luxury.*

Restaurant Elisenbrunnen (Friedrich-Wilhelm Platz) is the ideal way to take in the aesthetics of Elisenbrunnen, an early nineteenth-century thermal complex—severe neoclassic, dominated by a central dome—that was the core of the Bad Aachen spa when it was fashionable. The restaurant is quite as classic in style as the architecture, but it makes departures, as in Chili Con Carne Mexikanisches Gericht and Kalbssteak Florida. Terrace. *First Class/Luxury.*

Zum Schiffgen (Hühnermarkt 21) is smack in the historic center, on the square next to Marktplatz. German favorites (the daily specials are good value) and a terrace. *Moderate/First Class.*

Cafe-Konditorei Albert (Marktplatz 11) is for coffee and cake (try *Printen*—the town's gingerbread-like specialty), a snack, a light lunch, and a welcome respite. Central. *Moderate.*

SOUND OF MUSIC

Stadttheater Aachen (Theaterstrasse) is mock-classic—with a colonnaded portico—out of the early nineteenth century and smartly refurbished. Here you can see the local opera troupe, along with operettas, plays, and visiting attractions. Ask your hotel concierge what's on, not only at the Stadttheater but at other locations—he'll have schedules for performances of the Aachen Symphony and choral groups.

INCIDENTAL INTELLIGENCE

Aachen is closer to cities like Liège, Belgium, and Maastricht, Holland, than to any major German cities, with Cologne the nearest—about 40 miles. Further information: Verkehrsverein Aachen, the city tourist office, Bahnhofplatz 4, and on highways at the checkpoints linking Aachen with Belgium (at Lichtenbusch), and with Holland (at Vetschau).

3

Augsburg

Of Romans and the Renaissance

BACKGROUND BRIEFING

Still bearing the name of the Roman emperor who founded it as a military garrison 14 years before Christ was born, Augsburg, if not an august city, is a proud one. One has the feeling, walking along elegant Maximilianstrasse, that it was happier in earlier centuries—as a seat of considerably more political power and economic clout than it has now.

Augsburg's Golden Age embraced the Renaissance—a time when a pair of banking families, Fuggers and Welsers, financed Holy Roman Emperors, sponsored artists like Dürer and Holbein, and sparked the economic growth of a dynamic city.

Augsburg takes pride in the substance of its past. Its history includes more than emperors and artists. Luther came in 1530 to endorse the Augsburg Confession—the basic creed of Protestantism. The princes of the Holy Roman Empire came in 1555 to hammer out the Peace of Augsburg, a settlement of Catholic-Protestant issues arising from the Reformation.

A Free Imperial City during the long centuries of the Holy Roman Empire, Augsburg, like so many of its neighbors, became a part of the kingdom of Bavaria in the early nineteenth century. By that time the power of the Fuggers and Welsers had long since been dissipated. But if they are gone, they are not forgotten. Dürer painted the most illustrious Fugger—Jacob the Rich—and the portrait has remained on home base, in Augsburg, still the star of the gallery in which it hangs.

The Fuggers' money came from shipping, real estate, and silver, which they not only mined but traded. Jacob the Rich loaned huge sums to Emperor Maximilian (for whom the city's Maximilianstrasse is named), and helped bring about the designation of Charles V as emperor, by means of bribes to the prince-electors. The Fuggers became, as a consequence, the richest family in Europe, with political rights over their lands, and the right to coin their own currency.

They were not greedy. Their Augsburg largesse was not only for the arts but for the poor: they established the world's first low-income-housing project, which is still operating. The Welsers were not farsighted enough to commission a Dürer portrait, so they have not achieved the immortality of the Fuggers. Their leading light, one Bartholomäus Welser, was paid a debt owed him by Emperor Charles V in real estate instead of cash. What made the transaction memorable is that the land was not German but South American; virtually the whole of Venezuela. Herr Welser took his territory seriously, and sent men over to explore it. Gaining a substantial chunk of the New World proved not to be all that easy. There was a court trial over the matter that lasted a decade and a half, and in 1556 the Welser territory was returned to Charles V.

Matters of such global consequence are not a part of the contemporary Augsburg scene. What is more, because of its proximity to Munich—and that city's stiff competition—Augsburg gets relatively short shrift from tourists. Deplorable. The architectural and artistic heritage of the emperors and the bankers is not to be underestimated.

ON SCENE

Lay of the Land: Augsburg is a good-sized city; even its historic core is large, and has a number of top-rank destinations. If you want to become really acquainted with the city, give yourself time. The core, an irregular oblong, runs north-south. From the Bahnhof one proceeds eastward along Bahnhofstrasse to Königplatz and Bürgermeister-Fischer-Strasse a few blocks to

Maximilianstrasse, which runs perpendicular to it. This is Augsburg's grand boulevard—properly wide, punctuated by graceful fountains, lined by gabled and frescoed Renaissance mansions.

The main pedestrian shopping street—perky Annastrasse—is an offshoot of Maximilianstrasse. The two intersect where the towers of the landmark Rathaus, or Town Hall, and the playing waters of the sixteenth-century Augustus Fountain cross it. You're now in the heart of visitor Augsburg, with destinations like St. Annakirche, the Cathedral, and the Opera to the north, and still more points of special interest—museums and the *platz* beneath an ancient gate (Rotestor) to the south.

Dom (Hoher Weg): Augsburg's august cathedral, northernmost of our destinations, is an appropriate introduction to the city. For a millennium, it has dominated the cityscape with a pair of Romanesque spires, and an unusual Gothic apse, supported by flying buttresses. Note the bronze panels of the door at the south entrance. Within, you will be especially drawn to altar paintings by native son Hans Holbein the Elder. Across the broad court out back—there are Mozart concerts in summer—is the onetime bishop's palace where delegates—including Luther—hammered out the Augsburg Confession in 1530.

Heilige-Kreuz-Kirchen (Ludwigstrasse) are an oddity, and not the only such in the city—adjacent, similarly named churches, one Catholic, the other Protestant. The former, not surprisingly, is the elder, originally Gothic, but with baroque touches, not the least of which is a luminous Rubens *Assumption*. The neighboring Protestant Holy Cross Church went up in the seventeenth century, with paintings of that era, and a later—rococo—pulpit. Quite a pair.

Rathaus (Rathausplatz): The Town Hall is no less original than the pair of Holy Cross churches. It's a skyscraper out of the early seventeenth century with a bold multistory façade surmounted by a steeply gabled roof, a pair of spires adding church-like accents. Make a note of the architect; Elias Holl. His imagination was responsible for a good deal of late Renaissance Augsburg—including the arsenal and cloth warehouse.

St. Annakirche (Annastrasse) can be combined with a stroll on the main pedestrian-shopping street. The church, Protestant since the Reformation, was the core of a Carmelite monastery, where Luther had been a guest. Indeed, he's the subject of a Holbein portrait, a memorial of his visit. There are, as well, a pair of paintings by the elder Cranach, and a pair of chapels—one in memory of a rich goldsmith, the other dedicated to the even richer Fugger family.

St. Moritzkirche (Maximilianstrasse): As if to counteract the Swiss resort town with which his name is usually associated, Augsburg has a church named for St. Moritz—surely one of the few extant. This one's a felicitous Romanesque-Gothic-post-World War II meld that hangs together surprisingly well.

Fuggerhaus (Maximilianstrasse) went up in the early sixteenth century to house the most famed of the Fuggers, Jacob the Rich. Have a look at the courtyards.

Fuggerei (Kappeneck): Jacob Fugger lived in Fuggerhaus (above). With Fuggerei, he assuaged his conscience by building what the world has come to recognize as the first low-rent housing project. The catch was that to live in it you really had to be poor—and also take an oath that you would regularly remember Rich Jacob in your prayers. Hardly an inconvenience, given the rent, which continues to this day at about a dollar a year. There are three-score-plus handsomely gabled houses on the eight neat streets of the complex.

Schaezlerpalais (Maximilianstrasse) wants some of your time and understanding, because it can be confusing. It is, to start, a stunning rococo palace, with its most sparkling interior feature a ballroom—the *Festsaal*—that has, happily, been preserved in all of its late-eighteenth-century brilliance: gilded stuccowork complemented by gilt-framed mirrors and paintings—along with gilded sconces—on the cream-colored walls, a patterned parquet floor, and over it all a great oval of a fresco embedded in the ceiling. Shall we dance? Next, appropriately enough, comes the *Deutsche Barock-Galerie*—a series of chambers filled with baroque and rococo art—a Tischbein portrait of a blue-gowned eighteenth-century blonde; a pudgy sculpted angel from the same era, a miniature dolls'-house kitchen—gadget-filled. Then move along to an attached structure, the onetime St. Catherine's Monastery that now sees service as Augsburg's ranking museum, *Städtische Kunstsammlungen*. What you most want to see here is Albrecht Dürer's famous portrait of Jacob Fugger the Rich—black-robed, red-capped, and from his expression, obviously determined. Other Old Masters are on view here, too, including Rembrandt (a youthful self-portrait) and Augsburg-born Holbein the Elder.

Römisches Museum (Bäckergasse) is a two-for-one show. First is the setting—a onetime Dominican church of considerable Renaissance/baroque splendor. Desanctified, it has had its pews removed, its Corinthian columns, stuccoed ceiling, and soaring walls whitewashed. And—filled with souvenirs of Roman Augsburg busts, mosaics, weapons, and models of ancient buildings—it is a museum that combines style and content with art and artisanship.

Maximilian Museum (Annastrasse) occupies a complex that includes the Renaissance mansion that once housed Augsburg's second family of wealth—the very same Welsers who, for a brief period, owned what is now Venezuela. This museum tells the Augsburg story through objects saved over the course of many centuries, which are displayed with a sense of drama and history: intricately plotted maps, documents with their seals as impressive as their signatures, jewels and baubles by local smiths, sculpture and furniture, tools and trinkets. Fun.

St. Ulrichkirchen (foot of Maximilianstrasse) are another pair of same-name churches, one earlier Catholic, the other later Protestant. They're baroque remodelings of what was originally a fifteenth-century monastery. Beautiful, singly or in tandem.

SETTLING IN

Hotel Drei Mohren (Maximilianstrasse 40) was named the Three Moors when it opened in 1723 on the site of a sixteenth-century

Fugger palace. World War II leveled the rococo Drei Mohren, whose guests had included Mozart and Goethe, but its replacement, in understated 1950s modern, is a pleasure, from the comfortable guest rooms to the public spaces, including a top-rank restaurant, bar-lounge, and warm-weather terrace-café. Location is perfect. A Steigenberger hotel. *Luxury.*

Dom-Hotel (Frauentorstrasse 8) is nicely located, just north of the cathedral whose name it takes. There are nearly two score rooms, a good number with private baths, and a restaurant. *Moderate.*

Hotel Riegele (Viktoriastrasse 4) is a near-neighbor of the Bahnhof, lying between it and the core of town. Thirty-plus rooms, a number with baths. Restaurant. *Moderate.*

Hotel Post (Fuggerstrasse 4), on the street named for the great Renaissance family, is centrally situated, near St. Annakirche. There are more than 60 neat rooms, a number with private baths. Breakfast only. *Moderate.*

Holiday Inn (Wittelsbacher Park) has nearly 200 rooms with baths, a rooftop restaurant with super views. But you pay a price: An away-from-the-center location near the Kongresshalle convention center southwest of the Bahnhof. *Luxury.*

DAILY BREAD

Ratskeller (Rathaus, Rathausplatz) is a traditional-style restaurant in the basement of the landmark Town Hall. Fare is at once as hearty and as tasty as it is well priced. *Moderate/First Class.*

Fuggerkeller (Maximilianstrasse 38) is a next-door neighbor of the Hotel Drei Mohren, which operates it. Setting is ancient, old-school; food delicious. *First Class.*

7-Schwaben-Stuben (Bürgermeister-Fischer-Strasse 12) is a long-on-the-scene favorite with Augsburgers, heart of town, with regional specialties. *Moderate/First Class.*

Café Drexl (Maximilianstrasse 18) is a well-located, rest-the-feet spot for coffee, cake, a snack, or lunch. *Moderate.*

SOUND OF MUSIC

Stadttheater (Kennedyplatz) is posh: classic-style, late nineteenth-century, central—and for opera and operetta, as well as plays.

INCIDENTAL INTELLIGENCE

Ideally, this underappreciated city—often visited in connection with Romantic Road bus tours—should be given at least an overnight stay, preferably the better part of two days. If you can't manage that, come on a day trip from your Munich base, departing on an early train, staying the day, and returning that evening to Munich. *Further information:* Verkehrsverein Augsburg—the tourist board—Haldestrasse 12 (headquarters) and Bahnhofstrasse 7.

4

Baden-Baden

The Casino and the Cure

BACKGROUND BRIEFING

Well, there are Badens and there are Badens. But there is only one Baden-Baden.

And it is, perhaps, just as well. One doubts the planet could absorb more than one genuine article. For Baden-Baden is heady stuff.

Always has been. The Romans, with their uncanny thermal-spring-detecting apparatus, came upon this lush and lovely valley at the northern fringe of the Black Forest. Their mission was military—it was an army garrison that they set up—but they gravitated as ducks to water toward the mineral springs, and named their settlement *Aqua Aurelia.*

The very same Caracalla—whose great baths in Rome know contemporary fame as the setting for summer opera—was the last emperor to reign over Aqua Aurelia. Local German people—the Alemanni—took over in the third century, with the Christian Franks following. They gave the town its first castle and, more important, its current name. That was during the early Middle Ages.

Eventually, the Franks' palace was preempted by the upward-mobile Dukes of Zähringer, the very same who ruled Freiburg, at the southern fringe of the Black Forest (and the subject of a chapter in this book). Before long, the Zähringers had styled themselves margraves of Baden, settling into a castle atop a growing town that, by the late fifteenth century, had become a recognized watering place.

Like so much of Germany, Baden-Baden took a beating during the seventeenth-century Thirty Years' War. When England's Bath was enjoying its Golden Era in the eighteenth century, Baden-Baden was in the process of being rebuilt; its greatest epoch was to follow. In the early decades of the nineteenth century the town was more elegant than ever and its new Casino was destined to become at least as strong a lure as its waters.

The timing was propitious. The railway train had made the middle and upper classes mobile as never before. Baden-Baden's triple-threat combination—a location convenient to France, the Low Countries and Britain, not to mention the major German cities; the famous thermal spa; and games of chance in the opulence of its new Casino—attracted visitors of substance: reigning heads, petty princes, writers come to gamble (Dostoyevsky), composers to create (Brahms), moneyed bourgeois anxious to be the first from their block to rub shoulders with this crème de la crème clientele, all of them indulging overtaxed livers and trying their luck with cool, cool croupiers in the Casino.

No bombs dropped on Baden-Baden during World War II. But war's end saw the military drawn there. It has been headquarters for the French Command in Germany since the end of the war, and it is, as well, the site of a Soviet Army detachment, a Royal Canadian Air Force base, and British and American military teams. Who could fault any of them? Baden-Baden's charms are irresistible.

ON SCENE

Lay of the Land: A word first about the double Badens of the town's name. Why two, when a single Baden might do? It all has to do with history. The margravial family, at the time of the Reformation, split in two—one part Catholic (the Baden-Baden line) and the other Protestant (the Baden-Durlachs). The two names came into use primarily to distinguish these clans, with the town taking the name of the older Catholic margrave. And it stuck, because it distinguished the town from both the larger state of Baden, of which it was an entity (as in the case of New York, New York), and from other cities called Baden, both in Switzerland and Austria.

Now to the nitty-gritty. Start with the main railroad station. It's called Baden-Oos, and it's a 20-minute drive from town. (Be prepared for a steepish taxi tab to your hotel.) Once arrived, the situation changes. Baden-Baden is happily, handsomely (and verdantly) compact, especially if you arbitrarily chop it in two—tackle the commercial area of downtown first and then the adjacent uptown area of Casino, baths, and hotels, which can be easily negotiated on foot.

The Baden-Oos Bahnhof, north of town, is gained by Rheinstrasse, which, as it approaches the center, becomes Langestrasse and then the principal pedestrians-only shopping street after it crosses Hindenbergplatz. It leads into commercially important Luisenstrasse, and another square, Leopoldplatz. It is at this point that the downtown and the casino-baths-hotels areas converge.

Another major street, Sophienstrasse, leads east from Leopoldplatz to the historic part of the city with such monuments as its major church (Stifstkirche); ruins of the ancient Roman baths; the popular Augusta and Friedrichs Baths; and the elevated Neues Schloss—the margravial residence, housing a pair of museums.

Return, then to Leopoldplatz, head a bit west, and you're at the Kurhaus, the neoclassic building housing, among other things, the Casino. On either side of it are the Trinkhalle—where one may sip the Baden waters or tastier grape juice—and the city's opera house and next-door art gallery. Leading south from this complex, and following the Oos River, is tree-lined, parklike Lichtentaler Allee, along which are some of the leading hotels, not to mention sports facilities—tennis courts to riding trails.

Lichtentaler Allee's southern extremity is a onetime town—Lichtenthal—from which it takes its name. But it is now a part of Baden-Baden, with a monastery its most prominent landmark, and the house in which Brahms lived and wrote his Symphony No. 1 (*Lichtenthaler*) still another.

Due south: an especially scenic corner of the Black Forest, easily inspected by means of a rollercoaster-like highway—Schwarzwald Hochstrasse—cutting through it.

Kurhaus and Casino (Kaisersallee) are one and the same building. Actually, the latter is a part of the former. Call it what you will, do have a look, if not a play of the dice or a roll of the wheel. Without, it is white-colonnaded in the neoclassic style of the early nineteenth century when it went up, replacing an eighteenth-century structure that served a similar purpose. Within, it positively dazzles, and one is not surprised to learn that it was created by a theatrical set designer, a Frenchman named Charles Sechan, who was commissioned by a fellow Frenchman—imported to operate the museum—named Jacques Benazet. Sechan latched onto a theme—the French royal palaces—for his gaming rooms, which are fanciful variations (more robust than rooms of the original periods, but not vulgar) on some of the decorative styles of the last two centuries—Louis XIII through Napoleon III—with the gold and beige Louis XIII Hall of a Thousand Candles the most original of the group. Go for just plain sightseeing before the gambling begins, traditionally 10 A.M. to noon, wearing, of course, whatever you like. During gaming hours, though—traditionally the 12-hour period starting at 2 P.M.—gents want to wear ties as well as jackets, ladies doll up, and regardless of what's worn, a passport must be carried. (Don't expect a Baden-Baden resident to take you about. He or she can enter the gaming rooms only with a letter of permission from the Bürgermeister.)

The Casino's games are blackjack, roulette, and baccarat, with the minimum-value chip DM5, the maximum DM10,000 (except for baccarat, with a DM100 minimum). Croupiers are German citizens; they live on winners' tips, and work 30 to 45 minutes at a stretch, in conjunction with a "judge" stationed at each table. German, French, and English—in that order—are the official languages of play; Germans, Frenchmen, and Arabs constitute the bulk of the gamblers, with a sprinkling of Americans.

The baths and waters: North Americans are, for the most part, unfamiliar with and unattracted to thermal spas, at least for medical purposes. We mostly like to go and enjoy the peripheral amenities. And why not? Still, you may want to take advantage of the facilities in Baden-Baden for, say, a 24-hour course of treatment, to get the kinks out, or for a no-nonsense stay of a fortnight or so, as a result of a visit planned in conjunction with your physician. You or your doctor may want to consult the Baden-Baden Spa Medical Association, whose free English-language booklet, *Baden-Baden: A Health Resort and Centre of Rehabilitation,* describes facilities and types of treatment for various conditions—cardiovascular, gynecologic, neurologic, upper respiratory. German patients are in abundance, generally for stays of three weeks—the minimal time that German health insurance plans allow for a cure. Short-term visitors are advised that it can be invigorating to spend a couple of hours of a single day undergoing the basic routine—under the high-domed ceilings of atmospheric Friedrichsbad—embracing a range of steam-rooms and pools, followed by a wire-brush massage, a dunk in an ice-cold tank, terminating with a half-hour nap, swathed mummy-like in sheets and blankets. It's fun, and you'll feel top-of-the-world!

Here's how the facilities break down. The *Trinkhalle* (Kaiserallee 3), adjacent to the *Kurhaus-Casino,* is—aside from the ruins of the ancient Roman baths—the oldest; it's a very grand frescoed Pump Room, where one may drink the waters or choose grape juice, the latter as part of recently devised treatment programs administered in spring and fall. The *Friedrichsbad* (Romerplatz 1) went up in 1866 but is ultra-mod as regards equipment and facilities, and offers a variety of baths, massages, exercises, and the like. The *Augustabad* (Gersbacherstrasse 35) is the newest facility (1966) with a rooftop sun-terrace, sauna, and a range of facilities—mudpacks to underwater jet baths. Also, thermal, spa, and treatment facilities are attached to a number of the hotels. For literature in English, including the Baden-Baden Spa Medical Association's booklet, write: Thermalkurbäder, D-7570 Baden-Baden, Bundesrepublik Deutschland.

Neues Schloss Museums (Florinterberg): The so-called New Palace—to distinguish it from an even older one in ruins—is a baroque replacement of a French-battered Renaissance structure, of interest principally because it houses a pair of museums. One, dealing with the town's history back to prehistoric times, has quarters in the outbuildings, and is ugly and sadly substandard. The other—called Zähringer after the long-ruling margravial family—is in the palace proper, and is something else again; a repository of fine and decorative arts collected over the centuries by margraves and their families. I'm partial to the family portraits. But there are, as well, fine furniture; a cache of porcelain, mostly eighteenth-century, including some Meissen; and a hodgepodge of older objects—silver and crystal especially.

Kunsthalle (Lichtentaler Allee) is the municipal art gallery. Special shows, with varying themes and of varying quality.

Stiftskirche (Marktplatz) is the closest Baden-Baden comes to a cathedral. Still Catholic, it's a meld of Romanesque and Gothic, with a superb oversized crucifix dominating the choir, and tombs of (mostly Renaissance) margraves.

Brahmshaus (Maximilianstrasse 5 in the Lichtenthal quarter) is for Brahms buffs. Beginning in 1865, the composer spent 10 summers in residence, enjoying himself—from all accounts—and working away, with the output including the locally named "Lichtentaler Symphony" (No. 1). Several upstairs rooms are open, museum fashion, one with a plethora of Brahmsiana.

Kloster Lichtenthal (Klosterplatz, Lichtenthal) is nicely combined with a visit to neighboring Brahmshaus (above). It's a formidable complex, mostly dating back half a millennium, still inhabited by nuns. Worth seeing are the Klosterkirche, rather plain Gothic, set off by smashing works of art; and, in the main convent building, a retail shop wherein are sold a variety of liqueurs made by the sisters, and some of their handwork as well.

Schloss Favorite, a few miles' drive northeast of town, is an essentially baroque palace built by an early eighteenth-century margravine, which is at its best from without—the look is symmetrical and elegant—and in the kitchen, where the draw is a fabulous collection of porcelain. The state rooms lack a light touch, although there's an unusual hall of mirrors. You might want to go for a concert in summer, or for lunch in the café-restaurant on the grounds.

Schloss Neuweier, in the opposite direction as Schloss Favorite, is southwest of the center, and very old indeed. The look here is derring-do, knights-in-armor Gothic, starting with an encircling moat, continuing with the knights' regalia—armor, weapons, helmets, shields, banners—within. And a restaurant.

A Black Forest excursion: You need as little as a morning or afternoon; as a matter of fact, even an hour's drive will give you an idea of the surprising—and surpassing—beauty of the *Schwarzwald,* or Black Forest. What many transatlantic visitors least expect are the spectacular mountains of the region, tiny villages tucked in their valleys; hotels, ski lodges, restaurants, and cafés at scenic points. The highway cutting through the northern portion of the forest is the Schwarzwaldhochstrasse. It's less than 40 miles in length, with its highest parts at an altitude of some 3,000 feet. Signs direct motorists to well-marked walkers' trails that lead to lookout points, swimming pools—both indoor and out, ski lifts, and of course places for refreshment. Good bets for drinks or eats: Zum Alde Gott and Engel Gasthof in the half-timbered village of Sasbachwalden, modern Hotel Plättig at Plättig, and Hohenhotel Rote Lache, in Rote Lache.

Baden wine country: White wines of the Baden region are among Germany's foremost. Combine a trip through the vineyards with your Black Forest ramble. The wine route or *Badische Weinstrasse* southwest of Baden-Baden embraces villages among vineyards—you can sip and meet the locals.

SETTLING IN

Brenner's Park Hotel (Lichtentaler Allee): Even in a resort whose hotels are among the finest in Europe, Brenner's Park stands out. Along with Hamburg's Vier Jahreszeiten, I rank it as the finest in Germany. The park-like Lichtentaler Allee setting—a short stroll to the Kurhaus—is a joy in itself. The ambience of this longish, low-slung hotel—perky without being noisy, restful but never dull—is another plus. Public spaces are extraordinary. The look throughout is one of dramatic understatement, from off-lobby salons for private chats over coffee, to buzzy cocktail lounge, handsomely proportioned restaurant, and intimate specialty grill—of which more later. The 110 rooms and suites are opulent, their baths and adjacent dressing rooms enormous and gorgeous. There are, as well, a beauty of an indoor-outdoor pool, sauna, solarium, and gym. Add to that the Lancaster Beauty Farm, where cosmetic, massage, and yoga specialists offer tone-up programs embracing supervised exercise workouts, swimming, facial and mudpacks, yoga, figure control, and delicious reducing diets (which I've sampled) in conjunction with the hotel restaurant. Consider, too, Villa Stephanie, a self-contained, next-door health clinic, with its own medical staff (nine physicians are on staff), and the most modern equipment, with longevity injections one of several specialties. When all is said and done, though, Brenner's has become internationally preeminent for two principal reasons: superbly professional management and an abundance of skilled, smiling service. Bless it. Member Leading Hotels of the World. *Luxury.*

Hotel Badischer Hof (Langestrasse 47) is a onetime monastery transformed by the pan-German Steigenberger chain into one of its most distinctive hotels. (Indeed, if I were asked to select my two favorite Steigenbergers, they would be the Badischer Hof and still another ex-monastery, the Inselhotel in Konstanz.) The Badischer Hof, originally eighteenth-century, had the good fortune to be wrapped around an open galleried cloister. The clever Steigenbergers roofed it, and it's now the lobby-lounge, three dramatic stories in height, with a restaurant leading from it, and nearly a hundred spiffy rooms and suites reached from its upper corridors. Central. *Luxury.*

Hotel zum Hirsch (Hirschstrasse 1) is nothing if not Old Baden-Baden. The same family has been running it since the opening a few decades after the Thirty Years' War, back in the seventeenth century. The present building is a couple of centuries newer, but old-school: gracious lounges, chandelier-hung restaurant, bar with deep upholstered chairs, summer breakfast terrace, antiques-accented suites and rooms, and the Hirsch's very own thermal bath, whose healing waters are piped into the tubs of guest rooms. Central. *Luxury.*

Hotel Europäischer Hof (Kaiserallee 2) is the Steigenbergers' second Baden-Baden hotel. This one, though less historic and not as architecturally innovative as the Badischer Hof, is hardly to be overlooked, what with a central Oos River setting, vast lobby-lounge, 150 handsome suites and rooms, atmospheric bar, restaurant, and terrace café. *Luxury.*

Hotel Quisisana (Bismarckstrasse 21) occupies a turn-of-century structure, its façade a blend of gables and bays and wrought-iron balconies—converted into a combination hotel-spa, with panache. Public spaces and bedrooms are traditional but with contemporary touches. The restaurant is proud of its *nouvelle cuisine* menu, and each dish's calories are indicated. The spa goes beyond the requisite Baden-Baden pool-sauna-gym, sporting baths besides and assorted additional equipment. *Luxury.*

Appartementhotel Haus Both (Voglergasse 1) is just the ticket if you would like to settle in for a spell, and have a yen to do a bit of cooking. There are just seven apartments-for-two, with living room, bedroom, kitchen, and bath. The style is modern, the suites are named for cosmopolitan cities (including New York), and the management is welcoming. Central. *First Class.*

Golf Hotel (Fremersbergstrasse 113) conveys, by its name, a course of its own. Not so. But it is near Baden-Baden's 18-hole links, in a park-like environment at the edge of town. Indoors is nice, too—roomy lounges, smart restaurant, cozy bar, nearly 100 rooms with terraces, many with ravishing views. *Luxury.*

Waldhotel der Selighof (Auf dem Golfplatz) is, like the Golf Hotel above, a near-neighbor to the golf course, in a bucolic setting, at Baden-Baden's edge. The lounges are pretty, the restaurant moves outdoors in summer, there's a honey of a pool in the garden, tennis, and rooms tastefully decorated in 1950s modern. *Luxury.*

Hotel Parkvilla Kossmann (Kaiser-Wilhelm Strasse 3) is an eighteenth-century town house whose most celebrated guest came a century later—Chancellor Bismarck, if you please. This one has seen better days, but it remains clean and not without a certain charm. A number of rooms have their own baths. And many have, in addition, splendid views of the surroundings. Cordial owner-management. Restaurant. Central. *Moderate.*

Hotel Villa Sorrento (Lichtentaler Allee 58) would make a perfect setting for a neo-Impressionist movie. It's a stunner of an early-nineteenth-century house that must, in its heyday, have been very grand. Now, though, the spacious rooms—some with their own baths—are for paying guests who would like to stay on the town's fanciest thoroughfare, at a price. Breakfast only. *Moderate.*

Hotel Greiner (Lichtentaler Allee 88) lacks age and the ambience that comes with it, but compensates with agreeable rooms with shower and terrace—good-looking all of them—a cheery breakfast room (no full-service restaurant), and a central situation. *Moderate.*

Gasthaus zum Felsen (Geroldstrasse 43, Lichtenthal) is a no-nonsense guesthouse, away from the center in the Lichtenthal section of town. The lures are spotless rooms, some with their own baths, and a corking good restaurant—how many places can guarantee satisfaction as this one can, with the owner-chef one and the same? *Moderate.*

Kurhaus Schloss Beuhlerhoehe (Schwarzwaldhochstrasse, Bühl/Baden) is nothing less than a garden-encircled castle of yore on the highway cutting through the Black Forest, converted with panache into an 80-room-and-suite hotel, with a reputed restaurant, heated swimming pool; neighboring golf, skiing, fishing and hunting—with Baden-Baden but nine miles to the north. Member Relais and Châteaux. *Luxury.*

DAILY BREAD

Restaurant and Schwarzwald Grill (Brenner's Park Hotel, Schillerstrasse 6): The restaurant is good to look at; a vast, high-ceilinged room, in pastels, with picture windows looking onto the garden. Service is white-glove, albeit friendly. There are table d'hôte lunches and dinners, and an extensive à la carte menu with the range from Parma ham, oysters on the half-shell, and Beluga caviar through fresh Dover sole and roast partridge on into hearty apple pancakes or fresh raspberries. And what a wine list! The Schwarzwald Grill is something else again: intimate, Black Forest-pubby, with advance reservations usually required; specialities include stuffed local trout in Riesling, beef Wellington, duck Bigarade. With superb thick steaks and roast beef always on hand. Both *Luxury.*

Stahlbad (Augustaplatz) typifies Baden-Baden at its most stylish, intimate, and delicious. This is an old-timer with class. Framed prints—the series by France's nineteenth-century Boilly satirizing gourmands—line the walls. The table linen is pink and crisp, and there's a dewy-fresh red rose at each place. Everything I've sampled is delicious. A typical dinner: crab salad, Lady Curzon soup, lobster thermidor or veal steak, chocolate mousse. Distinguished wines. Central. *Luxury.*

Boulevard (Kurhaus, Kaiserallee) is at once sprightly, easy on the pocketbook, and right in the Kurhaus. The menu covers a wide range—German appetizers, soups, and entrées, on into international favorites like steak au poivre and mixed grill. Good-value daily specials. Super sweets. *Moderate/First Class.*

Sinner-Eck (Leopoldsplatz) is for well-prepared dishes; hearty soups, seafood and meat entrées, delicate desserts. Central. *Moderate.*

Zum Nest (Rettigstrasse 1) is a favorite with locals, who favor the French specialities, and visitors, who want to try the German dishes, especially roast venison. *Moderate.*

La Carrozza (Merkurstrasse 3) is indicated for pasta. Order the lasagna or the *paglia e fino*. Italian wines. *First Class.*

Café-Konditorei König (Lichtentalerstrasse 12): There are cafés all over the place, but the König is almost as much of an institution as the Kurhaus or Brenner's Park Hotel. Go for coffee, a glass of wine, a light lunch, an ice-cream sundae, afternoon tea, and, if you order nothing else, the extraordinary pastries. But go. *First Class.*

AFTER DARK

Casino (Kurhaus, Kaiserallee): Of course the Casino will be your first—and possibly your only—after-dark destination. I detail its lures on an earlier page. Suffice it to say at this point that you may go afternoon as well as evening—and in the morning, for an inspection tour, sans gaming.

SOUND OF MUSIC

Weinbrennersaal (Kurhaus, Kaiserallee): The opulent concert hall of the Kurhaus is the scene of frequently scheduled concerts given by the famed Baden-Baden Symphony, often with first-class soloists. Guest orchestras come to play, too. There are, as well, daily—sometimes even thrice-daily—concerts by the Baden-Baden Symphony in the Kurpark during the warm-weather months. Ask your hotel concierge not only to tell you what's on, but to give you a copy of the monthly activities guide; the cultural program is richly detailed.

Stadttheater (Goetheplatz): This beautiful house beautifully complements the neighboring Kurhaus. It was designed by a Frenchman in the mock-baroque style of the mid-nineteenth century, and opened with a bang; Berlioz selected it for the premiere of his opera, *Beatrice and Benedict*. Go for opera, ballet, plays.

INCIDENTAL INTELLIGENCE

Baden-Baden is very close to France: Strasbourg, with scheduled service to its airport, is only 40 miles distant; Stuttgart and

Frankfurt are the nearest German airports. Hotel guests are charged a Spa Tax, relatively minimal, with a Spa Card given in return, which is an "open sesame" for daytime Kurhaus concerts, drinks of thermal water at the Trinkhalle, and other attractions. *Further information:* Bäder-und-Kurverwaltung—the municipal tourist office—Augustaplatz 8, Baden-Baden.

5

Bamberg

Monument to an Emperor

BACKGROUND BRIEFING

He has been dead nigh onto a millennium, but no matter; Bamberg remains true to its hero: a Holy Roman Emperor named Heinrich, who was at once soldier, builder, monarch, ardent patriot, and true believer (at least we assume so, since he was sainted). And so, for that matter, was his Luxembourg-born wife, Kunigunde.

Bambergers can't be faulted for their Heinrichian bias. Their pet emperor—fourth of a dynasty of two score—made of this city not only a repository of architecture and art but a capital as powerful ecclesiastically as politically.

Born toward the end of the tenth century—at about the time that Bamberg first enters the records of history with a name corrupted from a founding noble family called Babenburg—Heinrich rose quickly, from duke of Bavaria to king of Germany to Holy Roman Emperor, respected by the Italians for military prowess, beloved of the Germans for loyalty to his homeland. And appreciated by the Bambergers for creating in their town—where he had inherited a castle from papa, Heinrich the Squabbler—a bishopric worthy of the home base of the Holy Roman Emperor. That the bishopric became important is an understatement. From the time of its founding in 1007, its incumbents ruled Bamberg—as prince bishops—straight into the early nineteenth century, when it was absorbed by giant Bavaria.

This political-spiritual prowess coupled with the mercantile wealth that came from a favored river location—in a fertile valley on the Regnitz near its junction with the Main—saw Bamberg develop, as well, as a center of art and culture. And so it remains to this day, blessedly spared World War II bombings, large enough to sport a sophistication that otherwise gem-like little towns like Rothenburg cannot claim, yet small enough so the visitor can come to grips with it in a relatively brief sojourn.

ON SCENE

Lay of the Land: No German city is a more felicitous distillation of the man-made and the natural. Bamberg is a jumble of architectural treasures, Romanesque through Renaissance into rococo, creating vivid silhouettes atop hills, drawing our eyes down curvy lanes, making bold statements in broad squares, even occupying a mini-island in the Regnitz River.

There are two of a number of things in Bamberg. Starting with the islands in the river: One—a tiny isle to the west—is just big enough to hold a building at once a landmark and a trademark of the town: the *Altes Rathaus*, or Old Town Hall. The other island—to the east—is big enough to constitute the bulk of another of Bamberg's "twos," the mercantile or east side of the Altstadt, or Old Town, in contrast to the ecclesiastical, or west side. There is, in addition, a second, or *Neues* (new) *Rathaus*. And a pair of onetime prince electors' palaces—one new, another old.

It's the eastern—nonecclesiastical—side of town that one sees first when one arrives by train. The Bahnhof leads from Luitpoldstrasse across the river over Luitpoldbrücke, to one of the most humming of Altstadt squares, Maximilianplatz, dominated by the Neues Rathaus designed by the same Balthasar Neumann responsible for the Residenz in Würzburg. Maximilianplatz—you may shorten that to Maxplatz as the locals do—is adjacent to an even more historic square, Grüner Markt, with a clutch of baroque monuments, including the Jesuits' Martinskirche, designed by the brothers Dientzenhofer who were responsible for a number of the seventeenth-century architectural treasures of the town.

Move along, toward the river, and the painted façade of the *Altes Rathaus*, on its own river island, looms against the hills of Bamberg's western quarter—the Domplatz complex dominated by the cathedral, and approached through Domstrasse; massive St. Michael's Monastery to the north; landmark churches, Obere Pfarrkirche and Stephanskirche, to the south.

But Bamberg is so much more than these major monuments. One wants to amble about—past half-timbered houses, on winding lanes, before façades of grander mansions, their oriel windows overhanging the streets; beneath the precise geometry of gabled Renaissance roofs, under sculpted arches of monumental gates, along gracious courtyards, with their cobbles worn from the myriad footsteps of centuries.

Try treading Domgasse, Karolinenstrasse, Roppeltsgasse, and Aufsessgasse—a hilly street with carved stone Stations of the Cross bordering it—and Judengasse, if only to see Böttingerhaus, an early-eighteenth-century mansion (peek into the courtyard) that is Bamberg's most beautiful specimen of residential baroque.

The Domplatz complex is the essence of Bamberg in and about a single square. Foremost—you see its extraordinary four-steeple silhouette from all over town—is the *Dom*, or Cathedral. It was begun by Bamberg's patron, Emperor Heinrich II, way back in 1012, rebuilt after a couple of fires a couple of centuries later, part Romanesque, part early Gothic, splendid without—the finely carved Prince's Portal, for example, is a gem—and within. What one wants most to see are the tombs of Emperor-Saint Heinrich and Empress-Saint Kunigunde by Tilman Riemenschneider; the Maria Altar, by still another great carver, Veit Stoss; the thousand-year-old tomb of Clement II, only pope buried in Germany; and, to end, the Diocesan Museum which occupies the Chapter House—another Bamberg work by Balthasar Neumann. See clothes that were worn by Heinrich II and Kunigunde, preserved all of these centuries, along with sculpture, stained glass, and other objects from eras Romanesque through baroque.

Move along in the Domplatz complex to another Bamberg museum, devoted to the city's history, and located, logically enough, in the Alte Hofhaltung, which is what the older of the two prince-electors' palaces is called. The collection—documents on yellowed parchment, gorgeous maps, civic paraphernalia—is no less evocative of ancient Bamberg than are this building's courtyard and the half-timbered houses that frame it.

End your Domplatz visit with its newest building, the immense baroque-era Neue Residenz, newer of the pair of prince-electors' palaces. Its showplace chamber is the Kaisersaal, with sumptuous frescoes, and plasterwork. (The esteemed Bamberg Symphony sometimes plays here.) But there is an entire suite of beautifully furnished and accessorized rooms, including an art-filled Chinese Room. And two bonuses: the first is an art museum, full of old German masters, Cranach and Hans Baldung Grien among them. The other is the State Library, with a selection of its illuminated manuscripts, prints, paintings, and miniatures.

Michaelskirche (Michaelsberg) had been the chapel of a Benedictine monastery dating to the eleventh century—another of Heinrich II's projects. The façade is essentially baroque, sheltering bits and pieces of earlier eras—including tombs of a long line of Bamberg prince-bishops. And the view! Look out at Bamberg below—the nearby Cathedral cluster, the Alte Rathaus on its river island, the Brunermarkt churches and mansions beyond.

Obere Pfarrkirche (Kaulbergasse) is mostly lacy Gothic, a major Bamberg church, its vaulted ceiling and elegant windows framing a quietly art-rich interior.

Stephanskirche (Stephansberg) is No. 4 of the four major hill churches that constitute the Classic Bamberg skyline. (The other three: Michaelskirche, Dom, Obere Pfarrkirche.) St. Stephan's, originally of the Heinrich II era, is now essentially baroque, and it is, as well, the principal Protestant house of worship, a distinction worth noting in a city governed for centuries by Catholic bishop-princes, and one that never recognized the Reformation.

Hoffmanhaus (Schillerplatz) is the onetime residence of E.T.A. Hoffman, the very same gentleman whose stories were the basis of Jules Barbier's libretto for the Offenbach opera *Tales of Hoffman*. Hoffman was, as well, a musician and painter, and Hoffmanhaus exhibits a good deal of his work. There's an across-the-street theater named for this native Bamberg son.

SETTLING IN

Hotel Bamberger Hof-Bellevue (Schönleinplatz 4) is the longstanding Numero Uno, a gracious house in the heart of the mercantile, or eastern, sector of town, near Brunermarkt. A good proportion of the 45 rooms have private baths; and there's a pair of corking good restaurants. *First Class.*

Hotel Alt Bamberg (Habergasse 11) is another nice heart-of-town house, traditional-style, with almost half of its 30-plus rooms containing private baths. Restaurant-bar. *Moderate.*

Hotel National (Luitpoldstrasse 37) is closer to the Bahnhof than the historic core, but with the advantage of private baths in all 40 rooms. Restaurant, bar. *First Class.*

Hotel Hospiz (Promenade 3) has a handy central mercantile-sector location, with two-thirds of its 30-odd rooms containing private baths. This is a church-supported hotel, one of a countrywide network, invariably good value if not always a barrel of laughs. Breakfast only. *Moderate.*

DAILY BREAD

Weinhaus Messerschmitt (Langestrasse 41) may connote—at least to people of a certain age—a World War II plane. But it shouldn't. This centrally situated restaurant, with a sumptuous paneled-wood ceiling and antique accessories that evoke the past, has been on scene since 1832. Fine wines, of course, but fine fare, too, with eel in sage a specialty. And this is a hotel as well, so that you may combine dinner with an overnight stay. *First Class/Luxury.*

Hotel Bamberger Hof-Bellevue Restaurants (Schönleinplatz 4) are congenial, atmospheric, nicely staffed, and with delicious German and international dishes. *First Class.*

Würzburger Weinstube (Zinkenwörth 6) is a core-of-town oldtimer, half-timbered without, beamed and pubby within, with terrace tables in summer. But the food—especially grilled fish—is super, too. *First Class.*

Theaterrose (Schillerplatz 7) is indicated for lunch after a tour of Hoffmanhaus or a performance at the E.T.A. Hoffman Theater. *Moderate/First Class.*

Café am Dom (Ringleingasse 2) is popular with foot-weary Domplatz trekkers. Stop for coffee, a drink, a snack, or a light meal. *Moderate.*

Brauerei Schlenkerlg (Dominkaner Strasse 6): An attractive source of Bamberg's typical smoked beer; have it with a snack. *Moderate.*

SOUND OF MUSIC

Kulturraum (Dominikanerstrasse) is a onetime Gothic church-cloister that the Bambergers have sensibly converted into their municipal concert hall-cultural center, the principal base for the widely renowned and widely traveled Bamberg Symphony, which plays also in the opulent Kaisersaal of the Neue Residenz.

E.T.A. Hoffman Theater (Schillerplatz) is home to visiting opera and operetta troupes from other German cities as well as to plays, in German of course, of its own resident repertory company.

INCIDENTAL INTELLIGENCE

Städtisches Fremdenverkehrsamt Bamberg—the municipal tourist office—is at Hauptwachstrasse 16.

6

Bayreuth

Vivat Wagner!

BACKGROUND BRIEFING

Never underestimate the power of a woman. Especially if she was a sister of Frederick the Great. Had not such a gifted lady—so adept at the arts, both fine and decorative, in the manner of her brother—happened along, then Bayreuth's other great personality would not have been part of its history either.

What happened to this unprepossessing central German town was that its unprepossessing early-eighteenth-century ruler—the margrave of Brandenburg—very shrewdly won the hand of the princess of Prussia. When the lady from Berlin got to provincial, culturally barren Bayreuth, King Frederick's sister Wilhelmina proved to be a chip off the old block, at once a builder-designer and a writer-composer. Among the margravina's monuments—in the intricate albeit graceful style of rococo that came to take Bayreuth's name—is a theater so startlingly handsome that it took the eye of composer Richard Wagner, in the course of his search for a headquarters for his operas.

By the time Wagner had changed his mind about the theater (it was too small-scaled for his expansive work), he had become enamored of the town. Margravina Wilhelmina's imprint—the theater, a pair of palaces in sumptuous gardens, a light rococo touch—was responsible for the choice of ancient Bayreuth as the site of the modern world's first annually scheduled music festival.

Wagner decided to remain and build a theater of his own. Ruthlessly exploiting the bizarre friendship that had developed with young, pathetically unbalanced King Ludwig II of Bavaria—who was so enamored of Wagner that he bombarded him with impassioned letters and used his opera plots as the decor themes for Neuschwanstein Castle—Wagner, with generous financial largesse from Ludwig, created his *Festspielhaus.* It opened in 1876. And so, as a consequence of this double-W combination—Wilhelmina and Wagner—Bayreuth was on the map.

It is at its most frenetic—hotel bookings are made many months in advance—during the Wagner Festival weeks, traditionally late July into late August, when action centers on Wagner's own theater. But the margravina's opera house has its annual moment of glory, as well: The Franconian Weeks merriment, usually beginning at the end of May, features works of composers contemporary with the early days of the theater—Mozart, Haydn, and Handel.

ON SCENE

Lay of the Land: Core of town is relatively compact. A pair of Bahnhofs—Altstadt, at the south edge, and St. Georg at the north—flank the center, whose heart is Marktplatz, set off by still-handsome buildings, Renaissance and baroque. The bulk of the city's monuments are in this district. But Wagner's theater is to be found in a less venerable quarter to the northwest.

Opernhaus (Richard-Wagner-Strasse)—or, to use its full name, Markgräfliches Opernhaus—is, along with Munich's Cuvilliés Theatre, quite the most extravagant rococo theater in Germany, and one of the loveliest in Europe. The ultimate in the case of big things coming in small packages—it seats only 500—this is a five-level jewel centered about the margravina's box, surmounted by a gilded canopy protected by two sculpted angels, a massive crown of Brandenburg-Bayreuth suspended between them. Regular daytime open hours, for a look-see even when there are no performances.

Festspielhaus (Grüner Hügel)—perched atop its own "Green Hill"—will not win a beauty contest (and never has) for its exterior. The interior, though, is not without interest. And not only because of its superb acoustics and vast stage. Wagner patterned it on the ancient Greek amphitheaters, even to the use of uncomfortable backless seats—wood replacing the Greeks' marble in this case. Though nothing like as beautiful as the great neoclassic architect Palladio's theater in the Italian town of Vicenza, the Bayreuth theater has similarities. There are daytime open hours, during nonfestival months. But this house looks its best when benches are occupied by black-tie festival fans, come to admire the boldly contemporary productions of such favorites as *Parsifal, Tristan und Isolde,* and the four-part *Ring* cycle, conceived by Wagner's grandsons/directors Wieland and Wolfgang, sung by world-renowned Wagner specialists, with orchestras led by equally celebrated conductors.

Neues Schloss (Richard-Wagner-Strasse)—behind a neoclassic façade—ranks with her opera house as a major work of the Margravina Wilhelmina. Allow a solid morning or entire afternoon here. First, visit the state rooms—in the margravina's delicate rococo style—with the stucco work especially grand, and furnishings top rank. To be seen, additionally, are the art gallery—with paintings (portraits especially) of the period, among its works: an absorbing museum of history, with souvenirs of the town's past; and for devotees of the master-composer, the Wagner Museum—with a piano he composed on, letters, and other Wagneriana.

Haus Wahnfried (Richard-Wagner-Strasse) is the classic-style Wagner residence, in whose garden are buried the master and his wife, Cosima. (Cosima's father, the composer Franz Liszt, is buried in the town cemetery.)

Hermitage is the country palace of the margraves and their ladies, well worth the few miles' excursion to the northeast, principally because of the contributions made by Margravina Wilhelmina—especially a Japanese Room filled with treasures of the Orient, some gifts from Frederick the Great. You'll like the contrast of the casual (English-style) and clipped-formal (French-style) gardens.

SETTLING IN

Goldener Anker (Opernstrasse 6) has the edge on location (next door to the margravina's opera house), tradition (signed photos of visiting Wagner Festival star singers and conductors are all about), and furnishings (lots of old pieces). Intimate in size, too; there are fewer than 30 bedrooms, no two alike and not all with bath. And a dining room, described below. *First Class.*

Hotel Bayerischer-Hof (Bahnhofstrasse 14) is bigger and perhaps grander than the Goldener Anker, but not as central. (It's near the main station.) There are 60-plus agreeable rooms (many with bath), a swimming pool, and a couple of restaurants, later recommended. *Luxury.*

Reichsadler (Bahnhofstrasse 23) is a smaller, less luxurious but comfortable near-neighbor of the Bayerischer-Hof. Restaurant. *First Class.*

Kolpinghaus (Kolpingstrasse 5) is conveniently located, with a restaurant, and a good number of rooms with bath. *Moderate.*

DAILY BREAD

Königshof (Bahnhofstrasse 23): Small but smart, and dotted with singers and musicians at Festival time. *Luxury.*

Dachgarten (Hotel Bayerischer-Hof, Bahnhofstrasse 14) is a nicely elevated spot for a first Bayreuth meal: it's actually a roof garden, affording views of town and offering a varied menu, mostly German but with international dishes, too. *First Class/Luxury.* (The hotel's *Weinstube* is pleasantly pubby, with hearty fare and *Moderate* tabs.)

Hotel Goldener Anker Restaurant (Opernstrasse 6) is especially amusing at Festival time, when performers pack it, along with fans. But at any time the old-school setting is attractive and the menu wide-ranging, steaks to schnitzels, with a fine wine list. *First Class.*

Wolffenzacher (Badstrasse 1) is heart-of-town, friendly, and with tasty meals including especially good soups. *Moderate.*

Jagdschloss Tiergarten (Tiergarten) is some three miles from town in the Thiergarten suburb, but worth the jaunt if you would enjoy dinner in the onetime parlors of a margravian hunting lodge, still smartly rococo. A good place for game. *Luxury.*

SOUND OF MUSIC

If it's Festival time—Wagner or Franconian Weeks—I repeat earlier caveats: book way, way in advance for hotels as well as performances, especially Wagner. At other times of year, ask your hotel concierge for current concerts and the like. If something is taking place at the margravina's Opera House, make a beeline for it.

INCIDENTAL INTELLIGENCE

Further information: Verkehrsverein Bayreuth, Luitpoldplatz 9.

7

Berchtesgaden

Eagle's Nest in the Alps

BACKGROUND BRIEFING

If one is of a certain age, the name of this Alpine village connotes one thing and one thing only: Adolf Hitler's mountain retreat during the hideous Nazi years. Well, so far as that goes, Berchtesgaden is having the last laugh. It has learned not only to live with the Hitler association, but to exploit it. This magnificently sited village—but 75 miles southeast of Munich—has become a visitor destination of no small consequence.

And with reason. Nazi connections aside for the moment, the major lure is the mountains, as was the case for many preceding centuries—first the medieval Augustinian monks, later their successors, whose leaders doubled as abbots and lay princes allied to the Bavarian royal house. Germany's No. 2 peak after the Zugspitze—the Watzmann—looms to the south, all 9,000 vertical feet of it. And so does the Hochkalter, still with a glacier on its slopes. The peak called Untersberg, unexpectedly surfaced in red marble, and the Lattengebirge chain are to the north. Near neighbors are a jewel of a lake, Königssee; salt deposits, the mining of which has been a regional income-producer for no less than eight centuries; Herrenchiemsee, one of the trio of nineteenth-century palaces built by Bavarian King Ludwig II (and the subject of a chapter of their own); the beautiful Austrian city of Salzburg; and the Obersalzberg, an on-high plateau that was the nerve center of Hitler's southern command, and its neighbor, Kehlsteinhaus, the Hitlerian residence.

ON SCENE

Lay of the Land: From Berchtesgaden village, one can make a number of excursions—via chairlift to the top of 6,500-foot Mt. Jenner; to the Schellenberger Ice Caves of Mt. Untersberg; to an ancient salt mine with an underground lake; to Königssee—along its waters and through the streets of its "capital," the pretty hamlet of St. Bartholomä; and to the Obersalzberg-Kehlstein complex.

Berchtesgaden Schloss is a village treat: a onetime monastery converted into a castle and then into a museum. Take some time here. Concentrate, first, on the Gothic-era hall which houses the art collection of a royal resident. To see are collections of sacred art, especially wood sculptures by Renaissance greats Tilman Riemenschneider and Veit Stoss. There are, as well, a series of furnished rooms, fifteenth through nineteenth centuries. And most special, a tranquil Romanesque cloister.

Hitler's complex: Just east of town, the Obersalzberg plateau can be reached either by bus or a short cable-car ride from the Bahnhof. By no means all of what Hitler—aided by crony Martin Bormann—built remains; a 1945 Allied air raid saw to that. But the ruins of a once-vast subterranean structure—including a suite reserved for Hitler and his mistress Eva Braun—are to be seen. From Obersalzberg—from which there are vistas of Berchtesgaden and the surrounding district—one takes a bus for Kehlsteinhaus, along a route through the rocky side of the mountain, which provides even more spectacular views. One transfers from bus to elevator for the last leg of the journey to the 6,017-foot summit. Kehlsteinhaus is now a café. Pause for coffee and cake; the region's peaks loom beyond, along with—on a clear day, at least—the Austrian city of Salzburg.

Königssee, a finger-like sliver of water tucked between peaks, is as much a "must see" in its way as are Obersalzberg and the chairlift ride to Mt. Jenner. Nowhere else on earth is the combination of snowy peaks and green-blue lake water more winning. Nor is any mountain village more photogenic than St. Bartholomä, with a little church out of a fairy tale, and restaurants—there are several at lakeside points—strategically situated for lunch-intermissions.

SETTLING IN

Hotel Geiger (Stanggass) is the longtime leader, operated by the same family for its century-plus history. Style is chalet traditional, furnishings largely antique, views ravishing. Accommodations come both with and without private bathrooms. The restaurant—local trout is the specialty throughout the region—is surpassed by none locally, and there are a pair of swimming pools. Member, Relais et Châteaux. *First Class.*

Hotel Demming (Sunklergasse 2) is a comfortable full-facility house. Most rooms have baths; restaurant, sauna, solarium. *First Class.*

Hotel Vier Jahreszeiten (Maximilianstrasse 20) is hardly to be confused with similarly named luxury hotels in Hamburg or even Munich, with which it's not connected. But it is worth knowing about; more than half a hundred rooms with private baths; restaurant; sauna-gym. *First Class.*

Gästehaus Grünberger (Hansererweg 1) is a commendable budget spot, with more than a score of rooms with bath. Breakfast only. *Moderate.*

Hotel Post (Weihnachtsschutzenstrasse 3) has no business being on a street with a name like Weihnachtsschutzenstrasse. As for the Post, it's agreeable: more than 20 rooms with bath; *Biergarten,* with meal service. *Moderate.*

DAILY BREAD

Hotel Geiger Restaurant (Stanggass) offers, in a setting full of old things, delicious fare, deftly served. *First Class.*

Kurhaus (Maximilianstrasse 9) is at its handsomest in summer, when its lovely terrace is open. At any time, the hearty meals are enjoyable. *First Class.*

Lockstein (Am Lockstein 1) is elevated, away from the center and with the advantages of super views from the terrace. Traditional menu. *First Class.*

Waldluft (Bergwerkstrasse 37) is for no-nonsense meals—solid and generally satisfying, at a good price. *Moderate.*

INCIDENTAL INTELLIGENCE

Berchtesgaden seems, on a map, more isolated than it is. There are daily trains out of Munich that make the trip in three scenic hours. *Further information:* Kurdirektion—the tourist office—is at Königsseer Strasse 2.

8

Berlin

West and East—
A Study in Bittersweet

BACKGROUND BRIEFING

The capital of Germany between the wars and of the German Empire and the Kingdom of Prussia in earlier centuries, Berlin today is half capital of absolutely nothing, the other half of Western Europe's only Communist state—of which it is a geographical part.

It is heady Dietrich-bittersweet, today's Berlin. It is Everyman's Europe. Oldsters who grew up with Hitler and goose-stepping Nazis in newsreels — and later in war — pinch themselves in disbelief. Youngsters, who may or may not have seen Helmut Dantine in old movies screened on TV, but who have certainly had some academic exposure to the city, find themselves in a classroom in Instant History.

And all at once. There it is: the Berlin of the arrogant Prussian kaisers. The Berlin of the Isherwood-Kurt Weill Time Between the Wars, the preposterous, terrifying Hitlerian Berlin, the ravaged Berlin of the World War II bombings, the contemporary this-very-minute Berlin, an almost diabolical gift of the Cold War, arbitrarily chopped in two, with its grotesque Wall separating capitalist from communist, East from West, Berliner from Berliner.

Berlin has had the same name for eight centuries. One of its most auspicious dates was 1415, when one Frederick of Hohenzollern became the elector of Brandenburg, first of a long line of royal rulers for whom Berlin would be home until World War I just half a millennium later. The religious-inspired Thirty Years' War, in the mid-seventeenth century, spread from what is now Czechoslovakia to a Berlin that it nearly leveled. The war brought remarkable modernity, though, in the reigns that followed. Elector Frederick William II, no longer content with his title (''electors'' were rulers who had the additional privilege of helping select the Holy Roman Emperors), styled himself ''king,'' and erected the still-standing Charlottenburg Palace for his queen, Sophia Charlotte.

Frederick II, the king we know as Frederick the Great, ascended the throne after the death of his militaristic and peculiar father, Frederick William I, in 1740. Frederick the Great's title was deserved. Eccentric and homosexual, he was a genius as well as a militarist (his longtime antagonist was the Hapsburgs' Maria Theresa of neighboring Vienna), a prolific poet and writer, an intellectual who was a close friend of Voltaire, a man with sophisticated taste in matters of art and architecture. (He built the still-visitable Sans Souci and Neues Palais at nearby Potsdam, and also drastically altered, added to, and improved upon his grandfather's Charlottenburg.)

The opulent style of decor he fostered still bears his name—Frederician rococo. (It is a pity that his arch-rival, Maria Theresa, had such poor taste in her palaces. Her Schoenbrunn is no Sans Souci.) *Der alte Fritz*—Good old Fred, as he was called—was to be more beloved of his people than any leader who followed.

Wilhelm I ascended the throne in 1861, and it was during his reign that all of the German states got together to form modern Germany (this was the era of the strong-willed Bismarck), with a consequent change in kingly title. Wilhelm became the first *Kaiser*, or emperor, of the new *Reich*, and Germany—indeed Europe—remained at peace for a record period, until 1914, when it fought the Allied Powers in World War I, suffered devastating defeat, and with its empire disbanded, started life anew as the Weimar Republic.

The Weimar period was Germany's initial attempt at democracy. It may not have been the best time in history to try a new form of government, for there was dissatisfaction with the terms of the Versailles Treaty, severe inflation, and heavy unemployment. Oddly, during this period when Berlin was representative of a nationwide economic and political nadir, it experienced an intellectual renaissance.

These were the years of Max Reinhart's emergence as a theater great, of Marlene Dietrich in classics like *The Blue Angel,* of film directors like Ernst Lubitsch, and of composer-writers like Bertolt Brecht, with his *Threepenny Opera.* The poets and writers published. The artists painted. Berlin café life was the envy of Europe. But it all came to naught. Or almost.

Austrian-born Adolf Hitler became chancellor of the republic in 1933 and before long assumed dictatorial powers. The Germany he had envisioned in his book *Mein Kampf* became a reality. Every facet of German life had to conform with the oppressive, repressive tenets of Nazism. The weak, ineffectual Weimar Republic had been transformed into one of the most horrendous police states in history, with anti-Semitism and an expansionist, militarist foreign policy its principal credos. By 1945, at the end of the Hitler-triggered World War II, 6 million Jews had died in Nazi concentration camps; much of Europe—including much of Germany and its capital—was destroyed; Hitler and his mistress, Eva Braun, had committed suicide in Berlin; and Germany had surrendered. The Allied Powers divided Germany into eastern and western sectors—and did likewise with its capital.

In 1948 and 1949, the Allies kept West Berlin alive with a remarkable airlift, their answer to Soviet efforts to isolate the city from the West. In the following decade, so many residents of East Berlin had escaped into West Berlin that Walter Ulbricht, then president of East Germany, erected a heavily guarded wall to keep his people in their own part of the city.

In late 1971, the four occupying powers—the Soviet Union, Britain, France, and the United States—got together to work out a new quadripartite agreement on Berlin. The Soviets agreed in writing to allow West Berlin to continue to exist as a Western outpost 110 miles within East Germany's borders and to cease harassment as long as Westerners agreed to cut down excessive political demonstrations. The agreement put it this way: "There shall be no use or threat of force in the area. . . . Disputes shall be settled solely by peaceful means. . . . The Four Governments agree that, irrespective of the differences in legal views the situation which has developed in the area . . . shall not be changed unilaterally."

And so the two Berlins continue to coexist. While East Berlin has had the help of its Soviet mentors in rebuilding over the years, West Berlin has had heavy injections of capital from West Germany and the West generally to keep it solvent as a showplace of democracy within the geographic confines of a Communist state.

Most West Berliners—if not most West Germans—continue to hope (theoretically, if not practically) for the day when Berlin will again be their capital (the president of West Germany has an official residence in Berlin, and the country's currency is West Berlin's currency). Many are lured to its good universities and the job opportunities in West Berlin's subsidized economy. Not all stay, though. West Berlin, with all its advantages and amenities, remains an island in not particularly placid waters, even though, in recent years, West Germany and East Germany have each come to officially recognize the existence of the other, and to exchange ambassadors. Even though West Germans—and West Berliners, with proper permission—may now travel to East Germany, East Germans do not enjoy comparable mobility.

Ideally, to appreciate—and to understand—Berlin, one settles in, in both West and East. And by that I mean one gets to know the eastern sector by means of residence in one of its excellent hotels—not just a skim-the-surface, superficial day excursion from the western sector. Such a quick visit, however, is preferable to no East Berlin visit whatsoever. Still, it is only by treating East Berlin—and for that matter East Germany—as one would treat any other travel destination—Paris, the Grand Canyon, Moscow, Acapulco, if you will—that one is able to appraise East Berlin fairly. It has to be given a fair shake, on its own.

That said, what follows in this chapter is a survey of the best of Berlin's disparate halves—a geopolitical entity unique in the world that, for better or for worse, not only functions but thrives, compensating with cultural and ideological distinction for what it lacks in the kind of conventional beauty common to most great cities.

A note on terminology: West Berliners have no objection to their part of the city being called West Berlin by visitors: they appreciate the fact that the designation makes for immediate geographical clarity. However, East Germans call their half of the city just plain "Berlin," without the "East." Or, as they invariably put it in official literature and on the directional road markers leading to their part of the city from throughout their country: *Berlin, Hauptstadt der DDR* (Berlin, Capital of the German Democratic Republic). What they want understood is that East Berlin is more than their chunk of a bigger city; it is the seat of government of their nation—unlike West Berlin, which no longer has that status, even though its citizens hope it will sometime again.

WEST BERLIN

ON SCENE

Lay of the Land: By and large—there are exceptions—you don't go to Berlin for the aesthetics. It may be said that a city heavily damaged in World War II could not possibly be handsome today. But that statement presupposes that contemporary architects are unable to create beauty. Berlin might have become more pleasing to look upon if different planners and designers had been in charge of rebuilding it. (One need only consider the job done in other German cities—Munich, Hamburg, Cologne, Düsseldorf, to name but four.) But we must take West Berlin as it is: an unlovely town that is not without pockets of fascination.

The principal thoroughfare—a street of small shops and large stores, cafés and restaurants, hotels and *boîtes*—is the Kurfürstendamm—long, wide, and with the ruined tower of turn-of-century Kaiser Wilhelm Memorial Church as its landmark. The church was left in ruins intentionally—as a reminder of the tragedy of World War II; adjoining it is a contrastingly modern church, the most interesting aspect of which is a series of striking stained glass windows.

The wise visitor establishes headquarters in one of the many hotels on or near *Ku-damm,* as Berliners call Kurfürstendamm.

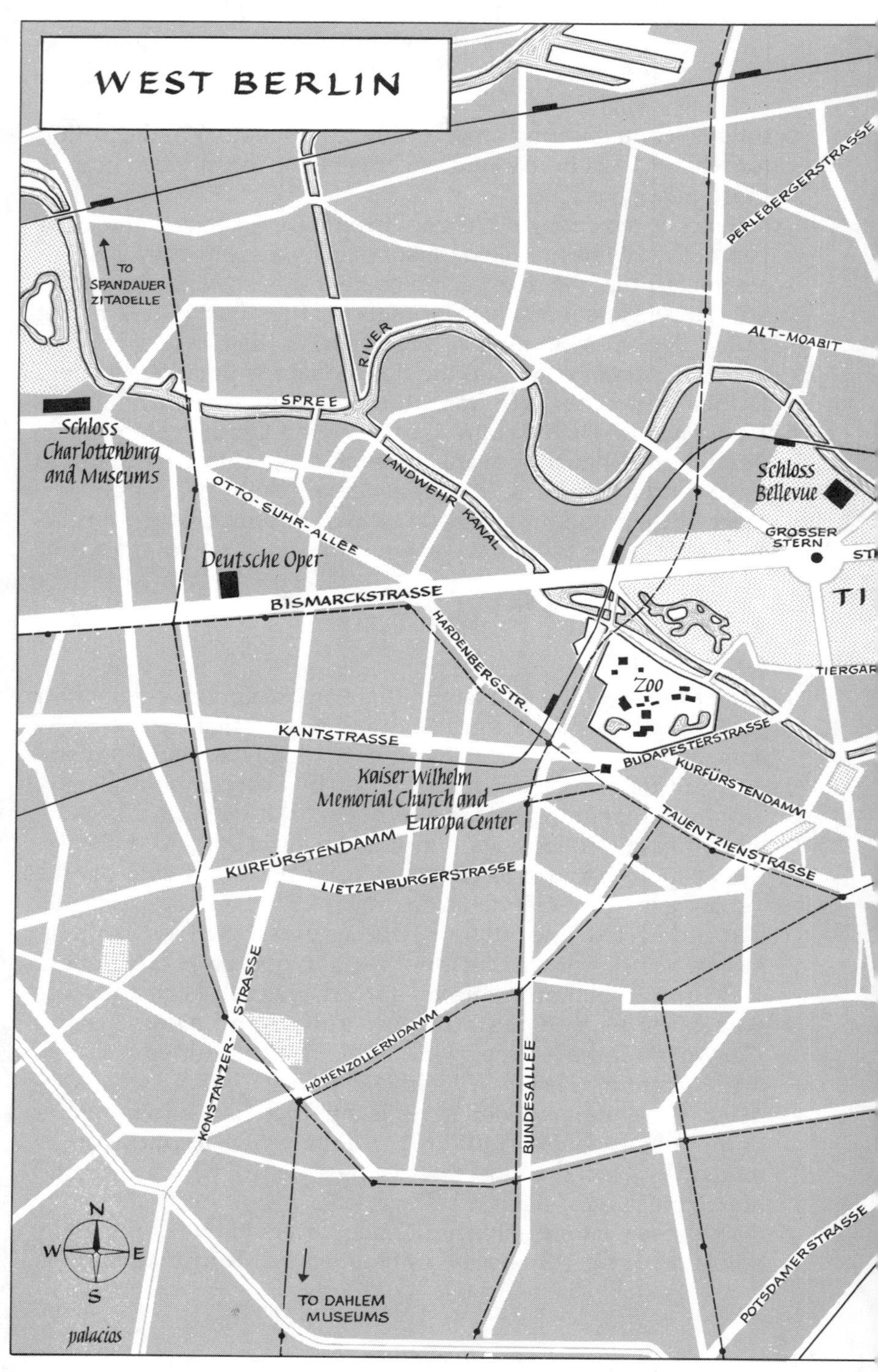
WEST BERLIN
TO SPANDAUER ZITADELLE
Schloss Charlottenburg and Museums
SPREE
RIVER
LANDWEHR KANAL
OTTO-SUHR-ALLEE
Deutsche Oper
BISMARCKSTRASSE
HARDENBERGSTR.
KANTSTRASSE
Kaiser Wilhelm Memorial Church and Europa Center
KURFÜRSTENDAMM
LIETZENBURGERSTRASSE
PERLEBERGERSTRASSE
ALT-MOABIT
Schloss Bellevue
GROSSER STERN
Zoo
BUDAPESTERSTRASSE
KURFÜRSTENDAMM
TAUENTZIENSTRASSE
HOHENZOLLERNDAMM
KONSTANZER-STRASSE
BUNDESALLEE
POTSDAMERSTRASSE
TO DAHLEM MUSEUMS
N
W
E
S
palacios

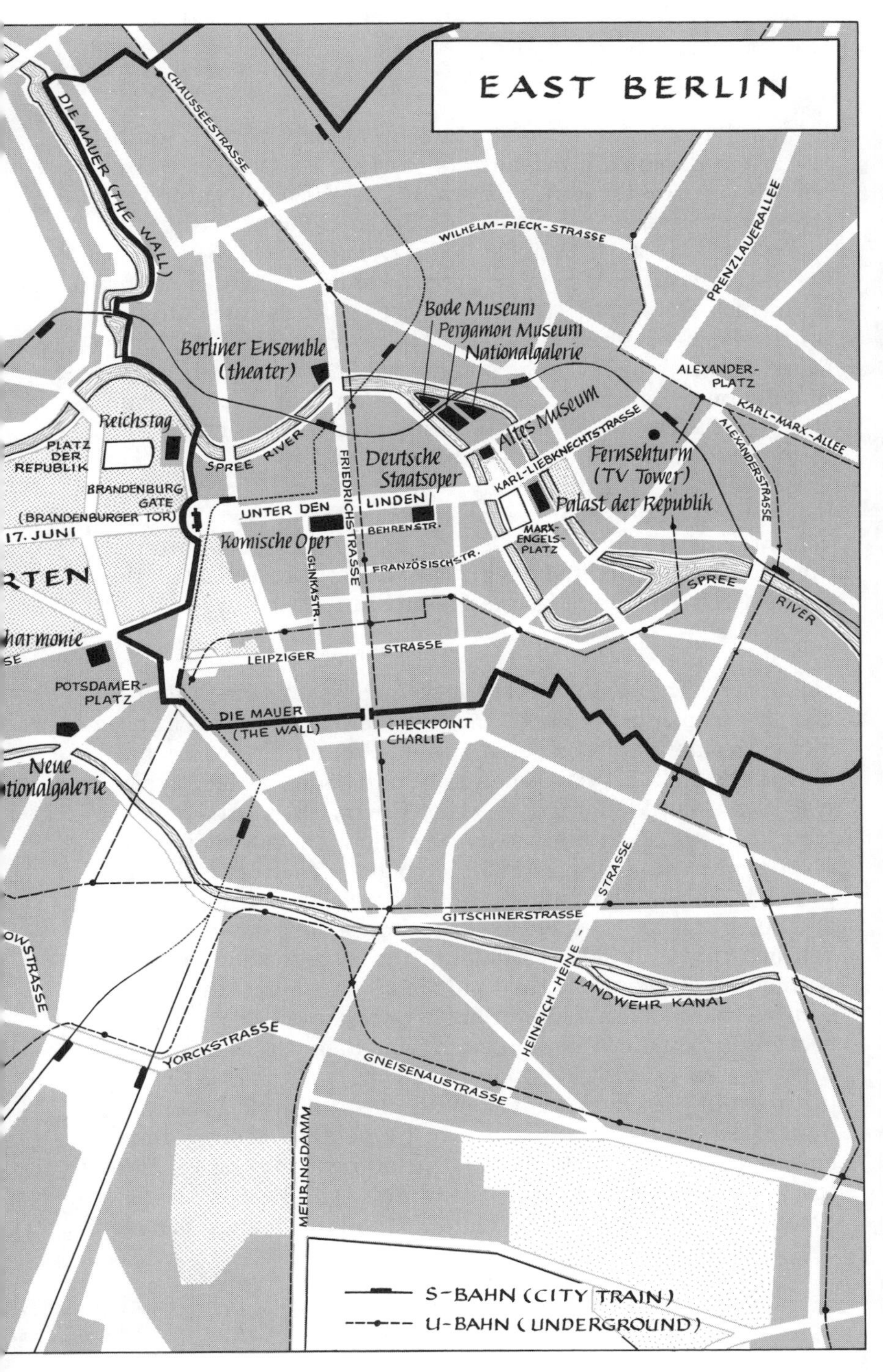

EAST BERLIN
CHAUSSEESTRASSE
DIE MAUER (THE WALL)
WILHELM-PIECK-STRASSE
PRENZLAUERALLEE
Bode Museum
Pergamon Museum
Nationalgalerie
Berliner Ensemble
(theater)
ALEXANDER-
PLATZ
KARL-MARX-ALLEE
Reichstag
Altes Museum
PLATZ
DER
REPUBLIK
SPREE RIVER
KARL-LIEBKNECHTSTRASSE
Fernsehturm
(TV Tower)
ALEXANDERSTRASSE
Deutsche
Staatsoper
FRIEDRICHSTRASSE
BRANDENBURG
GATE
(BRANDENBURGER TOR)
UNTER DEN
LINDEN
Palast der Republik
17. JUNI
Komische Oper
BEHRENSTR.
MARX-
ENGELS-
PLATZ
RTEN
GLINKASTR.
FRANZÖSISCHSTR.
SPREE
RIVER
harmonie
LEIPZIGER
STRASSE
POTSDAMER-
PLATZ
DIE MAUER
(THE WALL)
CHECKPOINT
CHARLIE
Neue
tionalgalerie
STRASSE
GITSCHINERSTRASSE
HEINRICH-HEINE-
OWSTRASSE
LANDWEHR KANAL
YORCKSTRASSE
GNEISENAUSTRASSE
MEHRINGDAMM
S-BAHN (CITY TRAIN)
U-BAHN (UNDERGROUND)

Just north of it is the inner-city park, Tiergarten, with its southern fringe dominated by the zoo, fronting Budapesterstrasse, which leads north from Ku-damm. Places one will want to visit are spread around, but the elderly Berlin U-Bahn, or subway, works well, is easy to negotiate, and will even take one to East Berlin. Tegel Airport, point of entry for most visitors, is not far north of town. Charlottenburg Palace, with its museums, is northerly also, albeit closer in. The extraordinary Dahlem Museum's complex is to the southwest. The two towers of the Brandenburg Gate flank Unter den Linden—East Berlin's main street—at the eastern edge of the Tiergarten, which is home both to the eye-filling eighteenth-century Belvedere Palace, where West German presidents stay when in town, and an ultramodern convention center. I've anticipated your next question: Where is Checkpoint Charlie—the celebrated cross-through point for the two Berlins? It's just east of Potsdamerplatz, at the southeastern end of the Tiergarten, on Friedrichstrasse.

Die Mauer (The Wall) is every first-time visitor's first destination. It was painted white by the East Germans to dress it up a bit for President Carter's Berlin visit in 1978, but that has not removed the chill. It's best taken in from Potsdamerplatz, which was, in pre-World War II days, what Times Square used to be to New York, and Piccadilly Circus to London. The massive ruined oblong hulk you'll see is all that's left of the old Kempinski. In its prime, it housed 10 restaurants and cabarets, each with a theme and decor of its own—a Vienna coffeehouse, for example, a Chinese tea garden, Wild West saloon, and of course a dance hall with an all-girl band, of the kind we all enjoyed in the movie *Cabaret*—based on a Christopher Isherwood short story. For background on the Wall—more, possibly than you may want or need as a casual visitor—stop in at *Haus am Checkpoint Charlie,* just west of the checkpoint. Behind its store-front façade the owner-directors—refugees from the eastern sector—have amassed thousands of documents, including many graphic photos, about the Wall, its impact on the city and East-West relations, and on remarkably ingenious methods of escape that have been undertaken.

Reichstag (Platz der Republik) and the *Soviet War Memorial* are best taken in tandem. The latter, built so soon after World War II that it stands in the western rather than the eastern sector of the city, is at once massive, graceless, and of interest more for its ironic location—and its 20-man contingent of Soviet army guards that change every two hours—than its beauty; it's built of bricks from Hitler's destroyed chancellory. You'll find it between the beautiful eighteenth-century Brandenburg Gate and the Reichstag, originally constructed in the late nineteenth century, in neoclassic style, to house the German Parliament. Arsonists partially destroyed it in 1933, at the start of the Hitler era, and more damage was done during World War II. For years the building lay in ruins. In the late 1970s, though, it emerged rebuilt and remarkable. The legislative chamber has been completely reconstructed, in slick modern style. But it is not to be entered at all—until West Berlin is once again the German capital. However, the rooms adjacent can be inspected; indeed, they constitute a remarkable museum of the city's political life over the centuries. Most requisite—with photographic blowups, reproductions of documents, old impedimenta—is the section having to do with the rise of Hitler and Nazism. There's one section in which you hear the Führer's voice while watching a film of him haranguing crowds at a rally. Creepy, but you owe it to yourself to go. Restaurant-café, too.

The Schloss Charlottenburg Complex (Luisenplatz) is one of Berlin's two underappreciated treasures. (The other is Dahlem, described below.) Charlottenburg is Berlin of old at its most sumptuous—the single major spark of elegance in the city's western sector that's open to visitors. It is, in addition, the site of no less than four museums, none overly large but each distinguished. A day, all told, is not too much time here. *The Royal Apartments* must be toured as the nucleus of a Charlottenburg visit; they embody the splendor of the eighteenth century. Charlottenburg had its beginnings with Elector Frederick II in 1701, but later in the century Frederick the Great made additions in the silvery rococo style he so liked. The palace was badly damaged during World War II, but the restoration—painstakingly slow, authentic, and skilled—has been superb. Visitable rooms include Frederick the Great's quarters in a wing he added to the palace—his study, library, and a waiting room. But there are additional salons: the Porcelain Room—with Chinese export wares completely surfacing the walls; and the long Oak Gallery—used today for gala receptions. There are portraits of resident royals throughout, mostly by Antoine Pesne, the court painter in the eighteenth century. *Belvedere* is the name of a charming eighteenth-century teahouse in the formal gardens of Charlottenburg. It's a good excuse for a garden stroll. The treat within is a cache of mostly Berlin-produced porcelain, eighteenth-century through Biedermeier. *Kunstgewerbe Museum* houses decorative arts. Locale is a ground-level palace wing, with ecclesiastical treasures out of the Middle Ages, Renaissance jewelry, and silver among the exhibits. *Antikenmuseum* (Schlosstrasse 1) is across the *Platz* from the main palace entrance, in a building of its own. Lures: objects of surpassing beauty from ancient Greece, Rome, and beyond, with delicate sculptures and gem-embedded gold jewelry the highlights. *Ägyptisches Museum* (Schlosstrasse 70) is, thanks to the glorious bust of Queen Nefertiti, Charlottenburg's most celebrated museum. But there's so much more here—busts of other monarchs quite as striking as that of Nefertiti, not to mention a recently acquired ancient temple gate—Kalabsha by name—to rival the Temple of Dendur at the Metropolitan Museum in New York, and, like its Met counterpart, a gift from the Egyptian government.

The Dahlem Museum Complex (Arnimallee 23) is so big as to be almost as confusing as the Charlottenburg cluster. And because, like Charlottenburg, it's away from the center, it is paid relatively scant non-German visitor attention. To see is a contemporary, exceptionally well-designed museum group that contains—as but one of its component parts—a picture gallery that is one of the world's greatest. Allot the bulk of your time—a half day easily—for paintings of the *Gemäldegalerie.* There are, to be sure, a fair number of Old Masters to be seen in East Berlin. But the fortunes of World War II were kinder to the western sector in this respect. Only the art museums of Munich, Hamburg, Frankfurt, Cologne, and East Germany's Dresden rank with this one: German painters in quantity, Dürer and Cranach and Holbein especially; Italians in abundance, Titian and Botticelli among them; Flemings like van Eyck, van der Weyden, and Rubens; Dutchmen, including a slew of Rembrandts; eighteenth-century French masters like Chardin and Watteau and Boucher, not to mention *Frederick the Great* by the same Pesne whose work fills that king's rooms at Charlottenburg. *Museum für Völkerkunde* is Dahlem's ethnographic gallery, and a stand-out, internationally. Americans will be interested in a feather cape that once belonged to Hawaii's eighteenth-century King Kamehameha I, along with North American Indian wigwams. There are, as well, bronze busts from Benin in Nigeria, Javanese shadow puppets, Chinese pottery horses, pre-Columbian sculpture, Colombian antique gold jewelry. *Museum für Islamische Kunst,* the Dahlem respository of Islamic art and artifacts, covers a wide gamut—from exquisitely embellished tile fountains and prayer niches to rugs and pottery. *Museum fur Indische Kunst* has one of the choicest collections of the arts of India outside of that country itself—miniature paintings, sculpture, textiles, jewelry, magnificent tombs. And there are still additional Dahlem collections: sculpture through the ages, Old Master prints and drawings, and Oriental art. Dahlem has a cafeteria, and a shop for cards and catalogues for all its museums.

Berlin Museum (Lindenstrasse 14) is a surprise, both as regards package (a stunner of a baroque townhouse) and contents. There are furnished-in-period rooms full of beautiful objects—paintings, prints, maps, documents, china, furniture, from rococo through Art Nouveau—the better to recount the city's history. Atmospheric restaurant-café.

Tegel Palace (Adelheidalle 19) was originally created by the brilliant early nineteenth-century architect-painter-designer Karl Friedrich Schinkel in the Prussian neoclassic genre. You see it today—rebuilt with imagination and style—as a Baroque country house, with the bonus of a museum whose unusual subject matter is plaster casts of classical sculptures.

Pfaueninsel Palace (Pfaueninsel) went up in the eighteenth century as a royal folly—or fantasy-castle, in the image of an Italian ruin, and was used by later monarchs as a summer home, on its own little island, called after the peacocks, a number of which still are resident.

Jagdschloss Grünewald (in suburban Grünewald) is a Renaissance hunting lodge that could be a period movie set. Furnished as it was when royalty used it as a retreat, beginning in the sixteenth century, its painting collection is a happy surprise; Cranach and Rubens are among the masters. If you go in winter, wear snuggies; there's no heat.

Plötensee Memorial (Stauffenbergstrasse) is, in its way, quite as moving an experience as the Dachau Concentration Camp Memorial (see the chapter on Munich) and the Reichstag Museum, recommended earlier in this chapter. It occupies what had been the second largest World War II execution chamber in Germany, where, during the Nazi era, some 1,800 political prisoners—including women and children, foreign as well as German—were hanged or guillotined. The building now houses a permanent exhibition, *Resistance to National Socialism,* which documents the anti-Nazi underground before and during the war. A simple stone memorial is dedicated to Hitler's victims, 1933-1945, with a stone urn alongside it, containing earth from concentration camps throughout the country. Very moving.

Jüdische Gemeinde mit Synagoge zu Berlin (Fasanenstrasse 79)—the seat of Berlin's Jewish community of some 7000 (it numbered more than 170,000 before World War II), at once a multi-function community center and synagogue. Stop in to pay your respects at its memorial to victims of the Holocaust—a wall of its patio where, beneath a Star of David and the simple legend, 1933-1945, are bronze plaques with the names of 21 Nazi concentration camps both within Germany and in German-occupied countries.

Nationalgalerie (Potsdamerstrasse 50) exemplifies for far too many visitors the fine-arts museum scene in Berlin. Local tourist authorities seem to promote it over the superior Dahlem Collection because it was designed by a name architect, Mies van der Rohe. And because its thrust is modern art—German Expressionists like Beckmann and Feininger, French Impressionists and post-Impressionists, including Picasso. All in all, the building is surely Mies's most prosaic—a dullish, late 1960s rectangle. And many German museums have better collections of work of these periods. See it only after you see the Dahlem, Charlottenburg, and Grunewald.

SETTLING IN

Hotel Bristol Kempinski (Kürfurstendamm 27): I can't imagine West Berlin without the Kempinski. Bearing the proud old name of a pre-World War II entertainment-restaurant-café complex (referred to above), it is post-war, but traditional, with the best location in town; 335 handsome and handsomely equipped rooms and suites, and a spacious lobby off of which are a very grand main restaurant, a spiffy grill (worthy of later comment), a gracious coffee-and-drinks lounge, a bar with music for evening dancing, and a Ku-damm café that is one of that busy street's busiest. I have always, over the years, found service smiling and professional. This is one of Germany's very best. Member, Leading Hotels of the World. *Luxury.*

Hotel Inter-Continental Berlin (Budapesterstrasse 2) opened as Berlin's first major post-World War II hotel in the late 1950s as the Berlin Hilton—which it remained until the late 1970s, when it became a franchise house of the well-known Inter-Continental chain, which undertook a thorough sprucing-up upon taking over. There are 350 rooms and suites with baths, a knockout of a pool-cum-sauna, a rooftop café with views and tea-dancing, and other dine-drink spots leading from the big, high-ceilinged lobby including Huguenot, one of Berlin's best restaurants. Central; the zoo is next door. *Luxury.*

Hotel Palace (a part of the Europa Center—with shops, restaurants, and the Berlin Casino, on Budapesterstrasse) is a house of considerable style and sophistication with a relatively intimate ambience (there are but 175 suites and rooms, invariably lovely) and inviting public spaces that include a main restaurant, a bar that's a major congregating spot, a pool/sauna, and a grill on which I comment later in this chapter. *Luxury.*

Hotel Steigenberger (Rankestrasse 30) is the contemporary, sleek-lined Berlin outpost of the Germany-wide Steigenberger chain. It is conveniently central—just a block from the Ku-damm, with some 400 functional rooms, bar-lounge and a pair of restaurants of which the Berliner Stube is recommended for local specialties. *Luxury.*

Hotel Ambassador (Bayreutherstrasse 42) is perhaps seven or eight minutes' walk from the Ku-damm. This is a relatively new hotel of medium size with the look of smart Danish modern. The 120 rooms and suites sport black-tile baths. There are an intimate grill, main restaurant, bar, and pool/sauna. *Luxury.*

Hotel am Zoo (Kürfurstendamm 25) has location—it's right in the heart of the Ku-damm—as its chief asset. This is an elderly house, competently updated. The lobby is smallish and inelegant, but the 145 rooms and suites are agreeable, and all have private baths. A café-restaurant, worth knowing about, is later described. *First Class.*

Hotel Savoy (Fasanenstrasse 9) is an attractive old-timer just off the Ku-damm. The 115 rooms and suites all have private baths. Convenient restaurant. *First Class.*

Parkhotel Zellermeyer (Meinekestrasse 15) is one-of-a-kind, post-World War II modern, with a high-ceilinged lobby, 140 inviting rooms and suites, especially nice restaurant and bar, and attentive management. Central. *First Class.*

Hotel Schweizerhof (Budapesterstrasse 21) is big (450 rooms and suites), busy, with a choice of places to dine and drink, and a pool. A fair walk to the Ku-damm. *First Class.*

Hotel Hamburg (Landgrafenstrasse 4) is friendly, contemporary, with 240 sprightly rooms (the singles are smallish), restaurant, bar; quite a walk to the Ku-damm. *First Class.*

Hotel Sylter Hof (Kurfürstenstrasse 16) is an across-the-street neighbor of the Hamburg, and fairly comparable as regards age, look, and amenities. Lots of singles. *First Class.*

Hotel Berlin (Kurfürstenstrasse 62) is a 264-room, full-facility house with an impersonal air that dissipates in the grill, which I mention later. Fairly central. *First Class.*

Hotel Alsterhof (Wurzbürgerstrasse 1) has some 80 compact, albeit cheerful and fully equipped, rooms, restaurant and bar, central location, smiling staff. *Moderate.*

Hotel Arosa-Airlines (Kurfürstendamm 68) has a Ku-damm location going for it, along with nearly 70 neat rooms, many with private baths. Breakfast only. *Moderate.*

Hotel Astoria (Fasanenstrasse 2) is on a street leading off the Kudamm, at its core. Thirty-plus rooms, many with private baths. Breakfast only. *Moderate.*

DAILY BREAD

Huguenot (Hotel Inter-Continental Berlin, Budapesterstrasse 2) is authentically and deliciously French, offering old-time and *nouvelle* dishes, and presenting them with flair, to the accompaniment of wines from one of the city's really extraordinary cellars. *Luxury.*

Kempinski Grill (Hotel Kempinski, Kurfürstendamm 27) is Berlin dining that is at once elegant (not commonplace in this city), delicious, and intimate. The *plats du jour*—saddle of veal, beef Wellington, roast duck—are good bets. So are the lobster specialties. Fine wines. *Luxury.*

Historische Gaststätte auf der Zitadelle (Spandau Zitadelle) is a stylishly updated suite of rooms in ancient Spandau Castle. The fare is German with an international flair. Fish soup is delicious, and sausage platters are special. Go for lunch. *First Class.*

Palace Grill (Hotel Palace, Europa Center) has the look of the Biedermeier decades of the early nineteenth century. Subdued, handsome, and with good things to eat, including steaks as you like them, grilled sole, hearty German dishes. Luscious desserts. *Luxury.*

Hardtke (Meinekestrasse 26) remains, year-in, year-out, an old reliable—and continually commendable—source of Berlin specialties, including *Eisbein* (pork knuckles and sauerkraut) and *Berliner Weisse* (an unlikely meld of beer with raspberry juice). Central. *First Class.*

Anselmo (Damaschkestrasse 17): I am always grateful to the Italians who immigrate to Germany and open restaurants featuring their cuisine. Especially if they cook well. Which is happily the case at this sprightly contemporary spot, near the Ku-damm, which is indicated for a variety of well-sauced pastas, with wines from the Peninsula to accompany. *First Class.*

Conti (Sybelstrasse 14) is a long-on-the-scene seafood house in an imaginative nautical setting, with pike soup—a traditional Berlin dish—a specialty. Entrées range from lobster to sole. Professional service. *First Class/Luxury.*

Berlin Grill (Hotel Berlin, Kurfürstenstrasse 62) is a few steps downhill, off the lobby—big, with an agreeable hum to it, and with classic German dishes its best bets, including Kalbsmedaillon Hotel Berlin—scallops of veal with sweetbreads, bacon, and mushrooms. Exemplary wines. *First Class.*

Hecker's Deele (Grolmanstrasse 35, off the Ku-damm) is a good bet for an agreeable lunch for dinner, Berlin-style. Attractive, friendly. *Moderate.*

Kranzler (Kurfürstendamm 18) is a long-established café-konditorei-restaurant that continues, year in, year out, to provide cheery and swift service, and tasty things to eat—full meals, ice cream, pastry, coffee, at any time of day through late evening. On a tourist-trod street like Ku-damm, not many places of this type come close. *Moderate.*

Weinkrüger (Hotel am Zoo, Kurfürstendamm 25) is whatever you want it to be—*Stube* for a glass of wine, café for a snack, restaurant for a simple meal. The look is pubby, the waitresses pretty, the location central. *Moderate.*

Reichstag Restaurant (Reichstag, Platz der Republik): Be the first on your block to eat in the handsomely restored nineteenth-century Reichstag (see above). This is a well-proportioned, high-arched room, with the daily specials usually a good bet. *Moderate.*

Weissbierstube (Berlin Museum, Lindenstrasse 14): The setting is a baroque mansion that's the city's historical museum (see above). Go for lunch—tasty salads, daily specials, delicious bread. Fresh flowers all about. *Moderate.*

SOUND OF MUSIC

Philharmonie (Matthaikirchplatz) is more than home base for the Berlin Philharmonic. This hall is, in addition, the finest work of contemporary architecture in Berlin, and one of the few truly superior, modern-design concert halls extant. You must not let its unconventional exterior throw you. It's inside you want to see. The auditorium is asymmetrical. The designer began with a hall of tremendous height and grouped his 2,200 seats in blocks, both above and below the platform on which the orchestra performs, which makes the orchestra appear to be tucked into the maze of seating areas. The foyer area—promenade section and café—is equally understated and inspired. Other concerts are in other settings, notably on summer nights, in the chapel of Schloss Charlottenburg.

Deutsche Oper Berlin (Bismarckstrasse 34) is the contemporary home—unremarkable architecturally—of the first-rank West

Berlin opera company. The repertory runs a delightfully wide gamut—Wagner's *Parsifal* through Tchaikovsky's *Pique Dame,* with a rich Italian core in between.

AFTER DARK

Schaubühne (Halleschen Ufer 32) has become celebrated, in recent seasons, as a center for avant-garde plays, both German and imported, including American. There are a number of other legitimate theaters, and a richly varied and constantly changing nightclub-cabaret-disco scene, of which the locals make much. Perhaps they are attempting to compensate for the fact that, for some reason or other, Berlin has fewer quality restaurants than any other large German city.

Spielbank Berlin (Europa Center) is West Berlin's heart-of-town casino, ultra-mod, invariably busy. The games are roulette, blackjack, and baccarat, and the hours are late.

INCIDENTAL INTELLIGENCE

You can, if you insist, take the train to West Berlin from West Germany; Hamburg is a good departure point. (Or make the trip in reverse.) But do not expect East German equipment to come anywhere near that of West Germany. Of course you may enter by car, as well, through East Germany, with whatever documents are required at the time of your trip; these usually include the so-called Green Card (international insurance). Much more sensible—the way most foreign visitors choose—is arrival by air. Under terms of the Allied-Soviet agreements, Lufthansa, the West German national carrier, still is not allowed to fly into Berlin. Only airlines of the occupying Western powers may do so; these are our own Pan American, Air France, and British Airways, which fly in not only from their own countries, but from other cities within West Germany—especially Frankfurt, Hamburg, Munich, and Nuremberg. Day tours from West Berlin to East Berlin and Potsdam are run by travel agencies. You may book on short notice through your hotel concierge; all you need to take with you is your passport and a minimum amount of marks specified by the East German government—the actual requirement varies from time to time. This money must be spent. You may also go on your own to East Berlin—again taking passport and abiding by the currency regulations currently in effect—simply by taking the U-Bahn (subway) from Zoo station in West Berlin, changing at Hallesches Tor to the Tegel line, and alighting in East Berlin at Friedrichstrasse station. Or you may enter East Berlin by car at Checkpoint Charlie (corner Friedrichstrasse and Zimmerstrasse). Any way you go, if you're a day visitor, you must—like Cinderella—be off to West Berlin from East, by midnight. That said, let me urge that instead you make a proper visit to East Berlin—staying a while in a hotel, possibly visiting other East German points, as well. *Further information:* Verkehrsamt Berlin—the West Berlin Tourist Office—is in Europa Center. For East Berlin—and more information on East Germany—read on.

EAST BERLIN

ON SCENE

Lay of the Land: The first-timer's reaction to East Berlin depends heavily on whether or not it is an initial introduction to a Communist state. If you've been to the Soviet Union or the Eastern European Communist lands, you'll find East Berlin more comfortable and its citizens more relaxed with non-Communist foreigners than those of other countries, save Hungary. On the other hand, if this is your first experience in the communist world, you must be prepared for an absolutely instant change from the West, as exemplified in West Berlin. (It is precisely this juxtaposition of the two lifestyles that makes Berlin unique. No other Communist capital but East Berlin is so geographically astride the West.)

Similarities to the western sector of the city will not, at first, be as apparent as differences. By that I mean the people speak the very same language, have inherited the very same centuries-old culture (variations have come only since World War II), and, for that matter, look very much the same. The East German standard of living is the highest of the Communist lands; people dress relatively fashionably and well, and are quite as immaculately groomed as their western neighbors. They live well (mostly in modern high-rise apartments) and eat well. They're well educated, though within the framework of their government's mostly orthodox and rigid Marxist ideology. And their cultural resources, in both the fine and performing arts, are extraordinarily rich, sometimes—as one discovers—surprisingly progressive in the Western sense.

Most important, perhaps, for the newcomer: East Germans do not have horns. They do not bite. They do not growl. They smile quite as often, I would guess, as West Germans. (The entire younger generation has known no way of life save communism in their land and in the neighboring Communist lands they are allowed to visit on vacations.) And they are, like most people anywhere, hospitable to foreigners: They welcome them both personally and officially (the United States and East Germany exchange ambassadors)

But there are other conditions to be prepared for. The Cyrillic alphabet will greet you on all multilingual official literature, for Russian—as in all Soviet bloc countries—is the second language, after German and before English and French. You'll see Soviet soldiers, too. As in all Communist countries where the state, through a variety of enterprises, controls the economy, the hubbub and noise and variety and vitality of Western commercial activity are absent. The streets of East Berlin are quieter, traffic sparser, and choice of destination—whether it be shops, cafés, or restaurants —more limited. There is the matter of sameness. Hotels are all a part of the same nationwide chain (it's called Inter Hotels) and they cater heavily to groups—mostly from fellow Communist countries. Menus in restaurants of the same category are fairly standard, countrywide, and because there still are not enough restaurants and cafés, they are invariably jammed, with *slow, slow, slow* service a consequence. (Pre-opera, -concert, or -theater tip: Dine *much* earlier than you would on the other side of Checkpoint Charlie: it will take you a lot longer.)

Arrangements for your visit? They're *all* made by the state's travel department, which promotes tourism and acts also as travel agent. The name: Reisebüro der Deutschen Demokratischen Republik, or simply Reisebüro der DDR. Headquarters is a tall office tower in the heart of town on Alexanderplatz, but every hotel in the country has a service branch for on-the-spot booking of tours, excursions, hotels, and the like.

To enter—except on the one-day excursions out of West Berlin—you'll need a visa and prepaid hotel accommodations. These may be booked through travel agents at home, who in turn make arrangements with the Reisebüro der DDR's United States representatives. (The principal U.S. representative is Koch Travel, 157 East 86th Street, New York, New York 10028.) Should you decide, while in West Berlin, that you would like to spend more than a day in East Germany, hop over, in the course of one of these excursions, to Reisebüro der DDR headquarters, or the travel-service desk of one of the East Berlin hotels, and make your arrangements on the spot. Generally, value for your dollar is excellent; East Germany is considerably less expensive than West.

Geographically, East Berlin is relatively uncomplicated, and in many respects more agreeable aesthetically than West Berlin. One misses West Berlin's verve, but the eastern sector is fortunate in having at least a nucleus of monumental buildings of the pre-war city, compared with almost none across the checkpoint.

The easiest way to orient oneself is to consider the Brandenburg Gate (actually just over the line, in West Berlin) a major landmark. It marks the terminus of East Berlin's most celebrated street, Unter den Linden, which cuts through it on a west-east axis. As it goes east, it passes Friedrichstrasse, which runs perpendicular to it, and which you will have heard of in West Berlin; it's the street on which Checkpoint Charlie is located, and on which you will find S-Bahn (surface rail) and U-Bahn (subway) stations. Not to mention the nearby Komische Oper, one of the two opera houses.

Unter den Linden—on which are lovely old buildings, such as the original Humboldt University and the Deutsche Staatsoper—ends at the principal square, Marx-Engels-Platz. It is dominated on the east by the massive Palast der Republik—an ultra-modern restaurant-and-café-filled, open-to-the-public government building; and on the north by Museum Insel, a conveniently located island on the Spree, a river that bisects the town. The island contains no less than a quartet of imposing pre-World War II buildings housing major museums.

Unter den Linden takes a new name—Karl-Liebknecht-Strasse—as it continues east, past the luxury Palasthotel and needle-slim Television Tower, to Alexanderplatz, with the towers of Hotel Stadt Berlin and the Reisebüro der DDR clearly in view, and the Hotel Berolina a near-neighbor. Ask at your hotel for the Reisebüro's excellent and free city map, and also for a copy of the biweekly What's On magazine, *Wohin in Berlin?* (whose map is very good, too). Now you're set to stroll about as you wish, when you wish, where you wish, with the heart of town easily negotiated on foot.

THE MUSEUM ISLAND MUSEUMS (Museum Insel): Come for the day on an excursion from West Berlin and you'll take in but one museum of this remarkable group (usually the Pergamon) which is housed in massively scaled late-nineteenth-century buildings that are a far cry from the ultra-mod Dahlem Museum complex in West Berlin. But these East Berlin museum buildings evoke the rich and powerful capital of the German Empire as the Dahlem—despite its treasures—cannot do. There are great works of art to be seen in both sectors of town. West Berlin comes out ahead on paintings, but East is not to be lightly dismissed in this area and has other spectacular exhibits. Here is how they break down:

The Pergamon Museum building houses the Antiquities Collection, with the Altar of Pergamon for which the building is named, and in addition the Near Eastern, Islamic, Far Eastern, and Folk. Skip the last two if you like. But the first three are requisites. The Pergamon Altar dates to 180 B.C. and hails from the city of Pergamon from which German archaeologists transported it, stone by stone, at the turn of the century. It is a city block in length, its vast staircase leading to a colonnaded shrine on a frieze-embellished base. The Near Eastern Museum's holdings are also monumental: First group includes a neo-Babylonian gate, walled roadway, and throne-room façade, all surfaced in brilliant enameled bricks dating to the seventh century B.C. Additionally: a Roman market gate of marble from the second century B.C. two magnificent arched-and-colonnaded stories in height, and about the size of the Pergamon Altar. The steep flight up to the Islamic Museum on the second floor is worthwhile—emphasis is on size, too: fragments of gates, palaces, and walls brought intact from the Islamic world to Berlin.

The Bode Museum has a number of different sections, too: If time is short, skip the Prehistory and Coin Museums, saving time for the Picture and Sculpture Galleries. The Early Christian and Egyptian Museums are also worthwhile if you can work them in. The Gemälde Galerie's paintings are second to Dresden's in East Germany: nothing like as extraordinary as what ended up in West Berlin's Dahlem after World War II, but hardly to be dismissed. Italian masters like Lippi, Bronzino, Moroni, Bassano, Canaletto, and Tiepolo; Low Countries greats including Rubens and Jordaens, Brueghel and Snyders, Cuyp and Seghers. You get the idea. The Skulpturen Sammlung's works are a top-caliber group, mostly German, and from the Low Countries, medieval through rococo, church altarpieces through classical gods and goddesses. The Frühchristlich-Byzantinische Sammlung's thrust is early Christian and Byzantine work—altar triptychs, huge mosaic frescoes from distant churches, icons and sarcophagi, with origins from Coptic Egypt to Italy. The Ägyptisches Museum's handsomest specimens include a honey of a minisphinx and a remarkable group of papyrus documents.

Nationalgalerie: This dead ringer for the Parthenon is a mixed bag as regards exhibits. Its range is eighteenth century through twentieth. There's some fine French work—Courbet, Rodin, Fantin-Latour, Degas, Vlaminck, Cézanne—and the rest is German. I like the big eighteenth-century views of Berlin, and the Anton Graff paintings of that same era. The nineteenth-century painters are mostly unfamiliar to us, until we get closer to our era with Max Liebermann and Lyonel Feininger.

Altes Museum is indeed *altes*—the granddaddy of the island cluster, going back to 1830, and fronted by a colonnaded row. The star of the show is a collection of a thousand Old Master drawings and many thousand additional prints from that era to ours. Hitch: they're not always on display.

Märkisches Museum (Am Köllnischen Park 5) is East Berlin's historical museum, with art and artifacts spanning the centuries—paintings, drawings, maps, porcelain, glass, and some charming music boxes.

Kunstgewerbemuseum (Schloss Kopenick, Kopenick) makes for an interesting half-day outing if one would like to see the industrial suburbs of the city. (You may go by train.) This museum—devoted to decorative arts—occupies a once-bucolic and still-handsome baroque palace out of the seventeenth century. There are two atmospheric floors full of fine furniture, silver, gold, pottery, and porcelain, all in a series of rooms with their original, somewhat sagging parquet floors and exuberantly frescoed and stuccoed ceilings and walls.

Tierpark (Am Tierpark in the Friedrichsfelde section, north of downtown) is East Berlin's zoo, and has its own subway station (Tierpark). Talk about carrying coals to Newcastle: lions born and bred on the premises—the big specialty—have been exported to Africa. The fauna run the gamut from buffalo to polar bears. Fun on a weekend, when local families are on hand.

Palast der Republik (Marx-Engels-Platz) is the splashy up-to-the-minute, multifacility government building that houses, among other things, the Volkskammer, East Germany's legislative chamber (have a look), not to mention halls for concerts and other public events (see *Sound of Music*), and a veritable galaxy of restaurants and cafés (see *Daily Bread*).

SETTLING IN

Palasthotel (Karl-Liebknecht-Strasse): Swedish architects designed this recent (1979) 600 room-and-suite house with unabashed capitalist luxury in mind. The accommodations, all of course with up-to-the-minute baths and air-conditioning, are smart Swedish modern. Amenities include a dozen restaurants, cafés French-style to *Bierstube.* And in addition, they include a swimming pool-sauna-solarium, a bowling alley, and—of course—the mandatory shops. Central and eye-opening. *Luxury.*

Hotel Metropol (Friedrichstrasse 150), only a couple of seasons older than the Palasthotel (above), was the first of the Western-style luxury houses. And what luxury! There are 340 suites (a couple with their own saunas) and rooms, pool/sauna/gym, and a variety of restaurants (including one I comment on later) and bars leading from the high-ceilinged lobby. An easy walk to both Deutsches Oper and Komische Oper. Shops. *Luxury.*

Hotel Stadt Berlin (Alexanderplatz) is a needle-like skyscraper of close to 1,000 rooms and suites, the leader in East Berlin before the Metropol and Palasthotel went up. A slew of dine-drink-dance spots, including a spiffy 37th-floor aerie. Shops. *First Class.*

Hotel Unter den Linden (Unter den Linden) is more intimate than the large hotels listed above and less elaborately equipped. The location is convenient—near both opera houses—and the principal restaurant, with its copper-hooded grill, is handsome. Lobby snack bar for snackers. Shops for shoppers. *Moderate.*

Hotel Berolina (Karl-Marx-Allee, off Alexanderplatz) is the senior house, in age, of our East Berlin group, even though it is a modern skyscraper, full-facility. *First Class.*

DAILY BREAD

Rotisserie (Palasthotel, Karl-Liebknecht-Strasse) offers elegance, *haute cuisine* (smoked brook trout, roast young pheasant, châteaubriand for two, sweets from the trolley), and skilled service. *Luxury.*

Spezialitätenrestaurant (Hotel Metropol, Friedrichstrasse) has a winning pub-like look: all dark wood, leather, and chrome. The fare is on the same sublime level as the Rotisserie at the Palasthotel. A good place to try East Germany's own red wine from Meissen. *Luxury.*

Panorama (Hotel Stadt Berlin, Alexanderplatz) is way, way up on floor 37, and a lovely view comes with the lunch. Order a

German specialty, if you require convincing that the native cuisine on both sides of the city's dividing line is similar. *First Class.*

Spreerestaurant (Palast der Republik, Marx-Engels-Platz) is the toniest eatery in this sprawling, very contemporary government facility. Mostly German fare, with the day's specials the best values. *First Class.* (Note also that there are two other full-service restaurants in this enormous, sprawling building—*Palast* and *Linden,* in addition to a *Weinstube, Bierstube,* milk-, coffee-, and ice-cream-bars.)

Moskau (Karl-Marx-Allee opposite Hotel Berolina) is for the genuine Russian article—borscht, shashlik, chicken Kiev, dry Georgian wines, too. *First Class.*

Ratskeller (Rathaus, Spandauerstrasse) is an atmospheric parlor out of the last century, not unlike its counterparts in West Germany. Good German fare, both beer and wine. Order the daily special. *Moderate.*

Ganymed (Am Schifferdam, next to Berliner Ensemble Theatre) is as appealing for its wines as for its food. This is a perfect introduction to the wines of East Germany's fellow Communist countries, especially Hungary, Bulgaria, and Romania. Steaks and salads. *First Class.*

Brecht-Centrum (Chausseestrasse) could be the parlor of a turn-of-century Berlin house. Menu features Berlin specialties. Small, attractive. Dinner only. *Luxury.*

Fernsehturm (Littenstrasse) is East Berlin's Television Tower. Like its counterparts round the globe, it has sources of sustenance, aloft—to capture the view—and below. Café and restaurant. *Moderate/First Class.*

Operncafé (Unter den Linden 5) is the city's most celebrated restaurant-landmark on its most celebrated thoroughfare, embracing café, proper restaurant, and a bar named for the adjacent opera house. *Moderate/First Class.*

SOUND OF MUSIC

Komische Oper (Behrenstrasse at Friedrichstrasse) looks, from the outside, like a fairly recent cinema. Within, this historic house has been exquisitely restored, with a brilliant rococo ceiling—supported by giant sculpted caryatids—framing an intimate auditorium, its red plush seats and curtain set off by ivory walls. To outlanders, the resident Komische companies—opera and ballet both—are not as well-known as those of the Deutsche Staatsoper, which is why I lead off with this East Berlin sleeper. Beg, borrow, or steal tickets to whatever is playing. There are no better voices anywhere in Germany—which is saying a lot. And the ballet's dancers have a light touch, à la Balanchine, not to mention a repertory with works by resident choreographer Tom Schilling that many of the international companies could do well by, including *Göttliche Komödie,* in which the male and female leads dance sans costume.

Deutsche Staatsoper (Unter den Linden) is the graceful neoclassic theater that was designed in the eighteenth century by the same architect—Knobelsdorff—whom Frederick the Great commissioned to create his Sans Souci Palace at Potsdam, among other Frederician works. It was badly bombed during World War II but painstakingly restored in period, reopening in 1955 with Wagner's *Die Meistersinger.* Both the opera and ballet companies of this house—while not as avant-garde as that of the Komische Oper—are top-rank. And, as with the Komische, sets, costumes, orchestras, direction are all superlative. Go!

Palast der Republik (Marx-Engels-Platz) is the site of symphonic and other concerts—by East German and visiting orchestras (usually from other Communist lands) in its striking Grosser Saal and Hauptfoyer. Concerts also take place in the two opera houses, and at other locales.

Berliner Ensemble (Bertolt-Brecht-Platz) is the Belle Époque-style theater wherein are performed the plays of Bertold Brecht—*Mutter Courage und ihre Kinder,* among others—and works by other masters including Shakespeare and Ben Jonson. In

German, of course. But that never stops Brecht—or other theater—buffs.

INCIDENTAL INTELLIGENCE

Interflug, East Germany's international airline, serves a number of communist and some capitalist European countries. Schönefeld Airport is but a few miles from town, and Interflug's city ticket office is at Alexanderplatz 5. Western European airlines flying into Schönefeld include KLM Royal Dutch Airlines and Scandinavian Airlines (SAS). Transfers from one's East Berlin hotel, or from Schönefeld Airport, can be arranged to West Berlin's Tegel Airport. *Further information:* Reisebüro der Deutschen Demokratische Republik, Alexanderplatz, Berlin, DDR; East Berlin City Tourism Information Office, Fernsehturm—that's the Television Tower—on Littenstrasse. And, in the USA, Koch Travel, 157 East 86th Street, New York, New York 10028.

9

Bonn

Campus to Capital

BACKGROUND BRIEFING

Poor Bonn. It is Germany's most unloved city, and surely the only European capital for which nationals of the country—nonresidents of Bonn, at least—feel somewhat contrained to apologize.

Actually, it is not all that bad a town. Not, at least, after one gets to know it, works a little to see what it is all about. What one discovers is that Bonn is not without facets of considerable interest, not the least of which is how it came to be the seat of the West German government.

The story you used to hear is that when World War II was over, and the longtime capital of Berlin was found to be plop in the middle of East Germany and under four-power occupation, West German Chancellor Konrad Adenauer—who had a house in the neighborhood of Bonn and had been a mayor of nearby Cologne—banged his fist on a table and said, simply but firmly, "Bonn it will be!" But Paul Zurnieden, in the book *Bonn: Federal Capital,* says that the true story wasn't that melodramatic, that at the time the selection was made Adenauer was not yet chancellor, and that there were other reasons for the German Parliamentary Council's close vote on May 10, 1949. On that day, Bonn got 33 of the council's votes, and Frankfurt, 29. What helped swing the votes to Bonn was the Berlin bloc, which voted for relatively obscure Bonn rather than for big-time Frankfurt because it feared that if Frankfurt won, it would remain the capital permanently, even after the day—sometime in the indefinite future—when the two Germanys would again be one. This fear existed not only because of Frankfurt's size and prestige but because of its historical eminence as well: for many years German kaisers were crowned there.

And so Bonn, which had been heavily bombed during World War II, and which had looked forward only to the day when it could resume its role as a provincial university center, found itself the command post of a vanquished Axis power about which the whole world was curious. It had never before known such attention.

What it may have lacked in eminence it made up for in age. Bonn goes back a thousand years to the time of the Romans who, in the middle of the first century A.D. set up a garrison called *Castra Bonnensia.* It lasted four centuries, and its successor, after an interval, was an early Christian community that became popular as a place of pilgrimage and gradually attracted commerce. Later centuries saw the electors of neighboring Cologne involve themselves in the growing by-then-fortified city. Twice in the fourteenth century the Bonn cathedral, or *Münster,* was the site of coronations. Bonn then came to serve as residence of the archbishops and electors of Cologne.

The Renaissance was an era of dramatic ups and downs, both temporal and spiritual; more than once the town was razed and rebuilt. Its golden period came in the eighteenth century—during the reigns of Cologne electors Maximilian Friedrich (famous for his contributions to fine arts and architecture) and Max Franz (a son of Austrian Empress Maria Theresa and patron of the young Beethoven).

That era saw the construction of buildings of grace and style that still remain Bonn's finest monuments. The founding of the present university came a century later, by which time Bonn had become part of Prussia. The city prospered to the point where, in the late 1800s, rich merchants and industrialists were attracted to it—they liked the bucolic Rhine-front setting—and built the great houses that stood the town in such good stead when the post-World War II government needed residences for such latter-day eminences as the federal president and the federal chancellor.

Fully a third of the town was destroyed by World War II bombs. But with its designation as capital after the war, a new prosperity came to the city. The German people have never quite accepted the indignity of such a relatively obscure town becoming their capital. But this did not stop the construction necessary to house government ministries. Civil servants from all over the republic moved to their new capital. When last I added them up, there were 111 diplomatic and consular missions in the city, ranging from Äthiopien (Ethiopia) to Zypern (Cyprus). The interaction of such a mixed group of people, representing every major faith, race, and culture on the globe, often results in a cosmopolitan community, particularly in an intellectual center like Bonn, with its respected university. But none of these groups seems to have had much effect.

There is no denying, its attributes notwithstanding, that Bonn lacks bounce. If things were not more lively and sophisticated in earlier days, one can well appreciate why Beethoven—native son No. 1—escaped to Vienna at the age of 22. Still, permanent residence and diplomatic long-term posting are one thing, a visitor-stay of a couple of days another. Bonn—as I will try to make clear—is not to be despised by any means.

ON SCENE

Lay of the Land: Bonn straddles the west bank of the Rhine, extending north to south. The heart of town, with the baroque old quarter, university, and pedestrians-only shopping area—centered on Remigiusstrasse between Marktplatz and Münsterplatz—is in the general vicinity of Kennedybrücke—one of three bridges across the Rhine. The Hauptbahnhof, not far west of this central area, is gained by Poststrasse from Münsterplatz.

Leading south, roughly paralleling the river, is the wide Adenauerallee, along which are a number of important public and semipublic structures. Adenauerallee leads to a prosaic modern shopping and office-building complex, Bonn Center, the core of the Federal Government—including Bundeshaus (the Parliament) and the ministries: it's called Regierungsviertel.

Another part of the city, Bad Godesberg, largely residential and full of diplomatic families, lies to the south, on the Rhine. Bonn is at its most charming in its historic central zone, which is where the pleasure visitor should establish headquarters.

Münster (Münsterplatz): This essentially Romanesque, five-tower church, in the heart of town, is Bonn's most spectacular architectural souvenir of old. The exterior alone is worth a walk-around. There is a soaring central spire, two rear towers framing a purely Romanesque apse, and an additional pair of towers—mini-towers, really—at the front entrance. The Münster spans nine centuries, and was the coronation church of two Holy Roman Emperors. You will want to pause in the tranquil cloister, and take a look at the strikingly arched crypt.

Beethoven's Geburtshaus (Bonngasse 20) rarely fails to win over even the most atonal and non-musical of visitors. As for the Beethoven buffs who enter the master's beautiful rococo birthplace, well, they rush for the Memorial Room in the attic—furnished only with a bust and wreath beneath it—to see the organ the master played in Bonn's still-standing Minoritenkirche. His last grand piano is there, too, as well as a host of paintings, miniatures, sculptures, scores, letters, documents, and other mementoes honoring the composer, including a register in which his birth on December 17, 1770, is recorded.

Rheinisches Landesmuseum (Colmantstrasse 14) is one of a number of this city's underappreciated museums, and a top-rank catch-all, embracing a wealth of antiquities dating to the Roman occupation of the region, as if to say to rival Cologne: You don't have it all! There are also works of art—fine and applied—of succeeding eras, including handsome eighteenth-century furniture, porcelains, and glass.

Kunstmuseum Bonn (Rathausgasse 7) is an unassuming little building that proves big things can come in small packages. Up you go to the second floor to feast your eyes on nothing less than a couple of dozen—the largest such cache extant—of the paintings of August Macke (pronounced *mack-ah*), Germany's most immediately likeable Expressionist painter of the early years of this century. Macke portrayed people in familiar settings. Or sometimes simply the familiar settings. Whichever, they are gay and bright and happy. Get hooked on Macke in Bonn, and you'll follow his work in galleries throughout Germany.

Ernst-Moritz-Arndt-Haus (Adenauerallee 79) lies behind a flower-filled garden half the length of a football field and lovingly tended. It goes back to 1819, the start of the Biedermeier period of design that continued almost to mid-century, with furniture in burled, light-hued woods with a fillip or two more of exuberance than that of the severe neoclassic period immediately preceding. This house, with a view of the Rhine, is a joyful two-floors-full of nineteenth-century Bonniana—paintings and prints, bibelots and books, chandeliers and cameos, not to mention the superb furniture. One of the most thoroughly engaging house-museums in Germany.

Rathaus and Universität: This is simply a suggestion for an agreeable walk, starting in Marktplatz (go early in the morning and catch the produce market), primarily to see the pink, gold, and white rococco façade of the little *Rathaus.* This is the Town Hall from whose steps heads of state invariably speak on Bonn visits—John F. Kennedy, Charles de Gaulle, and Queen Elizabeth. From Marktplatz cross the street called Am Hof, and you're in Hofgarten, an inner-city park that had been the gardens of the palace of the electors of Cologne. The University of Bonn occupies the main palace—long and broad and baroque. From here, if you're game for a longer hike, follow Poppelsdorfer-Allee, a knock-out of a tree-lined avenue that connects the electors' main palace with still another onetime royal residence, Schloss Poppelsdorfer; they're architecturally related but the Poppelsdorfer is easily visitable within. Reason: it's the university's Mineralogical Museum; you may not hanker after the rocks on display, but the interiors are a pleasure.

Regierungsviertel is, as I mentioned earlier, the tongue-twister of a name for the Federal Government quarter. There is nothing here of earth-shaking architectural or otherwise aesthetic significance. The *Bundeshaus* (Gorresstrasse 15)—Parliament—is a onetime teachers' college that's kept primly whitewashed. It used to be open to visitors when not in session, but the terrorism of recent years has resulted in an apprehensive attitude toward guests. At any rate, the Federal Republic's legislature is comprised of the Bundesrat, the upper chamber whose members are appointed to it by the ten Länder, or states, as well as West Berlin; and the Bundestag, the 496-seat lower house, whose members are elected to four-year terms by universal suffrage. As for national leaders: the two houses jointly elect the president for a five-year term. The official presidential residence is the house of a mid-nineteenth-century industrial tycoon, and it bears his name: *Villa Hammerschmidt* (Adenauerallee 135); you may drive by and peek—it's not open to the public. The chancellor of the Federal Republic—the actual leader of the government, not unlike a prime minister—is chosen by members of the lower house, the Bundestag, alone. The major political parties, as of course you know from reading the papers, are the Social Democrats and the Christian Democrats. The Free Democrats are No. 3., with the newer radical Green Party increasingly consequential. Official residence of the chancellor had been, since Bonn became the capital after World War II, still another mid-nineteenth-century mansion. Called *Palais Schaumburg* (Adenauerallee 139), it had earlier been home to a sister of the last kaiser, Wilhelm. Now, though, it's home to no one, but is used for government parties; not open to the public. The chancellor lives in a spanking modern chancellery, the *Bundeskanzleramt* (Bundeskanzlerplatz) which opened in 1976.

Doppelkirche (Dixstrasse, in nearby Schwarzreindorf) is worth a pilgrimage, at least for the visitor curious enough to seek out an ingeniously conceived upstairs-downstairs church constructed some 800 years ago, which remains a place of extraordinary beauty. Original frescoes cover the Romanesque arches and altars of both its *Oberkirche,* the upper church, and *Unterkirche,* the church directly beneath it, with railed octagonal openings allowing upstairs worshippers to look below; and vice versa!

SETTLING IN

Hotel Königshof (Adenauerallee 9) is as close as contemporary Bonn comes to a sense of style. In this case, it's post-World War II modern—subdued and unobtrusive, but holding up well both in the public areas (including a Rhine-view restaurant with terrace, of which more later) and the 100 rooms and suites. Location is a five-minute walk from the heart of town. You're in luck if a diplomatic reception takes place during the course of your stay. Station yourself in the lobby or front garden to watch chauffeured limousines drive up to the portico—each with its national flag fluttering from the hood—to drop off ambassadorial passengers, with ballet-like precision. There are more than 100 delegations, all told, and each country has an assigned permanent number on its license plate; locals memorize the numbers. *Luxury.*

Sternhotel (Marktplatz 8) has as its principal advantage a Marktplatz location, next door to the *Rathaus,* with its own terrace-café on the square. The inside is nothing fancy, although there's a nice restaurant, and most of the 65 comfortable rooms have their own baths. Good deal, this. *First Class.*

Hotel Bristol (Poppelsdorfer Allee at Prinz-Albert Strasse) is more beautifully equipped than it is beautiful—a big, ultra-mod, overdecorated house, not quite central, with 120 generous rooms and suites with bathrooms, indoor-outdoor pool/sauna, top-category restaurant, basement pub, and late-hour coffee shop. *Luxury.*

Hotel Beethoven (Rheingasse 24) is compact, modern, nicely located near the river (with fine views of it from the restaurant), but some of its singles and doubles—please note—contain sinks and showers but no toilets. If you want the complete bathroom package, specify so. *Moderate.*

Hotel Bergischer Hof (Münsterplatz 23) is well situated in the shadow of the Münster, and a good number of its nearly 30 rooms do have private baths. Restaurant. *Moderate.*

Hotel Gross (Bonngasse 17) is hardly as big as its name would indicate but there are a score of rooms, some with private bathrooms, and a location that could not be more central. Breakfast only. *Moderate.*

Hotel Dreesen (Rheinaustrasse 1, Bad Godesburg) is a rambling riverfront house—old school and agreeable—that may be worthwhile if you have a car, or are visiting friends in Bad Godesburg. Bedrooms are its chief treat, especially those with balconies overlooking the Rhine. (Even some of the baths have balconies.) There's a riverfront terrace-café, as well as a picture-window restaurant, whose fare is not as enticing as its setting. *Luxury.*

Hotel Godesburg (Auf der Godesburg 5, Bad Godesburg) is a novel contemporary hotel cleverly appended to what remains of the Godesburg, a thirteenth-century castle on a promontory overlooking the Rhine. At least go for a look at the ancient castle tower and take in the view. *First Class.*

Steigenberger Hotel (Am Bundeskanzlerplatz 5) is a graceless contemporary box that is, at least in the opinion of one former guest, the least successful of the pan-German Steigenberger chain. There are 160 rooms and suites, places to dine and drink, and a pool. Location is out in the government quarter, adjacent to a shopping center with all of the atmosphere of one, say, in Brandon, Manitoba. Recommended only to the traveler on government business, who wants to be a hop and a skip from the ministries. *Luxury.*

DAILY BREAD

Schaarschmidt (Brüdergasse 14), in an atmospheric old house, is a sensible choice, to be taken in tandem with the opera, of which it's a near-neighbor. Forget that German name: when it comes to the fare, this place is for French specialties like roast lamb in the Gallic manner, or Charolais beef in mustard sauce. French and German wines. *Luxury.*

Beethovenhalle Restaurant (Theaterstrasse 3) is the spacious Rhine-view dining room of Bonn's modern concert hall, with an attached terrace, and fine views. Fare is competent German and international. *First Class.*

Petit Poisson (Wilhelmstrasse 23) is a French winner—and not only for fish, as its name suggests. *First Class.*

Grand Italia (Bischofsplatz 1) is a welcome reminder of the peninsular republic to the south. Have a comforting bowl of minestrone and a plate of pasta, with an Italian wine. *Moderate/First Class.*

Restaurant Royal (Hotel Königshof, Adenauerallee 9) is this handsome hotel at its handsomest, a quiet, contemporary environment with two thrusts: a good international kitchen and a smashing view of the Rhine, which it and its open-air terrace overlook. *Luxury.*

Im Bären (Acherstrasse 1) is for big steins of beer and delicious grilled sausages, of which no visitor to Germany that I know has ever tired. Fun. *Moderate.*

Die Pantry (Wesselstrasse 5) is ideal for a casual meal; its feature is a help-yourself salad-buffet. Good fish dishes, too. Central. *Moderate.*

Café-Konditorei Dahmen (Poststrasse 19) is Bonn's traditional café leader—redolent of the last century, with super pastries to accompany your coffee. *Moderate.*

Bonner Kaffeehaus (Remediostrasse): ersatz nineties, with mobs of locals. Go for coffee or a meal. Location is the main pedestrians-only shopping street. *Moderate.*

SOUND OF MUSIC

Beethovenhalle (Theaterstrasse) is a strikingly contemporary hall, appropriately named for Bonn's favorite son, and home base for the city's distinguished Orchester der Beethovenhalle.

Central and on the Rhine. With a restaurant that I've recommended above.

Theater der Stadt Bonn (Am Boeselagerhof 1) is a well-designed, medium-sized, modern house whose resident opera troupe is of surprisingly high caliber. Even Germans from other parts of the country—who are patronizing toward their federal capital—are impressed with productions of the Bonn Oper.

INCIDENTAL INTELLIGENCE

Bonn shares an international airport with nearby Cologne, and is connected with the other German cities on Lufthansa's domestic and European routes. Cologne-Bonn International Airport is 17 miles northeast of the capital with which it is linked by regularly departing airport buses. If you've flown transatlantic to Frankfurt or Düsseldorf, Lufthansa's Air Express train will take you from those airports to Bonn. This is as good a Rhine River port as any for cruises of varying lengths. *Further information:* Werbe-und-Verkehrsamt der Bundeshauptstadt Bonn—boiled down, that means city tourist office—is at Münsterstrasse 20, Bonn.

10

Bremen

Proud and Hanseatic

BACKGROUND BRIEFING

The Hanseatic League, though never formally dissolved, has not had a meeting since 1669. It is all very well for us New Worlders to regard that association of medieval northern European trading towns as a rather dry chapter in a history book. But Bremen has never quite gotten over its eminence as a leading League light.

Still styling itself the Free Hanseatic City of Bremen—*Freie Hansestadt Bremen*—it is, especially when combined with its sister city, Bremerhaven, a major world port. At the same time, Bremen is Germany's smallest *Land,* or state—in other words, a city-state in an era when such governmental entities are rarities.

But Bremen has always been rather special. It was an archbishopric as early as the ninth century—a time when the archdiocesan territory ranged through all of Scandinavia. In the seventeenth century, by which time the Hanseatic League's eminence had waned, the town moved right along, gaining status as a Free Imperial City of the Holy Roman Empire.

Later centuries saw its maritime power strengthen until, by the middle of the nineteenth (in partnership with Bremerhaven) it had gained world status. It reacted to the privations following

World War I by again distinguishing itself—as a short-lived (1918-19), albeit sovereign, socialist republic.

World War II left its mark on Bremen: heavy destruction. But matchless monuments remain, some original, some restored. And the city has regained its former wealth, pride, and, if one may say so, at this point, North German arrogance, coupled with an inferiority complex that comes from being a close neighbor of giant Hamburg. If it is true that anything Bremen does, Hamburg does better, it is also true that the smaller city is far from being a small-scale imitator of the larger.

Enough is worth visiting in Bremen to warrant a couple of days in residence, as long as one does not expect a barrel of laughs. This is a city that most of the time takes itself seriously. What light touches one does encounter are more self-conscious than spontaneous.

ON SCENE

Lay of the Land: Considering its size—a fairly substantial city—Bremen's central area is relatively compact, and for the hardy, walkable. The trick is to establish headquarters at a centrally situated hotel. There are a number near the Hauptbahnhof, where many visitors arrive. From the station, one may walk into the historic zone by proceeding south along Bahnhofstrasse, continuing as it changes its name to Sögestrasse, eventually touching base with Marktplatz, off of which—perpendicular to pedestrians-only Sögestrasse—leads the commercially important Obernstrasse. Another street of major visitor interest—Böttcherstrasse—runs in the same direction of Sögestrasse, and is likewise reached by Marktplatz. Schnoor, the name of a street that is still another must-see, is to the south and east, and might well be taken in along with a visit to the Kunsthalle, an art museum situated in Wallanlagen, the green belt that fringes downtown, to the north. Bremen's, southern frontier is the Weser River; regularly scheduled boat tours of the harbor depart from Martini Pier, due south of Marktplatz.

Rathaus (Marktplatz) is the building of which Bremen is proudest. It melds Gothic and Renaissance styles, making just the statement that pleases Bremen's burghers. It says, as no press release or color booklet could: "We are a very rich city and have been so for half a millennium." The façade on Marktplatz is one of Europe's most beautiful—elegantly gabled, richly sculpted, multi-arched at street level. The ground-floor hall, open as a kind of public market and with a simple, beamed-ceiling decor, is Middle Ages in origin. The Upper Hall on the second floor is open only to scheduled guided tours, worth looking into if one would see the city's most beautiful interior. Immense ship models hang from the ceiling amid brass chandeliers. There are, as well, a quartet of stone-fringed portals, museum-caliber historical frescoes, and a gem of a spiral staircase leading to a room called the Golden Chamber—anticlimactic after the approach to it.

Roland Statue (Marktplatz) has been, since it went up in the fifteenth century, a symbol of Bremen's independence and pride. Roland is a larger-than-life medieval knight (his height is 16 feet). You can't miss him—and won't want to.

St. Petri Dom (Marktplatz) is the graceful twin-spire church that dominates Marktplatz along with the Rathaus. It is the Catholic cathedral of this largely Protestant city, not one of Germany's most beautiful but hardly to be ignored. It's a millennium old, with a lovely rose window, an oddball interior embracing a pair of naves separated by a wall, some recently discovered frescoes and floor tombs, a museum of its treasures, and its own answer to world Egyptomania—a crypt jam-packed with a freaky collection of mummified bodies, mostly dating to the fifteenth century.

Schütting (Marktplatz) is still another Marktplatz monument, a honey of a sixteenth-century work that went up as a merchants' guild and today serves a similar function: it's the Bremen Chamber of Commerce. Pop inside.

Bürgerschaft (Marktplatz) strikes a jarring note in the Marktplatz: an architecturally prosaic mod-look structure—with a façade more glass than steel—that serves as parliament of the *Land*, or city-state, of *Bremen*. If you haven't seen a *Land* legislature in session elsewhere in the Federal Republic, visit Bremen's. The 100-member legislative chamber is up a flight, severely clean-lined, but not unlike others you've seen in other democratic lands.

Böttcherstrasse, a deftly restored ancient street—heart of downtown—is Bremen at its most light-hearted. And it has a lot more than zippy, bright-look shops and cafés. There is, first of all, a set of chimes that ring thrice daily—traditionally at noon, 3 P.M. and 6 P.M.—and there is the frosting on the Böttcherstrasse cake: a late-Middle Ages mansion—seven stories, gabled and shuttered—that houses a pair of extraordinary museums. The first comprises a series of Renaissance rooms, furnished with collections of silver, pottery, pistols, sculpture, and, as a bonus, a room full of Cranach paintings—seven by my count. Keep moving, though. Soon you're in the other museum, this one devoted to paintings of another era—the late nineteenth century—by Bremen's own Paula Modersohn-Becker, who created portraits and still-lifes in the manner of the French Impressionists, but in her own winning style, and whose work is celebrated Germany-wide.

Kunsthalle (Am Wall 207) is Bremen's principal art museum, a bit away from the center, but important for two aspects of its collection. First is the strength of its Dutch Old Masters—Rembrandt, Terborch, Cuyp among them—along with a sprinkling of other nationalities—Germany's own Cranach through Italy's Tiepolo. Then there are Impressionists and their contemporaries—Van Gogh, Vlaminck, Utrillo, to name some—with German Expressionists, such as August Macke. Later artists: Picasso, Léger, and Dufy.

Schnoor, an ancient street being restored with considerable panache, is quite as much fun as Böttcherstrasse, but with a personality of its own. The antique houses are less grand, mostly doll-sized, and now sheltering trendy shops—specializing in gourmet foods, made-on-premises candies, one-of-a-kind crafts—as well as engaging cafés and restaurants, with affluent artists and artisans in residence on upper floors. Give it an hour or two.

Focke Museum (Schwachhauser Heerstrasse 240) is a fairish taxi or streetcar hop from downtown; I wouldn't suggest it if it weren't outstanding. This is Bremen's folk-historical museum. It occupies a cluster of venerable country houses set in their own little park, and it's lovely. The main building has the oldest objects—armor, shields, swords, and daggers, ancient coins and religious sculpture, portraits of early patricians and their ladies, painted glass and etched crystal, models and paintings of ships in profusion. Still another building recreates rococo Bremen by means of a series of exquisitely furnished eighteenth-century rooms. With a restaurant, of which more later; and a barn, windmill, and farmhouse—all nineteenth century—in the garden.

SETTLING IN

Hotel Columbus (Bahnhofplatz) is, for my money, No. 1 in town: handsome, quietly contemporary, with 140 rooms and suites, tapestry-lined lobby, maritime-style basement bar-lounge popular with locals and visitors alike, a pair of exemplary restaurants, and cheery service. Location is opposite the station, convenient to the heart of town. *Luxury.*

Hotel zur Post (Bahnhofplatz) is an across-the-platz neighbor of the Columbus, with an equally convenient location, a look more compact and mod, brisk service, nearly 140 agreeable rooms and suites, nice restaurant and bar, indoor pool and gym. *First Class.*

Überseehotel (Wachstrasse 27) is a winner: a step from Marktplatz, at once central and good-looking (the motif is imaginative modern), with full baths, restaurant, and bar-lounge. *First Class.*

Bahnhofshotel (Bahnhofplatz) is a house worth knowing about in the budget category; well-located, with some 30 comfortable rooms; breakfast only. *Moderate.*

Park Hotel (Bürgerpark) is at the bottom of my list. First, because its away-from-the-center location—pretty to be sure, in a pretty park—isolates it from the city's core. One needs a car or taxi to go back and forth. Second, because its location—with no competition nearby—appears, sadly, to have affected the quality of the service, or so it seemed on my most recent stay. This is a post-World War II building, understated modern, of that period, to the point of blandness, with the bar its best-looking room. *Luxury.*

DAILY BREAD

Ratskeller (Rathaus, Marktplatz) is the long-on-the-scene and long-celebrated restaurant in the bowels of the *Rathaus,* embracing a series of atmospheric chambers, with one of the most extensive wine cellars in Germany, and a wide-ranging menu, with dishes both hearty (sauerbraten) and delicate (grilled sole). If you're going to have but one Bremen lunch or dinner, it should be here. *First Class.*

Schnoor 2 (Schnoor 2) occupies a handsomely restored and decorated antique house on a street mentioned earlier for interesting restored structures and joie de vivre. One lunches or dines in snug booths tucked into a maze of crannies on two low-ceilinged levels. Both fare and service are professional. Order Bremen's most noted specialty, cream of crab soup. And either fish or the meat specialties. *Luxury.*

Martini (Böttcherstrasse 2) is the ideal eatery on this interesting street. The look is peppy modern, the menu full of delicious specialties (steaks are memorable), and the tabs *Moderate.*

Stadtrestaurant (Hotel Columbus, Bahnhofplatz) is the pubbier of the excellent pair in this hotel, with tasty favorites—*Wiener schnitzel,* veal steak, delicious soups and desserts. *First Class.*

Focke Museum Restaurant (Schwachhauser Heerstrasse 240) is probably the handsomest restaurant in town, stylish country-look, with fare to match. *First Class.*

Alt-Bremer Brauhaus (Katharinen Klosterhof 32) is included here only because tour groups, and often unsuspecting individuals, are steered to it. It is to Bremen what the tourist-packed, schmaltzy beer halls are to Munich: drearily atypical. Food is dull and heavy, music deafening, entertainment embarrassing, if only for the sight of unsmiling, unescorted ladies dancing together. *Moderate.*

SOUND OF MUSIC

Theater am Goetheplatz (Goetheplatz) is Bremen's opera house, with a repertory company offering a traditional range—Wagner to *A Turk in Italy;* musical comedies, too.

Stadthalle (Hollerallee) is the boldly modern hall used for concerts of all kinds.

Puppentheater (Wüstestatte 11) is a winsome house in the Schnoor district for puppet plays, including *Pinocchio* and *Rumpelstiltskin.* Kids' matinees and evening performances.

INCIDENTAL INTELLIGENCE

Bremen is an easy day-long train excursion from Hamburg, if you would hit only the highlights. Worth noting, too: it's one of the select network of West German cities served by Lufthansa. Neuenland Airport is but three miles from town, and is connected with it by tram. *Further information:* Verkehrsverein Bremen—the city tourist office—has its own building on Bahnhofplatz.

11

Cologne/Köln

Rhineland's Chief Charmspot

BACKGROUND BRIEFING

Cologne is its cathedral, and its cathedral is Cologne. In no other major European city that I know of, save perhaps Milan, does the life of the town so revolve around its principal religious edifice. (These two cities have still another matter in common: in each, construction of the great Gothic cathedral began in the Middle Ages and was not completed until the last century.)

If Cologne is enamored of its *Dom,* it remains attached, too, to its quite respectable origins. It reminds today's visitors that a couple of millennia back it was the "Rome of the North." Kölners will go on to tell you that their town knew sophisticated plumbing and hygiene and architecture and communications as long ago as did ancient Rome. Roman remnants still are everywhere to be found, even in long-unturned earth that is dug when new buildings go up.

The Romans first came as soldiers. In the century before Christ they built a garrison on the Rhine that was—in the century after Christ—to become a proper colony. Indeed, *Colonia* it was named by the emperor of the moment, Claudius, who appended his name and that of his locally born empress to the official title: *Colonia Claudia Ara Agrippinensis.* It's no wonder that

that four-word mouthful found itself shortened simply to *Colonia*—and that is the name that stuck.

The Romans settled into their northern headquarters for some four centuries, eventually losing control to Germanic Franks who took over in the fifth century what had for some decades been the seat of a Christian bishop. Later, under Charlemagne, the bishopric became an archbishopric, with secular as well as spiritual power.

The archbishops of Cologne—who were to evolve as prince-electors of the Holy Roman Empire—came to rule a Rhineland realm. Indeed, they became so smug that the local officials they antagonized forced them to move their palace, at first to nearby Brühl (where its rococo splendor remains a joy to visit), and later to neighboring Bonn (where it now houses the university).

By that time Cologne had long since made its mark, not only spiritually (work started on the cathedral in the thirteenth century) but politically and economically as one of the few Hanseatic League members that was not a seaport. Like many German cities, Cologne fell into French hands in the late eighteenth century and then reverted to German control—the king of Prussia took over in the early nineteenth.

As a part of Prussia—and later as a part of Bismarck's German Empire—Cologne grew rich, rich enough indeed to finally complete its cathedral while amassing wealth as a manufacturing center and terminus for transport—both river and rail. During the decade and a half before the Nazis, the city's mayor was the very same Konrad Adenauer who was to become the post-war Federal Republic's first chancellor. (Adenauer is remembered as the mayor under whom the ancient university was reestablished, the confining outer fortifications of the city replaced by a green belt, and its intellectual vigor developed.)

World War II was bound to be disastrous for so strategically valuable a center. Something like 90 percent of the city was destroyed by virtually unrelenting Allied bombings. Even during this period, the cathedral played a major role, thanks to the voice of a fearless priest—Joseph Frings, who was archbishop of what had become the world's second largest diocese after Milan. Cardinal Frings, in 1943 and again in 1944, had the courage to lash out, from the cathedral pulpit, at Nazi persecution of Jews as "an injustice that cries to the heavens."

Even after World War II, Cardinal Frings's sermons from the cathedral pulpit were global news. In 1946, while his countrymen were still struggling to rebuild their land and their lives, filching food and provisions in the process, he reassured them that "in an emergency, the individual may take what he desperately needs for his survival and his health, so long as he cannot provide it through other means." The sermon became a contemporary German classic, even adding a slang word—*fringsen,* connoting an illegal act of self-preservation—to the German vocabulary.

Post-war reconstruction has been a remarkable achievement, and—not unsurprisingly—the cathedral has served as the focal point. (It was closed for restoration and rebuilding for more than a decade—from war's end until 1956.) This is a made-to-order tourist town: easy to grasp, and to negotiate geographically; with splendid monuments of its past, all of which are easily accessible; well-equipped in both creature comforts and after-dark diversion; and with a perky populace, at ease with foreigners. Cologne is one of Germany's most immediately likable cites.

ON SCENE

Lay of the Land: I've already made clear the dominant role of the cathedral. It occupies its own square right in the heart of the action (by that I mean due west of the Rhine). Hohenzollernbrücke, one of three principal Cologne bridges, crosses in the cathedral's shadow. Trains roll right into still another cathedral near-neighbor: the Hauptbahnhof. Hotels—major, middling, modest—cluster about the cathedral, as do a pair of museums (including the outstanding Römisch-Germanisches). Additionally, it is from the cathedral that one approaches Cologne's delightful pedestrians-only shopping streets: Hohestrasse, the High Street, runs south, a good quarter-hour's walk to an intersecting street (running perpendicular to it) called Schildergasse; Schildergasse continues the pedestrians' route westward to the vast square called Neumarkt. Most places the visitor will want to explore are within the area delineated by this route; you can

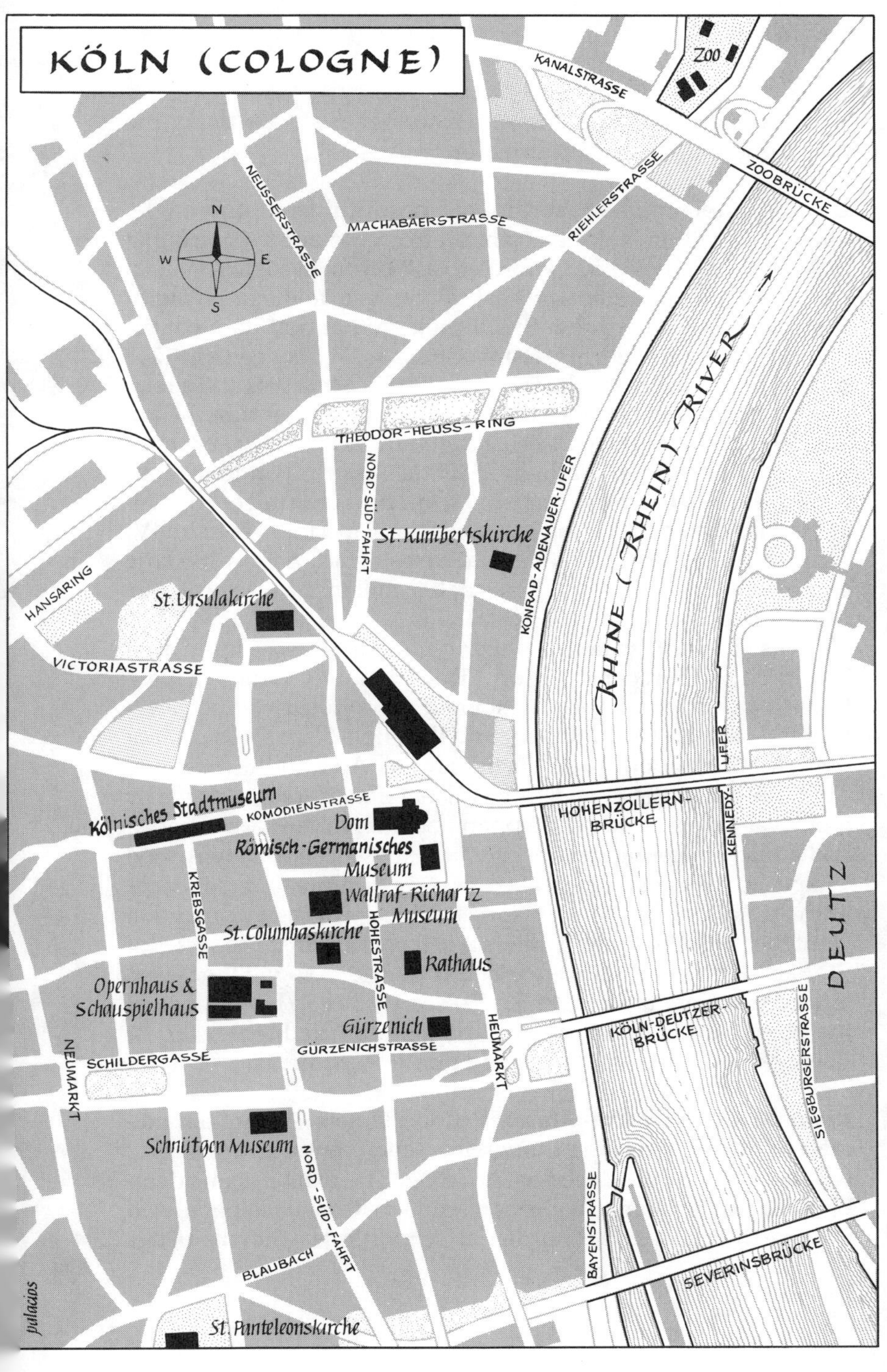

KÖLN (COLOGNE)
ZOO
KANALSTRASSE
ZOOBRÜCKE
RIEHLERSTRASSE
NEUSSERSTRASSE
MACHABÄERSTRASSE
N
W
E
S
THEODOR-HEUSS-RING
NORD-SÜD-FAHRT
KONRAD-ADENAUER-UFER
RHINE (RHEIN) RIVER
St. Kunibertskirche
HANSARING
St. Ursulakirche
VICTORIASTRASSE
KENNEDY-UFER
HOHENZOLLERN-BRÜCKE
Kölnisches Stadtmuseum
KOMODIENSTRASSE
Dom
Römisch-Germanisches Museum
KREBSGASSE
Wallraf-Richartz Museum
St. Columbaskirche
HOHESTRASSE
Rathaus
DEUTZ
Opernhaus & Schauspielhaus
Gürzenich
HEUMARKT
KÖLN-DEUTZER-BRÜCKE
SIEGBURGERSTRASSE
NEUMARKT
SCHILDERGASSE
GÜRZENICHSTRASSE
Schnütgen Museum
NORD-SÜD-FAHRT
BAYENSTRASSE
SEVERINSBRÜCKE
BLAUBACH
St. Panteleonskirche
palacios

walk almost everywhere in central Cologne, always using the twin cathedral spires for orientation.

Dom (Domplatz) is extraordinarily beautiful from any angle, without as within. (Not to mention from the air, if you're that lucky.) People have been known to ask for Dom-view rooms in the Dom Hotel next door so that they can take in the façade with their breakfast and—when it's illuminated and at its most romantic just before retiring. (I am one such.) Work began in 1248 on this great Gothic landmark. (The Gothic style was still a relatively bold departure from the Romanesque at that time.) Construction continued, with some halts, until the early sixteenth century, when there was a long hiatus—more than three centuries—before the romanticism of the nineteenth century inspired a move to finish the job. The Prussian king, Wilhelm IV, came from Berlin in 1842 to signal a fresh start, and in 1880 the completed Cologne Cathedral—half a millennium after it was begun—received worshipers.

It was worth the wait. (And worth the years it was closed after World War II for reconstruction.) The splendidly vaulted nave—flanked by aisles with lovely stained glass in their windows—leads to a massive Gothic choir and the High Altar. Pause at that point for the golden Three Magis' Shrine. And don't hesitate to catch the art in the chapels—*Virgin and Child with the Magis,* by medieval Cologne master Stephan Lochner, in the Lady Chapel, and a huge millennium-old crucifix in the appropriately named Chapel of the Cross. There is a stairway of more than 500 steps to the tip of one of the twin spires, which you may or may not want to negotiate. (New Yorkers will recognize that the spires of St. Patrick's Cathedral are variations on the Cologne theme; so indeed is the architecture of St. Patrick's.) But do have a look at the objects in the treasury—ravishing illuminated manuscripts, finely carved ivory, gold-threaded priests' vestments.

Römisch-Germanisches Museum (Roncalliplatz 4) is an immediate neighbor of the Dom, though it is seven centuries younger. I speak only of its ultra-modern building. The exhibits considerably predate the Dom; they're souvenirs of Roman Cologne, and it's worth bucking the hordes of school kids—they're better behaved than many of ours might be—to take in what is probably the most frequently visited museum in the Rhineland. Star of the show is a mosaic floor—the Dionysian Mosaic it's called—from a second-century house that stood at the very spot where the museum stands. Originally in the house's dining room, the mosaic embraces 32 panels—of fruit, flowers, animals—with representations of the god Bacchus (Dionysos to the Greeks) dominating. But there's so much more in this museum—a coin with the head of Empress Agrippina, the locally born wife of founding Emperor Claudius; pottery and busts, tablets and markers, cameos and jewels, vases and kitchen gadgets. The two-level layout is worth seeing in itself, with mock-ups of entire rooms from ancient Roman houses, where tables are set as they might be in Home Furnishings at Bloomingdale's or Marshall Field's. And there are clusters of portable stools scattered about. Pick one up and take it to wherever you like, then sit and observe—or ponder.

Erzbischöfliches Diözesanmuseum (Roncalliplatz 2) is another museum neighboring the Dom. Operated by the archdiocese, it is small but treasure-filled, with church art of the Middle Ages, including an exquisite *Madonna and Child* by the same Stephan Lochner who painted the altar in the Dom and a smiling sculpture of St. Nicholas—to name two.

Wallraf-Richartz Museum (An der Rechtschule): Before you enter the museum, take a peek at its next-door neighbor, restored fourteenth-century Gothic *Minoritenkirche*—severely handsome. Then ready yourself for an art museum that ranks not only with the two Germanys' best—Frankfurt's Städel, Berlin's Dahlem, Munich's Alte Pinakothek, Dresden's Picture Gallery—but is right up there with Europe's leaders. Named for its founders—the former an art collector, the latter a rich merchant—the museum celebrated its 150th birthday in 1974. It constitutes a survey of painting, medieval to contemporary. The quality is as outstanding as the quantity. There is a rich menu here. You start with the works of German artists such as Dürer, the Cranachs, and Stephan Lochner, who did several of the altars here. Move, then, to some of the medieval greats of the Low Countries—

Massys, van Cleve, Bosch, and others—and to the baroque paintings of that region: still lifes by Brueghel, landscapes by van Ruysdael, and works by Rubens and Van Dyck, Teniers and Snyders, Jordaens and de Vos. Not to mention some beautiful Rembrandts, including a self-portrait.

There are works by rococo Italians like Canaletto and Tiepolo, rococo Frenchmen like Boucher and Rigaud, Spaniards like Murillo and de Ribera, and later French immortals beginning with Corot and continuing with Renoir, Cézanne, Manet, Bonnard, Monet, Pissaro, Sisley, and Vuillard. The German Expressionists have a strong representation—Kirchner especially—as have contemporary Americans—even including the almost frighteningly life-like sculptures of his fellow-citizens by Duane Hansen, and paintings by Frank Stella and Morris Louis. Half a day here is not too much. Cafeteria, for coffee breaks or a light lunch.

Schnütgen Museum (Cäcilienstrasse 29): The concept of an ancient desanctified church as a setting for an art museum is not all that novel. In other European countries one comes across collections ranging from Greek sculpture to wrought-iron work from the Renaissance in onetime sanctuaries. Nowhere else, though, that I know of has a church been converted into a museum with more panache—and indeed with more striking beauty—than the Schnütgen, current occupant of a twelfth-century Romanesque/Gothic church called Cäcilienkirche—St. Cecilia's. Alexander Schnütgen was a Cologne priest whose hobby was sacred art. At the time he served—the latter decades of the last century—the city's church lofts and sacristies still bulged with brilliant art of the Middle Ages. In the course of his work he was in a position to come across—and collect—objects that in many cases would have been sold to foreign collectors. When he died early in this century he bequeathed an extraordinary collection to the city. Its home has been St. Cecilia's (with a wing added) only since World War II. The plaster walls above the stone arches of the nave have been whitewashed, the better to show off the art, and the visitor is as moved by the environment as by the exhibits. There are covers of carved ivory missals, pages from illuminated manuscripts, incense burners of brass, saints carved from stone and wood, emotion-charged Madonnas and crucifixions, stained glass and altarpieces, embroideries and priests' chasubles, monstrances, and candelabra. Please go.

Kölnisches Stadtmuseum (Zueghausstrasse 1): The arsenals that must have been commonplace in most European cities probably suffered a common fate: they were blown up. The only other one I know of, still standing, is a beauty in Venice. But it's not open to visitors. Here in Cologne, though, the arsenal has been turned into the city historical museum. It's special. Two floors of maps, etchings, paintings of earlier centuries, with guns, armor, and all manner of Cologniana. If you like city historical museums in historic settings, you'll like Cologne's.

Apostelnkirche (Neumarkt) is, first, alliterative—Rhineland Romanesque—and second, striking. It's massive and imposing without—on a major city square—and within you'll want to admire the spacious choir and oddly low-slung nave.

St. Panteleonkirche (Waisenhausgasse) is a page out of a fairy tale—twin-towered Romanesque that goes back 1,000 years. There are a treasury of masterworks, and delightful *faux marbre* (fake marble) interior accents from the much later baroque period.

St. Ursulakirche (Ursulaplatz) is Romanesque, with its Golden Chamber a worthy destination. (Get the key from the verger, after promising, of course, to return it.) A dazzler.

Rathaus (Judengasse): The City Hall is disappointingly modest for a city as otherwise impressive as Cologne. Still, it dates to the fourteenth century, although there are later additions. The façade is more eye-filling than the interior.

St. Severinkirche (Severinstrasse) is distinguished by a graceful front spire—tall and square—and a pair of twin mini-spires. A Romanesque-Gothic meld full of artworks.

Antoniterkirche (Schildergasse) is a little church you'll want to pop into in the course of shopping strolls on pedestrians-only Schildergasse. Restored Gothic with memorials to victims of two World Wars, and works by German moderns like Ernst Barlach. Moving.

Zoo (Riehlerstrasse): Cologne's zoo is well over a century old, but today's version is post-World War II. If you're in town on a weekend, go—not only for the animals (especially the monkeys and birds, not to mention the fish in the aquarium) but to mix with the local citizenry, as well. *The Botanical Garden*—with lush tropical and subtropical vegetation in its greenhouses—is an adjacent bonus.

SETTLING IN

Dom Hotel (Domkloster 2) could not be more aptly named. You can almost touch the cathedral from those rooms that face it. And it's very grand. Indeed, few German hotels have such tastefully appointed rooms and suites—there are 150. With all of this going for it, it's not surprising that the reception staff and concierges are spoiled and can be hoity-toity: bar-lounge is friendlier, if not the restaurant. Cathedral-view terrace-café. *Luxury.*

Excelsior Hotel Ernst (Domplatz) is the other of the pair of spiffy hotels flanking the cathedral. It's a mite more distant from the Dom than the Dom Hotel, and one has the feeling that reception and concierge staff here try to be friendlier than the competition. The nearly 150 rooms and suites are handsomely traditional, mostly Louis XV and Louis XVI in style. There are a kicky bar and a pair of restaurants, the basement *Keller* and another exceptional enough to rate further comment. Member, Leading Hotels of the World. *Luxury.*

Hotel Inter-Continental Cologne (Helenestrasse 14): Like its sister Inter-Contis in five other major German cities, this is a smartly operated modern house that works well from the accommodations—some 300 suites and rooms, with all the HIC comforts—on to amenities that include a nifty high-ceilinged indoor pool-cum-café, capacious bar-lounge that's a major gossip-spot with locals, and a pair of restaurants—one of them an informal *Bierstube* that's fun. I wish the location were more central; still, it's but a 15-minute walk to the cathedral. *Luxury.*

Hotel Mondial (Berchergasse 10) has the advantages of modernity—200-plus fully equipped rooms and suites, a convenient restaurant, café, and bar; and an ideal near-cathedral situation. *First Class.*

Senats Hotel (Under Goldschmied 9) is still another sensible choice: half a hundred rooms with baths; restaurant. Modern. Very central. *First Class.*

Hotel Europa am Dom (Am Hof 38) is a modern house built over a medieval cellar called Treppchen-Keller, which it operates as a wine restaurant with music. Above ground, there are 100-plus rooms, almost all with baths, and some with terraces affording smashing views of the neighboring cathedral. Main-floor restaurant-café, too. *First Class.*

Hotel am Augustinerplatz (Hohestrasse 30) is no-nonsense modern. By that I mean all 110 rooms have a bath or shower; there's a convenient bar-lounge, and prompt breakfast service. Splendidly central. No restaurant. *Moderate.*

Hotel Ludwig (Brandenburgerstrasse 24) is a cheery, good-value house that you like from the moment you're welcomed with a smile at reception—which doubles as a bar from whose fridge you may order liquid refreshment. The rooms are small but nice, and many have private baths. Very central. *Moderate.*

Hotel Berlin (Domstrasse 10) has private baths in a good number of its 90 functional rooms. *Weinstube*/restaurant. Location is north of the cathedral. *Moderate.*

Hotel Thielen (Brandenburgerstrasse 1) is a pair of joined, updated houses with the decor crazy but cozy. Half a dozen rooms have their own baths: there's a big basement shower room for occupants of the other rooms. Very friendly management. Central. *Moderate.*

DAILY BREAD

Hanse Stube (Excelsior Hotel Ernst, Domplatz) is Cologne's most successful thrust at elegance, all dark paneling with a coffered ceiling framing mauve-velvet banquettes and mock-Hepplewhite chairs. The menu is an international jumble—mixed grill out of London, lobster Newburg out of Paris, local variations on the sauerbraten theme. Exceptional wines. *Luxury.*

Die Bastei (Konrad-Adenauer-Ufer 80) is attractive for the river view as much as for the food, which is good. Try the house's chicken-breast specialty, and don't pass up dessert. *Luxury.*

Chez Alex (Muhlengasse 1) is a taste of la belle France, in an inviting environment. If you've a yen for *quenelles de brochet*—rarely encountered in *Allemagne*—place your order here. Or roast duck. French pastries and wines. *Luxury.*

Alfredo (Tunisstrasse 3): No foreign food is more consistently excellent in Germany than that of Italy. Alfredo's—for delicious pastas and the house's pride, *saltimbocca romana*—is a case in point. Smiling service. *First Class.*

Opernterrassen (Brüdenstrasse 2) is a handsome terrace restaurant-café, next to the opera, with the hearty main-course fare (veal and pork specialties) no less good than the salads and sweets. *Moderate.*

Alt Köln (Trankgasse 7) is just opposite the Dom, next door to Excelsior Hotel Ernst. It's a cluster of connected chambers, old-style and welcoming. Order soup, a schnitzel, a steak. Clientele is loquacious, a blend of locals and visitors. *Moderate/First Class.*

Ratskeller (Rathaus, Rathausplatz 1)—not unlike its sister City Hall restaurants Germany-wide—an ever-reliable of hearty sustenance, appetizingly presented, good to eat, and, in cost: *Moderate.*

Café Kranzler (Brüderstrasse) is an outlet of a nationwide chain whose stock-in-trade is pastry—excellent pastry—along with snack selections, and, if you like, proper meals. With the bonus of an Opera House location. *Moderate/First Class.*

Krüh (Am Hof 12) is one of many typically Cologne, brewery-operated tavern-restaurants, with scrubbed-wood tables, paneled walls, open fire in winter, and full restaurant menu, including the overfermented beer called *Früh Kölsch,* the cheese sandwich with mustard on a rye roll called *Halben Hahn* (half-chicken, which of course it is not), the potato pancakes called *Rivkoche,* and *Hämchem*—a pork-and-mashed-potatoes platter. *Moderate.*

Gastätte Haus Toller (Weyerstrasse 96) is an easy subway ride to Barbarossaplatz from the cathedral (and a good excuse to try the handsome U-Bahn). Setting is a venerable house, furnished in baroque style, and you've no choice but to order the only entrée: pigs' knuckles; they're delicious. A salad tossed in a dill dressing accompanies, along with home-brewed beer. *Moderate.*

Café-Konditorei Reichard (Domplatz): Grab a table, take in the façade of the cathedral, over coffee—better yet, cappucino—with a slice of the house's own *Kuchen,* or a snack. *Moderate.*

SOUND OF MUSIC

Opernhaus und Schauspielhaus (Brüderstrasse) is a good-looking two-theater building with a distinctive sloping façade framing its huge revolving stage. Oper der Stadt Köln, among Germany's best, performs a richly rounded repertory—*Der Barbier von Sevilla* and *Der Fliegende Holländer* through *Don Carlos* and, if you please, our own Cole Porter's *Kiss Me Kate.* The Schauspielhaus part of the complex is a drama theater, with plays from its repertory; visiting troupes also appear, some performing in exotic languages like English.

Theater Kefka (Aachenerstrasse) is—along with a similar theater in Copenhagen's Tivoli Gardens—one of the few remaining European pantomime groups. Special.

Gürzenich (Martinstrasse) is originally Gothic, deftly updated into a multipurpose hall that's home to the globally esteemed Gürzenich, Cologne's principal symphony. You're in luck if your visit coincides with a Gürzenich concert.

INCIDENTAL INTELLIGENCE

The handsome international airport—Cologne/Bonn—is shared with the federal capital, but it's closer (11 miles) to Cologne, with which it's linked by regularly scheduled airport buses. If you've flown transatlantic to Frankfurt, you may take Lufthansa's Airport Express train, along the Rhine—with commentary en route, about the castles and splendid scenery—to Cologne. If you haven't liked service on your Lufthansa flight—or, for that matter, if you have—you're in the right town. The airline's administrative headquarters is here, in its own skyscraper, on Von Gablenz Strasse, in the quarter called Deutz. This city is also the home port of the Cologne/Düsseldorf Rhine Navigation Company, with departures from the pier between Hohenzollern, and Deutzer bridges. Go on a 24-hour trip to Mainz (which will take you past the romantic castles bordering the Rhine); better yet, plan longer cruises. There are one-day excursions, too. These include a boat-train combination, leaving in the morning by steamer, for Koblenz (the subject of a chapter in this book) and returning by rail from that city in the evening. *Further information:* Verkehrsamt der Stadt Köln—the city tourist office—is located at Am Dom—opposite the cathedral's main door.

12

Dinkelsbühl

Big Things in Small Packages

BACKGROUND BRIEFING

Laugh at its name if you like. The fact remains that dinky Dinkelsbühl is an extraordinary souvenir of the Middle Ages. We must be grateful indeed that even before the Industrial Revolution, with so much urban razing of the old to make way for the new, Dinkelsbühl had become something of a Bavarian backwater.

Which is hardly to say that it had not known eminence. Dinkelsbühl goes back to the eighth century when a local warrior-farmer founded it, on the banks of the Wornitz River. Ere long it had become important enough—located where two medieval trade routes converged—for aggressive Hungarian invaders to covet it. As a protective measure, a moat was built. Later came the first of its famous encircling walls, as trade—between Holland and Italy on one route and between Poland and France on the other route—made it all the more vulnerable.

As the Middle Ages progressed, Dinkelsbühl achieved status as a Free Imperial—and thereby self-governing—City within the Holy Roman Empire. And, as the Renaissance developed, so did the town, with guildhalls and merchant mansions lining its streets, and a new defense system—formidable walls punctuated by towers and gates—that remains to this day.

The post-Napoleonic era saw Dinkelsbühl pass to the then Kingdom of Bavaria. Its only subsequent invaders were romantic artists from nineteenth-century Munich, eager to paint fortifications and lanes and half-timbered houses. The artists have been succeeded by tourists, with Dinkelsbühl now a stop of no little importance on the Romantic Road that embraces Bavaria's most beautiful small cities.

ON SCENE

Lay of the Land: Not everyone arrives on a Romantic Road tour bus. The rail traveler arriving at the Bahnhof will be at the southern edge of town, beyond the walls. The town is a bit north, along Romantischestrasse from the Bahnhof to the towering gable of Wornitztor, an entry gate that visitors have known for half a millennium. Wornitztor leads to Altrathausplatz, the square named for the old town hall—now a school—that dominates it. Altrathausplatz leads into Dinkelsbühl's principal north-south thoroughfare, Segringerstrasse, and that runs all the way to the northern tip of town and the gate that takes its name, Segringertor. Follow Segringerstrasse, gate to gate, possibly detouring at Bauhofstrasse, for an eastward hike to still another gate, Rothenburgertor. In between you will find the currently used Rathaus and Heilige Geist Hospital with its own Gothic church and the town's historical museum nearby.

Wherever you walk—and you must not hesitate to explore any Dinkelsbühl street or square (Marktplatz, Lutherstrasse, and Turmgasse especially)—the look is lovely, with architectural styles ranging from Gothic through Renaissance to baroque. By that I mean the engaging angles of gabled roofs, painted oriel windows protruding from houses' upper stories, fresco-decorated walls, wrought-iron signs—some gilded, some not—swinging from over the heavy doors of shops and inns and *Stuben.*

St. George's Church, where Altrathaus leads into Segringerstrasse, is often called a cathedral. It is not. But it has the grandeur associated with churches that are the seats of bishops. And when one considers Dinkelsbühl's modest size, it is all the more remarkable. St. George's, which dates to the fifteenth century, was planned by burghers as a way to dramatize the town's mercantile prowess. Its tower is Romanesque in style. But the rest of St. George's is undiluted Gothic. Fan-vaulting frames the triple nave of a 235-foot-long interior. There are outstanding works of art: a high-altar crucifixion by Wohlgemuth, who taught Dürer; a Madonna sculpted of wood, attributed to the master of that medium, Würzburg's Tilman Riemenschneider; a moving pietà—Christ, descended from the cross, in his mother's arms—that dates to the Middle Ages; and in one chapel a fifteenth-century work in stone of the Last Supper.

Dinkelsbühl Museum (Spithalhof) occupies a series of historic chambers in the Heilige Geist Spital complex, and is full of centuries-old town art and artisanship: paintings and pottery, sculpture and coins, documents and tools.

SETTLING IN

Hotel Deutsches-Haus (Wienmarkt 3) is, after St. George's Church, the principal visitor destination in Dinkelsbühl. This is a fifteenth-century dazzler: its façade half-timbered, with painted decorations. As important is the inner sanctum, with a baker's dozen rooms, some with private baths, and an atmospheric restaurant. *Moderate.*

Hotel Goldene Rose (Marktplatz) is quite as venerable as Deutsches Haus. It was September 19, 1891, when Queen Victoria spent the night, as management proudly informs us. There are a score of rooms, the nicest in town, some with bath, and a fine restaurant. *Moderate.*

Hotel Eisenkrug (Lutherstrasse 1) is quite as scenically—and centrally—situated as its competitors; a dozen chambers, some with bath; attractive restaurant. *Moderate.*

DAILY BREAD

Zur Sonne (Weinmarkt 11) for solid meals in a core-of-town setting. *Moderate.*

Goldener Hirsch (Weinmarkt 6): An aged house: filling food, at the right price. *Moderate.*

SOUND OF MUSIC

Stadthalle is the town's concert hall/auditorium. There are summer performances by the town's own theater troupe in *Wehrganggarten*.

INCIDENTAL INTELLIGENCE

Verkehrsamt Dinkelsbühl, the town tourist office, is on Marktplatz.

13

Düsseldorf

Underappreciated Elegance

BACKGROUND BRIEFING

Its name is not especially catchy—not to ears accustomed to the English language. No, Düsseldorf—meaning simply village on the Dussel River—does not at all sound like what it is: the medium-sized city that comes closest to reflecting the German urban dream.

Omit the Big Three from the picture—by that I mean Munich, Hamburg, and Berlin—and there's not a city in Germany that stands out like this one. It is, like a number of German cities, architecturally delightful and intellectually rich. But it is blessed with two more attributes less easily found in Germany: apparently innate senses of both style and humor. If there's a German town that knows the light touch, this is it.

Not that great age—as European history goes—is one of Düsseldorf's special charms. The Romans, who settled in at the rivalrous, neighboring Rhine city of Cologne, avoided Düsseldorf. It was not much heard from—or about—until the early eighth century, when the Benedictines opened a monastery in the neighborhood. That became the nucleus for a lay settlement, and by the twelfth century the current name found its way into extant documents. A century later and Düsseldorf was officially chartered as a city. Political eminence was a while in coming.

Fifteenth-century dukes—especially the Bergs and Cleves—made it their seat, and in the seventeenth century it changed hands. The regionally powerful Wittelsbach clan—the very same who were kings of Bavaria until World War I—took over as palatine electors, and one of the clan—Johann Wilhelm or Jan Wellem, as he still is known to Düsseldorfers—became a symbol of the spirit of the city: gregarious, wise, generous, sophisticated. Jan Wellem and his successor, Karl Theodor, developed the town, collected art, and built rococo castles. Townspeople still regard an equestrian statue of him—in front of the Rathaus in the Old Town—with affection, for it was in that quarter that he would often spend evenings with his subjects over glasses of wine in pubs that still exist.

The latter decades of the eighteenth century—when the Napoleonic Wars began to change the face of Europe—saw the French occupy Düsseldorf. (Indeed, Napoleon himself was a visitor, and who is to say that this first manifestation of *la présence française*—and another following World War I—have not contributed to the city's sophistication?) It became a grand duchy with the grand duke Joachim Murat, an aide and brother-in-law to Bonaparte.

The post-Napoleonic Congress of Vienna resulted in Düsseldorf's absorption by Prussia, and as the nineteenth century progressed, so did the city, developing into an industrial-commercial complex of considerable power. World War I was followed by a four-year French occupation. In World War II the Allies made strategically valuable Düsseldorf the target—in a three-year period—of 243 air raids.

Considering that more than half of the city was destroyed not more than a few decades ago, today's Düsseldorf—capital of the state, or Land of North Rhine-Westphalia—is a miracle of recovery, rehabilitation, restoration, refurbishing—all the "R" words that connote, in this case, sprightly success in living the urban life.

ON SCENE

Lay of the Land: This city of half a million, though exceptionally well laid out, is not so compact that you can easily take in all of its core on foot. Distances can be substantial. It's easiest to get an idea of geography by considering the Rhine as the city's western frontier. (Three bridges cross it—Theodor-Heuss-Brücke, to the north, Oberkasselerbrücke going south, and then Rheinkniebrücke.) If you're arriving on a Köln-Düsseldorfer Rhine River steamer—as many visitors do—you'll tie up at the line's own pier between Theodor-Heuss and Oberkasseler bridges, at Rheinpark. If your arrival is by plane, you'll enter town from the airport to the north. And if your means of entry is train, it will stop at the Hauptbahnhof, at the southeast part of town, facing Konrad-Adenauer-Platz. From the station, the core of the city is approached from Friedrich-Ebert-Strasse, which, as it goes northwest, becomes Steinstrasse after crossing Oststrasse. Steinstrasse continues inward, crossing another north-south thoroughfare, Berliner Allee, before it reaches Königsallee, the heart-of-downtown boulevard through which flows a swan-populated canal.

Königsallee—or simply "Kö" as the locals refer to it—leads north to Hofgarten, a lovely inner-city park that was the garden of the Elector's Palace in earlier centuries. Today, a number of Düsseldorf attractions fringe it.

The southern flank of the Hofgarten gives on to a thoroughfare called Elberfelderstrasse which, as it goes west, changes its name. As Bolkerstrasse, it leads west into still another part of town appealing to visitors: the Altstadt, or Old Town. Limited to pedestrians, lined with pubs and cafés and restaurants, Bolkerstrasse ends at Marktstrasse, and Marktplatz, whose major monuments have already been mentioned—the much-beloved equestrian statue of Elector Jan Wellem, and a building blending the Renaissance with the baroque: the Rathaus, or Town Hall. The waters of the Rhine—ever busy with the flow of river traffic—are due west.

Königsallee, the north-south boulevard with a stream rather than pavement as its central artery, extends half a dozen glamor-packed blocks from the Hofgarten south to Graf-Adolf-Platz. Set off by fountains and statues and plane-tree-lined, the "Kö" is a heady mix of marvelous places to spend money. And make no mistake, money is spent on the "Kö." It's taken from the banks that line it on one side for use on the other, at grand jewelers and trendy boutiques and pricey restaurants and beamed pubs and pavement cafés. It's fun to wander about, if only to see how many blue-chip names one recognizes: Georg Jensen silver, Alfred Dunhill doodads, Luisa Spagnoli dresses, Yves Saint-Laurent suits, Emilio Pucci prints, Charles Jourdan shoes, Mädler luggage. Not to mention locally operated emporia of considerable panache, in which are sold a range of wares, togs to toys.

Kunstmuseum Düsseldorf (Ehrenhof 5) occupies an interesting Bauhaus structure out of the twenties, and is worth the trek to the northern tip of the Hofgarten—location is between the garden and the Rhine. The paintings are Old Masters and German Expressionists. There is a huge and marvelous *Venus and Adonis* by Rubens, and works, as well, by Van Dyck, van Ruysdael, and Steen of the baroque period in the Low Countries, and earlier Flemish luminaries like Massys and van Cleve. The Germans are represented by Cranach, the Spaniards by Goya, the Italians by Tintoretto, the French by Boucher, to name some. If it is not a great collection—there are many more substantial elsewhere in Germany—it is impressive enough, since it is balanced by German moderns like Beckmann, Kirchner, Nolde, Macke, Corinth, Kandinsky, and Feininger.

Only a sampling of drawings and engravings—medieval through modern—are on display at a given time; German representation—especially Dürer, who did so many—is happily heavy. And so is Italian.

And glass: This is one of Europe's best collections: delicate ancient Roman pieces on through to America's Louis Comfort Tiffany's Art Nouveau, from the turn of the century.

Kunstsammlung Nordrhein-Westfalen (Schloss Jägerhof, Jacobistrasse 2) more or less rounds out the painting scene in Düsseldorf. To start, though, the setting: a nifty rococo town palace. And then the art. There are a pair of departments. The first is mainly French moderns, with—according to my count—no fewer than a dozen Picassos, as well as works by Bonnard, Matisse, Léger, and Chagall, not to mention Gris and Dali. Then cross the Atlantic to New York and its contemporary school:

Sam Francis, Morris Louis, Kenneth Noland, Ellsworth Kelly, Frank Stella, Jasper Johns, Jackson Pollack—to name some, and to convey the impression that yes, indeed, the gang's all here.

Then—to change the subject and the floor—there is a perfectly beautiful cache of Meissen, the most celebrated of the eighteenth-century German porcelains. The stars of this show are a pair of subdued canines—pugs named Mopse and Kissen, seated on pink porcelain cushions.

Stadtgeschichtliches Museum Düsseldorf (Bäckerstrasse 7) is, unless one is a master of the German tongue, more fun to amble through than to pronounce. Set in a nicely restored eighteenth-century town palace, its subject matter is the history of the city—as interpreted by all manner of objects—ancient coins; pieces in silver, gold, and copper; etchings and maps; splendid pieces of furniture spanning the centuries; portraits of local luminaries through the ages; paintings of Düsseldorf scenes, such as an 1880 interpretation of Marktplatz—with the Rathaus behind the landmark Jan Wellem statue—that could be a view of today, save for the century-old clothes of shoppers in the flower stalls.

Hetjens Museum (Palais Nesselrode, Schulstrasse 4) occupies still another rococo palace, named for the family who may well have inspired the Nesselrode pie. The Hetjens is very special. It houses the collection of a nineteenth-century industrialist who, from childhood, indulged his interest in the fine and applied arts by studying and collecting, with ceramics his specialty. He bequeathed the collection to the city of Düsseldorf at the turn of the century, and it was moved into the impeccably restored Palais Nesselrode only in 1969. Understand at the start: this is not simply a couple of dozen pieces of German porcelain—Meissen, for example, as at Schloss Jägerhof and many other museums in Germany. Herr Hetjens collected specimens of ceramics from all over the world, and from all periods, so that what one sees here is a unique international survey—-ancient Egypt and ancient Anatolia, for example, through the European Middle Ages, on into the ceramics of Islam and of Africa, the Orient and the Americas, with later acquisitions from contemporary ateliers.

Goethe Museum (Jägerhofstrasse I): In the chapter on Frankfurt, I unreservedly recommend Goethe's house—now operating as a museum—not so much because it was Goethe's as because it illustrates how affluent German bourgeois families lived in the eighteenth century. This museum, however—despite its setting in a proper, though restored rococo palace—is strictly for Goethe fans, of which North America has many fewer, in proportion, than has Germany. Now, then, if you *are* a devotee of Goethe, this is for you: original manuscripts, first editions, personal correspondence, and other memorabilia. Lots more even than in the documents section of the house in Frankfurt.

Schloss Benrath (Schlossallee, in the Benrath suburb) is a good 10-mile haul from the center. But if you would like to see how an eighteenth-century prince-elector (Karl Theodor, the gifted builder-successor to Jan Wellem) took his ease in the country, then have a look. The period is rococo—with a formal garden surrounding a palace that's bigger than it appears. Look down at the intricate parquet floors, and look up at the splendid stuccowork of the ceilings as you move about. Be sure to take in—among others—the bedrooms of the elector and the electress, and a special upstairs treat: a balconied chapel.

SETTLING IN

Hotel Breidenbacher Hof (Heinrich-Heine-Allee 36) reflects Düsseldorf's style and sophistication as does no other hotel in this city of exemplary hotels. The accent is on seventeenth- and eighteenth-century antiques throughout—lobby, grand stairways, wide corridors, not to mention the 150 rooms and suites, each with a snazzy black-and-white tile bath of exceptional luxury. Management is skilled, location central, service white-glove. Amenities include a bar and pair of restaurants, one of which is singled out for further comment in a later paragraph. Member, Leading Hotels of the World. *Luxury.*

Hotel Hilton International Düsseldorf (Georg-Glock-Strasse 20): The pity of the Hilton is its away-from-the-center location. If you've a car, or don't mind hopping taxis to and from downtown, you'll be very happy in this extraordinarily handsome house, one of the most outstanding in the top-rank Hilton International chain—most of whose properties round the world I'm familiar with. This is a winner, starting with a dramatic high-ceilinged lobby, right on to the welcoming guest rooms, and a range of facilities such as indoor-outdoor pool-with-sauna, coffee shop with the look of a stylish restaurant, still another restaurant worthy of later comment, zingy bar-lounge with a grand prix motif, and a bit of the Casbah—called 1,000 Nights—in the subterranean disco. *Luxury.*

Hotel Inter-Continental Düsseldorf (Karl-Arnold-Platz 5): Besides Hilton International, still another leading U.S-headquartered hotel chain is represented in Düsseldorf. Like the Hilton, the Inter-Conti (to use the sensible abbreviation coined by the Germans for this company's hotels throughout their country) is away from the center, but it compensates for whatever inconvenience its location may present with one of the most crackerjack managements of any hotel I know in Germany. Everything works like a dream in this house—from reception to room service, with a restaurant that is one of the best in town (I single it out for later comment), coffee shop, intimate bar, capacious heated pool with chaises for summer sunning, sauna-gym. *Luxury.*

Hotel Nikko (Immermannstrasse 41) is a touch of Nippon in Düsseldorf, a spanking modern, heart-of-town hostelry operated by Japan Air Lines. There are 300-plus spacious rooms and suites in beige with pastel accents; a spectacular lobby, busy bar-lounge, restaurants both Occidental and Oriental. (Why not a dinner of, say, sushi or tempura or sukiyaki, with rice wine?) Fresh flowers everywhere. *Luxury.*

Parkhotel (Corneliusplatz 1) is an old-timer, traditional-style, with a superb central situation. Things run large here—lobby, guest rooms, restaurant, bar-lounge, summer terrace-café. The Steigenberger management, in whose chain this is a link, emphasizes solid comfort over elegance. *Luxury.*

Hotel Excelsior (Kaiserstrasse at Kapellstrasse) has a natty, nifty look to it—smart lobby-lounge, inviting restaurant, and some 60 good-looking rooms, with the doubles especially generous. Overlooking the Hofgarten. Central. *First Class.*

Hotel Savoy (Breitestrasse 2) is a well-regarded middle-category house, at once full-facility and central, with comfortable rooms with baths, chandelier-hung restaurant, dark, paneled bar. *First Class.*

Hotel Uebachs (Leopoldstrasse 3) is smallish, cheery, and on a side street easily walkable from the center. Many rooms with bath. Restaurant. *Moderate.*

Hotel an der Oper (Heinrich-Heine-Allee 43) is enviably well-situated—directly opposite the opera house, heart of town. Functional rooms, many with bath. Breakfast only. *Moderate.*

Hotel Münch (Königsallee 90) is the ideal house for the budget-minded—on the smartest street in town. A good number of the 40-plus rooms have private baths. Breakfast only. *Moderate.*

Hotel Plaza (Karlstrasse 4) is intimate—there are about 30 rooms, a number of private baths—and nicely located in the center, below the Old Town. Breakfast only. *Moderate.*

DAILY BREAD

Walliser Stuben (Aderstrasse 46) hides its haute cuisine capabilities behind the attractive albeit unpretentious look of a Swiss mountain tavern. But it is not to be underestimated. The menus abound in classic dishes—fresh foie gras, a soup of truffles, filet of beef in a pepper sauce, the freshest of green vegetables, delicate pastries, and a cellar of Swiss as well as German wines. Tables are illuminated by candles in brass sticks, and every dish comes to the table under a copper hood. In my experience, one of Germany's best restaurants. *Luxury.*

Müllers und Fest and ***KD*** (Königsallee 14) are a pair of restaurants with the same address and management. The former is up a flight and the more formal and expensive of the pair—with its menu at once elaborate, extensive, and traditional. Everything, invariably, is delicious, the house's own seafood cocktail or turtle soup, lobster Newburg or an authentic Italian saltimbocca, soufflés-to-order for dessert. Or the simpler *plat du jour. Luxury.* KD, at street level, is mod-look, with an abbreviated, less expensive menu. The *plats du jour* are invariably good bets. *First Class.*

La Rotisserie (Hotel Inter-Continental Düsseldorf, Karl-Arnold-Platz 5) is the ideal choice for a candlelit, deftly served dinner. Choose either traditional German fare—a hearty schnitzel, perhaps—or order any old number of authentically French dishes. Splendid desserts on the trolley. Fine wines. *Luxury.*

San Francisco (Hotel Hilton International Düsseldorf, Georg-Glock-Strasse 20) could be a West Coast dance hall in a period movie—high-ceilinged, opulent, amusing. What you want to order is the specialty of the house: steak imported from Colorado—New York Sirloin, Porterhouse, or T-bone, with a baked potato and California-style salad, preceded by a shrimp cocktail. The locals love it. *Luxury.*

Orangerie (Bilkerstrasse 30) occupies an authentically venerable house on an authentically venerable street. It is very posh indeed. The name of the game is haute cuisine, with two table d'hôtes featured, one just plain expensive (seven courses excluding coffee), the other *very* expensive (eight courses, sans coffee). Quail salad, caviar-accented *quenelles, bisque d'écrevisses,* sweetbreads *à la moutarde:* all very tasty. But this is upper-echelon expense-account territory, with tabs—very pricey indeed. *Luxury.*

Breidenbacher Eck (Breidenbacher Hof Hotel, Heinrich-Heine-Allee 36): This is a witty, delicious spot, a kind of Art Nouveau environment, with tables illuminated by orange-silk-shaded lamps, and the menu original and satisfying—snails as you know them from France, eggs Benedict as you know them from

Chicago, mixed grill as you know it from London, desserts as you've come to love them in Germany. *First Class.*

La Brochette (Königsallee 48) : Another upstairs-downstairs operation, on a less lofty scale than the Müllers und Fest combination. La Brochette is the elevated section, and ideally you get a table at the picture window overlooking the "Kö." Order one of the day's specials—a lamb stew, perhaps, or roast pork, preceded by oysters on the half-shell, and followed with a sweet and coffee. *First Class.* Or choose the less costly Café Hemesath.

Grand' Italia (Hüttenstrasse 30) is the not immodest title of (you guessed it) a source of dependable Italian food—pastas and veal dishes, most especially. Italian wines, too. *Moderate.*

La Charmargue (Marktstrasse 12, in the Old Town) is ideal for a fine Gallic repast of, say, onion soup, entrecôte with French fries and really good French bread, with a French wine to accompany. *Moderate.*

Brauerei Gatzweiler (Balkerstrasse 63): As good a choice as any for a hearty German meal with beer in a robust setting. Pea soup and sausages with sauerkraut are the house specialties. *Moderate.*

Zum Uerige (Bergerstrasse 1) is a light-hearted, exuberant *Bierstube*—large, noisy, and amusing, for food as well as for brew. *Moderate.*

Zum Schiffchen (Hafenstrasse 5) is a good Old Town dinner choice. The setting is a seventeenth-century house, the tables scrubbed wood, the specialty—aside from the house's beer—is sizzling, grilled pork. *Moderate.*

Capri (Balkerstrasse at Hunsrückenstrasse, Old Town) is a pizza joint. But what a pizza joint! Step right in, say *ein Pizza mit Salami, bitte* to the counterman, and see if what you're served isn't the best slice you've had between, say, Naples and your hometown. *Moderate.*

Café Bittner (Königsallee 18): Have coffee and pastry or a snack upstairs, and consider buying the house's own chocolates—locals call them the best in town—from the counter at street level, though they're quite expensive. The popular café, however, is *Moderate.*

Nachrichten Treff (Königsallee 77) is a café-bar—amusing *fin de siècle*—with journalists among its regulars, the better to read the honest-to-goodness news tickers on the premises, and to buy the flown-in English newspapers. In summer, "N.T." as locals call it, has tables outside for crowd-watching while nursing a *Bier,* bullshot, Bloody Mary, or Irish coffee—these last are specialties. *Moderate.*

SOUND OF MUSIC

Opernhaus (Heinrich-Heine-Allee) is the handsome headquarters of the company that is an interesting—and high-caliber—joint venture of the neighboring cities of Düsseldorf and Duisburg. It's called Deutsche Oper am Rhein, and its repertory runs a broad gamut, mostly classical, with annual cycles of works by Mozart, Wagner, and Janàcek. Resident ballet troupe, too. The house is heart-of-downtown, modern, with its auditorium in tones of coral and gray, and a vast intermission promenade salon-cum-bars.

Rheintonhalle (Hofgartenrampe) has a confusing name. It is, as often as not, called Tonhalle, with the "Rhein" omitted. A 1978 conversion of the older Rheinhalle, its walls are surfaced in blonde wood—also the material for an unusual canopy over the stage, which has seats behind it, as well as in front. Düsseldorf's symphony is first-rate, not surprising in a city where Mendelssohn, Schumann, and Brahms all participated in the Lower Rhine Music Festivals, still a highlight of the city's music scene. Additional concerts are held in *Robert-Schumann-Saal,* which is located adjacent to the riverfront Rheinterrasse.

Schauspielhaus (Jan-Wellem-Platz): The city's principal drama theater is a futuristic dazzler, and you want at least to pass by its façade. Plays, of course, are in German, but architecture buffs will be interested in this structure, from the low-slung undulating exterior to the offbeat, pillared interior of the Grosses Haus, larger of two auditoriums. Location is near the southeast edge of the Hofgarten, next to the slick Thyssen skyscraper.

INCIDENTAL INTELLIGENCE

Düsseldorf is linked with the U.S. via Lufthansa's daily nonstop, transatlantic service from New York, with service also, from Miami and Toronto. Lohausen Airport is five miles, or a 20-minute taxi ride, from the City Air Terminal at the Hauptbahnhof, with which it is connected by regularly scheduled airport bus service. And there's a convenient rail link to the city, too. *Further information:* Verkehrsverein der Stadt Düsseldorf—the city tourist office—is at Konrad-Adenauer-Platz 11 (Arcade) and in the Hauptbahnhof.

14

East Germany

Potsdam
Dresden
Leipzig

BACKGROUND BRIEFING

The eastern sector of Berlin, major city and capital of the German Democratic Republic, is the subject of half the chapter devoted to that city, for the convenience of the reader who will, in all likelihood, take in the greater city in the course of a single visit.

But, there are three other significant East German cities without which a book such as this would be incomplete. Potsdam, nearest to the capital, stands out because of two ravishing Frederick-the-Great-built palaces, and a much later royal residence wherein was signed the European World War II peace treaty. Dresden, though still not rebuilt completely as a result of World War II destruction, re-emerges, nonetheless, as one of the important art cities of the planet. And Leipzig, also ravaged during World War II, continues as the site of immense annual international trade fairs—one spring, the other autumn—that have been a tradition since 1165; in other words, for more than eight centuries.

None of these East German cities has quite the sophistication of East Berlin, which is not only the capital, but the recipient of cultural crosscurrents—unintentional, and perhaps, officially, unwanted—from the western half of town, which is as capitalist and cosmopolitan as any principal Western European metropolis. All things being relative, we find East Berlin lacking West Berlin's vibrance, and these provincial East German towns even more detached from the hubbub we take for granted. Soviet soldiers are all about, and the Russian language is a required study in the schools. It's No. 2 after German, coming before English and French, even on postcards and tourist leaflets.

Vehicular traffic on the streets is sparser than we're accustomed to, there are fewer shops, and—though the well-stocked department stores are a major exception—less merchandise than in the West. Hotels are part of the same countrywide, state-fostered Inter Hotels chain we knew in East Berlin. There is more similarity in the restaurants and cafés than is the case in our part of the world. And the efficient government travel department—through its service desks in the hotels—has a tourism monopoly.

Guides, as in the capital, are optional. One may wander and explore at will. An East German visa is required. Vouchers for hotels, tours, and the like are purchased in *advance* from one's home travel agent, from the Reisebüro der Deutschen Demokratischen Republik (Alexanderplatz, Berlin, DDR), *or* from one of the Reisebüro's principal U.S. representatives, which include Koch Travel, 157 East 86 Street, New York, New York 10028. Visa applications are handled by travel agents, along with hotel and tour vouchers. (Germans resident in the U.S. intent on visiting East German relatives are subject to additional red tape—which includes requesting relatives to obtain local police approval for their visit. Ask your agent, the Reisebüro, or the East German Embassy at 1717 Massachusetts Avenue, N.W., Washington, D.C. 20036, for details.)

Getting to the provinces? Go on one of the Reisebüro's package tours, which will have included East Berlin. Or go on your own. You may drive in a car rented in East Berlin, take the train, or—in the case of Dresden only—fly from East Berlin on Interflug, the national carrier. Potsdam may be visited on day-long excursions out of West Berlin, but they are of necessity quite abbreviated, not unlike the West Berlin-originated excursions to East Berlin.

POTSDAM

Potsdam, an attractive town lying to the southwest of Berlin (and—ironically, today—closer to West Berlin than East), first became a royal seat in the seventeenth century, under an elector of Brandenburg. But it sprang to life for the first time less than a century later when Prussian King Frederick II—Frederick the Great because of his prowess in battle, and his remarkable aptitude in such areas as architecture, interior design, literature, and fine arts—got bored with residence at Charlottenburg Palace in Berlin.

Frederick hired the same architect-designer, Knobelsdorff, who had worked for him on expanding Charlottenburg and who had designed the opera house (now in East Berlin), to reconstruct the old so-called Potsdam Town Palace (alas, destroyed in World War II). Knobelsdorff was to create a get-away-from-it-all retreat—albeit palatial—that Frederick called by the French name Sans Souci (without care).

Sans Souci is but one of two palaces Frederick built in Sans Souci Park. The other, completed later in the same century, and not a Knobelsdorff work, is the new, or Neues Palais. Ideally, one takes both in on a single visit—the two are connected by a scenic park walk—and also covers the more important outbuildings that are appendages.

Sans Souci—considered the Knobelsdorff masterwork and the epitome of Frederician rococo, as refined by the talented monarch—surmounts a hill that doubles as, of all things, a vineyard, with half a dozen levels of vines still growing. A single-story rectangular pavilion, the palace is entered in the center beneath a cupola, which covers a marble-walled vestibule ringed with white columns that are topped by gilded Corinthian capitals. A tour takes one through one ravishing room after another—the Concert Room is one of the best, with wall frescoes that include one of Sans Souci and its vineyards. There are also a dark, paneled library, a picture-hung *Kleine Galerie,* and rooms that were occupied by Frederick and his not infrequent house guest, the French philosopher Voltaire. Throughout, furnishings, paintings, stuccowork, sconces, and chandeliers are museum-caliber.

Of Sans Souci's auxiliary buildings, the finest is the *Bildergalerie,* a high-ceilinged adjacent pavilion in which Frederick put together what is believed to be the first collection—anywhere—of paintings displayed in a building built specifically for that purpose. The paintings are hung in rows, one above the other, so that it's hard to distinguish them. But it may be worth your while to invest in a copy of the gallery's catalog, for there are some fine works in the maze, including no less than a full dozen by Rubens, seven by Van Dyck, with Cranach, Caravaggio, Bassano, Reni, Lotto, and Tintoretto represented in this granddaddy of the art museum.

The *Chinesisches Teehaus,* another Sans Souci satellite, is a delightful conceit, a kind of retreat from the retreat: frescoed, furnished, and accessorized in the then much-emulated Chinese style. Have a walk through the park to the *Neues Palais,* which Frederick planned with a specific political purpose. Much bigger than Sans Souci, and primarily a residence for the royal family—rather than just for himself and personal guests, as was Sans Souci—the Neues Palais was a kind of edict to the people in which their monarch, to compensate for the privations of the Thirty Years' War, extolled the power, strength, and glory of the Prussian royal house. If it has not the subtle appeal of the smaller palace, the Neues must still be given its due. Of course it can be argued that its façade—heavy with the weight of an interminable series of rooftop sculptures—is ostentatious. But the interior is superb: a typically rococo shell-walled entrance hall; the long Marmorgalerie, with the checkered marble floor for which it is named; the pale-green and gold Konzertzimmer with the exercise in geometry that is its parquet floor; the Ovales Kabinett, whose bowl-shaped ceiling could be a fragile piece of porcelain; and, most memorable, the theater—a semicircle wherein gilded caryatids (not unlike those in East Berlin's Komische Oper) support a ceiling fringed by white plaster angels carrying golden garlands, a brilliant ceiling-sunburst framing the whole.

Schloss Cecilienhof is something else again: as royal palaces go, a relatively modest house, built while World War I was raging, as a home for Kaiser Wilhelm II's brother—the crown prince of the realm—and his English-born wife, who was the inspiration behind its style, that of an English country house in the manner of the Tudors. The princely family remained in residence through most of World War II, after which the Allied Powers selected the palace for the meeting already immortalized by the history books as the Potsdam Conference—at which the peace treaty was drawn up.

That portion of the palace where the treaty delegations met is operated by the East German government as a museum. One sees the studies and reception rooms of Churchill (and his successor at the conference, when British governments changed, Clement Atlee), of the Soviet Union's Stalin, and of America's Harry Truman. The beamed, mock-Tudor hall in which the delegations deliberated at a circular table is still covered with the flags of their countries.

Very cleverly, the residential wing of Cecilienhof has been converted by the government into a rather charming hotel, which takes the palace's name. It's the ideal place to stay overnight in the course of a Potsdam visit, and its restaurant—once a palace dining room—is first-rate and has an á la carte menu as well as daily specials. *First Class.*

Much bigger and more typical of the East Germany-wide Interhotels chain is luxury-category *Hotel Potsdam,* a full-facility tower, with attractive public spaces—including a beamed Weinstube, bar with dancing, and several hundred rooms with baths.

Further information: Verkehrsamt Potsdam—the city tourist office—is at Klement-Gottwald-Strasse 24.

DRESDEN

Dresden, farthest south of our trio of cities, is a place of pilgrimage for admirers of art, opera, and classical music. The opera company is the best provincial troupe in East Germany, and it ranks with those of the Deutsche Staatsoper and the Komische Oper in East Berlin. Dresdener Stadtkapelle—the city's symphony—dates to 1548, and visited the United States in 1979, when its principal concert was in the United Nations General Assembly Hall. Any capsule history of the art in this longtime capital of the electorate, and later kingdom, of Saxony must begin with the first of a line of royal collectors, Elector George, who reigned in the early decades of the sixteenth century. The art-filled *Kunstkammer* of a succeeding elector, Augustus, followed later in that century. But it was Augustus the Strong—first of the electors to become king not only of Saxony but of Poland as well—who became the greatest of Saxony's collectors, in the early decades of the eighteenth century.

Indeed, it was a sampling of Augustus's treasures that constituted the first cultural exchange between the East German government and the United States: a ravishing—albeit limited—sampling of Dresden's art went on display at three U.S. museums—opening the new East Wing of Washington's National Gallery, then moving to New York's Metropolitan and to San Francisco's Palace of the Legion of Honor in 1979.

The Splendors of Dresden, as the loan show was called, opened American eyes to the Elbe River city of which little had been heard since before World War II, when it was reputed to be one of Europe's loveliest. Bombs devastated Dresden during the war, but its core is being rebuilt—slowly but well—according to original plans. (A stroll along the Elbe, past the Cathedral and not yet fully restored Opera House, evokes the Dresden of the last century's romantic and the eighteenth-century's Italian painters.) And its core-of-town museums—whose wealth was only hinted at in the American show—are in themselves reason enough for a visit to East Germany. They warrant a minimum of two full days, and a third would not be amiss.

The Zwinger (Postplatz) is an extraordinary rococo palace-complex—dating from the reign of Augustus the Strong—that, with a nineteenth-century addition, houses three museums. The exterior—sculpture-dotted façades, fountain-centered courtyards—is a major Dresden treat. Inside, go first to the Picture Gallery, whose Old Masters collection is on a par, to name only German museums, with West Berlin's Dahlem, and the galleries of Munich, Hamburg, and Frankfurt. The Italian and Dutch works are exceptional. Rafael's *Madonna di San Sisto* is what people make a beeline for first. But there are so many others—Titian's *Lady in White,* Mantegna's *Holy Family,* Rubens and Holbein, Boccaccio and del Sarto, Correggio and Giorgione, Veronese and Tintoretto, Canaletto and Tiepolo. There are

Dürers and Cranachs among the Germans, van Eyck and van Cleve among the Flemings, Rembrandt and Van Dyck, Velásquez and Murillo, Poussin and Watteau, and—among much else to excite—a painter whose name—Liotard—you may not know, but whose *Chocolate Girl* is the very same lady you see on Baker's Cocoa boxes. The Zwinger's second museum, the Historical Collection, is the ultimate in derring-do armor displays, with its metallic coverings for horses especially spectacular. And its third repository, the Porcelain Collection, is a series of connected galleries begun by Augustus the Strong, among whose accomplishments was the establishment of the china factory situated in the neighboring city of Meissen.

Move, then, to a building called *Albertinium* (Neumarkt). Its major museum, on a par with the Zwinger's Picture Gallery, is the *Grünes Gewölbe*, or Green Vault—so called because of the wall color of its original home, and containing what must be the world's most exquisite collection of objects fashioned of ivory, gold, silver, precious stones, and enamel, surpassing even that of the Residenz in Munich. A St. George, for example, of white enamel and amethyst, with his dragon an enameled blue embedded with a giant ruby. A golden sword, its handle encrusted with emeralds and diamonds. An entire Mogul ceremonial procession in miniature, the potentate dominating from his sapphire-set canopy atop an ivory-carved elephant. Go upstairs, next, for a survey course in the art of the nineteenth century—Frenchmen just before the Impressionists, like Courbet, on to Monet, Manet, and Renoir. Germans of this era—Corinth, Nolde, Dix. There's more to the Albertinium—check the basement, filled with sculpture, ranging from Greek, Roman, and Etruscan through the rich Middle Ages on to works by modern France's Rodin and modern Germany's Wilhelm Lembruck. With more, as you exit: a selection of the Albertinium's enormous collection of prints, drawings, and engravings mostly from the German and Italian Renaissance.

Schloss Pilnitz (a taxi ride from the center, on the north side of the Elbe) was the summer palace of the electors and kings of Saxony from the eighteenth century until the monarchy ended with World War I. Part of the complex is eighteenth-century oddball—with heavy Indian and Chinese influence not unlike England's Brighton Pavilion—and part is late eighteenth-century classicism. Bonus: a wonderfully eclectic mix of paintings and art objects from Middle Ages through Art Nouveau, on permanent display.

Allow time to stroll Dresden's pedestrians-only *Pragerstrase,* which links the hotel area with the historic core. Pop into restored monuments like the baroque-era Dom, still in operation as the Catholic cathedral, and with art treasures of its own. Hotels are all modern towers, not unlike those in sister East German cities. Best is Leningradstrasse's *Hotel Newa (Luxury)* with an especially nice restaurant. The first-class Pragerstrasse trio of hotels—*Bastei, Königstein,* and *Liliehstein*—are all modern breakfast-only houses, which are served by the *International Restaurant* and cafeteria, coffee- and ice-cream-bars in the vicinity. *Hotel Astoria* (Ernst-Thalmann Platz) is older and *Moderate*-category, but with a restaurant worth knowing about. And don't forget the *Dresden Oper;* book tickets at your hotel immediately upon arrival. Nearby Meissen's Gothic cathedral is one of East Germany's finest old churches, and the Meissen porcelain factory has a retail shop, which may or may not have any stock on hand when you visit; most of the production is exported to hard-currency countries, including West Germany, where prices are astronomical. *Further information:* Verkehrsamt Dresden—the city tourist office—is at Pragerstrasse 10.

LEIPZIG

Leipzig, once beautiful, once mellow, is East Germany's second city. Heavily damaged during World War II, the rebuilt Leipzig—centered between the Hauptbahnhof and Platz der Republik to the north and Rossplatz to the south—is not without something of an agreeable bustle, and there are pockets of interest: a restored old *Rathaus* (Marktplatz) with an interesting municipal historical museum up a flight; *Thomaskirche,* the 1,000-year-old Gothic church where Bach (his works are performed there to this day) directed the choir, and where he is buried; a trio of atmospheric and ancient restaurants: *Auerbachskeller*—in which Goethe set a scene in *Faust* (Grimmaischestrasse 2), *Kaffebaum* (Kleine Meischergasse 4), and *Burgskeller* (Madlerpassage); and a symphony orchestra—the famous Gewandhaus—whose conductors have included Felix Mendelssohn, Wilhelm Furtwangler, and Bruno Walter. Hotels, for this internationally famed twice-a-year fair-city, are oddly disappointing and inadequate, given the visitor traffic. Best are the Novotel chain's fairly modern *Hotel Stadt Leipzig* (Richard Wagner Strasse), unprepossessing albeit modern *Hotel am Ring* (Karl Marx Platz), and *Hotel Astoria* (Platz der Republik), at once grim and ugly; and the newest: Japanese-built *Hotel Merkur.*

There are two Trade Fair areas, one downtown (Messehäuser der Innenstadt), one away from the center (Messegelände); and visitors bound for the fairs—at the beginning of March and the beginning of September—traditionally find entry red tape relaxed for them. (Travel agents can let you know the current requirements.) Business travelers come from some three score countries to what is the largest of the Communist world's trade fairs. *Further information:* Verkehrsamt Leipzig—the city tourist office—is at Sachsenplatz 1.

15

Frankfurt

Substance Sans Style

BACKGROUND BRIEFING

Frankfurt's problem is image. Self-image.

Other German cities—virtually all—made comebacks after World War II destruction, devastation, and debasement, some, of course, more spectacularly than others. Frankfurt has, too—as an all-Europe transport hub (some half a hundred international airlines fly to its frenetic airport), as an international banking center, rich from commerce and manufacturing, not to mention the foreign currencies of its visitors—for whom it usually is, for better or for worse, an introduction to Germany.

What they find, these anxious-to-be-impressed newcomers, is a city which has eschewed the éclat and style of, say, cities such as Hamburg, Munich, Cologne, or Düsseldorf, in favor of solid comfort and substantial resources, cultural as well as commercial.

The difficulty for the brief-term explorer is cutting through the prosaic to find the plums.

Frankfurters themselves rarely help. (Expatriates say it is the stolid personality of the native Hessian people that has a lot to do with this anything-but-ebullient city.) You will rarely be told by locals that their art museum is one of the top handful in all Germany, with a Continent-wide reputation, as well.

Cathedral? Frankfurt's—containing hardly inconsequential art treasures—comes as a surprise. Citizens seem content to present their town and their fellows as plain as the proverbial old *Schuh*. A pity for the premier port of air-entry to a top-rung European country.

Still, it was not always so, in this city which was a kind of co-capital with Aachen for Charlemagne, where Holy Roman Emperors were long crowned and plans for a modern pan-German union were hatched; where Rothschilds and their fellow bankers amassed great fortunes, where trade fairs—drawing all of Europe and more recently the rest of the planet—have been a tradition since the Middle Ages.

And—hardly to be forgotten—this is where the Romans settled nearly a thousand years ago. Within two and a half centuries, native Germans—the same Alemanni who routed the Romans in other German towns—took over, with the native Franks succeeding them half a millennium later.

The end of the eighth century saw Charlemagne dominating the Frankfurt scene, ruling the empire—then Frankish, later to become the Holy Roman Empire—while strengthening the role of the Catholic Church.

Political eminence complemented commercial dominance. By the early thirteenth century, merchants from all over Europe were attending Frankfurt's trade fairs. A century later, the reigning Holy Roman Emperor designated Frankfurt's extant St. Bartholomew's Cathedral as the place for electing emperors. A couple of centuries thereafter, when wealthy Frankfurt had long since been a self-governing Free Imperial City, its cathedral became the imperial coronation site, with the archbishop elector of neighboring Mainz officiating, and a dinner following at the Römer, which is what Frankfurters have long called their City Hall. (The name relates to emperors being crowned ''Kings of the Romans'' there.)

Native son Johann Wolfgang von Goethe—poet, playwright, novelist, scientist—described the opulent coronation ceremonies for Emperor Joseph II in his autobiography. That was in 1764—not long before the last Frankfurt coronation, which occurred in 1792. After the Congress of Vienna, Frankfurt became the seat of the parliament of the newly formed German Confederation.

The Confederation created by the Congress of Vienna as a replacement for the Holy Roman Empire—was a loosely knit union of some two score German states. Its breakup was begun in, of all places, its capital, Frankfurt, when the liberally sponsored Frankfurt Parliament convened in 1848-49, intent on forging a strongly united pan-German state. What resulted, instead, was the Prussian-dominated North German Confederation, which in 1871 became the German Empire—with Frankfurt a part of it.

In that same year, Frankfurt was back in the political limelight as the setting for the Treaty of Frankfurt, which concluded the ugly Franco-Prussian War. Two wars later—World War II—strategically important, industrially powerful Frankfurt suffered air raid after air raid, to the point where the heart of the city—one of the most beautiful in Europe, if etchings, paintings, and scale models are accurate—was almost entirely destroyed.

Rebuilding was not as successful aesthetically as in other German cities. Still, today's Frankfurt deserves more of the visitor's attention than most believe it is worth.

ON SCENE

Lay of the Land: For a big city—its population, with outlying areas, hovers around the million mark—Frankfurt is relatively easy to negotiate, even on foot. The spacious Hauptbahnhof is at the western frontier of downtown, fronting the square called Am Hauptbahnhof, which is flanked by streets named for Düsseldorf and Basel. From the station, one heads directly into the center via one of three east-west streets. One, Taunusstrasse, is the most direct route to the principal square, Hauptwache, with a major U-Bahn (subway) station and nearby shopping streets including pedestrians-only "Fressgasse" (actually Karl-Bacher-Gasse, and full of cafés, restaurants, and food shops), and Goethestrasse—wherein are concentrated the bulk of Frankfurt's smarter shops. Another, Kaiserstrasse, is shop-lined and strollable. The third, Münchenerstrasse, is the most direct route to Theaterplatz and the opera house, called Städtische Bühnen (Municipal Stages).

Most of the places one wants to visit lie east of Theaterplatz, west of Schumacherstrasse, and south of Hauptwache, bordered on the north by the Main River. The Main is crossed by

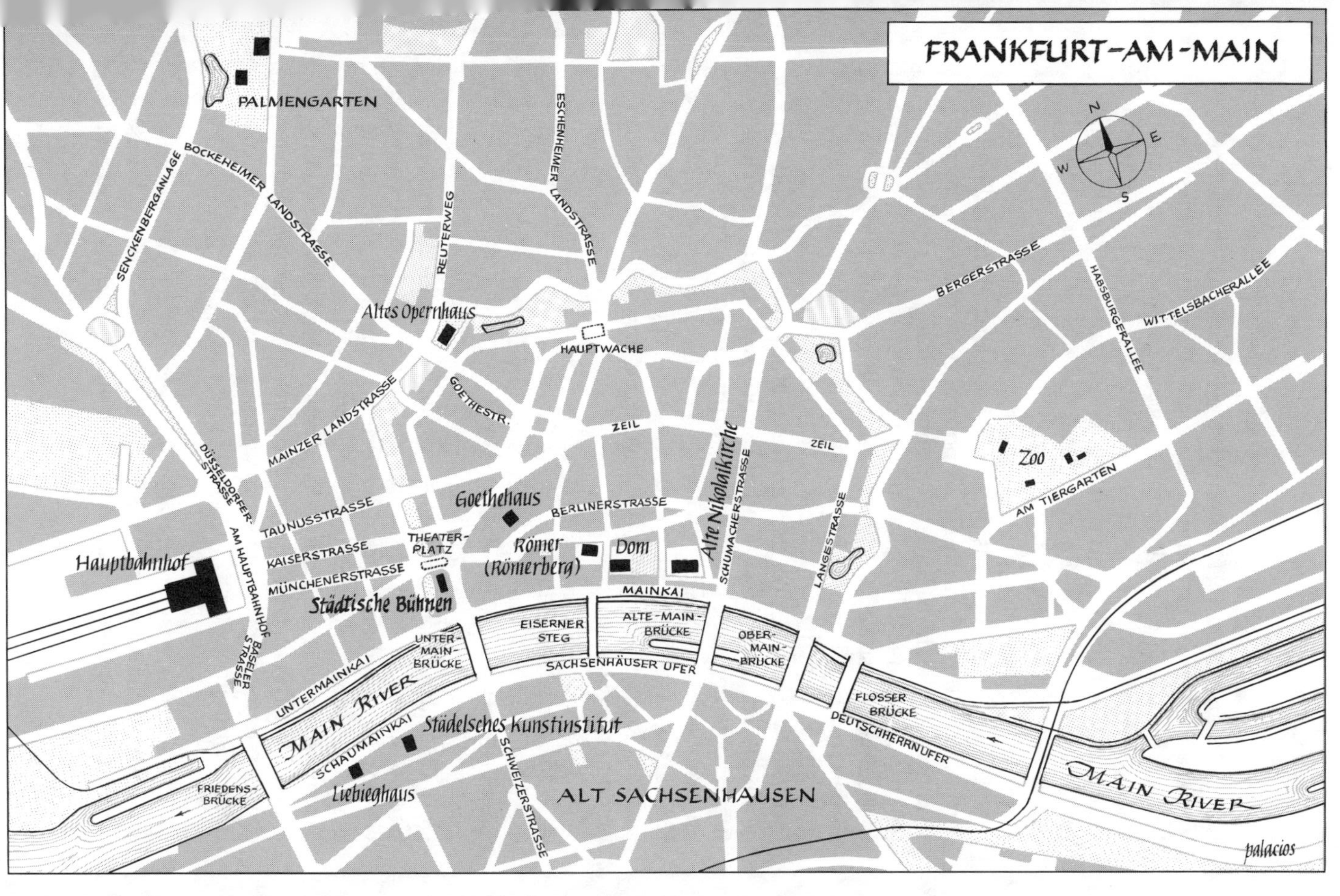
FRANKFURT-AM-MAIN
N
E
S
W
PALMENGARTEN
BOCKEHEIMER LANDSTRASSE
SENCKENBERGANLAGE
REUTERWEG
ESCHENHEIMER LANDSTRASSE
BERGERSTRASSE
HABSBURGERALLEE
WITTELSBACHERALLEE
Altes Opernhaus
HAUPTWACHE
GOETHESTR.
MAINZER LANDSTRASSE
ZEIL
ZEIL
Zoo
AM TIERGARTEN
DÜSSELDORFER-STRASSE
AM HAUPTBAHNHOF
TAUNUSSTRASSE
Goethehaus
BERLINERSTRASSE
THEATER-PLATZ
Römer (Römerberg)
Dom
Alte Nikolaikirche
SCHUMACHERSTRASSE
LANGESTRASSE
Hauptbahnhof
KAISERSTRASSE
MÜNCHENERSTRASSE
Städtische Bühnen
MAINKAI
EISERNER STEG
ALTE-MAIN-BRÜCKE
OBER-MAIN-BRÜCKE
UNTER-MAIN-BRÜCKE
BASELER STRASSE
SACHSENHÄUSER UFER
UNTERMAINKAI
MAIN RIVER
FLOSSER BRÜCKE
DEUTSCHHERRNUFER
SCHAUMAINKAI
Städelsches Kunstinstitut
SCHWEIZERSTRASSE
FRIEDENS-BRÜCKE
Liebieghaus
ALT SACHSENHAUSEN
MAIN RIVER
palacios

half a dozen bridges. Three of these are important to visitors. You'll find yourself crossing Untermainbrücke or Eisernersteg-brücke for visits to no less than five conveniently situated museums. And you may traverse Altebrücke to take in the amusement district named Alt Sachsenhausen. Frankfurt's pretty botanical park, Palmengarten, is to the northwest of downtown, while its outstanding zoo lies to the east.

The Römer (Römerberg) is on the Römer square and is Frankfurt's city hall, an embarrassingly poor post-World War II reconstruction of what must have been a fine building, in a fine square (many of whose historic buildings were renovated and meticulously restored as a part of a costly three-year project concluded in 1983), but which now looks more like a scenic backdrop for a schmaltzy operetta. Or mostly. The façade has, in fact, the best exterior on the square, with a quartet of sculpted emperors above its mock-Gothic balcony, a red and blue clock tucked between the top gable. Within, the seat of government is an unlovely mass of post-World War II *moderne*, on whose Kaisersaal walls there are children's-book-type murals of 50 or so Holy Roman Emperors, Charlemagne onward, who broke bread in the original hall.

Alte Nikolaikirche (Römerplatz) is this old square's most successful building, without as well as within. It's smallish, squarish, single-steepled Gothic. Do go in.

Dom (Marktplatz): Frankfurt's simply but tastefully restored Gothic cathedral—St. Bartholomew's by name—deserves more visitor attention than it gets. The tiered wedding-cake of a dome is a beauty, and within there are such works of art as a fifteenth-century sculpted altar scene of the dying Virgin Mary, and a ravishing Van Dyck, *Descent from the Cross.* Not to mention the chapel where the prince-electors voted in a whole slew of Holy Roman Emperors.

Goethehaus (Grosserhirschgraben 23) is Frankfurt with its most unabashed charm: a smartly furnished five-story rococo townhouse that warrants the attention not only of Goethe buffs (of which America, proportionately, has many fewer than the German-speaking lands), but of any visitor curious about how a prosperous family would have lived in a major eighteenth-century German city. Goethe fan or not, one wants to see the desk in the room he used as a study. But so much else is of interest—authentically accessorized kitchen, red damask chairs of the company-best upstairs drawing room, museum-caliber furniture throughout—beds and bureaus, clocks and cabinets. Note the fine paintings, drawings, and silhouettes on the walls. The adjacent museum—smaller than the Goethe Museum in Düsseldorf—is a repository not only of documents relating to Goethe and his work, but of paintings and sculptures of Frankfurt's favorite favorite-son.

Städelsches Kunstinstitut (Schaumainkai 63): With a sampling of historic Frankfurt behind you (above), you're ready for what, in my opinion, is Frankfurt's most important attraction—an art museum that has less than a handful of peers in Germany and is one of Europe's best. The collection of a civic-minded eighteenth-century banker was its nucleus. Forget about the aesthetics of the gawky and ungracious late nineteenth-century Städel building. Concentrate on the art: a survey of painting roughly from Rogier van der Weyden through Pablo Picasso, mostly in a score of second-floor galleries. The Italians include Fra Angelico, Giovanni Bellini, Carpaccio, Botticelli. The Flemish primitives—van Eyck, David, and Memling as well as van der Weyden—are superb. There are works by German Renaissance masters—Stephan Lochner, Grünewald, Altdorfer, Baldung, the Holbeins, the elder Cranach, and of course Dürer. Baroque? How about some paintings from the Low Countries: Rubens, Rembrandt, Hals, van Ruysdael? The French are well represented—Clouet, Lorrain, Poussin, with a brilliant pre-Impressionist, Impressionist, and post-Impressionist collection, Corot and Courbet through Monet and Renoir into Matisse, and German Expressionists—Macke, Kirchner, Beckmann, Corinth. Cafeteria and a shop with postcards and catalogues the most expensive of any in Germany.

Leibieghaus (Schaumainkai 71) is for sculpture what the Städel is for paintings: a world-class collection, in a onetime baronial mansion. The range is Egyptian (reliefs from ancient tombs) through Greek (a memorable goddess Athena) and Roman (busts of assorted nobles) into Europe's Middle Ages (a local eleventh-century carved-wood crucifixion), and then beyond to the Renaissance (a Tilman Riemenschneider *Virgin and Child,* with a brilliant baroque-rococo grouping. And ancient China as a bonus.

Museum für Kunsthandwerk (Schaumainkai 15) is Frankfurt's extraordinary—and pathetically underappreciated—decorative arts museum. The setting is a Schaumainkai mansion dating to the eighteenth century. But the range of the collection extends from the Middle Ages through to the present, with Asian works as well. There are beautiful objects—medieval cupboards, baroque commodes, rococo desks, neoclassic chairs, Art Nouveau (*Jugendstil* in German) settees. The fine arts are also represented, especially paintings of eighteenth-century Frankfurt. This museum's short-term exhibitions take place in Karmeliterkloster—a onetime cloistered convent—nearby at Munzgasse 5.

Bundespostmuseum (Schaumainkai 53) is, along with the Swiss Postal Museum in Berne, the best such that I know, even if you're an American who has no particular affection for the contemporary postal system of your native land. This one is an amusing mix of all manner of things relating to the German mails—insignia and signs, postal carriages and trucks (models and the real thing), posters and prints, notices and forms, stamps and seals. Plus one of the rare museum exhibits of which I'm aware anywhere in West Germany (the Reichstag Museum in West Berlin is a major exception) having to do with the Hitler era—a model of a swastika-embellished mail truck out of the thirties.

Zoologischer Garten (Alfred-Brehm-Platz): Frankfurt's zoo is special and worth a journey from downtown, especially for the dramatically designed Exotarium—open-air living spaces for certain of the resident population. Go on a weekend to mix and mingle with the Frankfurters. An aquarium, too. Snack spots.

Palmengarten (Palmengartenstrasse) is Frankurt's counterpart of London's Kew Gardens: a rambling park filled with some 12,000 varieties of plants and flowers (including orchids) and trees. As close in Germany as you'll get to a tropical island. Restaurant, café. Lovely.

SETTLING IN

Hotel Inter-Continental Frankfurt (Wilhelm-Leuschner-Strasse 43): Well, you've got to give the Inter-Conti credit for ingenuity. When it became clear that there was a need for more space than it had in its main building, with no space available next door, the hotel chose a site across the street, and connected the two by means of an underground tunnel. Result: Germany's largest hotel—with more than 800 rooms and suites, in a location that is a hop and a skip from the Hauptbahnhof and the river, and a fairly comfortable walk to the heart of downtown. The high-up accommodations are the ones to shoot for—they have super views of the city and the Main. Traditionally furnished suites are a specialty, the better to please visiting executives. There are a trio of restaurants (posh Rotisserie, moderately priced Brasserie, pubby Bierstube), two bar-lounges, and a heated pool. *Luxury.*

Hotel Frankfurter Hof (Am Kaiserplatz) has one of the handsomest façades in town—mock-Renaissance with an arched arcade facing Kaiserplatz. Within, it is full-facility, a Steigenberger hotel that is not the best in the Germany-wide chain, but has the advantage of the most central location in Frankfurt. The 460 rooms are comfortable, as are the nearly 30 suites. There is a choice of restaurants—one French, another international-hotel-style, still another (this, the most fun) a German *Stube*. And a couple of bars. Competent, though rarely cheerful, service. *Luxury.*

Parkhotel (Wiesenhüttenplatz 28) is a pair of buildings, one elderly and traditional, the other mod. There are close to 300 rooms and suites that are not exactly aesthetic triumphs. The principal restaurant is worthy of comment later. Bar-lounge, terrace-café. Near the Hauptbahnhof. *First Class.*

Savoy Hotel (Wiesenhüttenstrasse 42) is a modern house near the station with an attractive lobby; 150 fully equipped rooms, bar and disco, pair of restaurants, the better of which—the grill—is handsome. *First Class.*

Hotel Schwille (Grosse Bockenheimerstrasse 50—also known as Fressgasse) is heart-of-town on the pedestrians' shopping street earlier recommended for its restaurants, cafés, and food stores. This is a perky little house, with a vast *café-konditorei;* 60 pleasant rooms, more than half of which have bath or shower and toilet; and a big breakfast room. I like. *Moderate.*

Hotel National (Baselerstrasse 50) charms. Which is not often the effect of a Frankfurt hotel. This is a lovely old schoolhouse, antiques-accented throughout (including the wide corridors). There are nearly 100 rooms, with the doubles proportionately more capacious than the singles—at least the singles I've seen. Inviting restaurant. Near the Hauptbahnhof. *First Class.*

Hotel Continental (Baselerstrasse 50), another Hauptbahnhof neighbor, is nothing to write home about, but fills the bill for standard-class shelter. There are some 70 rooms, and it should be noted that some of the singles, confusingly enough, have sink and shower but no toilet. Others have sink only, still others, the works. Doubles are all fully equipped. Small restaurant. *Moderate.*

Hotel Hessischer Hof (Friedrich-Ebert-Anlage 40) pulls off a trick very well; it's a traditional-style house within—even to the point of a restaurant decorated with antique Sèvres porcelain—and plain contemporary without. Location is just opposite Messegelände—the fairgrounds north of downtown—with a clientele heavily fairgrounds-oriented. This is a honey of a hotel—rambling lobby, tea lounge, stylish accommodations (there are just 115 rooms and suites), not to mention the gilded Sèvres in glass cases lining the restaurant's walls. *Luxury.*

Hotel Münchner Hof (Münchenerstrasse 46) is unprepossessing and small, but all of its bright rooms have bath or shower and toilet, there's a good restaurant, and the location is central. *Moderate.*

Hotel CP Frankfurt Plaza (Hamburgerallee 2) is a tower embracing 600 rooms and suites, up near the fairgounds; it fills a need as regards the accommodation of quantities of congress delegates and visitors in town for the annual book and other trade fairs for which Frankfurt is celebrated. Restaurant, coffee shop, bars, views from on high. A link in the commendable Canadian Pacific chain, all of whose home-territory hotels I've lived in, in the course of researching and re-researching *Canada A to Z. Luxury.*

Hotel Maingau (Schifferstrasse 38) is across the Main in Sachsenhausen, a district dotted with simple restaurants, bars, cafés, and the like. If you like this part of town you may be interested in this updated house, with agreeable rooms, many with bath. Restaurant. *Moderate.*

Frankfurt Airport Sheraton Hotel (Rhein-Main International Airport): A *really* luxurious 555-room-and-suite hotel at an airport? Answer is a resounding yes. This is a stunner of a Sheraton, for which you must book well in advance. German and other businessmen keep it filled, flying in for conferences with colleagues, which take place in the hotel's meeting rooms, then spending the night without going near town, and flying away in the morning. Good restaurant, coffee shop, bar-lounge. *Luxury.*

Steigenberger Airporthotel (Flughafenstrasse 300, near Rhein-Main International Airport) is an attractive link in the Steigenberger chain, with 350 modern rooms and suites, several tempting places to eat and drink (including a historic inn, adjacent, where meals are served alfresco in summer). Note, though, that you need a bus to get to the air terminal from here (the hotel provides them). Whereas at the Sheraton you're *at* the air terminal. *Luxury.*

DAILY BREAD

Rotisserie (Hotel Frankfurt Inter-Continental, Wilhelm-Leuschner Strasse 43): Go in the spring, and you'll be able to order Frankfurt's first fresh asparagus of the season—a tradition at this smart restaurant. Go autumn through winter, for game, including saddle of venison, roast pheasant and partridge. Super steaks and seafood, as well. *Luxury.*

La Truffe (Parkhotel, Wieshüttenplatz 28) is at once elegant and delicious, with fare a masterful mix of German traditional, with France's *nouvelle cuisine.* Exceptionally handsome presentation. *Luxury.*

Ernos (Liebigstrasse 15) represents what might be called hard-core French, in the very best sense. There are lovely traditional dishes, appetizers through sweets (with careful attention to sauces). And interesting specialties, including perch sautéed in white wine. *First Class.*

Mövenpick (Opernplatz 1), one of a number of similarly named restaurants in German cities, is of Swiss origin. I have found its food to be delicious—the inspiration is French, it would seem, more than Swiss—service punctilious, prices fair. You're not going to get a better entrecôte—with a sauce bordelaise—or more delicious potatoes dauphinois, in Paris, or even Geneva. *First Class.*

Brückenkeller (Schützenstrasse 6) is an atmospheric wine tavern—antiques-accented the better to add authenticity—with traditional German fare that can be, when required, delicate, or if indicated, heavy. No better source in Frankfurt of German wines. Festive. *Luxury.*

Chez Henri (Sevignystrasse 31) is the place to go when you're in a distinctly Gallic mood, with an appetite for the genuine French article—onion soup, roast duck, a chocolate soufflé, perhaps?—in an attractive setting. French wines, too. *Luxury.*

DaFranco (Elbestrasse 5): Italian fare is invariably delicious in Germany, principally because it's prepared by Italian-born chefs who double as *padrones*. Da Franco does well from pastas—in a wide range and nicely sauced—to veal specialties. End with a rich *zuppa inglese. First Class.*

Alten Limburg (Römerberg) occupies elaborate quarters in a seventeenth-century half-timbered house in the heart of the historic district. Order a stein of *Eisbier*—a premium-priced brew that is presumed to have been processed from melted snow (thus its name)—and one of the table d'hôte specials: consommé, pork chops, French fries, and salad, for example. *Moderate.*

Hahnhof (Berlinerstrasse 64) is ideal when you want a proper meal downtown, and at a price. Liver-dumpling soup, say, along with veal steak, and a glass of the house's Pfalz-region dry white wine. *Moderate.*

Der Fundus (Theaterplatz) is for lunch while exploring central Frankfurt, before or after the opera. The look is contemporary-café, but you can order a substantial meal. *Moderate.*

Gumpelmann (Am Salzhaus, near Kaiserstrasse) is old-style, with wooden booths and soft lighting. The schnitzels are tasty, the location central. *Moderate.*

Hauptwache 68 (Hauptwache) is center-of-the-action on the main square, at the U-Bahn station. Pluses are the steak and mixed grill, and a counter, for single diners in a hurry. *Moderate.*

Konditorei am Goethehaus (Grosserhirschgraben 21): Land sakes, a Japanese konditorei? Well, the proprietors are Japanese. And at lunch the food is mostly of Nippon—and good. Go at other times for delicious—and proudly German-style—pastries, *mit Kaffee oder Tee. Moderate.*

Café Hauptwache (Hauptwache): The gracious baroque building in the center of the Hauptwache is seventeenth century and is beloved by Frankfurters. Linger for coffee and something to eat, and watch the passing parade. *Moderate.*

Café Kranzler (Hautwache 7) is a favored old-timer, recently reopened, with chocolates and pastries for sale on the street floor, and the café—for casual meals and pick-me-ups, on two. *First Class.*

Lorsbacher Tal (Grosse Rittergasse 49, in the Sachsenhausen quarter across the Main) is as good as any of the multitude of the so-called cider restaurants in this tacky-touristy district. (The cider has alcoholic content, though less than beer.) Standard menu is pork chops, sauerkraut, mashed potatoes, with the cider served in blue-and-gray pottery pitchers—the only touch of charm that I can perceive in this colorless genre of Frankfurt restaurant. *Moderate.*

Schlosshotel (Hainstrasse 25, Kronberg) is for a gala evening out of town, to a pretty town 12 miles from Frankfurt. You'll dine in great style in a pre-World War I palace built by Kaiser Wilhelm for his mother, Empress Frederick—as opulent as when nonpaying guests like Queen Victoria (the empress's mum) slept under its roof. *Luxury.*

AFTER DARK

Städische Bühnen (Theaterplatz) is Frankfurt's post-World War II opera house, of no special aesthetic distinction in and of itself, but the home of an increasingly respected repertory opera troupe (the range is wide—Bizet through Wagner) along with a ballet company that has become a national leader due to the reshaping by U.S. choreographer-director John Neumeier. Plays also, in German, of course.

Alte Oper (Opernplatz): Frankfurt's longtime Opera House, a magnificent neo-classic structure that was built in 1880 at a cost estimated at about $32 million, seriously damaged by Allied firebombs during World War II, has been painstakingly rebuilt—essentially following original plans—at a cost double the original. Although bearing its initial name, Alte Oper is today a concert hall. (Both the Chicago Symphony and the Vienna Philharmonic played at the gala 1981 reopening.) The musical fare is pop as well as classical. Try to take in a performance.

Jahrhunderthalle (Höchst) translates as Century Hall and is a principal setting for concerts of the local and visiting symphonies. Location is the suburb of Höchst, six miles west of the center. There's a first-class restaurant here that is ready for pre-performance dinner. (Other concerts take place in churches, museums, and a variety of other locales.) Ask your hotel concierge for the monthly publications *Das Programm in Frankfurt* or *Frankfurter Wochen Schau.*

INCIDENTAL INTELLIGENCE

Frankfurt's Rhein-Main International Airport is six miles from town. There is train (S-Bahn) service as well to town. In the city, buy your ticket *before* boarding (either subway or streetcar) from automatic vending machines in stations. Here's how: select color of your destination, then depress button of the corresponding color, inserting exact fare, amount of which is posted on the machine. Good luck! *Further information*: Verkehrsverein Frankfurt—the municipal tourist office—has its main office at Hauptwache on Level B, with information offices at the Hauptbahnhof and at the airport.

16

Freiburg and the Black Forest

Adjacent Town-and-Country Beauty

BACKGROUND BRIEFING

The West German Freiburg's problem is one of identity. It's one of three European cities similarly named. There's a Swiss Freibourg—spelled the French way—and an East German Freiburg, as well. Travelers from across the Atlantic tend not to think very much at all about any of the trio, let alone the subject of this chapter.

But they should: Freiburg-im-Breisgau—to use its complete designation to distinguish it from sister Freiburgs—is a lovely town. A small-scale metropolis at the southern tip of the Black Forest—still virtually an unknown quantity to North Americans—it combines a number of attributes. A king-size mountain—gained by funicular—in its own back yard is one. The get-away-from-it-all resorts of the Black Forest constitute a second. A perky populace—perhaps made cosmopolitan over the centuries thanks to the proximity of both France and Switzerland—is still another.

The founding fathers were a ducal family called Zähringen, who created the Swiss Freibourg and Switzerland's Berne, as well—way back in the early twelfth century. Medieval urbanists, you might call them. The Zähringen dukes knew a good location. Freiburg, with the Black Forest to the north and the Rhine just beyond, could not help but be a handy trading depot.

Locally mined silver and bronze helped swell the town's coffers, as did a cache of garnets, converted on the scene to jewels for grand European ladies, including Marie Antoinette, who made a Freiburg layover, en route from Vienna to Paris to become dauphine of France.

Rich burghers built a rich city, whose mercantile guilds became politically strong. When the Zähringens' successors, the unpopular counts of Urach, misbehaved, the guild forces engineered allegiance to the Austrian House of Hapsburg, with which Freiburg remained aligned, from the fourteenth century to the eighteenth.

With ups and downs, to be sure. But they did create a soaring cathedral in the fourteenth century, a university in the fifteenth-century that is still held in high esteem today, and a Freiburg-based Diet of the Holy Roman Empire.

But the seventeenth-century Thirty Years' War made Freiburg a battlefield in which both German and later Austrian forces were defeated by the French. A century or so later, in the course of the War of the Austrian Succession, the French once again gave Freiburg a drubbing. It set about rebuilding for a second time, and remained intact until the era of the World Wars. The bombing attacks of World War I were nothing compared with those of World War II—in 1944—when much of the historic center was tragically shattered. But post-World War II decades have seen a meticulous restoration; today central Freiburg has not only the look but the ambience of its earlier centuries.

ON SCENE

Lay of the Land: Freiburg's historic core is agreeably compact—an almost perfect square in the center of the greater city. One can easily walk the entire area. The Hauptbahnhof fronts Bismarckallee at the northwest corner of the Altstadt, or Old Town. From it, one can walk easterly into the action via either Roastrasse or Eisenbahnstrasse, both of which lead past Colombi Park and then the major north-south thoroughfare it faces, which is important—or at least long—enough to have two names: Werderring and Rotteckring. An ancient street—lined by medieval buildings—called Trumstrasse leads from Rotteckring into a major square, Rathausplatz, and the Town Hall for which it is named. From Rathausplatz one may continue a walk eastward, via Franziskanerstrasse, first crossing the main commercial thoroughfare of the city—Kaiser-Josef-Strasse—to Marktgasse, continuing east to Münsterplatz.

From Münsterplatz, go south. Take Herrenstrasse a short way until it comes upon a meticulously restored old street called Oberlinden. The landmark there is a thirteenth-century gatetower, Schwabentor, overlooking a square named for it. The tower adjoins a cable-car station for ascent of Freiburg's municipal mountain, Schlossberg, with spectacular views, especially to the east.

Münster (Münsterplatz): Freiburg's cathedral took a full three centuries (thirteenth to sixteenth) to build. The finished product was well worth waiting for. Start at the rear, looking up at its twin towers. They're the oldest part, dating from 1200, and originally housed chapels. Gradually, authorities evolved the idea of using them as the rear of a greater church, in the Gothic style, which was then in its infancy. Thus the main body of the cathedral culminating in the western tower evolved. There are three sections—the lowest and eldest is relatively unadorned, the middle is a graceful octagon, and the top is a lacy spire.

The porch, just beyond the finely carved doorway, is a Middle Ages sculpture museum in and of itself, with a number of exquisite groups. Some of the most striking are a bevy of Wise and Foolish Virgins and a cluster devoted to what were then the "liberal" arts: grammar, dialectic, rhetoric, geometry, music, arithmetic, and astronomy.

The interior of the church—splendidly vaulted and with a window-illuminated choir visible through the long nave—is filled with art treasures. You'll find your own favorites. Mine are a sculpted *Madonna and Child* over the front portal, just as you enter the nave; the stained glass, especially that of the transept; a Hans Baldung Grien painting, *Crowning of the Virgin,* on the High Altar; and Holbein's *The Adoration of the Magi* in the University Chapel.

Münsterplatz: Your visit to the *Münster* completed, pause outside for a look around its square. Head first for one of its celebrated sausage stands, and order a grilled wurst; they're delicious. Wander about, then, taking in the façades of the spectacular Kaufhaus—a gilded, gabled, and turreted Gothic beauty, with opulent reception rooms and a concert hall. And the two rococo structures: Wenzingerhaus (now a music conservatory) and the Archbishop's Residence.

Augustinermuseum (Salzstrasse) ranks with the *Münster,* and that is going some. And in more ways than one, for it began life at just about the same time the *Münster* did—in the thirteenth century—and with the same function: as a church. Or, more properly, an Augustinian monastery, a part of which was a Gothic chapel. It is the site now of one of the most extraordinary—and extraordinarily beautiful—art museums in Germany. The major thrust, in this town of the Middle Ages and the Renaissance, is the art—fine and applied—of those two periods. But the range extends into the baroque, rococo, romantic, and contemporary eras as well. You will want to give the Augustiner time. The chapel alone is a work of art; and so is the cloister. A fierce, wood-carved prophet of the thirteenth century, a Renaissance sculpture group depicting the Death of the Virgin, and a rococo St. Sebastian in plaster typify the works of plastic art. Paintings are no less stunning—a medieval *Annunciation,* brilliantly colored Matthias Grünewalds, a Hans Baldung Grien veiled *Madonna and Child,* illuminated manuscripts and rococo frescoes, nineteenth-century drawings and oils of the nearby Black Forest, paintings by such twentieth-century German masters as August Macke, Karl Hofer, and Otto Dix; stained glass and gold and silver; porcelain, and furniture in gaily painted rooms of the last century, out of Black Forest peasants' houses.

Museum für Völkerkunde (Gerberau 32) is across the square from the Augustinermuseum and a remarkable repository of ethnographic art—a rare Benin mask out of Nigeria, pre-Columbian works that rival those at the Anthropology Museum in Mexico City, serene Japanese Buddhas, South Seas artifacts. (The same building houses a natural history museum.)

Schwabentormuseum (Schwabentor): Schwabentor, the gate-tower mentioned earlier, houses a winsome mini-museum whose subject matter is *Zinnfiguren*—antique figures fashioned of tin. Have a look.

Adelhausenkirche (Adelhausenplatz) is the handsomest of the city's baroque churches—an outgrowth of a Gothic chapel that is exuberant and art filled.

Neues Rathaus (Rathausplatz) is hardly new, despite its name. It is richly detailed baroque, but it's been the Town Hall only since the turn of the century. A carillon concert takes place daily at noon. And in summer there are theater performances in the inner courtyard.

SETTLING IN

Colombi Hotel (Rotteckring 16): The Colombi comes on, at first glance, as low-key, what with its modest seven-story post-World War II façade, and an agreeable but unassuming lobby. But the 85 rooms and suites, one finds, are handsomely equipped; there are both ground-floor café with bar-lounge and a Colombi Park-view restaurant on the mezzanine, one of the best in Freiburg. Location is perfect—for both station and heart of town. And service: I have found none kinder in Germany. *Luxury.*

Novotel Freiburg (Karlplatz): If Novotel Freiburg is atypical of the town—not because it is contemporary but because it is garish-contemporary—it has attributes that place it second only to the distinguished Colombi. These are a central location (views of the *Münster*), 115 fully equipped though cramped rooms, restaurant, bar-lounge, top management by the French Novotel chain, and a friendly staff. *Luxury.*

Hotel Jägerhäusle (Winterstrasse 89) needs qualification. It's my third choice for two reasons. First is architecture. So few modern hotels are innovative that credit is due exceptions. Its designers selected a striking site—on a promontory above the city. They built horizontally, and the hotel blends into a park-like setting.

Second is the interior, which though not unique, has an upside-down arrangement, with guest rooms on floors below the lobby. The swimming pool is down there too. One sees it through a glass wall from reception. Restaurant and terrace-café, with views of town; stark white bedrooms with primary-color accents, tennis. *Luxury.*

Hotel Rappen (Münsterplatz 13) evokes Old Freiburg. Location is on the square dominated by the cathedral, style is traditional, ambience intimate (only a score of rooms, mostly charming and with private baths). There are a pair of restaurants (mentioned later), and a terrace-café. *Moderate.*

Hotel zum Roten Bären (Oberlinden 12) dates from the year A.D. 1120—no newcomer to the Freiburg scene! Location, on ancient Oberlinden, is as atmospheric as the hotel, which has some 30 rooms, recently refurbished so that all now have private baths. The restaurant is celebrated; more about it in a later paragraph. *Moderate.*

Hotel am Rathaus (Rathausgasse 6) is smack in the center, near Rathausplatz, small-scale, with 20-plus rooms, (many with bath), cozy restaurant. *Moderate.*

DAILY BREAD

Weinstube zur Traube (Schusterstrasse 17) occupies a sturdy house that dates back a few centuries. The look is understated, but you know, once you've been seated, served an aperitif, and given a chance to study the menu, that you're in an exceptional restaurant. Lunch or dinner might include lobster bisque, grilled Black Forest trout, a Baden-region white wine, a festive dessert, and with coffee a snort of the local *Kirschwasser. Luxury.*

Ratskeller (Kornhaus, Münsterplatz): Freiburg's Ratskeller is not in the Neues Rathaus—which I've recommended you take note of above—but in an older, more impressive building on Marktplatz. There are a series of period rooms for dining within, and a warm-weather terrace on the square, as well. Steaks with Yank titles are specialties here. How about a Buffalo Bill

Peppersteak or a Colorado-Cut Sirloin? German fare, too. *Moderate/First Class.*

Zum Falken (Rathausgasse 2) is a combination restaurant-*Weinstube*-small hotel. It occupies ancient quarters adjacent to Rathausplatz. Old prints on wood-paneled walls accent a room that features the house's own vintages and soups, veal specialties, rich desserts. *First Class.*

Zum Roten Bären (Oberlinden 12) is the restaurant—and major—part of the twelfth-century hotel mentioned above. The management claims it's the oldest continuously operated eatery in Germany. Food is solid German—roast goose, schnitzel, game. Big wine cellar. *First Class.*

Hotel Rappen Restaurant (Münsterplatz) is the dining room of the hotel I've already recommended. Decor is out of the neighboring Black Forest and the food delicious, especially specialties like pepper steak, pheasant, duck. Good-value full-course meals. *Moderate/First Class.*

Löwen (Herrenstrasse 47): Why not an unassuming but hearty lunch or dinner in the handsome restaurant of a small, midtown hotel? Order the planked-platter special: steak, grilled *Wurst,* and a salad. And ask for a glass of wine—do try the dry German reds. *Moderate.*

Weinstube zur Gichelschmiede (Inselstrasse 1): You'll like this old house with a honey of an oriel window without and a trendy atmosphere within. Go for a glass of wine, a snack, or a meal. Central. *Moderate.*

Steinmetz (Kaiser-Josef-Strasse) is Freiburg's longtime No. 1 café-konditorei. Cake, coffee, snacks. *Moderate.*

SOUND OF MUSIC

Stadttheater (Sedanstrasse at Werderring) is the colonnaded opera house; ballet, operetta, pop events, as well.

The Freiburg Philharmonic performs in the Kaufhaus (Marktplatz) and in the Stadthalle congress/concert hall. The Münster is the setting for performances of the Bach Chorus.

ESCAPE TO THE BLACK FOREST

Germany's best-kept holiday secret, the Black Forest, or Schwarzwald, is more a region of mountain-fringed and verdant valleys than the woodsy domain its name suggests. From Baden-Baden, at its northern fringe, one may—as I explain in the Baden-Baden chapter—spend a delightful day or even half day motoring along a highway called the Schwarzwald Hochstrasse, which cuts through the beauty spots of the forest's northern section.

From Freiburg, the forest's southern metropolis, the visitor does well to plan an even more ambitious Black Forest sojourn, selecting one of a number of delightful hotels in various categories located at strategic points in the forest—usually in and about a village out of a fairy tale.

If there is a single destination in the forest that is captivating to sightseers, it is the sumptuous church and monastery called St. Peter, which is found in the village of the same name. It could have been transplanted right out of Bavaria, so splendidly does it typify the opulent, eighteenth-century ecclesiastical style of that region. In the church, note the angel-flanked gold altars, both high and side, and the gallery-encircled library, whose ancient volumes are surmounted by a fresco-filled ceiling—arched and graceful. Stay at the *Hotel Sonne,* operated by a family, as are virtually all of the inns in the Forest. There are lovely views from the bedrooms, and solid fare in the dining room. *Moderate.*

St. Peter is but a few kilometers east of Freiburg. Continue an additional few miles east to a hotel-filled trio of villages—Friedenweiler, Titisee-Neustadt, and Hinterzarten. Their lures, aside from natural beauty, are the range of accommodations they offer. *Baers Hotel und Kurhaus,* in Friedenweiler, is solid, old-fashioned, and welcoming, with handsome places to dine and drink, swimming pool and health spa, and—as an added dividend—a Romanesque church out of the twelfth century. *First Class.*

Titisee is at once the name of a village and an idyllic lake bordered by evergreen forests and hotels. *Treschers Schwarzwald Hotel am See* is low-slung, rambling, and decorated in what one might call very stylish rustic. There's an indoor-outdoor pool, evening dancing and entertainment, thoroughly attractive rooms, lakeside restaurant (with summer terrace) that is one of the best in the region, and skilled management. *Luxury.*

Still another Titisee hotel, the *Adler-Post,* is aged (the same family has run it since 1850), central (in the village) and intimate, with fewer than 40 no-two-alike rooms, inviting restaurants, indoor pool/sauna. *First Class.*

Hinterzarten, third village of our contiguous trio, offers an exceptional range of hotels. The *Thomahof* is chalet-style, smallish but full-facility, and *Moderate. Hotel Weisses Rössle* is traditional-style (it was originally founded in 1347), set in its own spacious garden, and *First Class.* Then there is *Parkhotel Adler,* one of whose VIP guests—and there have been many—was an eighteenth-century Hapsburg princess en route to France to marry and eventually become queen of France: Marie Antoinette. Today, Parkhotel Adler consists of but 80 guest rooms and suites—each distinctive and beautifully decorated—along with no fewer than half a dozen dining rooms ranging from casual *Stube* to the Forest's best haute cuisine restaurant. Additional facilities include an indoor-outdoor pool, a health club, and even a bowling alley. With a sun-dappled terrace-café for summer meals and drinks. And management that is as skilled as any that you could find in Germany. Member, Leading Hotels of the World. *Luxury.*

Still a fourth village, an agreeable drive to the southwest of Hinterzarten, is hotel-and-restaurant-dotted Badenweiler. Here, I recommend a stop—at least for a meal if not a relaxing overnight or two—at *Hotel Römerbad,* operated by the same family—the Fellman-Lauers—since 1825. This is a handsome old-world house, with 111 no-two-quite-alike rooms and suites, distinguished restaurant, pools within and without (summer lunches are served around the latter), tennis, riding, and nearby golf; a multi-facility fitness center-cum-sauna, even an on-premises Estée Lauder beauty salon. Member, Leading Hotels of the World. *Luxury.*

INCIDENTAL INTELLIGENCE

The city tourist office—Verkehrsamt der Stadt Freiburg im Breisgau—is at Rotteckring 14, next to the Colombi Hotel, and is an information source for the Black Forest as well as the city. Nearest airport with scheduled service is not in Germany but in Basel, Switzerland.

17

Garmisch-Partenkirchen

Splendor in the Mountains

BACKGROUND BRIEFING

Towns straddling Alpine valleys, massive snowy peaks hovering over them, don't simply happen, say, in the manner of stage sets in Romberg operettas. If Garmisch-Partenkirchen is a mouthful to pronounce, it's a chapterful, as regards its pedigree.

The historians and archaeologists have it all figured out, or at least enough of the outlines to know that prehistoric tribes—the Illyrians—were quite as awestruck a good two millennia ago by the physical splendor of the neighborhood as we are today. So were war-like Celts who followed them, and just after the birth of Christ—name-dropping Romans who first put the Partenkirchen part of our twin towns on the map as Partanum.

Later centuries saw it thrive as a garrison on the military road between Augsburg and the Brenner Pass, and some centuries later the Garmisch part of the package was settled as Germareskove. It had become the seat of local ruling nobles by the eighth century. Dukes of the same Wittelsbach family that was to rule Bavaria until the early decades of our own twentieth century built a castle in the area some 900 years ago. Before much longer, the region became a church center and then it became a trading post of consequence.

Those powerful families of Augsburg to the north—the Fuggers and the Welsers—used Partenkirchen as a midway point on the route that linked their city with Italy. At the same time, Garmisch thrived by negotiating the moving goods on rafts along the waters of its Loisach River on the north-south axis.

The seventeenth-century decades of the Thirty Years' War were bad news for Garmisch. Indeed, it was not until after Napoleon changed the map of Europe in the early nineteenth century that the twin villages again became upwardly mobile, as a part of Bavaria. Some decades later, technology helped. The rail connection with Munich put Garmisch and Partenkirchen within easy reach of the nature-adoring German middle and upper classes. Tourism became the principal local industry, and it has remained so on into this century. The two towns combined politically, the better to make a united front in their successful campaign to host the 1936 Winter Olympics. Those games—remembered in political as well as sports annals for the outrageous spectacle of the interminable swastika-dominated parades and rallies of the Nazis—gave the area a permanent winter-sports complex and a reputation as a major Alpine resort, the Hitlerian association notwithstanding.

With nearby Munich an international air terminus, post-World War II Garmisch-Partenkirchen began to attract foreign as well as German visitors—skiers in winter, just plain nature-lovers the rest of the year. Today, though the combined population of the twin towns remains small—some 30,000—this is a destination to be reckoned with. There are some 10,000 tourist beds in the area, and a network of a baker's dozen cablecars and cogwheel trains that scale six ravishingly beautiful peaks, including Germany's highest: the 9,787-foot-high Zugspitze.

The miracle of modern Garmisch-Partenkirchen is that success has not gone to its head. If one forgets the altitude of the peaks overhead, the ambience remains low-key, rural Bavarian. Even the better hotels are smallish in scale, not without an intimate quality. Locals seem glad you came all the way to see them—and show it. And they retain their old ways—annual folk festivals (Garmisch in July, Partenkirchen in August), a thriving folk theater, their own dialect, the same costumes their grandparents wore (at least on holidays). And what is more: an impressive municipal symphony and a casino that ranks up there with the poshest. I like.

ON SCENE

Lay of the Land: Tradition and habit die hard in the mountains of Bavaria. The united towns of Garmisch and Partenkirchen are one town. And yet they are not one town. Confusing? A little. Simplify the situation in this way: The combined political entity is shaped like a butterfly, with the wings at their broadest in the south. Lying between the wings—Partenkirchen on the east, Garmisch on the west—is the Bahnhof they share, central as it can be. (And, again conveniently, with the Zugspitzebahnhof—for rides to the top of the Zugspitze—right next door.)

Bahnhofstrasse leads from the Bahnhof—but in two directions. One going due east connects with Partenkirchen's main street, Hauptstrasse, and other major Partenkirchen points of interest, such as its Baurentheater-Museum, and, of all things, a mountain-climbers' school.

Return to the Bahnhof and take the other Bahnhofstrasse, leading due north, and after a long block, turning a corner to the west, where it continues into the heart of Garmisch, and towards landmarks such as the Kongresshaus/Konzertsaal on Richard-Strauss-Platz, the casino on Marienplatz, and the Hallenschwimmbad, or indoor swimming pool, on Achenfeldstrasse. Bahnhofstrasse, when it reaches Marienplatz, becomes Zugspitzstrasse—Garmisch's Main Street. Now, on which of the two wings of the butterfly will you want to light? They're both attractive, and each has strategic advantages. Garmisch is probably the more central. By that I mean that one can walk to more places of interest from its hotels. Partenkirchen, on the other hand, is more convenient for the excursionist who would visit destinations from St. Antonkirche in the hills just above town, on the east, to the castles of Mad Ludwig in the area, like Linderhof and Neuschwanstein, to which I devote more description later.

Old Garmisch-Partenkirchen is not to be underestimated, and is best undertaken at the start of a visit, before one ascends to the mountains. *Alte Kirche* (Hausbergstrasse) has a needle-like

Romanesque spire, but is somewhat newer Gothic within, its ace in the hole a series of frescoes from which layers of paint were recently removed, to reveal paintings of startling beauty. *St. Martinkirche* (Marienplatz) is more what one would expect to find in the Alps—a typically exuberant specimen of Bavarian rococo, its main altar a busily carved and gilded masterwork, its ceiling embellished with fine frescoes. Across the "frontier" is still another lovely church, Partenkirchen's *Pfarrkirche* (Ludwigstrasse). It is, to be sure, mock-Gothic—out of the last century. But it's filled with art treasures: gilded multipanel high and side altars, and paintings dating back several centuries. *St. Antonkirche* quite literally hugs the side of a mountain overlooking Partenkirchen. It's a pilgrimage church out of the eighteenth century, and one passes Stations of the Cross on the hilly approach, and memorial plaques to local lads lost in World Wars I and II on the way. Within, one finds the grandeur of rococo, especially in a fresco that covers the entire ceiling, a life-size likeness of Christ on the cross, and an organ whose pipes are framed in gilded carved wood. The major work is a sculpted *Pietà*—Christ, descended from the cross, in his mother's arms, an angel hovering overhead—that is as moving as it is beautiful. And just outside the church is Café Panorama; pause for coffee, cake, and a view of town and peaks, before you descend. *Heimat Museum* (Ludwigstrasse, Partenkirchen) is just opposite the Pfarrkirche (above) in a venerable house filled with arts and crafts of the local Werdenfels region, medieval sculpture through rococo furniture.

Olympic installations: The Olympic Ski Stadium is worth the trip from the center of town. It's enormous—about 100,000 spectators can watch the action—and with a pair of Olympic ski jump platforms, one long (240 feet), the other shorter (180 feet), with a smaller third jump for learners. The Olympic Ice Stadium must accommodate more skaters than any other single block of ice. It embraces a trio of rinks with a grandstand that can hold 12,000. A sight, even when empty. Its neighbor is a remarkable indoor-swimming-pool complex, Alpspitz Wellenbad by name. There's machinery for making waves, a solarium, an adjacent outdoor pool, and of course a café.

Ascending the Zugspitze: Trains for the 70-minute cograilway run from the Zugspitzebahnhof (next to the principal Bahnhof) and depart, most of the time, hourly on the hour. The route is through the pretty valley of Garmisch-Partenkirchen and up the flank of the Zugspitze almost to its summit. The train ride terminates at Hotel Schneefernerhaus, 8,100 feet heavenward, and if you've left town after breakfast, you'll be ready for lunch at the hotel and a look at the surrounding peak and the town, way, way below. From the Schneefernerhaus, take the four-minute cable-car ride (departures about every half hour) that transports you to the very top of the Zugspitze—some 10,000 feet from sea level. This is where you'll want to relax. Enjoy the sun on the terrace, have coffee or a drink, and while the light is still good, prepare for descent on still another cable car, this one departing half-hourly for the 10-minute ride down to a station at Eibsee, a lake in the valley that's an easy bus or taxi ride from town.

Visiting other peaks in the area: There's a generous choice. After the Zugspitze, many visitors choose the summit of the mountain called *Wank.* A funicular takes you on a 20-minute ride from its Partenkirchen terminal, 5,874 feet upward to a spectacular sun-terrace, where you'll want to try and develop an Alpine tan while marveling at the views. Still other cable cars link the valley with *Eckbauer* (4,079 feet), *Graseck* (2,978 feet), and *Kreuzeck* (5,452 feet).

Winter versus summer: Garmisch is gorgeous, whatever the time of year. Winter is busier—and more crowded—in this winter-sports capital of Germany. (The crowding comes not so much from the skiers as from their skis and poles.) Even then, though, you need not be a skier to have a great time. The locals have mapped out trails for walkers—all you need are sturdy boots. But you may prefer to undertake your sightseeing via cable car, reserving energy for the congenial *après ski* routine of the evenings. In nonsnowy months the region is walking territory. Locals climb at the drop of one of their feathered hats. So do Germans from other parts of the country. Join them. Or, if you're a lazybones, simply steep yourself in the scenery from the windows of the cable cars and from the summits of the peaks which they ascend.

Oberammergau, a woodcarvers' village with medieval origins, is an agreeable 10-mile excursion from Garmisch (Munich is 50 miles distant). Its setting—in a high Alpine valley bisected by the Laine River and encircled by dazzling peaks—is easy on the eye at any season: verdant in summer, brilliantly foliaged in fall, snowy white (and ski-able) in winter. What one wants to take in are the traditional-style painted fronts of venerable houses on central streets, the Heimat Museum of antique, hand-carved crèches; the eighteenth-century frescoes and stuccowork of Pfarrkirche, the principal church; and last but hardly least, Passionspielehaus, the 5,200-seat theater whose vast stage is partly open-air and in which Oberammergau's globally celebrated Passion Play takes place, 9 A.M. through 5 P.M. daily, late May through late September, once every decade, in the years ending with zero. Performers are some 1,400 villagers, with the morning's act delineating Christ's life through the Last Supper and his arrest, following Judas's betrayal; and the afternoon act depicting his trial by Pontius Pilate, through the Crucifixion, Entombment, and Resurrection. The play was first performed in 1634 as part of a vow taken by villagers thankful for being spared by the Black Plague. Recent productions—especially that of 1970—aroused international controversy, with Jewish groups singling them out as anti-Semitic, and promoting boycotts. The script was rewritten for 1980, largely to the satisfaction of both Catholic and Jewish authorities. Annual turnouts in recent decades have totaled about half a million, with advance booking—possibly in connection with specially organized package tours—advised. Where to stay? *Hotel Alois Lang* (St. Lukas Strasse 15) is No. 1, traditional-style, garden-fronted, full-facility, with two score rooms; it's *First Class,* as is *Hotel Bold* (König-Ludwig-Strasse 10). Two *Moderate*-category houses are *Hotel Wolf* (Dorfstrasse 1) and *Hotel Schilcherhof* (Bahnhofstrasse 17). As for restaurants, *Weinstube Bems* (St. Lukas Strasse 5) is a standout *(First Class),* with *Gasthof Stern* (Dorfstrasse 33) a good *Moderate*-category eatery.

SETTLING IN

Posthotel Partenkirchen (Ludwigstrasse 49, Partenkirchen) is a rococo treasure-trove—a house that went up in the mid-eighteenth century as a stopping-off point for mail carriages and mail carriers. Horses were watered and changed there, and more often than not the night was spent, so a fresh start could be made the following morning. Today's Posthotel is a delight: the town's most luxurious hotel, as striking for its architectural detail—paneling, stuccowork, gaily frescoed façade—as for furnishings and accessories. There are only 55 rooms and suites, so the ambience is intimate and the service personal. No two rooms are quite alike, but they're all antiques-accented: many have views of the snowy peaks. There are three restaurants, each handsomer than the next, and are worthy of further comment; also a *Weinstube* and historic neighbors—like the Pfarrkirche and the Heimat Museum, on the same quiet street. *Luxury.*

Clausing's Posthotel (Marienplatz 12, Garmisch) is smack in the center of Garmisch, as it has been since 1624, when it opened as a tavern. You like it before you enter: the façade is pink stucco with a deep overhang of the roof protecting a lineup of eighteenth-century statues in between the upper-floor windows. Bedrooms vary in size and decor, but they're invariably comfortable. There are a trio of antiques-filled restaurants (I comment on them in a later paragraph), a bar that has long been a major congregating point; and a watch-the-crowds-go-by café-terrace, enclosed in winter. *Luxury.*

Partenkircher Hof (Bahnhofstrasse 15, Partenkirchen) is rambling, elderly, and welcoming, with nearly 70 attractive rooms (many with views), inviting lounges, cozy bar, terrace café, and indoor pool, as well as one of the best restaurants in the region; more on that later. *Luxury.*

Hotel Forsthaus Graseck (Vordergraseck 23, Garmisch): My habitual preference for centrally situated hotels notwithstanding, I place the detached Forsthaus Graseck near the top of my Garmish-Partenkirchen grouping because it's such fun to reach and/or exit from: unless you climb the mountain it straddles by foot, the only access is by cable car from Garmisch, some 2,700 feet below. Bedrooms are contemporary with Alpine accents. There's a mix of restaurants and bars, pool, sauna and—I save best for last—sumptuous views of the town below and of Alpine peaks, beyond, from a deckchair-equipped sun terrace, and from tables of the terrace-café. *Luxury.*

Hotel Obermühle (Mühlstrasse 22, Garmisch) is intimate (there are less than 40 rooms) and handsome, with a bonus of one of the best restaurants in the combined towns. And lovely service. *First Class.*

Hotel Wittelsbach (Von-Brug-Strasse 24, Garmisch) is old-fashioned where it should be old-fashioned—high-ceilinged lounges, chandelier-hung restaurant, friendly staff. And more contemporary where that's what's indicated: sleek indoor pool, glassed-in terrace-café, up-to-date baths with all the rooms. Many rooms have balconies; the views are scrumptious. *First Class.*

Hotel Alpina (Alpspitzstrasse 12, Garmisch) is contemporary, yet has traditional lines. It's delightful in summer, when one can swim and sun at the big outdoor pool. There's also another pool within, with sauna; restaurant, bar, 45 attractive rooms. *First Class.*

Hotel Bellevue (Riesserseestrasse 9, Garmisch) is away from the center in its own garden with the mountains as a backdrop. No two rooms are alike, all have baths, some have kitchens. A pool with bar and a pair of handsome breakfast rooms. No restaurant. *First Class.*

Hotel Staudacherhof (Hollentalstrasse 48, Garmisch): On a residential street, mountain-backed, with both indoor and alfresco pools, rambling lounge, picture-window breakfast room, and agreeable bedrooms, all with baths. *First Class.*

Hotel Zugspitz (Klammstrasse 9, Garmisch) is compact, genial, modern, and central. Many of its functional rooms have baths, the lounge is cozy, and there's a dinner-only restaurant, in addition to breakfast service. *Moderate.*

Hotel Brunnthaler (Klammstrasse 31, Garmisch): Just the ticket for the traveler wanting a neat room (not all have baths) in a small, friendly setting; lobby-lounge, bar. Breakfast only. *Moderate.*

Gasthof Fraundorfer (Ludwigstrasse 24, Partenkirchen) is noted for the conviviality of its restaurant (about which more later), but the management is so kind and the location—on a historic Partenkirchen street—so agreeable: a nice spot for a budget stay, recently refurbished; not all of the rooms have baths. *Moderate.*

DAILY BREAD

Reindl Grill (Hotel Partenkirchner Hof, Bahnhofstrasse 15, Partenkirchen): If its decor is not as exquisite as one or two other Garmisch-Partenkirchen eateries, the Reindl Grill has its food going for it. Your Lady Curzon soup will be quite as delicious as your escargots Bourguignonne, Swiss *Bundnerfleisch,* bouillabaise, or *Wiener schnitzel.* And you may always have a superb steak with French fries. Desserts are opulent, cheese selections unusually copious (they are paid little heed as a course in most German restaurants), and the wine list first class. If you order the daily table d'hôte, *First Class;* otherwise, *Luxury.*

Clausing's Posthotel Restaurants (Marienplatz 12, Garmisch) are so beautiful to look upon that you owe yourself a dining experience here. Choose brass-chandeliered Die Klause (with old postmens' horns suspended from the ceiling); light and lilting *Zirbelstube,* with a painted-beam ceiling and Bavarian frescoes on the walls; or Poststuberl, pewter plates on the ledges of its walls. Menus are similar in all three, with a whole card of game specialties in season, a copious à la carte, and good value table d'hôtes. Depending on your order: *First Class* or *Luxury.*

Stahls Badstuben (in Garmisch's Alpspitz Wellenbad—the municipal swimming-pool complex) is a worth-knowing-about, late-hours restaurant-café, with an extensive menu of German and international favorites. *Moderate.*

Gasthof Drei Möhren (Ludwigstrasse 15, Partenkirchen) is typical Country Bavarian in style, albeit with sophisticated Bavarian cuisine at its most delicious; smoked-on-premises salmon, roast local venison, and a memorable lemon sorbet are a few of the specialties. *First Class.*

Gasthof Fraundorfer (Ludwigstrasse 24, Partenkirchen) is a paneled chamber, with hearty fare, and nightly entertainment. Table d'hôte and à la carte. Fun. *Moderate.*

Café-Konditorei Krönner (Achenfeldstrasse, Garmisch) is for coffee-cake and people-watching in Garmisch. *Moderate.*

Café-Konditorei Lievert (Ludwigstrasse 18, Partenkirchen) is the Partenkirchen counterpart of Krönner. Views of its valleys and the Pfarrkirche, across Ludwigstrasse. *Moderate.*

Café Panorama (St. Anton, Partenkirchen) is the next-door neighbor of the eighteenth-century pilgrimage church (recommended earlier) on the slope of a mountain at the edge of Partenkirchen. After you hike up, pause for coffee, cake, and views of town and peaks from the terrace. *Moderate.*

SOUND OF MUSIC

Konzertsaal (Kongress-Zentrum, Richard-Strauss-Platz) is the contemporary city concert hall, a part of the convention center. Go for the local symphony and visiting attractions.

Kurtheater (Richard-Strauss-Platz, Garmisch) is the city's opera house/theater.

Spielbank (Bahnhofstrasse, Garmisch) is the casino—for roulette and baccarat, that reopened in 1984 in smart new quarters.

Baurentheater (Gasthof Rassen, Ludwigstrasse, Partenkirchen): Twice weekly performances—traditionally Sunday and

Thursday—of the region's centuries-old folk theater. Watch from your table, with a giant stein of beer at hand.

INCIDENTAL INTELLIGENCE

I've already mentioned how close Munich is—51 miles. Innsbruck, Austria, is even closer—35 miles. And Mittenwald (the subject, like Munich, of a chapter in this book) is near enough—but 15 miles—a comfortable day's excursion, if you like. *Further information:* Verkehrsamt Garmisch-Partenkirchen—the municipal tourist office—Bahnhof, Garmisch-Partenkirchen.

18

Hamburg

Germany's Best-Kept Urban Secret

BACKGROUND BRIEFING

Big does not always connote great. But in Hamburg's case it does. The Federal Republic's largest city is its best-kept urban secret: a metropolis sparkling with grace and excitement that has still to achieve the international touristic fame of sister cities like Berlin, Munich, and Cologne.

Odd, this hiding of its light under a bushel. Understandable, perhaps, if it were a town tucked into the interior. But Hamburg is a North Sea port of consequence—still proudly styling itself *Frei und Hansestadt Hamburg* even though four centuries have elapsed since the powerful Hanseatic League, of which it was a founding city, became dormant.

By the time Hamburg and neighboring Lübeck (itself the subject of a chapter in this book) created the mid-thirteenth-century alliance that was to expand as the Hanseatic League. Hamburg had grown substantially. It had been founded three centuries earlier as a military bastion—a castle called Hammaburg—believed to have been built by Charlemagne as a defense against invading Slav forces.

Its location—at a point where the Alster and Elbe rivers converge, just inland from the latter's mouth in the North Sea—proved to be considerably more than militarily strategic.

Hamburg blossomed as ships laden with German cargoes sailed north up the Elbe; and those bearing goods from the north made their way south into the German heartland.

The Catholic church used the town—seat of an archbishop since shortly after its founding—as a base for missionary activity throughout northern Europe. As the merchant class grew richer with the growth of the Hanseatic League during the Renaissance, Hamburg developed Germany's first stock exchange. The city became increasingly cosmopolitan, extending hospitality to waves of immigrants from lands as diverse as England (clothiers, who had been expelled from Antwerp), Portugal (refugee Jews), and Holland (fleeing Protestants).

The baroque era of the seventeenth century saw the strength of the Hamburg-dominated Hanseatic League ebb. The following century—the eighteenth—was when Hamburg forged trading ties with America that are still strong. The French came as occupiers in the early eighteenth century, as they did in much of Germany. In 1815, Hamburg joined the German Confederation, created by the Congress of Vienna to replace a defunct Holy Roman Empire. Like the rest of the north, it later cast its lot with the German Empire through World War I. At the termination of that conflict it found itself—but only until the year 1919—a sovereign socialist republic.

World War II saw Hamburg—understandably a key Allied target—heavily bombed, largely destroyed. More than 50,000 of its citizens were killed. Reconstruction in the decades following was a success economically and aesthetically. Some 18,000 ships—flying flags of 90-odd countries—annually steam between Hamburg's magnificent harbor and some 1,100 ports on coasts of all continents.

This is Germany's largest port. This is Germany's largest city, save Berlin. And this is one of Germany's two city-states. (The other, Bremen, is much smaller, the subject of a chapter in this book.) Hamburg's *Rathaus* is as much a state legislature as a city hall. The chief burgomaster doubles as president of the Senate upper house, whose members—senators—have the rank of ministers of the *Land,* or state, of the Federal Republic and are elected by members of the lower house—the *Bürgerschaft*—

which has the same status in the federal framework as the legislatures of a big *Land* like, say, Bavaria.

Very special, Hamburg. More beautiful, to be sure, than Berlin: less ebullient, admittedly, than Munich. The pity is that in far too many instances its reputation as a visitor destination centers around the live sex shows of the red light district. This in a city with the style and sophistication—not to mention cultural resources near the top in an all-Europe ranking. Of course, spend an evening in the raunchy Reeperbahn. But stick around long enough to give Hamburg a fair shake.

ON SCENE

Lay of the Land: Central Hamburg covers considerable territory, but one gets to know it rapidly, thanks to major landmarks, both man-made and natural. There are two contiguous innercity lakes, the Aussenalster—the larger and more northerly—and the Binnenalster. The Kennedy and Lombard bridges cross the strip of land that divides them. The core of the city lies roughly between Binnenalster to the north and the harbor—leading from the Elbe River—to the south. The Hauptbahnhof fringes downtown at its eastern frontier. From it, two busy shopping streets—pedestrians-only Spitalerstrasse and (parallel to it) longer Monckebergstrasse (with department stores and bigger shops)—lead west. The latter proceeds directly to Marktplatz, which is dominated by the bulk of the neo-Renaissance Rathaus. A number of pleasantly walkable thoroughfares crisscross this district, which borders the Binnenalster. One, Ballindamm, lining the lake's eastern shore, is dotted with pricey shops. Another, Jungfernstieg, constitutes Binnenalster's southern bank. Its attractions include a pair of pavilion-like cafés that extend over the water. On Binnenalster's western shore, you will find Neuer Jungfernstieg with hotels, boutiques, and access to the street called Colonnaden, named for the pillars supporting the arcades through which its boutiques and cafés are entered. Two worthwhile destinations are in this area: the opera house and the concert hall. Poseldorf, Hamburg's toniest neighborhood—you'll want to scout its Milchstrasse shops—is a fair distance north, between a main thoroughfare called Mittelweg and the Aussenalster. The Reeperbahn with its sex shows lies to the

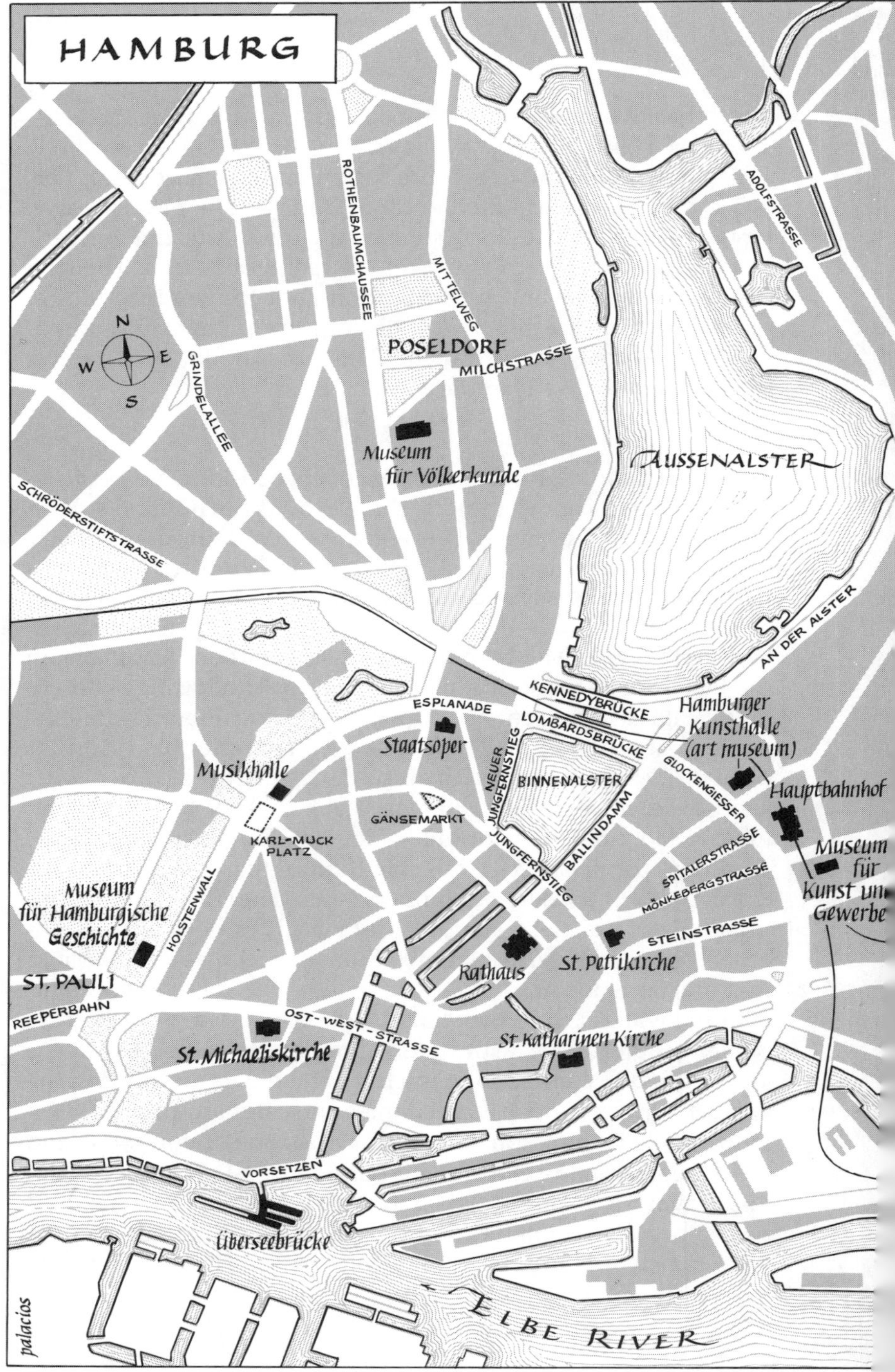

HAMBURG
N
W
E
S
ROTHENBAUMCHAUSSEE
MITTELWEG
POSELDORF
MILCHSTRASSE
ADOLFSTRASSE
GRINDELALLEE
Museum für Völkerkunde
AUSSENALSTER
SCHRÖDERSTIFTSTRASSE
AN DER ALSTER
KENNEDYBRÜCKE
ESPLANADE
LOMBARDSBRÜCKE
Hamburger Kunsthalle (art museum)
Staatsoper
NEUER JUNGFERNSTIEG
BINNENALSTER
GLOCKENGIESSER
Musikhalle
Hauptbahnhof
GÄNSEMARKT
BALLINDAMM
KARL-MUCK PLATZ
JUNGFERNSTIEG
SPITALERSTRASSE
Museum für Kunst un Gewerbe
MÖNKEBERGSTRASSE
Museum für Hamburgische Geschichte
HOLSTENWALL
STEINSTRASSE
Rathaus
St. Petrikirche
ST. PAULI
REEPERBAHN
OST-WEST-STRASSE
St. Michaeliskirche
St. Katharinen Kirche
VORSETZEN
Überseebrücke
ELBE RIVER
palacios

southwest, an easy walk for sailors from ships in port—who have made its reputation. Museums, major churches, and other points of interest are scattered about; by no means are they all easily walkable from hotels. The modern U-Bahn (subway) system is the easiest means of public transport; its stations are well marked on the Hamburg Tourist Office's free city map. The station called Landungsbrücken, for example, is adjacent to the harbor. Tip: Starting your visit with a boat tour will provide you with a taste of Hamburg's bracing maritime flavor.

Touring Hamburg harbor (St. Pauli Landungsbrücken): Here is the city at its most animated, cosmopolitan, exciting, and beautiful. Especially if the sun is strong, the water blue, and the clouds billowy. You're seeing one of the world's top six, right up there with New York, Rotterdam, London, Antwerp, and Marseilles. And it has virtually all been constructed since World War II, when it was 80 percent destroyed. There are dry docks and floating docks, rubber-tire-surfaced ferries bobbing at the hulls of mammoth freighters, the sleek white passenger liner *Prinz Hamlet* cutting through the traffic en route to England's Harwich, crews of in-port vessels waving to other crews—and to you... And flags! If a country has a merchant marine, you're bound to see its colors in Hamburg harbor: India and Norway, East Germany and the Philippines, China and Greece, Britain and Poland, America and France. Tours, usually lasting an hour, are made on larger excursion-type boats and smaller launches. The latter are available for hire on short notice; your hotel concierge will help you book one. Tip: go in the morning, concluding with a fish lunch at a harbor restaurant.

Rathaus (Marktplatz): Talk about opulence! This Renaissance-style palace—and palatial it is, all 647 rooms of it—went up at the turn of the century, but only after 4,000 piles were sunk in the ground to support it. Regularly conducted tours take oh-ing and ah-ing visitors through the major interiors—halls in which the Senate and Bürgerschaft of the city-state deliberate, reception rooms hung with tapestries and murals and portraits of upstanding citizens, immense chandeliers suspended from gilt-edged coffered ceilings.

Hamburger Kunsthalle (Glockengiesserwall 1) has the odd distinction of being a next-door neighbor to the Hauptbahnhof. What other major art museum can make that statement? Hamburg's, make no mistake, is major—in a class with its counterparts in Berlin, Munich, Frankfurt, and Cologne, in Germany; and near the top in any all-Europe ranking, as well. You need a leisurely morning or afternoon here. There's an upstairs café for snack pauses. And two floors of galleries. Start with the medieval Germans—a number of works by the painters known simply as Meister Bertram and Meister Francke. Move along to Cranach and Holbein, Van Dyck and Rubens, Rembrandt and van Ruysdael, Canaletto and Tiepolo, Boucher and Fragonard, an elegant Spanish courtier by Goya, romantic and Expressionist Germans—Friedrich through Baumeister. The familiar French names are represented—Rousseau and Léger, Sisley and Delaunay. Half a dozen Edvard Munches, and Picasso, of course. Look for the two lovely Vuillards of Hamburg—one of each of the inner-city lakes, Binnenalster and Aussenalster. Note the harbor as interpreted by France's Albert Marquet in 1909. And sculpture: strong on Germans like Lehmbruck and Barlach, but with France's Rodin, Maillol, Arp, England's Moore, Italy's Marini, and America's Calder imparting international flavor.

Jenish-Haus Museum (Baron-Voght Strasse 50): A politician who had both taste and money built this neoclassic stone mansion in the early decades of the last century. It operates today as a museum—the most beautiful of any of the German townhouse museums that I know. There are three floors of rooms that dazzle with elegance. Styles range from Art Nouveau and Victorian through to Biedermeier and Empire, with rococo and baroque salons, too. Note especially the pale, gray-on-white stuccowork of the sumptuous dining room. And take a stroll in the park, where the house stands.

Museum für Kunst und Gewerbe (Steintorplatz) is Hamburg's decorative-arts museum and an extraordinary repository—furniture, accessories, porcelain, over a range of centuries, and from the Orient as well as the Occident: a Japanese teahouse, a

Biedermeier parlor, a whole room full of Picasso ceramics and posters and tapestries, fine Renaissance objects, and what has to be the biggest and most diverse collection extant of Art Nouveau (*Jugendstil,* in German)—furnished room after furnished room of it. Special treat: A turn-of-century café—original lighting fixtures, carved-wood back bar, the works—has been moved into the museum and returned to service; buffet lunch or a snack.

Altonaer Museum (Museumstrasse 23 in the Altona district) is a delightful hodgepodge showing the history and culture of the region. There's a strong maritime section—ships in bottles, model ships, ships' prow sculptures, ship prints. A massive grouping of costumes, mostly nineteenth century. And most impressive: a series of interiors from regional farmhouses dating as far back as the eighteenth century, with gaily decorated walls and ceilings. As at the Kunst und Gewerbe, the special treat is eats. You lunch or snack in a completely transformed thatch-roofed, brick-walled farmhouse of ancient vintage, with its original furnishings, and waitresses dressed in duds of the period.

Museum für Hamburgische Geschichte (Holstenwall 24), the Hamburg Historical Museum. Its standout exhibit, for me, is the entire forward half of an early-twentieth-century cargo ship. Climb to the bridge, walk through the captain's quarters, wardroom, galley, crew's bunks below. Even read a full week's menu that's posted. There's a lot more—antique fire engines through infants' cradles. But my notes sum it up: "The Geschichte is too big to be fun." And, for the most part, it is.

Hagenbecks Tierpark (Hagenbeckallee): I don't know of a better reason to try out Hamburg's U-Bahn than the zoo—about 20 underground minutes from the Hauptbahnhof to its own station. Not as remarkable in design as Frankfurt's, hardly as central as Berlin's, but with a population of 2,500, representing well over 300 species, in a pretty park-like setting. And yes, the elephants are feedable.

St. Michaeliskirche (Krayenkamp 4) is nothing less than Hamburg's most beautiful church. North German baroque, with style and scale. Restored twice—once before World War I, after a fire, then after World War II bomb damage. Both times, obviously, with love. Note the tower, a sculpted St. Michael over the front door, and inside-sunburst-topped altar, pulpit, organ, Corinthian columns.

St. Jacobikirche (Jacobikirchof 22) is well-restored Gothic, with art treasures within. Of special note are a trio of altars and a remarkable antique organ.

St. Petrikirche (Speersort 10) is distinguished by its splendid steeple that dominates a red-brick façade. Gothic and more than once rebuilt, its stark white interior is the perfect foil for works of art, including a chapel altar, a sculpted Madonna of the fifteenth century, and an eye-filling pulpit.

Sunday morning fish market (St. Pauli): Sundays-only, and the earlier the better. (Try arriving between 8:30 and 9.) This is Hamburg's answer to the Paris Marché aux Puces, Rome's Porta Portese, London's Portobello Road. I tend to make a beeline for the grilled sausage stands, but there are other delights as well: fruits and flowers, candy and cake, balloons and bulbs, T-shirts and tote bags, jeans and umbrellas, ducks and doves, geese and rabbits, ceramics and copper—not to mention a selection of very noisy goats and kids. Most fun is watching fishermen sell just-captured shrimp, eels, and flounder from their own boats. With mobs of Hamburgers of all ages.

Lübeck, Travemünde, and Bremen: Lübeck and Bremen are two nearby ancient cities of considerable substance and significance (especially the first), and are subjects of chapters in this book, as is Travemünde, the Baltic Sea resort-adjunct of Lübeck. They are each convenient for one-day trips (train or otherwise) from Hamburg.

SETTLING IN

Hotel Vier Jahreszeiten (Neuer Jungfernstieg 9) is, to state its case at the outset, the ultimate German hotel. Still owned by the family that opened it at turn-of-century, it is the very model of the traditional-style luxury house, with the accent and emphasis at all times on luxury. The location, on a modish street flanking the Binnenalster, is a hop and a skip from the opera and the concert hall, with the best shopping streets equally close, and even the Hauptbahnhof and department stores walkable. There are a pair of spacious lobby-lounges (one perfect for morning coffee or a pick-me-up cup of tea), and just 200 rooms and suites, with the minimum-rate singles no less perfectly appointed than the larger accommodations. By that I mean thermometers to reveal the temperature of your bath water (they hang over the tub), curtains to keep shower water from spritzing the bathroom (not common in Germany!), washcloths (also uncommon in Germany), and when your breakfast tray comes, cozies both on boiled egg and coffee pot, the better to keep them hot. Fresh flowers, too. Antiques line the wide corridors and accent the rooms. There are a quartet of restaurants—each matchless in its way and the subject of later comment; and a bar. I don't know of management more professional or service more kind—anywhere. An all-Europe leader. Member, Leading Hotels of the World. *Luxury.*

Hotel Atlantic Kempinski (An der Alster 72) is the big white landmark of the Aussenalster, an elderly house with a situation more handsome than convenient (you're just far enough from the heart of downtown to want to ride rather than walk), and with the look—and facilities—of the old-style grand hotel, delightfully updated. There are 325 tasteful rooms and suites (if you're a head of state, or a tycoon, consider the three-room presidential digs), indoor pool-sauna, courtyard that turns café in summer, busy and buzzy bar, convenient coffee shop, and principal restaurant so good that I comment on it later. Member, Leading Hotels of the World. *Luxury.*

Hotel Inter-Continental Hamburg (Fontenay 10) combines the finesse of the city with the know-how of the round-the-world U.S.-headquartered Inter-Continental chain. Hamburg's Inter-Conti is sleek, white, and mod without, subdued traditional within—from large lobby-lounge to rooftop restaurant-bar that's worthy of additional comment on a later page. The pool—an indoor-outdoor combination—is beautiful. Convenient late-hours coffee shop. And the more than 300 rooms and suites are attractive and full-facility. *Luxury.*

Hotel Hamburg Plaza (Marseillerstrasse 2) opened with a bang in the mid-seventies as Loews Hamburg Plaza (I covered the festivities) but later became a part of Canadian Pacific's hotel chain. But this sleek tower is not going to remind you of Quebec City's Château Frontenac or Victoria's Empress. It's unabashedly contemporary with nearly 600 zingy rooms and suites (many with smashing views), Hamburg's handsomest hotel coffee shop, popular bar-lounge, and posh Tudor-style English Grill. Pool and sauna, too. A 10-minute walk to the center. *Luxury.*

Hotel Reichshof (Kirchenallee 34) is queen bee of the cluster of hotels adjacent to the Hauptbahnhof and the heart of downtown. It's a winner, with a warmly old-fashioned lobby, wide corridors leading to good-sized, nicely furnished rooms with up-to-the-minute baths; bar wherein guests lift elbows with thirsty Hamburgers; restaurant of which more later (it's that good) and my favorite feature: schmaltzy violin music for late-afternoon coffee drinkers at tables in the lobby between 5 and 6 P.M. *First Class.*

Hotel Alster Hof (Esplanade 12) occupies understatedly good-looking quarters on a quiet street just off the Binnenalster, not far from the Vier Jahreszeiten in the poshest part of downtown. There are just under 100 agreeable rooms and suites (the singles have showers rather than baths), inviting restaurant and bar. I like. *First Class.*

Hotel Baseler Hospiz (Esplanade 11) is next door to the Alster Hof, with easy-to-take ambience—low-key lobby-lounge, bright mod-look restaurant with lowish tabs, bar, and rooms with balcony views of the waters of Binnenalster. *First Class.*

Hotel Europäischer Hof (Kirchenallee 45) is in the Hauptbahnhof area with 300 contemporary rooms and attractive public spaces that include a restaurant, *Weinstube,* and bar. Sprightly service. *First Class.*

Hotel Kronprinz (Kirchenallee 46) is updated-elderly, near the station; a majority of its rooms have private baths or showers. The Schiffer Borse Restaurant here is one of Hamburg's most atmospheric, and the subject of later comment. *First Class.*

Hotel Alte Wache (Adenauerallee 25) is not far from the Hauptbahnhof, and easily walkable to the core of downtown. Its lure is single rooms with private baths. A good number of the total of 75 are in this popular category. Breakfast only. *Moderate.*

Hotel-Hospiz St. Raphael (Adenauerallee 41) is a neighbor of the Alte Wache but farther from the Hauptbahnhof. It's church-affiliated and has a somewhat sticky-sweet institutional air. But there are 120 modern rooms, many with private baths. Restaurant. *Moderate.*

Hotel Metro (Brehmer Reike 14) is near the Hauptbahnhof, with half a hundred functional rooms, a number with private baths. Breakfast only. *Moderate.*

Hotel Jacob (Elbchaussee 401) comes at the end of this group only because it's not central. Therein lies its appeal, however. This is an eighteenth-century manor house furnished mostly in period, with antiques-accented rooms and suites (many with panoramic views), a river-view restaurant that occupies a spacious terrace in warm weather, and a cozy bar. Very special. *Luxury.*

DAILY BREAD

W. Schumanns Austernkeller (Jungfernstieg 34): To call this one of a kind is to understate: It's a long, narrow affair, with a side aisle off which are a series of enchanting booth-like salons, each a minor masterwork of turn-of-century Art Nouveau. Note pictures on the walls of opera divas and actresses from times past. And don't neglect the fine fare—oysters, as the name of the restaurant implies, but a wide-ranging menu, meats as well as seafoods. Old-fashioned service. No credit cards, I learned the hard way. *Luxury.*

Überseebrücke (Uferpromenade) is as appealing for the setting—a modern glass-walled pavilion, on the Elbe, with splendid views of the action in the harbor—as for the fare: fresh seafood that is nowhere better in this seafood city; the grilled sole alone is worth the trip. More harbor action at lunch than in the evening. *Luxury.*

Ratsweinkeller (Rathaus, entrance on Gross Johannistrasse): Hamburg's Town Hall restaurant is the best all-round of any such I know of in Germany. It's vast and super-looking, with ship models suspended from its high, arched ceilings. Service is unobtrusive and speedy, and there's a wide-ranging menu embracing the city's seafood and other specialties, omelets to steaks. Daily full-course specials are excellent buys, the winecard an easy lesson in German vintages. *Moderate/First Class.*

Haerlin (Hotel Vier Jahreszeiten, Neuer Jungfernstieg 9) is the Vier Jahreszeiten's main restaurant, a gracious Louis XV pavilion with big windows overlooking the Binnenalster. Animated at lunch, with the menu embracing classic favorites—German, French, Italian, Swiss—invariably delicious, deftly presented and served. Try the *médaillon de veau,* Mozart-style. Or the cabbage-sausage-vegetable triumph, *choucroute garnie.* Exceptional wines, from throughout Europe. The same hotel's paneled *Grill,* with similar menus, is indicated for dinner, with the intimate *Keller*—belowstairs—ideal for post-opera or post-concert supper and dancing. All three are *Luxury.*

Schiffer Börse (Hotel Kronprinz, Kirchenallee 46, opposite the Hauptbahnhof) is, after the Ratsweinkeller, just about the most atmospheric of centrally situated restaurants—all dark woods, brass chandeliers, and suspended ship models. Seafood is king here, but not exclusively. Lively. *First Class.*

Ponton (St. Pauli Landungsbrücken) overlooks the dock where harbor-tour boats are boarded; ideal for a seafood lunch after your excursion. *Moderate/First Class.*

Fontenay Grill (Hotel Inter-Continental Hamburg, Fontenay 10) can be the basis of a gala Hamburg evening. Start with drinks in the adjacent cocktail lounge of this rooftop restaurant. Move along, then, for a dinner with panorama. Specialties are international—steaks through schnitzel—and served with flair. *Luxury.*

Brücke (Hotel Atlantic Kempinski, An der Alster 72) is the handsome, high-ceilinged, principal eatery of this exemplary hotel. Go for lunch and order the day's special from the trolley—truffled beef Wellington perhaps, with the mushrooms called *chanterelles.* Or *coq au vin.* Or roast venison. Skilled service. *Luxury.*

Finnlandhaus Restaurant (Esplanade 41): Credit the Finns with appreciating good views—in this case of Hamburg, its harbor and the pair of inner lakes, from this attractive resaurant twelve flights up. Appetizers (why not accompany yours with *aquavit,* Finnish-style?) are especially good, and so are seafood entrées. Well located, just west of the pair of bridges traversing the lakes. *First class.*

Bavaria Blick (Beinhard-Nochstrasse 2) is atop a harbor-view brewery. Fun for a supper—steak, fish, preceded by the house's special snails—after the opera or concert with a night view of the port as a bonus. *First Class.*

Broders Hanse Stube (Mittelweg 172, Poseldorf) embraces a tempting delicatessen below and a tavern-type restaurant upstairs. Go for lunch or whenever hunger pangs strike. Posh neighborhood. *First Class.*

Hotel Reichshof Restaurant (Kirchenallee 34, opposite Hauptbahnhof) is a touch of yesteryear, with the à la carte printed in no less than seven languages. Good-value daily specials. Friendly. *First Class.*

Alsterpavilion (Jungfernstieg 54) protrudes over the waters of the Binnenalster, and is at once a café for coffee or snacks and a full-service restaurant. Convenient. *Moderate.*

Die Pantry (Kirchenallee 19): Steaks, sandwiches, salads, at the counter if you like. Zingy. Central. *Moderate.*

Café Condi (Hotel Vier Jahreszeiten, Neuer Jungfernstieg): You'll go as much for its early-nineteenth-century Biedermeier furnishings as for its mouth-watering pastries with coffee. Light lunches, too. And if you can afford them, take home a box of the cafe's famous chocolates. *First Class.*

Café-Konditorei Engels (Alsterarkaden): A heart-of-town source of between-meals sustenance—coffee and cake to be specific—in a Louis XVI setting. *First Class.*

Café-Konditorei Kaul (Mönckebergstrasse) is for feet wearied in nearby department stores. (Karstadt is directly opposite.) Coffee and cake, snacks, light lunch. *Moderate.*

Sagebiels Fährhaus (Blankeneser Hauptstrasse 107) is a scenic ferry ride from downtown, perfect for a Sunday lunch in the country—in an antiques-furnished, eighteenth-century Elbe-view house in village-like Blankenese. Order one of the daily specials. *First Class.*

Hotel Jacob Weinrestaurant (Elbchaussee 201) is still another bucolic suggestion: you'll enjoy the beautiful dining room of this eighteenth-century manor house turned hotel. In summer, lunch on the terrace, over the water. *Luxury.*

SOUND OF MUSIC

Hamburgische Staatsoper (Dammtorstrasse 28) has a history spanning three centuries—it's one of the planet's great companies. The current house is a post-World War II replacement for what was, according to photos, a gracious old-school theater. This one has all the technical advantages. And if it has no special aesthetic pluses, one forgives it, given the direction, singers, and wide-ranging repertory: from a zany *Barber of Seville*—dating to the period of the 1960s-70s when Rolf Liebermann ran the house before taking over the Paris Opera—to a concertized version of *Norma.* And the ballet: recent seasons have seen it spring to eminence under the direction of Milwaukeean John Neumeier, who had earlier put the Frankfurt Opera Ballet into shape, and who also choreographs for the Stuttgart. His specialties are full-length pieces like *Don Juan* and *Romeo and Juliet.* Tickets are difficult to come by. Get your hotel concierge to help immediately upon arrival.

Musikhalle (Karl-Muck-Platz) is the turn-of-century, baroque-style hall near the opera house that is home to most symphonic concerts, those of the century-and-a-half-old Philharmonie Hamburg, especially. It contains large and small halls, the latter for chamber programs. Still other concerts of other orchestras take place at the State Academy of Music (Harvestehuder Weg 12) and in historic churches.

AFTER DARK

Reeperbahn is the name of the street in the near-harbor St. Pauli quarter that all the world knows for its explicit sex shows. The best is at *Cabaret Colibri;* others, with similar fare, are at *Salambo, Regina,* and *Tabu.* Shows generally last 90 minutes, running continuously from 7 P.M. to 4 A.M. and admission includes a drink. To answer your question: Yes, you will see a man and a woman engaging in the sex act on the stage. And, yes, there are package tours available. Nearby *Herbertstrasse*—behind a vast screen, the better to keep the kiddies away—is where ladies sit in the picture windows of houses of prostitution, so you'll know what you're getting into, gents. *Grosse Freiheitstrasse* is still another street where women make themselves available, moving about without and thus more accessible for conversation than their behind-glass associates on Herbertstrasse; they each have a private room upstairs. There's a branch of the *Wienerwald* restaurant chain on Reeperbahn that's adequate for snacks and supper. Bars scattered about are mostly pick-up joints and can be dangerous.

INCIDENTAL INTELLIGENCE

You can fly Lufthansa daily from New York to Hamburg. Fuhlsbüttel International Airport, eight miles north of town, is connected with it by regularly scheduled airport buses to the Town Terminal near the Hauptbahnhof. There's luxury passenger-ship service between Hamburg and the English port of Harwich every other day. Passage takes 20 hours. *Further information:* Fremdenverkehrzentrale—the Hamburg Tourist Office—is at Hachmannplatz 1 (near the Hauptbahnhof, with information offices in the Hauptbahnhof and at the airport.

19

Hannover

Handsome and History-Laden

BACKGROUND BRIEFING

Think Hannover and you think of the four Georges—that quartet of monarchs who because of a freakish twist of history reigned as kings of England and of a small northwest German state that has otherwise known relatively little celebrity.

What gave Hannover its moment—better say century-plus—of glory was this: A late seventeenth-century nobleman—Duke Ernest Augustus of the ruling Hannover family—was honored by the big boss Holy Roman Emperor and promoted. He was made an elector, which meant that he could participate in the choosing of the heads of the Holy Roman Empire, that his realm would be called an electorate, and that his status was nearly that of a king. What he did, then, was marry a king's granddaughter—Sophia, whose father was king of Bohemia and whose mother was not only the Bohemian queen, but the daughter of England's James I. In 1701, the Parliament in London settled the succession to the English throne on Sophia and her descendants.

As a consequence, in 1714, after the death of the childless Queen Anne, Sophia's son (whose German name was Georg Ludwig) became George I of England and the ruler of his native Hannover as well. George I was more popular at home, where he spent considerable time, than in England. His English subjects would have preferred him to speak their language, and they were not fond of his German mistresses, nor of the manner in which he divorced—and cruelly imprisoned for life—his queen, Sophia Dorothea.

George II, who learned some English, was less unpopular with his English subjects. He was succeeded by his grandson, vastly more English—indeed English-born—George III, who never got around to visiting his Hanoverian realm. The fourth George was even less Teutonic. His brother and successor, William IV, was the last of the Anglo-Hanoverians. William's successor—a niece named Victoria—had to content herself with but one throne—the English one—for a Hanoverian regulation—the so-called Salic law—barred women from succeeding.

And so it developed that Hannover was to have only two kings who were exclusively its own before it was annexed, in the mid-nineteenth century, by the more powerful kingdom of Prussia. Later, along with the rest of Germany, it became part of the pan-German Empire, which became the post-World War I republic.

World War II saw the city badly damaged by bombs. But there has been skillful restoration, and today's Hannover is at once politically important as capital of the state, or Land, of Lower Saxony *(Niedersachsen)*, economically dominant as a center of industry and commerce, and the site of a centuries-old annual trade fair that draws participants from the world over. Increasing numbers of visitors enjoy this handsome city's smile and bounce.

ON SCENE

Lay of the Land: You can't walk everywhere in this substantial city of half a million. But the core is relatively compact, and exceptionally well planned. The planning becomes apparent immediately upon arrival, at least if one has come by train. The Hauptbahnhof faces Bahnhofstrasse. Running north-south, it has been transformed into what is called a *passerelle:* a pedestrians-only shopping mall some 800 yards in length, and a double-decker one, at that, with two levels of shops running the entire distance. At the end is the town's most popular congregating place, the square called Kröpcke, off of which runs Georgstrasse, which leads to the Opera House, theaters, and a café-restaurant-shops district. At Kröpcke, Bahnhofstrasse becomes Karmarschstrasse and leads into a major east-west thoroughfare called Friedrichswall that runs perpendicular to it. At Friedrichswall's eastern fringe is Leineschloss, a handsome old palace now seeing service as the Lower Saxony Parliament. On the south side of this street are such landmarks as the Neues Rathaus—the so-called new Town Hall that will be described later—and the eminently strollable park it fronts, named Machpark. There are also a lovely lake within its bounds and a pair of major museums. Still another landmark is Hotel Inter-Continental Hannover, the across-the-street neighbor of the Town Hall. Herrenhausen Gardens, Hannover's most famous visitor attraction, are in the northwest part of town, too far to reach on foot, but by no means to be missed, and for that reason the very first of our suggested Hannover destinations.

Herrenhausen Gardens: Imagine the grounds of Versailles, outside Paris, without the palace. That, with some important differences, is Herrenhausen today. The magnificent summer palace of the Hannoverian electors—and later, kings—that went up in the baroque and rococo eras several centuries back was a casualty of World War II bombs. Certain buildings adjacent to the palace were untouched or have been restored, and the formal gardens are back in all their glory—with 125 gardeners to keep their formal flower beds and clipped lawns immaculate.

This is how the Herrenhausen complex breaks down: The major formal garden—*Grosser Garten*—is the horticultural showplace, restored and operated by the municipal authorities according to the original baroque designs of the seventeenth century. It includes 125 acres of formal flower beds and lawns, in an area bordered on three sides by a moat, and on the fourth by a geyser-like fountain, whose single jet spray of 267 feet is Europe's highest. It looks like a giant mosaic of considerable splendor. It is not for nothing that garden professionals rank this garden with those of Versailles and Vienna's Schonbrunn.

Still another area of the complex, the *Georgengarten,* is parklike, in the manner of the grounds of English country houses. A circular, Greek-style pavilion with Ionic columns is in the center of this plot.

The third major area, *Welfengarten,* also English-style, is the setting for a onetime royal palace—mock-Gothic in the fashion of the mid-nineteenth century—that is now Hannover's technical university.

Fourth, but hardly last of the major landscaped areas, is the *Gartentheater,* an alfresco theater—still used for concerts and plays in summer and restored to its original baroque design, with green hedges and gilded sculpture taking the place of walls and pillars, and seats for nearly 1,000 spectators.

Remaining Herrenhausen buildings: There are three of note. *Wallmodenschlossachen* is a late-eighteenth-century palace that had been home to Count Wallmoden, an illegitimate son of King George II. It now houses a museum devoted to the works of a nineteenth-century artist—Wilhelm Busch—whose works are little known to foreigners. Go for the building if not the paintings. *Galeriegebäude*—simply the Gallery in English—is all that is left of the old royal palace, and it is not to be dismissed. A sumptuous, fresco-decorated hall, grandly baroque, that was the living quarters of Electress Sophia—mother of the first of the English-Hanoverian kings—it is still in service as a 686-seat concert hall. I've saved the best for the last of this buildings-trio: Known variously as *Fürstenhaus* (prince's house) and *Herrenhausen Museum,* it more often than not is missed by visitors, despite the fact that more than any other single destination in town it brings to life the rococo period when the Georges—especially I and II—were rulers of both England and of Hannover. If I had time for but one Hannover interior, this would be it: an extraordinarily beautiful eighteenth-century palace, with 10 furnished-in-period rooms, each filled with art treasures. The entrance hall has larger-than-life portraits of George III and Queen Charlotte, attributed to Gainsborough. There are other portraits by Germans like Johann Zoffany and Sir Godfrey Kneller, who made their fame and fortunes in England in the eighteenth century.

Niedersächsisches Landesmuseum (Machpark) is the quadruple-threat *Lower Saxony* repository. Three of its four parts will not be of particular interest to the nonspecialist: natural history à la Chicago's Field Museum or New York's American Museum of

Natural History; ethnology—art and artifacts of South American, African, and Asian cultures; and ancient Lower Saxony civilization—mostly prehistoric. That leaves the Gallery of Paintings and Sculpture—and it's one of the best in Germany. There is both quality and quantity, with the range wide—medieval church art (including wood sculptures by Würzburg's Tilman Riemenschneider), works by Old Masters including Rubens and Rembrandt, Poussin and Renni, on through into exceptionally strong modern German work—Lovis Corinth and Max Liebermann with 25 works each, as well as such greats as August Macke, Emil Nolde, Wilhelm Lembruck, and Max Beckmann. Foreign masters Picasso, Dufy, Klee, Chagall, and Munch are represented too; and the sculpture is exciting—Rodin through Henry Moore.

Kestner Museum (Trammplatz, at the entrance to Machpark) is another mixed bag, and of exceptional quality. Housed in a modern building that's in strong contrast to the Neues Rathaus almost next door, it runs a gamut of the applied arts, Egyptian and ancient Greek through to this century's graphics. It is at its best from the medieval centuries onward—Madonnas in gold, silvery brocades, cloisonné bowls, even carved-wood choir stalls—from the Middle Ages; Renaissance glassware, baroque jewelry, rococo porcelain, with an especially generous presentation of Meissen. And a second-floor café.

Historische am Hohen Ufer Museum (Pferdestrasse 6) occupies imaginatively converted quarters dating to the Middle Ages. It tells Hannover's story with wit and style by means of costumes and carriages (including a crown-topped golden coach of the eighteenth century), furniture and farm tools, paintings and porcelain, even a player piano from the Roaring Twenties—which, when fed Pf 50, plays ragtime.

Marktkirche (Marktplatz) is the city's finest church, an utterly beautiful Gothic masterwork, whose interior—walls, pillars, and vaulted ceiling—is entirely of unadorned red brick. Exquisite gilded medieval triptych on the altar.

Altes Rathaus (Marktplatz), Hannover's old Town Hall, is Marktkirche's near-neighbor and near-contemporary: Gothic with unusual gables that are actually pencil-slim turrets of graduated height. The restaurant within is recommended in a later paragraph.

Neues Rathhaus (Trammplatz, at entrance to Machpark): The new Town Hall was new at the turn of the twentieth century. It's just the species of mock-Renaissance, both in grandeur and scale, that you would expect Kaiser Wilhelm II to dedicate—and he did. The heroic façade—richly ornamented—is the best of the building. A mammoth, gilded dome and two smaller side towers create the silhouette that has become a Hanoverian trademark. There's a scale model of the city in the lobby, and the 327-foot-high dome has an observation platform.

SETTLING IN

Hotel Inter-Continental Hannover (Friedrichswall 11), just opposite the Neues Rathaus, with the core of downtown just around the corner, is the city's preeminent hotel, with nearly 300 rooms and suites (some of the latter are furnished in antiques); spacious lobby; inviting bar-lounge; a quintet of restaurants, one a coffee shop that serves Germany's most lavish buffet breakfast; another a cozy *Bierstube;* still another a café-konditorei, and the fourth singled out for later recommendation. *Luxury.*

Kastens Hotel Luisenhof (Luisenstrasse 2/3), founded a century and a quarter back, is traditional, with more than 200 attractive rooms and suites, a pair of restaurants, one of which is described below, congenial bar, central situation. Very nice. *Luxury.*

Hotel am Leineschloss (Am Markt 12) is smack in the heart of downtown, and a touch of contemporary Denmark in Germany, with teak furniture by respected Danish designers like Arne Jacobsen and Hans Wegner; even the lighting fixtures and textiles are from the kingdom to Germany's north. Some 70 attractive bedrooms, all with private baths. Breakfast only. *First Class.*

Hotel Mussmann (Ernst-August-Platz 7), just opposite the station, is an older house that has nicely updated itself; the 100 rooms are cozy, and all have private baths; nice lobby. Breakfast only. *First Class.*

Central Hotel Kaiserhof (Ernst-August-Platz 4) is another neighbor of the station. It, too, is elderly, with neat little lobby, modernized rooms, all with baths. Full café-konditorei. *Moderate.*

Hotel Europäischer Hof (Luisenstrasse 4) is an unpretentious house near the station that absolutely shines, with neat-as-a-pin bedrooms with baths, a little lobby, and inviting breakfast rooms. *Moderate.*

Hotel am Stadtpark (Clausewitzstrasse 6) is at the bottom of my group because it's away from the center—in the Stadtpark, near the Stadthalle concert hall/convention center. This one's a skyscraper ever so mod, with 250 functional rooms and suites, restaurants, bar, sauna, indoor pool. *First Class.*

DAILY BREAD

Prinz Taverne (Hotel Inter-Continental Hannover, Friedrichswall 11) is the not-often-encountered restaurant that is pure luxury, from, say, appetizers of smoked salmon or caviar or fresh foie gras to entrées like thick U.S.-cut sirloins, English ribs of beef, German venison, Italian veal, on through to feather-light dessert soufflés and delectable pastries. Wine cellar. An intimate setting and impeccable service. Bravo, Inter-Continental! *Luxury.*

Georgenhof (Herrenhäuser Kirchweg 20) is out at Herrenhausen Gardens, and a perfect choice for lunch in conjunction with a visit to the Gardens and the Herrenhausen Museum. This is an authentic antique of a house transformed with finesse into an exceptional restaurant. Old serving pieces—bowls, pitchers, and plates of pottery and copper and pewter—are interspersed with fresh flowers in a series of intimate rooms giving onto a garden, where there are tables in summer. Cooking, dominantly German, has a light touch with game, poultry, and pork entrées. Or perhaps entrecôte with sauce béarnaise. When last I visited, credit cards were not accepted. *Luxury.*

Ratskeller (Altes Rathaus, Marktplatz) is among the handsomer and more atmospheric of German City Hall restaurants. And that's saying a lot. This is a spacious unit of vaulted rooms, with crisp white linen, quick waiters, and fare as hearty or simple as you would like—from consommé followed by an omelette, to mixed grill with fried potatoes. Beer or a wide wine choice. *Moderate/First Class.*

Grillroom (Kastens Hotel Luisenhof, Luisenstrasse 2/3) offers a wide-ranging international menu. Specialties are grills of beef, pork, and chicken from the open-to-view copper-hooded kitchen. *First Class.*

Bakkarat Spielbank Restaurant (Machsee) is an away-from-the-center drive, and the setting for a festive, international-style dinner, perhaps combined with games of chance in the adjacent casino. *Luxury.*

Mövenpick Café Kröpcke (Kröpcke at Georgstrasse): A branch of the Swiss-run, Germany-wide restaurant chain (Mövenpick) that has teamed with the city's most beloved old café (Kröpcke) at the central Kröpcke Square. There's a terrace for ice cream or coffee and cake, and for people-watching; and a big restaurant within. Everything is tasty. Tabs mostly *Moderate.*

Coq d'Or (Luisenstrasse 4, in Europäischer Hotel building) offers Gallic ambience and Gallic food—*truite aux amandes,* for example, or a delicious quiche. Good *soupe à l'oignon gratinée,* and French wines, too. *First Class.*

Altes Brauhaus (Bahnhofstrasse 5) is an old-reliable, all-purpose eatery—for standard German stick-to-the-ribs favorites, reliable steaks, tall steins of beer. *Moderate.*

Die Insel (Machpark): An appealing café at the shore of the heart-of-town park's own pretty lake. For a pause—coffee or a snack—between museum bouts. *Moderate.*

SOUND OF MUSIC

Staatstheater (Rathenauplatz, at Georgstrasse) is Hannover's remarkable opera house: a substantial neoclassic structure out of the mid-nineteenth century, elegantly colonnaded and statue-studded without. A post-World War II restoration within created a part-contemporary, part-traditional setting. Repertory classic *(Don Pasquale)* and contemporary *(My Fair Lady)*. Ballet and symphony orchestra.

Stadthalle (Stadtpark) is a concert hall/convention center with massive dome in a park a short ride from the center.

Herrenhausen Gardens: The baroque-era alfresco *Gartentheater* and the Royal Palace pavilion called the *Galeriegebäude* are the scene of plays (including Brecht and Shakespeare, albeit in German), opera (Britten to Handel), concerts, ballet, and fireworks, mid-May into September. And the *Grosser Garten* is usually illuminated after evening performances. Programs for the season are published in English by the Hannover Tourist Office, Ernst-August-Platz, usually five months in advance.

INCIDENTAL INTELLIGENCE

Hannover is one of the lucky German cities served by air; Lufthansa flies to its Langenhagen Airport, seven miles from downtown, with regular bus service to and from the Hauptbahnhof. *Further information:* Verkehrsbüro Hannover—tourist office of the city is at Ernst-August-Platz 8.

20

Heidelberg

Consequences of The Student Prince

BACKGROUND BRIEFING

Heidelberg's blessings are its history, its setting, a clutch of nineteenth-century poets and painters who romanticized it (apparently for eternity), and an early-twentieth-century American operetta called *The Student Prince.* The consequence of this combination is an endless flow of tourists to one of Germany's most visited smaller cities.

Fair enough. Still, when one considers that Heidelberg—almost unique among German towns—has not suffered from the destruction of a war since the seventeenth century (it was not touched during World War II)—and when one ponders its long, rich history, well, there is surprisingly little to inspect, if not to experience.

Which is hardly to say that one should omit Heidelberg from a German itinerary. Its picture-postcard panorama of castle, town, and river is lovely. But it is worth noting that the aesthetic pickings—the intellectual stimulation, if you will—of today's Heidelberg are relatively slim, in contrast to, say, Regensburg, Freiburg, Bamberg, or Kassel, to name a quartet of towns at random.

It is not surprising that nothing save a copy of the jawbone of the pre-historic Heidelberg Man—*Homo heidelbergemsos—*

remains. Nor are there souvenirs of the Roman encampments in the area 2,000 years back. There are, to be sure, remnants of the medieval Christian centuries among the illuminated manuscripts of the University Library (I am partial to a miniature of St. Peter on his papal throne that dates to 980).

It was, to be sure, from early Christians—monks who built a monastery on the hill above the Neckar where the ruined castle now stands—that Heidelberg gained its name, a corruption of the *Heiligenberg,* or Holy Mountain, of the friars. That elevated eminence did not go unnoticed by lay leaders. By the thirteenth century a fortress had replaced the monastery. A regional bishop turned the mountain over to a nobleman—the Count Palatine—one of whose successors, a century later, became one of the seven rulers privileged to cast votes to determine selection of Holy Roman Emperors. The first of these electors—Ruprecht I—founded what is Germany's oldest and most celebrated university.

Heidelberg was making the transition from Renaissance to baroque, still reacting—like the rest of seventeenth-century Germany—to effects of post-Reformation conflicts between Catholic and Protestant princes. The Thirty Years' War—which involved not only the various German states but France, Sweden, Denmark, Bohemia, the Low Countries, and Spain—occupied three early-seventeenth-century decades, ending with much of Germany weakened, plundered, and destroyed, and with Heidelberg a focal point of this long succession of international intrigues and battles. The castle, by this time a showplace, was not damaged until later in the century—1689—when the French did a job on it and the town below it as well.

The eighteenth century saw the permanent departure of the electors from Heidelberg Castle—first to Mannheim, later to Munich. And a simultaneous rebuilding of the town and the university, in good time for the romantic movement of the nineteenth century. Poets, painters, even musicians settled in. Goethe made eight Heidelberg visits, Karl Maria von Weber and Brahms composed, England's Turner painted. Mark Twain spent a late-nineteenth-century summer, and in the early twentieth century a chap called Meyer-Fürster wrote a play called *Old Heidelberg,* which Sigmund Romberg picked up as the basis of his now-immortal operetta *The Student Prince.*

That did it. Heidelberg's reputation as a tourist destination of consequence was made. Enough so, it seems, to have attracted the attention of rich Americans like Henry Ford, who contributed heavily to the building of a new university campus just before the dark era of the thirties. After the war, the United States—this time through its army—was again attracted to Heidelberg, which became the headquarters for U.S. European forces.

We still are not without representation on the scene. One hears as much American English in this town as in any in Germany.

ON SCENE

Lay of the Land: One reason for Heidelberg's touristic success is its geographic simplicity. You can't get lost. The Neckar River serves as the northern boundary of the historic core of town, with the castle—*Das Schloss*—looming over the town's southern fringe. The Hauptbahnhof is at the west end, in a modern quarter beyond the ancient sector. It fronts a street called Kurfürstenanlage, which leads straight into the center. Running roughly parallel is the city's main thoroughfare, Hauptstrasse. The bulk of the city's monuments—except for the on-high *Schloss* and the across-the-river promenade called Philosophenhöhe (go over to get the view)—lie on either side of Hauptstrasse between two squares, Bismarckplatz and Karlsplatz.

Three bridges cross the Neckar. Two are important. Theodore Heuss Brücke, the westernmost, leads to the new campus of the university. And the central Alte Brücke—the fifth to be built on the site, and dating to the late eighteenth century—leads to Philosophenhöhe, and is in and of itself a major Heidelberg landmark.

The newer part of town—west of Bismarckplatz—is a good walk from the core. But getting around the center on foot is a pleasure. You may even walk up to the *Schloss,* although the cable-car ride is at least as enjoyable—and easier. And up top, there's a car park, for motorists.

Das Schloss (The Castle) is a complex vast enough to confound and confuse—if you let it. What is worth remembering is that—to this viewer at least—it is at its best from afar: across the river, say, on Philosophenhöhe, with the silhouette of the town and the Alte Brücke spanning the Neckar. Get up closer and it's at its most spectacular from without: the largely Renaissance buildings have superb façades. The mostly ruined state of the castle group is thanks not to Allied World War II bombers—as is usually the case in Germany—but to French forces of Louis XVI that attacked Heidelberg in the late seventeenth century.

Concentrate on the exterior of the Friedrich Building—pedimented windows, niches with life-sized sculptures of royal inhabitants, a double-gabled roof; note the equally sumptuous façade—with nothing but air behind it—of the Ottheinrich Building; stroll the gardens; the views of town and river are classic. Then pop into the Friedrich Building. Its lures include the planet's largest wine barrel and an assortment of state rooms, most of them authentically, if not magnificently, restored to what they were in the seventeenth century. There are corridors with stuccoed ceilings, salons with the intricately worked door frames that were a Renaissance specialty; some fine porcelain stoves, not a few tapestries, a chapel, and an unlikely musuem. This last—*Deutsches Apotheken-Museum*—is a kind of national pharmaceutical museum, founded during the Hitler era in Munich, and moved to its present home, a baker's dozen of Castle rooms, after World War II. It is easy to assume that this museum is going to tell you more than you ever wanted to know about pharmacy—German pharmacy at that—but if you have a feel for the rococo era of the eighteenth century, you'll be delighted, if only because of the paintings and furnishings, which include deftly designed cubbyholed drug cabinets, and multidrawered prescription desks.

Kurpfälzisches Museum (Haupstrasse 97) translates as Museum of the Electoral Palatinate, and is, to simplify, the City Museum. It is, as well, one of the most charming smaller-city museums in Germany. I'll take it over a tour of the Castle any day of the week. It's a palace—Palais Morass, by name—in its own right, dating to the early eighteenth century. The city took it over at the turn of this century, retaining its original decor and a lot of its original furnishings. The staircase is sumptuous. The upstairs ballroom could be in a Robert Adam stately home in England. Other rooms are in the original rococo, and the decorative objects—furniture, rugs, porcelain, draperies, stuccowork—range from that era through the Biedermeier decades approaching mid-nineteenth century.

The collection? There are paintings by modern Germans like Nolde and Germany's eighteenth-century Angelica Kauffmann, and a host of later romantic views of German towns and castles. Also represented are England's Lawrence (a portrait of Metternich) and Turner (a view of—you guessed it—Heidelberg), Dutchmen Hals and van Ruysdael; Italians Guardi and Canaletto; and the museum's supreme treasure, a church altar from the sixteenth century depicting Christ and the Twelve Apostles, by the master Würzburg sculptor, Tilman Riemenschneider. With a garden restaurant, later recommended.

Universitätsbibliothek (Grabengasse) is by no means ancient itself—it dates to the turn of the century—but it is full of venerable exhibits from its own shelves. Especially important is a group of illuminated manuscripts that were formerly in the royal library of the electors.

Heilig-Geist-Kirche (Marktplatz) is the town's preeminent church, with a simple but handsome Gothic-vaulted interior, and a bulbous baroque steeple. Electors were for long buried here, but the French destroyed all but two of their tombs in their seventeenth-century rampage.

Rathaus (Marktplatz) is gracious baroque. Enter to see the impressive Grossesaal, or Great Hall, of this originally seventeenth-century landmark.

Jesuitenkirche (Grabengasse) has as pretty an interior as Heilig-Geist-Kirche; it's exuberant baroque—gilded Corinthian capitals atop the columns of the nave, elegant pulpit, the oversized frescoes typical of the Counter Reformation.

Kornmarkt is the square just east of Marktplatz, as you move along Hauptstrasse. It's framed by baroque houses, with a fountain statue of that era, that Heidelbergers have dubbed the Kornmarkt Madonna, in the center. Lovely.

Königstuhl is the name of the mountain behind and above the castle—at an altitude of some 1,700 feet. It's fun to take the same mountain railway line from Kornmarkt that you may already have taken to the castle. Stay on for Königstuhl Station, long enough to steep yourself in the panorama of castle, town, Neckar, and the countryside beyond.

A trio of out-of-town excursions: Heidelberg is a convenient base for day-or-less excursions of your own making, to two significant destinations, and a relaxing third, each an easy drive west of town. *Speyer Dom,* or cathedral, takes the name of the pretty Rhine River town in which it is situated. It is nothing less than an all-Germany ecclesiastical masterwork, purely and sublimely Romanesque, and boasting advanced age (the cornerstone was laid by an emperor in 1027), Imperial patronage over a range of centuries, and just plain good luck—by which I mean it escaped World War II bombing. There has, however, been considerable restoration (as at Mainz Cathedral [Chapter 27], with unfelicitous nineteenth-century frescoes unnecessarily ringing a magnificent, elegantly proportioned nave) but the essential grandeur and unity of style remain, from a series of royal tombs in the multi-arched crypt, through to lovely niches of the apse, beyond to the cathedral's setting: a hill over the Rhine, its slim towers—a pair each front and rear—visible for miles around. *Historisches Museum der Pfalz,* packed with colorful lore of the Palatinate region, and with a separate section on regional wines, is a near-neighbor of the cathedral. *Backmulde* (Karmeliterstrasse 11) is a convenient, moderate-priced restaurant for a lunch break. *Die Deutsche Weinstrasse*—a few miles to the west of Speyer—embraces a clutch of unpretentious villages punctuating vineyards of the Palatinate, with *Deidesheim* as agreeable as any for an overnight stop. Charming *Deidesheimer Hof* (First Class), has an excellent restaurant, and steps away are the little Town Hall and Gothic-era St. Ulrich's Church. A day's amble through villages like Forst, Ruppertsberg, and Niederkirchen—with stops for wine-tasting at taverns en route, and at open-to-visitors vineyards—is diverting. *Schwetzingen* is a quiet little town, not far east of Speyer whose ace-in-the-hole is an extraordinary eighteenth-century palace, *Schloss Schwetzingen,* the longtime seat of regional rulers, or Electors, one of whom, Carl Theodor, ordered architect Nicolas Pigage to surround the palace with a magnificent formal garden and—at least as significant—design a still-in-use auditorium, *Rokokotheater,* contemporarily noted for fall-through-early-spring seasons of Mozart Chamber Concerts. Stroll through the French-style garden, noting besides a wealth of classical-style sculpture, a mock Chinese bridge spanning a canal; a Temple of Apollo, complete with grottoes, waterworks and stairwells; an elegant, Pigage-designed bathhouse whose classic-style interior remains open; and a Pigage Arabian Nights fantasy-variation on, of all things, a mosque. End with a tour of the four-level Rokokotheater, noting the exuberantly fresoced ceiling—above a crystal chandelier, and *faux-marbre* pilasters framing the stage's proscenium. Have lunch at the palace complex's *Schlosscafé, (Moderate)* or—for a tasty proper meal—at *Gasthof Zum Ritter,* Schlossplatz 1. *First Class.*

SETTLING IN

Hotel Europäischer Hof (Friedrich-Ebert-Anlage 1) is Heidelberg's only luxury hotel. And the fact that it has no competition in its category appears to have spoiled it not a whit. Set in its own grounds, a scenic six- or seven-minute walk from the core of town, this is a beauty of a traditional-style house—overstuffed chairs in beamed lobbies, portraits of eighteenth-century luminaries on the walls, a main restaurant that merits additional comment later on, a warm-weather dining terrace, beautifully paneled *Stube* for casual meals, and bar that's a nice change from the studenty ones in town. Not to mention 100 rooms and suites—some in the original 115-year-old main building, some in a newer wing—that are at once capacious and quietly opulent, with gorgeous baths. *Luxury.*

Hotel Hirschgasse (Hirschgasse 3): I seldom recommend non-central hotels, but the Hirschgasse is special. It goes back to the fifteenth century, was updated—if that's the term—in the eighteenth, and again in recent decades, so that now all of the 30-plus rooms—no two just alike—have private baths. There's a rustic restaurant within, and another on the terrace in warm weather, from which one has views of castle and river. *First Class.*

Hotel Schönberger Hof (Untere Neckarstrasse 54) is a delight: an atmospheric heart-of-town house deftly transformed into an intimate hotel-restaurant. There are fewer than a score of rooms, all with private baths, and there is hospitable management and a restaurant so good it warrants further comment. *First Class.*

Hotel Höllander Hof (Neckarstaden 66): You can reach out of your window—well, almost—and touch the Alte Brücke from the Holländer Hof. It's a seventeenth-century house with a central location, recently renovated, with nearly half a hundred attractive rooms, all with private baths. (Half a dozen are specially equipped for handicapped travelers—a high proportion even for far larger hotels.) In addition, there's a top-notch restaurant. Affiliated with a Germany-wide chain of church-related hospices. *First Class.*

Hotel am Schloss (Swingerstrasse 20 at Kornmarktplatz) is nondescript modern as regards design, but it's central, all 21 rooms have baths, and from the rooftop terrace you'll see the Schloss almost directly overhead. Breakfast only. *Moderate.*

Hotel Acor (Friedrich-Ebert-Anlage 55) occupies a cluster of contiguous houses a few minutes' walk from Hauptstrasse. Cozy accommodations, many with bath. Breakfast only. *Moderate.*

Hotel Regina (Luisenstrasse 6): A little charmer, this. Just 18 recently updated rooms, all of which have private baths. Situation is between the Hauptbahnhof and the heart of town, which is a fair walk. *Moderate.*

Hotel Atlas (Bergheimer Strasse 63) is, perhaps, overbold in its box-like sleekness—it is a contemporary, 114-room house—for tradition-bound Heidelberg. But it fills a need for functional accommodations; rooms are decent-size and pleasant, the attractive restaurant makes a specialty of buffets at breakfast, lunch and dinner, there's a bar-lounge, and you may walk to the center of town in ten or twelve minutes. *First Class.*

Hotel zum Ritter (Hauptstrasse 178) is way, way at the bottom of this select grouping and rates space here only so you'll know I've not passed it by. Its claim to fame is an intricate Renaissance façade. Within are a hotel and restaurant that exploit the landmark setting, with bedrooms that can be absurdly tiny and poorly maintained and—if my experience is typical—service that is barely civil. *First Class.*

DAILY BREAD

Hotel Europäischer Hof Restaurants (Friedrich-Ebert-Anlage 1) constitute Heidelberg dining at its grandest. The main dining room is traditional in style, with white-glove service. And every entrée has interesting accompaniments; for example, the breast of pheasant is stuffed with truffled goose liver. *Kurfürstenstube* is a paneled tavern with a similarly appealing menu and a terrace for summer meals. Exceptional wines. *Luxury.*

Hotel Schönberger Hof Altdeutsche Weinstube (Untere Neckarstrasse 54) is the top-rank restaurant of a top-rank hotel. Traditional German specialties are prepared and served with a light touch in a smart setting that draws both knowing locals and visitors. Follow the proprietor-chef-host's suggestions for both food and wine. *First Class.*

Kurpfälzisches Museum Resaurant (Hauptstrasse 97): The charming restaurant of a charming museum in a rococo palace, with a beautiful garden for summer meals. Perfect for lunch—order a veal or poultry dish or the daily special—and explore the museum. *Moderate/First Class.*

Zum Güldenen Schaf (Hauptstrasse 67): The Golden Fleece embodies the essence of old Heidelberg—wood-paneled, busily decorated, with a menu embracing local specialties that's just the ticket for simple snacks through multi-course dinners. Delightful service. *Moderate/First Class.*

Weinkrüger (Hauptstrasse near Marktplatz) is at once pubby and elegant—no mean feat in a German *Weinstube.* The crowd is buzzy, the food delicious (there are steaks as well as more Teutonic dishes), and the wine-card is special. *First Class.*

Hotel Holländer Hof Restaurant (Neckarstaden 66) is antiques-accented with super views of the Alte Brücke and the Neckar River. Good-value menus. *Moderate/First Class.*

Zum Roten Ochsen (Hauptstrasse near Karlsplatz): If you're going to have a snack, drink, or meal at one student haunt, make it the Red Ox—the Roten Ochsen—which has been attracting thirsty scholars since 1703, and they all appear to have carved their initials on the tables. Go after dinner for a drink. The same family has run the place for six generations. *Moderate.*

Café Seppi (Hauptstrasse at Karlplatz) is another university pub of considerable vintage—some 200 years—with documentary evidence on the walls, and a smiling, good-natured clientele that welcomes foreigners. *Moderate.*

Ristorante Toscana (Marktplatz) is a good place to go when you crave something distinctly non-German, in this case pizza, or a pasta with Italian wine. *Moderate/First Class.*

Café-Konditorei Knösel (Haspelgasse at Fischmarkt) is a near-neighbor of Heilig-Geist-Kirche. The lure is delicious pastries and coffee. *Moderate.*

Heidelberg Castle Restaurants: Take your choice of the *Burgfreiheit* or the *Weinstube Schloss,* and expect hungry fellow-tourists to raise the decibel count and crowd the tables, as anxious for the view as you are. *First Class.*

SOUND OF MUSIC

Stadthalle (Theaterstrasse) is a turn-of-century house where Heidelberg's opera, repertory theater companies, and symphony perform; it's central. Additional concerts take place in the auditoriums on the old and new university campuses, and in churches.

INCIDENTAL INTELLIGENCE

In summer, boat excursions on the Neckar and on the adjacent Rhine are a good way to see Mannheim and Worms. Pier is near the Stadthalle. The city's Tourist Information Office is adjacent to the Bahnhof.

21

Kassel

Westphalia's Royal Riches

BACKGROUND BRIEFING

You haven't heard of it. And a visit to it is not part of your plans. Rethink your plans: this sleeper of a town is handsome, hospitable, and extraordinarily rich in art treasures. Location is midway between Frankfurt and Hannover.

Kassel is no upstart. Before the twelfth century had ended, it was a properly chartered city. During the stormy Renaissance it found itself a political center, as the seat of the landgraves—later electors—of Hesse-Kassel. With a court in residence, culture was bound to flower—and it did. During the early eighteenth century, when Napoleon was deputizing relatives to govern in his stead, Jérôme, the youngest of the brothers Bonaparte, found that older sibling Napoleon had arbitrarily dissolved his marriage to an American he had met in the States, and matched him with Catherine of Württemberg. Result: Jérôme became king of Westphalia for the period 1807-13, and lived in a sumptuous palace that is the high point of a contemporary Kassel visit.

Later years saw Hesse united with Nassau, as a province of the German Empire; Kassel became the capital. During World War II, by which time Kassel had become a manufacturing center of consequence, it was heavily bombed. Post-1945 restoration has been remarkably innovative. Kassel takes credit for having pioneered the heart-of-town pedestrian shopping zone that has become an urban German commonplace.

ON SCENE

Lay of the Land: For a city with a population hovering about the quarter-million mark, Kassel occupies a disproportionately large area. A good four miles divide the two areas of principal visitor interest—downtown, and the bucolic, mountain-backed western edge of town, where are the ingredients that give Kassel its cachet.

Downtown makes for pedestrian pleasure. Arrive at the Hauptbahnhof and you have only to walk a little southeast on Kurfürstenstrasse before it becomes a handsome walkers-only shopping promenade called Treppenstrasse, which extends to still another such thoroughfare perpendicular to it, Königstrasse. Walk west on Königstrasse a few blocks and you find monuments like the Rathaus and major downtown museums. Walk east and you pass the opera house en route to circular Königsplatz. Don't forget the Fulda River; it runs roughly parallel with Königstrasse, separated by a few streets. Amble over at one point or another, breaking your journey at one of the cafés with views, high above the Fulda.

The "other" Kassel is a car, taxi, or bus ride out the thoroughfare called Wilhelmshöhe, to the district from which that avenue takes its name. It centers about Wilhelmshöhe Palace and a wooded mountain preserve out back called Naturpark Habichtswald. Hotels are positioned in both sectors of town; you'll have to make up your mind as to which of them you'll headquarter in. Stay downtown and you're in the center of the urban action. Book at a Wilhelmshöhe hotel and you're in the heart of something very special. Just what? Read on.

Schloss Wilhelmshöhe is an eighteenth-century palace—arc-shaped with the focus of its central section a beautiful colonnaded portico, and its setting the clipped lawns of an 800-acre park. What is worth appreciating at the outset is that there are three distinct aspects of Wilhelmshöhe; to do each justice it's well to devote a day to the complex. Here they are:

1. *The state rooms of the palace* are Kassel's best-kept touristic secret. This is the onetime home of the landgraves—and later the electors—of Hessen, and in the early nineteenth century, of Napoleon's brother Jérôme during his short-lived reign as king of Westphalia. Restoration of the rooms and their period furnishings has been a multimillion-Deutschmark project of the current *Land* government, and it has resulted in one of Germany's most breathtaking palace interiors. The state rooms have their own entrance. They total about a score, and they're filled with treasures of art and artisanship—portraits of royal residents, sculpture, silver, crystal, porcelain—as well as with furniture, Louis XVI through Empire. Pick your favorite: throne-surmounted audience room, chandelier-hung dining room, more than one *Schlafzimmer,* with beds elegantly canopied; or the royal bath with murals and a sunken marble tub.

2. *The palace art gallery—Staatliche Kunstsammlungen Kassel* to use its proper name—with its own entrance, occupies a spacious wing of the palace that was refurbished especially for the purpose. Nowhere in Germany is a major collection of paintings more handsomely hung.

The Rembrandts—totaling 17, more than in any other German museum outside of West Berlin's Dahlem—are a special pride; among them are profiles of Saskia, the painter's wife, in a floppy hat; of the Holy Family behind a stage-like curtain; and of the artist as a very young man. And more: Dürer's matchless portrait of Elsbeth Tucher, Altdorfer and Rubens, Van Dyck and Jordaens, Hals and Van Ruysdael, Tintoretto and Murillo, Cranach and van Cleve, Rigaud and Titian, whose portrait of a scarlet-garbed-and-plumed nobleman is one of his greatest works.

3. *The Hercules Monument* is a stupendous likeness of the Greek god of strength and courage, surmounting its own classic-style pavilion that is, all told, more than 230 feet high. Italian-designed, it was erected by an eighteenth-century ruler to complement the palace that it overlooks. At its base is an ingenious system of cascades and fountains that connect the elevated statue with the terrain below. Have a look from on high (you may drive up) or from the palace. At 2:30 P.M. on most

summer Wednesdays, Sundays, and holidays, the water flows, full force, to a fountain at the base of the mountain.

Schloss Löwenburg is a near-neighbor of the palace at Wilhelmshöhe, which it could not resemble less. A romantically minded eighteenth-century landgrave built it to evoke a partially ruined castle out of the Middle Ages. And there it is: distressed façade built right into it, looking very much like the genuine article. Treats within are a museum of arms and armor; a mini-chapel, and a series of rooms—for lounging, dining, sleeping—with superb furniture, art objects, and various accessories.

Brüder-Grimm-Museum (Schöne Aussicht 2) will not come as a surprise if you've translanted its German name. Yes, indeed, this is the city of the Grimm Brothers of fairy-tale immortality. Librarians for the royal court, they wrote much else, but clicked with their *Kinder-und Hausmärchen,* published in 1815. They were a trio—Ludwig Emil, Jacob, and Wilhelm, but only the last two wrote the tales. The house is chock-a-block with Grimmiana, including editions of their classic in a multitude of languages.

Neue Galerie (Schöne Aussicht 1) is a century-old, classic-style pavilion with a severely handsome—and modern—interior, whose best feature is a collection of German Expressionists—such late-nineteenth- and early-twentieth-century greats as sculptor Ernst Barlach and painters Kirchner, Nolde, and Corinth.

Hessiches Landesmuseum, Tapetenmuseum (Brüder-Grimm-Platz 5) are a pair of decorative-arts museums sharing quarters in an atmospheric turn-of-the-century building. The Tapetenmuseum is the better known because its subject matter—wallpaper—is unique, as museums go, with antique specimens and wallpaper-manufacturing equipment, too. Sadly, it doesn't work. Not as it should. The effect is more retail show-room than repository of art objects. The Hessiches Landesmuseum is more successful, if less celebrated—with beautiful pieces, medieval through the nineteenth-century's Biedermeier: a don't-miss, with the eighteenth century especially strong. On your way out, ask to see the little *Astronomy Museum* in the same building, if only for its gorgeous antique globes.

SETTLING IN

Schloss-Hotel Wilhelmshöhe (Schlosspark 2) is not a castle-turned-hotel, which one might be led to believe, given its title. The name simply conveys the location: across the road from Wilhelmshöhe Palace, with views of it—and the Hercules Monument—from the rooms. Low-slung and modern, this house is quietly, winningly charming, with the rooms—both guest and public—as attractive as the service is engaging, with a restaurant about which I comment later. *First Class.*

Hotel Reiss (Am Hauptbahnhof): No. 1 downtown. There are 100-plus smartly furnished rooms and suites, a trio of commendable restaurants, bar-lounge, sprightly management. *Luxury.*

Parkhotel Hessenland (Obere Königstrasse 2) is a neighbor of the *Rathaus,* at the end of Königstrasse, near the downtown museums and opera. The look is scrubbed-up modern. Restaurant, bar, neat rooms. *First Class.*

Hospiz Treppenstrasse (Treppenstrasse 9) is on the pedestrians' shopping street described earlier, in the core of town. It's one of the group of Germany-wide hotels called hospices, which, though independently owned, are church-sponsored. This one has no restaurant; breakfast only. Rooms—many with private baths—are modern. *Moderate.*

Schloss Schönfeld Hotel (Park Schönfeld) is a charming onetime manor house—the style might be described as Teutonic-accented English Georgian—within a city park, and not inconvenient for Kassel exploration. Reliable restaurant and attractive bar-lounge. *First Class.*

Kurhotel am Habichtswald (Im Druseltal 12) is a modern, three-building cluster near, but still a taxi ride away from, Wilhelmshöhe Palace. This is ultra-mod, full-facility—restaurants, bar-lounge, indoor-outdoor pool, attractive bedrooms with baths. *First Class.*

DAILY BREAD

Dache (Obere Königstrasse 4) is a restaurant-café of exceptional quality. There are full-course specials each day, and an à la carte, with the veal and poultry specialties outstanding. The candy section sells chocolate discs, foil-wrapped, embossed with the Kassel trademark, the Hercules Monument. Or go for cake and coffee in the café. *Moderate/Luxury.*

Ratskeller (Rathaus, Obere Königstrasse) is at once atmospheric (location is the Town Hall), cheery, and good value, with broiled steaks and chicken among the specialties. Extensive wine list. *Moderate/First Class.*

Alt Kassel (Hotel Reiss, Am Hauptbahnhof) is a handsome room, its wood-paneled walls inset with blowups of scenes from the Kassel of the last century. Fare is both German and foreign: a hearty schnitzel, for example, or a grilled sole. *Luxury.*

Schloss-Hotel Wilhelmshöhe Restaurant (Schlosspark 2): The tone is understated, the waiters discreet but kind, the fare without surprises, but delicious; and the prices right. Order from a wide range—consommé and an omelette or a full-course lunch or dinner. *First Class.*

Via Veneto (Treppenstrasse 16) is ever-reliable Italian, with authentic (and authentically sauced) pastas, fresh salads, Italian wines. *First Class.*

Café Paulus (Friedrichsplatz) is a favorite with downtown shoppers, for coffee or lunch. *Moderate.*

SOUND OF MUSIC

Stadttheater (Am Friedrichsplatz) is Kassel's ever so modern two-theater opera house: the larger for opera, concerts, and ballet; the smaller for plays.

Wilhelmshöhe Park Concerts are generally held daily except Monday, May through September.

Löwenburg Palace Concerts are traditionally held on Saturday evenings in the courtyard.

INCIDENTAL INTELLIGENCE

Verkehrs-und-Wirtschaftsamt der Stadt Kassel is the city tourist office, with headquarters in the *Rathaus,* Kassel, and branches in the Hauptbahnhof and at Friedrichsplatz.

22

Koblenz

Straddling Two Great Rivers

BACKGROUND BRIEFING

The wonder of Koblenz—given its situation at the confluence of such important rivers as the Rhine and the Moselle—is that it is not a metropolis. History has decreed otherwise. However, this pretty—and pretty quiet—port town has not had an uneventful past. Nor a short one. Koblenz spans a score of centuries—it was founded in 9 B.C. The man who gets credit for starting things was a Roman general named Nero Claudius Drusus Germanicus, or, if you prefer, Drusus Senior, to distinguish him from other members of an illustrious clan.

The city's name then was *Castrum ad Confluentes*—Castle at the Confluence. Over the centuries it became Germanized to the present Koblenz, possibly during the early Middle Ages when a spate of Frankish kings settled in. Top-echelon clergy followed them, frequently converging upon Koblenz for conferences. And then—for no less than eight centuries—the city was ruled by the powerful archbishops of nearby Trier.

Its subsequent fortunes have been similar to those of the rest of German territory. Koblenz has seen French occupation under Napoleon, and has paid allegiance to the later pan-German empire of the kaisers. The post-World War I years saw an entire decade of Allied occupation. World War II brought heavy bombings. The city has done a conscientious restoration job. Today's visitors will enjoy a brief stopover in the course of a Rhine River cruise—the most scenic section of the Rhine lies between Koblenz and Mainz—or in the course of a rail or motor journey.

ON SCENE

Lay of the Land: The core of town—the Hauptbahnhof—lies east of the Rhine and south of the Moselle, a fair distance inland from the two rivers, but closer to downtown than the pier at which the Rhine steamers dock. (Ship passengers may walk to the center, however, if they do not consider a 20-minute hike overlong.) The river-flanking Rheinanlagen—leading all the way to the elevated point at which the rivers meet—is agreeable for strolls, and so, for that matter, are the inland streets. You can walk past a sumptuous eighteenth-century palace known simply as the Schloss to locals, or past an even older structure—originally a Jesuit school and with a splendid staircase—that is now the *Rathaus,* on Casinostrasse, at Jesuitenplatz.

Ehrenbreitstein Fortress is the only one of my suggested destinations not in the center of the city, but it is by no means the least important. Reach it by chair lift from town if you're adventurous, or take the surface route, over Pffandorfer Bridge. You go for three reasons. First, the fortress, most of it early nineteenth century, but with origins in the tenth. Second, the view, not only of low-slung Koblenz—its church spires piercing the sky—but of the Rhine, several of its legendary castles most definitely included. And third, you go for the Middle Rhine Museum, whose collections tell the Koblenz story beautifully, embracing paintings by regional artists, along with historic furniture and furnishings.

Deutsches Eck—or Corner of Germany if you would translate—is the historic name for the point at which the Rhine and Moselle converge. Walk to it from the center of town or as part of your stroll along the riverfront Rheinanlagen. You will already have had super vistas of the neighborhood if you've visited Ehrenbreitstein Fortress, so you may not want to ascend the stairway (there are more than 100 steps) to the viewing base. On the other hand, you may, if only for the perspective of Ehrenbreitstein from across the river.

Alte Stadt: Koblenz's oldest quarter—the old city—more or less lines its Moselle shore, from Deutsches Eck east on the Balduin Bridge across the Moselle. If your approach is from Deutsches Eck, make it on foot along river's-edge Moselanlagen. You'll want to take in a trio of ancient churches as well as the venerable fortress just beneath the Balduin Bridge called Alte Burg; it's home to the Rhine Museum—full of aged art and artifacts in an atmospheric setting. Two of the three churches are Alte Burg neighbors: Liebfrauenkirche, a twin-tower Gothic Romanesque beauty, and Florinskirche, somberly Romanesque. The third and the most remarkable is Kastorskirche, adjacent to Deutsches Eck, and a felicitous Romanesque-Gothic meld, with fan-vaulting framing such treasures as a rood-screen portrait of the church's name-saint, Castor, and a luminous Madonna painting.

SETTLING IN

Hotel Kleiner Riesen (Rheinanlagen 18): Happiness in Koblenz is a riverview room in this smallish river's-edge hotel with terrace, a hop and a skip from where the river boats tie up, and a good quarter-hour's walk to the center of town. The look is of solid, old-fashioned comfort, nothing pretentious. Breakfast only. *First Class.*

Pfälzer Hof-Continental (Bahnhofsplatz) is a neighbor of the railway station and from it one may easily walk into the center. Half a hundred comfortable rooms, not all with private bath; breakfast only. *First Class.*

Hotel Trierer Hof (Dienhardplatz) dates to the late eighteenth century and is strategically located near the heart-of-town Schloss and Stadttheater—both its contemporaries. Rooms are spacious if not elaborate, and the welcome warm. Breakfast only. *Moderate.*

Hotel Union (Löhrstrasse 73) is heart-of-town and comfortable, convenient to almost everything. More than 40 rooms, many with private baths. *Moderate.*

Diehls Hotel, though the city's most luxurious, has the disadvantage of being across the Rhine in a location not to every visitor's liking—it's especially inconvenient without a car. Still, there are pluses. Ehrenbreitstein Fortress is a near-neighbor, and there are idyllic views of river and city from restaurant and lobbies, as well as from most bedrooms—not all of which, incidentally, have private baths. *First Class.*

DAILY BREAD

Weinhaus Hubertus (Florinsmarkt 54) is venerable, woodbeamed, and has just the kind of hearty fare you would expect in so welcoming and old-fashioned a setting. Good soups, rich desserts, and filling entrées. *Moderate.*

Rhein-Mosel-Halle Restaurant (Julius-Wegeler-Strasse) is smartly modern in decor, with a menu at once German and international. A good place for a steak. *First Class.*

Im Wurstkessel (Firmungstrasse 12) is for a lunch or evening meal of, say, spicy *Mettwurst,* with rye bread and a glass of wine or two. Pubby. *Moderate.*

Café Rheinanlagen, on the Rheinanlagen promenade at Rhine's edge, is for coffee, drinks, lunch, or afternoon snack—on the terrace, with the river below. *Moderate.*

Weindorf: Koblenz is not only at the confluence of two great rivers: it stands between the great wine-producing regions that take these rivers' names. Weindorf is a complex of *Weinstuben,* where one tastes and samples to one's heart's content, often to musical accompaniment. Setting is edge of the Rhine, just below Rhein-Mosel-Halle. *Moderate.*

SOUND OF MUSIC

Rhein-Mosel-Halle is Koblenz at its most contemporary: a handsome garden-flanked multipurpose hall for concerts, meetings, and the like, with a commendable restaurant.

Stadttheater: The municipal playhouse is an eighteenth-century theater—styled after the theater in the palace of Versailles—that has been deftly adapted to modern use. Worth a look, or perhaps an evening, even if your German is not up to snuff.

INCIDENTAL INTELLIGENCE

Koblenz is a good take-off point for the exploration of nearby Rhine River castles and vineyards. Visitors on Rhine River cruises might find it convenient to break their journeys here, spend a night or two seeing the city, its environs, and possibly the Moselle area, too, and then reboard a river steamer to conclude the cruise. All as a consequence of made-in-advance arrangements. *Further information:* Fremdenverkehrsamt Koblenz—the city tourist office—is at the Hauptbahnhof.

23

Konstanz

Ancient Town,
Lovely Lake

BACKGROUND BRIEFING

Terminology and geography first, because it can be confusing. There is, to start, a vast 208-square-mile, 41-mile-long inland sea—called Bodensee, in German; Lake Constance, in English—bordering a trio of German-speaking lands: Germany, Switzerland, Austria. There is a town on that part of its shoreline bordering Germany called Konstanz, in German; Constance, in English. It is that town—a lovely one, confusing nomenclature notwithstanding—of which we speak at this point. On other pages, two additional Lake Constance towns are accorded chapters: Lindau and Meersburg. And the lake itself is a destination of import; excursion boats ply its waters to and from towns in all three countries bordering it.

The town of Konstanz surprises not so much with its beauty—to be expected in this corner of the planet—as with its historical importance in the European ecclesiastical scheme of things.

What happened was that the Catholic church in the early fifteenth century found itself with three priests claiming to be the lawful pope. That was two too many. The crisis—which came to be called the Great Schism—had to be resolved. One of this trio, who styled himself John XXIII (more than four centuries ahead of still another John XXIII), called a meeting in 1417 to straighten things out. His collaborator, the Holy Roman Emperor, chose the site—the town of Konstanz.

It is likely that Konstanz has never since been the focal point of so much hubbub. The upshot of the deliberations was that all three claimants—Gregory XII, Benedict XIII, and John XXIII—lost out. It was still a fourth priest who became Pope Martin V.

Other matters were attended to, as well. The Bohemian religious reformer, Jan Hus—who had widely attacked abuses of the clergy—was brought to trial, condemned for heresy, and, along with his colleague Jerome of Prague, burned at the stake. (He became, as a consequence, an immortal Czech hero.)

Today's visitor wants to remember that Konstanz was on scene centuries before the schism conference. The ancient Romans transformed it from a fishing hamlet into a fortress. The Holy Roman Empire honored it as an Imperial City. The church awarded it a bishopric. And today, quantities of visitors honor it with their presence.

ON SCENE

Lay of the Land: Set up headquarters in a centrally situated hotel and you can walk everywhere. Konstanz is compact, with the lakefront dominated by a municipal park, Stadtgarten, on one side of which is an ancient structure, Konzilgebäude—site of the schism conference—and on the other, a centuries-old ex-monastery that is now the No. 1 hotel. The Bahnhof is just below the Konzilgebäude. A short walk along Bahnhofstrasse brings us to the Rosgartenmuseum. The other major town monument, the single-spire *Münster,* or Cathedral, is an agreeable stroll away—via Neugasse, then along two streets with historic houses lining them: Hussenstrasse and Wessenbergstrasse.

Rosgartenmuseum (Rosgartenstrasse): If you've time for but one interior to visit in Konstanz, this should be it: an intact fifteenth-century hall that was built by the obviously rich guild of the town's butchers. The council chamber up a flight—with its original paneled walls and the light coming in through fine leaded windows—is worth the entrance fee in itself. But there are treasures—mostly medieval—among the two floors of exhibits, including a carved-wood *Madonna and Child,* a local master's painted interpretation of *The Nativity,* pewter and silver, engravings and pottery. Upon exiting, look in on neighboring *Heilige Geist Kirche,* if only to see the frescoes in which Augustinian monks—the original proprietors—told their order's story.

Münster (Münsterplatz) is an oddball Romanesque-Gothic-Renaissance-baroque meld. The single-steeple exterior is this church at its best. Within are a baroque pulpit and a main altar, which was a gift of the fabulously rich Fugger family of Augsburg.

Hus Haus (Hussenstrasse) is the unprepossessing house in which Bohemian church reformer Jan Hus boarded while being tried for—and convicted of—heresy at the Council of Konstanz half a millennium back. It's now a Hus memorial.

Birnau Basilica (Birnau) is a few miles from town at Birnau. And worth a pilgrimage. The setting alone—the white stucco and orange-tiled-roof rococo church framed by the blue waters of the lake with the snowy Austrian Alps opposite—is superb. Within is a magnificent specimen of southern German rococo, as fine as any to be found in neighboring Bavaria, where this style of church originated. Note ceiling frescoes, *faux marbre* columns, side chapels.

Isle of Mainau*—Insel Mainau* in German—is a surprise package, with a novel historic twist. A 110-acre blaze of subtropical gardens with baroque palace and church, the island is owned and operated by a titled relative of the Swedish royal family—Count Lennart Bernadotte. With the collaboration of his countess and a large professional staff, the count runs Mainau as a botanical garden. A causeway connects it with the mainland. Allow time for a walk among the orange and palm trees, rose gardens, and flower beds. The rococo palace chapel warrants inspection, too, and there's a restaurant (see *Daily Bread*) that's pleasant for lunch.

SETTLING IN

Inselhotel (Auf der Insel 1) is a major treat: a fourteenth-century monastery transformed by the Steigenberger chain into a hotel that is eminently and contemporarily comfortable, the while retaining enough of its original architecture and decoration to evoke a rich history. The 100 rooms and suites are spacious and full-facility. But it's the public areas that fascinate: the monks' vaulted and frescoed chapel is the ballroom. The cloister remains, paintings and all. Ancient architectural motifs have been retained in the restaurants (see *Daily Bread*), and the gabled roofs of the façade are those of old. Go in summer, so you can sun on the lakeside terrace and swim from the hotel's own beach. *Luxury.*

Hotel Deutsches Haus (Marktstätte 15) is No. 2 in town after the Insel—but a way, way down No. 2, smallish and unused-to non-German-speaking guests. It has spacious rooms (many with baths), a convenient restaurant, and heart-of-town location. *Moderate.*

Hotel Barbarossa (Obermarkt 8) has great age if not an abundance of luxury to recommend it; it is a fifteenth-century building with fine façade, 50 rooms (some with bath), restaurant-pub, super location. *Moderate.*

Hotel Seeblick (Neuhauserstrasse 14) is about the same size as the Barbarossa. Many rooms have bath and terrace. And there is a swimming pool and tennis court. Breakfast only. *Moderate.*

Hotel Drachenburg-Waaghaus (Gottlieben, Switzerland) is a hotel of such unusual style and beauty that I mention it at this point for readers with cars. Bordering the lake, a few miles drive from Konstanz in little Gottlieben, this is a half-timbered mansion with some of Europe's most exquisitely decorated bedrooms; styles vary from Renaissance to Louis XVI. Excellent restaurants, too. *Luxury.*

DAILY BREAD

St. Stefanskeller (Am Stefansplatz 41) occupies the cellar of a mellow house, heart of town. With its beamed ceiling, paneled walls, and tables candlelit and flower-embellished, it is a joy to look upon. With fare to match, mostly French-accented, thanks to a Gallic owner-chef who prepares light-touch *nouvelle cuisine* specialties and more traditional dishes. You can't go wrong with the tournedos Bordelaise and potatoes Dauphin-style. The cheese board is one of Germany's best. Fine wines. *Luxury.*

Casino Restaurant (Seestrasse 21) is the casino at its grandest—a well-proportioned lakeside room that serves dinner in style; specialties include veal steak and excellently prepared local fish. *Luxury.*

Dominikaner-Stube (Inselhotel, Auf der Insel 1) is a baroque-accented room illuminated by brass chandeliers; international dishes and German specialties are available along with very good wines. (Before your meal, have a drink in the hotel's Zeppelin Bar, named for the nineteenth-century count who invented the airship. He was an observer with the Union army in the U.S. Civil War and was born on the premises in 1838.) *Luxury.*

Konzil-Gaststätte (Konzilgebäude) is a café-restaurant with terrace in the historic Konzilgebäude, on the lakefront. *Moderate/First Class.*

AFTER DARK

Casino (Seestrasse 21) is smart, lakefront, and with a good restaurant recommended above. Go for blackjack and roulette, a drink, or, if you like, dancing.

INCIDENTAL INTELLIGENCE

As good a lake port as any for excursions by boat to Meersburg and Lindau (subjects of chapters), and to other points on the German, Austrian, and Swiss sides. *Further information:* Verkehrsamt Konstanz, Bahnhofplatz 6.

24

Lindau

The Middle Ages on an Island

BACKGROUND BRIEFING

Take a mountain-backed inland sea (Lake Constance) where three nations (Austria, Switzerland, Germany) converge. Pop a smallish island into it near its northern shore. Populate it with people grown so rich in trade and so politically strong that they came to meld masterworks of art and architecture from medieval Gothic through the rococo of the eighteenth century. The result: Lindau. By the time it built an Art Nouveau-style—or, as the German say, *Jugendstil*—railway station toward the end of the nineteenth century, it had begun to rest on its laurels, and proudly show itself off as an unabashed tourist center.

And why not? Lindau has earned a breathing spell. Its origins go all the way back to the ninth century. That's when legend says a nobleman endowed a monastery that was later to compete for eminence with commercial interests on the island. Indeed, Lindau's history—up to the early nineteenth century, when Napoleon stepped in—was one of monks versus merchants. A few stellar political moments were interspersed. Under Emperor Maximilian's League of Swabian Towns, Lindau was home to the Imperial Diet in the fourteenth century. But by and large, its eminence was commercial. It could not have been otherwise, given its location on the German side of Lake

Constance with German-speaking Austrians and Swiss—to whom it shipped goods—as its immediate neighbors.

Cavernous warehouses lining the lakeshore gave way, in the mid-nineteenth century, to hotels. A brisk visitor traffic was developing as the railroad became a favorite method of transportation for Europe's vacationing middle and upper classes.

Modern times? Insular Lindau has remained, blessedly, quite as it always has been, though it has grudgingly made a few concessions, such as electricity and modern plumbing. There has been expansion into new quarters of the city on the mainland, with which the island city—*Inselstadt* as it calls itself—is linked by two bridges.

Germany is not without ancient towns that have resisted modernization; two other Bavarian localities—Rothenburg and Dinkelsbühl—immediately come to mind, and there are others. What makes Lindau special is its island situation at a deliciously scenic point where three nations meet. A single caveat: If you can, go in the uncrowded months—anytime but summer.

ON SCENE

Lay of the Land: The beauty of Lindau, is that, try as you might, in this compact island city, you can't get lost. Assume you've arrived by train. The Hauptbahnhof is at the southwest edge of town, adjacent to the harbor—Seehafen—which is a landmark of special beauty. Two nineteenth-century monuments guard its entrance: a sculpted, larger-than-life Bavarian Lion and the so-called New Lighthouse (new in contrast to the nearby thirteenth-century Meng Tower, whose beacon had long guided ships). The harbor's Seepromenade, lined with hotels and cafés, is nearly parallel with the two major—and much longer—streets: Ludwigstrasse (with its eastern extension, venerable Fischergasse) is the closer and Hauptstrasse, now a delightful pedestrians-only shopping thoroughfare, as well as the historic core of the city, is farther inland. Two important squares of Lindau, Marktplatz and Schrannenplatz, are, respectively, to the east and to the west of Hauptstrasse.

Altes Rathaus (Reichsplatz), the Old City Hall, is a major work of art. A gabled Renaissance pile, it is distinguished by decorated façades, rear (on Schneerberggasse) as well as front (on Reichsplatz). The former wall embraces both sundial and clock, as well as murals depicting the fifteenth-century Imperial Diet that took place within. The latter façade is graced by a bold exterior stairway to the second floor, with still another gilded clock and another historical frieze above. Go inside for a look at the council chamber in which the Diet delegates deliberated, and a sampling of the antique books—there are nearly 20,000—in the city library.

Zum Cawazzen (Marktplatz) is the name of a rococo palace that houses the Lindau Municipal Art Museum. The collections—carved wood saints out of the Middle Ages, exquisite paintings Gothic through baroque, furniture in handsomely accessorized period settings—range over half a millennium of Lindau history.

Stefanskirche (Marktplatz), a neighbor of the art museum, is an odd meld: Gothic-arched windows through onion-steeple baroque tower. It's Protestant, with a next-door Catholic counterpart that is, in its way, as handsome.

Peterskirche (Schrannenplatz) is a neighbor to Diebesturm—German for Thieves' Tower—a Middle Ages prison with a pointed roof surrounded by a quartet of oriels. It's the church—a quietly lovely gem of a Romanesque structure that is Lindau's oldest—that houses the so-called Lindau Passion frescoes, the only such work extant by the elder Holbein, whose son, Hans Holbein the Younger, became celebrated for work done in England.

SETTLING IN

Hotel Bayerischer Hof (Seepromenade) is the flagship of a trio of hotels under the same owner-management that is directly on the harbor, with views of the lighthouse and Bavarian Lion from its restaurant, terrace, and front rooms. It's a bit more luxurious than its partners with attractive suites and rooms, most with baths, and a commendable restaurant that moves to a terrace in summer. *First Class/Luxury.*

Hotel Reutemann (Seepromenade) is No. 2 in the Seepromenade trio, with an inviting lobby-lounge, congenial bar, excellent harbor-view restaurant, old-fashioned service. *First Class.*

Hotel Seegarten (Seepromenade) is the third of the harbor-view trio, with the lowest tariffs, yet comfortable and attractive. There is also a full-facility restaurant. *Moderate.*

Hotel Helvetia (Seepromenade) is still another well-located house, overlooking the harbor, with 50 agreeable rooms—many with bath—and a terrace restaurant. *First Class.*

Hotel Goldenes Lamm (Schafgasse 3) occupies an ancient house on an ancient street that is identified by a swinging wrought-iron frame enclosing a gilded lamb. There are two score shining rooms, some with and some without baths, and an atmospheric restaurant. *Moderate.*

Hotel Bad Schachen (Bad Schachen) is a rambling good-looker of a resort spa in its own verdant park a few miles west of town. There are 140 comfortable and spacious rooms, most with baths; lakeside restaurant, pool, and sun terrace, cozy bar-lounge, and memorable vistas of Lake Constance and the Alps. But you have to want to be isolated from the action. Summer only. Member, Leading Hotels of the World, Relais et Châteaux. *Luxury.*

DAILY BREAD

Restaurants of Seepromenade hotels — Bayerischer Hof, Reutemann, Seegarten, Helvetia—are traditional, featuring German national and Bavarian specialties, with international favorites, too. Each has a view of the harbor. Tabs range *Moderate* through *Luxury.*

Goldenes Lamm (Schafgasse) is the restaurant of the Goldenes Lamm Hotel, and is nothing less than a national historic monument, with credentials dating its founding to the year 1422. Hearty favorites on the menu, good wine, copper lanterns. *First Class/Luxury.*

Weinstube Frey (Hauptstrasse 15) is a High Street favorite, and has been one as long as anyone in Lindau can remember. Wood beams and paneling, hearty fare. *Moderate.*

Zum Sünfzen (Hauptstrasse) is better eaten in than pronounced, at least by non-German-speakers. Big, welcoming, and *Moderate.*

Spielbank Restaurant (Oskar-Groll-Anlage 2) is the rather grand, rather pricey eatery of the away-from-the-center lake-view casino (see below), with both international and German dishes, glossy service, lake-and-Alps views from the tall windows; agreeable for a candlelit dinner. *Luxury.*

SOUND OF MUSIC

Stadttheater (Barfüsserplatz): Leave it to little Lindau to appreciate how old buildings can be put to contemporary uses. Its city fathers took a fourteenth-century Gothic church that the Franciscans vacated during the Reformation, restored it, and transformed it into a handsome 800-seat theater, with an additional concert hall occupying what had been the choir. Take in a performance if you can.

Harbor concerts, by the municipal orchestra, take place nightly except Monday on Seepromenade, against a backdrop of lake, lighthouse, and Bavarian Lion, May through September.

AFTER DARK

Spielbank (Oskar-Groll-Anlage 2) is the Lindau Casino, a contemporary pavilion that allows for an evening of roulette and blackjack on the shores of Lake Constance, with a recommended restaurant in connection (see above).

INCIDENTAL INTELLIGENCE

Train and bus service, of course. But you may arrive or depart by Lake Constance steamers, as well. Service is by modern vessels operated by the German, Austrian, and Swiss national railroads to lake ports of the three neighbor nations, including Germany's Konstanz and its satellites, Mainau Island and Meersburg. In summer, sightseeing boats, some stopping at the prettier ports, are regularly scheduled. Further information: Verkehrsamt Lindau—the city tourist bureau—is at the Hauptbahnhof.

25

Lübeck

Cool, Correct—
and Cultured

BACKGROUND BRIEFING

A thousand years is a lusty old age for a city. Especially one that has been destroyed several times in that span. Lübeck—way north near where West Germany shares a frontier with both Denmark and East Germany—has always bounced back. Its first razings were early on in its history; its most recent devastation was, if not a razing, heavy destruction from World War II bombs. Visit Lübeck today, as a newcomer, and you wouldn't know it. Its core—on a Manhattan-type of island, between the Trave and Wakenitz rivers and canals leading from them—is Instant Middle Ages, one of the greatest of northern-European evocations of that period.

One senses immediately upon arrival that Lübeck was rich—from the look of the elegant patrician palaces, dazzlingly beautiful churches, gabled merchant houses reflecting the solidity of their successful bourgeois residents. And from the ambience: Lübeckers are mostly cool, correct, and distant with visitors. Their behavior is perhaps most charitably summed up as a residue of the powerful medieval centuries when this city was the leader of a confederation of northern ports called the Hanseatic League, and was itself governed by a wealthy merchant aristocracy, whose rise and fall native son Thomas Mann chronicled at length in the novel *Buddenbrooks.*

Lighthearted Lübeck is not. Nor is it conveniently located in the center of tourist territory. This is a destination for the traveler for whom the beauty of architecture and art of past centuries—in a remarkably cohesive environment—transcends the attitude of a host populace not always at ease with guests.

ON SCENE

Lay of the Land: Historic Lübeck is encircled by water. Various bodies with various names are linked by bridges with the mainland, on which the Hauptbahnhof is situated—at its western edge. A pair of principal thoroughfares—parallel with each other—cut across the heart of town, north to south: Breitestrasse and Königstrasse. The principal square, Marktplatz, is in the center of things. Distance from the Hauptbahnhof to Marktplatz is a bit long for a walk. But once gained, the center is walkable. Indeed, one is hard put to come upon a street without architectural impact—baroque houses on Grosse Petersgrube, Renaissance gabled houses on Wahmstrasse, charming artists' houses on Hundestrasse, flying-buttress-like constructions arching over narrow Siebentequerstrasse. And still-in-use homes for the aged—built around flowered courtyards that date back centuries—on Glockengiesserstrasse, Dr. Julius-Leber-Strasse, and Wahmstrasse—to name a trio.

There are a pair of landmark gates out of fairy tales: Holstentor, twin-towered and formidable, on the west edge of town between the Hauptbahnhof and Marktplatz, and Burgtor, a medieval mini-skyscraper guarding the Old Town's northern flank.

Rathaus (Marktplatz): Lübeck's Town Hall reflects its seven centuries. It is the old city at its most spectacular: a mix of Gothic, Renaissance, and baroque united by street-level galleries fringing Marktplatz. Enter to see portraits of early city luminaries in the foyer and the baroque council chamber; and note the splendid covered staircase—a Renaissance gem—without.

Marienkirche is Marktplatz's other major monument. Its slim twin steeples—each punctuated by five-vertical rows of Gothic windows—are no less striking than its elongated flying buttresses. Treasures await within—fan-vaulting overhead, a 1959 crucifix that blends beautifully with the main altar, restored frescoes of old over the choir, gilded medieval altars in side chapels and, most exciting, in this mammoth interior, the sense of majestic scale.

Dom (Mühlendamm): Lübeck's cathedral, oddly enough not centrally located like Marienkirche, is not unlike that church. It is about the same age, and its silhouette—thanks to a pair of slender steeples—is similar. There has been a fine post-World War II restoration and one wants especially to note the crucifix above the main altar. Unlike the contemporary cross in Marienkirche, the *Dom's* is fifteenth century and one of the city's single most important art works.

Jacobikirche (Koberg) is still another Gothic masterwork, single-tower, capacious, with a fifteenth-century carved-stone altar in the south chapel—Brömbse—named for the family whose members it depicts. The high altar is striking.

Heiligen-Geist-Hospital (Koberg), a neighbor of Jacobikirche, has a façade like no other in town: low-slung Gothic, with five pinnacle-like spires distinguishing it. Special draw within is a series of perfectly beautiful fourteenth-century frescoes covering the walls of the chapel, just inside the front entrance.

Katharinenskirche (Königstrasse) is the fourth of the quartet of major Gothic churches. The exceptionally high windows of its nave and apse are almost more beautiful from without than from the interior. The rood screen is surmounted by a dramatic giant cross.

St. Annen Museum (St. Annen Strasse 13) went up in the early sixteenth century as a convent, but before it became a museum it was a workhouse and a prison. There are newer additions, but the vaulted Gothic halls and cloister house the core of the collection: Gothic church altars, medieval sculptures, paintings, other souvenirs of old Lübeck—including toys; and an exceptional series of period Lübeck rooms, with furniture and accessories representing a succession of epochs, medieval through the distinctive German Biedermeier of the earlier nineteenth-century decades.

SETTLING IN

Hotel Lysia (Beim Holstentor) is, as its address indicates, a neighbor of the landmark gate (earlier described) and a nice walk from the heart of town. It's modern, with some 160 attractive rooms and suites and an inviting lobby; pair of pubs, one mainly for drinking, the other with dancing; and a commendable restaurant. *First Class.*

Hotel Kaiserhof (Kronsforderallee 13) is a onetime private villa—turn of the century—that has been transformed into a cozy, comfortable hotel, with no-two-alike rooms and suites, some of them extra large; pleasant lounges; and although there is no proper restaurant—only breakfast is served—a well-equipped sauna compensates. Location is in a residential quarter away from the center. *First Class.*

Hotel Stadtwache (Mühlenbrücke) is a small, older house that has the advantage of a heart-of-town location and a restaurant whose fare is part German, part Chinese—not the most usual of combinations. So-so. *Moderate.*

DAILY BREAD

Das Lübecker Haus (Kolk 3) combines atmosphere and ambience with solid fare, good wine, and—not to be taken lightly in Lübeck—friendly service. The house is Renaissance and the restaurants' furnishings—beneath a broad-beamed ceiling—are mostly antique, too. *Moderate.*

Stadtrestaurant (Hauptbahnhof): Don't let the railroad station address throw you. The restaurant has its own entrance, and it's up a flight. This is one of Lübeck's best traditional-style eateries, with a heavy local following. There are four good-value, set-price meals each day, and a top-rank à la carte—schnitzels through steaks. *Moderate* to *Luxury.*

Café Belle Étage (Hauptbahnhof) is a pretty konditorei—for coffee and delicious baked-on-premises cakes, as well as for ice-cream specialties and snacks. Adjacent to the Stadt restaurant, which operates it. *Moderate.*

Haus der Schiffergesellschaft (Breitestrasse 2) is a sixteenth-century house with the setting at least as beautiful as the food is good. Traditional specialties. The pork stew is tasty. A good wine list. *First Class/Luxury.*

Ratskeller (Rathaus, Marktplatz) is a good bet in Lübeck, as are Town Hall restaurants generally, throughout Germany. The lure is an attractive setting, professional service, solid fare, and the prices: *Moderate.*

I. G. Niederegger (Breitestrasse 89) is at once a retail shop selling the world-famed Niederegger marzipan candies (reputed to have been created by this Lübeck firm's founder in 1806 and which are sold all over Germany and abroad) and a café-konditorei that is a congregating place for locals and visitors alike. The cakes are as good as Niederegger's almond-based marzipan. *Moderate.*

Café Junge (Breitestrasse 27) is still another Lübeck institution—a konditorei for baked goods, coffee, other sustenance. *Moderate.*

Das Schabbelhaus (Mengstrasse 48) is the most celebrated of the town's restaurants in antique houses. There is no denying its good looks, or, for that matter, its good food; the grilled filet of sole is masterful. But success, coupled with the Lübeck propensity toward gruffness of manner with strangers, seem to have taken its toll. Chilly. *Luxury.*

SOUND OF MUSIC

Stadttheater: Lübeck's turn-of-century opera house is home not only to opera but to ballet and musical comedy as well.

Church Concerts: The city's beautiful Gothic churches, which you will have visited, are often put to good use as settings for concerts of classical music.

AFTER DARK

The Casino, in the neighboring seaside resort town of Travemünde—subject of a chapter of its own—offers roulette and blackjack, not to mention its own *boîte.*

INCIDENTAL INTELLIGENCE

Travemünde, northern Germany's premier seaside resort, is Lübeck's next-door neighbor. I mention it at this point because Lübeck visitors might want to stay in its hotels (they are bigger and more luxurious), play at its casino, or, for that matter, arrive at or depart from Travemünde by ship; there is scheduled Baltic Sea service to and from all of the Scandinavian countries. *Further information:* Lübeck Touristbüro—the town tourist office—is at Rathaushof 14.

26

Mad Ludwig's Bavarian Castles

Neuschwanstein
Herrenchiemsee
Linderhof

BACKGROUND BRIEFING

There were to have been four, possibly five: the idea was a ring of romantic castles in the Bavarian Alps—places to which deranged King Ludwig II could retreat from his capital at Munich, either alone (his usual preference) or, upon occasion, with special friends. Only three castles were built before 1886, when Ludwig was found mysteriously drowned at the age of forty. But what a trio they are! And how ironic that they have become a major magnet for visitors—something their creator-builder never intended.

Hundreds of thousands journey into the Bavarian wilderness each year to trek through what Ludwig had termed his "holy places." "They should not be seen by the mob," he said, according to biographer Wilfred Blunt (*The Dream King: Ludwig II of Bavaria,* Viking Press 1970), "because that would 'desecrate and defile' them."

Ludwig—who obsessively supervised the architectural and interior design of the castles to the minutest detail—came by his bent for building naturally enough. His family, the Wittelsbachs, had ruled Bavaria—as dukes, electors, and later kings—from the twelfth century. Both Ludwig II's father, Maximilian II, and his grandfather, Ludwig I, were patrons of the arts. Papa

Max, when Ludwig was a boy, was interested enough in Germany's distant Gothic past to purchase a former Alpine palace—Hohenschwangau—and refurbish it in the mock-Gothic fashion of the early nineteenth century. It was here that Ludwig spent enough of his childhood to become obsessed by the past.

As he grew up, his Gothic tastes attracted him to the operas of Richard Wagner and eventually to Wagner himself, to whom he became almost irrationally devoted—as their published correspondence of many years would seem to make abundantly clear. Endowed with a creative, albeit damaged, mind, young Ludwig began his reign with promise. Before long, though, his interest in politics and government diminished in favor of the building program that was to consume virtually all of his attention—except for occasional flirtations with young men, mostly servants and soldiers—and a great deal of money.

As expenditures mounted, Ludwig's behavior became increasingly erratic. Unlike the long withdrawal at Windsor Castle of widowed Queen Victoria, who never neglected her role as constitutional monarch, Ludwig's actions became increasingly unacceptable to the Bavarian government.

Eventually the government appealed—successfully—to the king's Uncle Luitpold, who agreed to act as regent after Ludwig's withdrawal from the throne by reason of insanity. A medical commission bent on proving his insanity incarcerated the king in Schloss Berg, a lakeside country castle, under the care of a physician-observer named Bernhard von Gudden. On Sunday, June 13, 1886, when the king and the doctor had not returned from an afternoon walk, a search party was organized. Their drowned bodies were taken from Lake Starnberg late that night. The mystery of the two deaths still has not been solved.

But what of Ludwig's legacy? Long regarded as wild excesses, or a demented man's fantasies, the three palaces, now that they have stood nearly a century, have come to be recognized by art historians and critics as remarkably successful—and original—interpretations of the architectural and interior-design styles of earlier centuries. Ludwig, who supervised his architects, designers, and artisans meticulously, is now sharing posthumous credit with them for the castle trio. In each case his choice of setting—an isolated island on an Alpine lake for Herrenchiemsee, a peaceful valley for the intimacy of Lindenhof, a rocky crag for bold Neuschwanstein—has won increasing approbation.

And so has the artisanship that went into the design of the palaces and their furnishings. The Disney people have unabashedly based the trademark castle of their amusement parks on Neuschwanstein. And sketches, blueprints, and drawings of all three castles and their contents—along with some of the objects themselves—were the subject of a 1979 traveling show that had runs at such prestigious museums of the decorative arts as London's Victoria and Albert and New York's Cooper-Hewitt.

Access: Neuschwanstein/Hohenschwangau and Linderhof are best reached by means of bus-tours out of Munich and Garmisch-Partenkirchen, while Herrenchiemsee is closer to Berchtesgaden, with which it combines admirably.

NEUSCHWANSTEIN—most visited of the trio, especially by North Americans who know of it from adaptations at California's Disneyland and Florida's Disney World—is some 70 miles southwest of Munich, half that distance from Garmisch-Partenkirchen. It is a next-door neighbor to Hohenschwangau—not one of Ludwig's castles, but rather an ancient one restored by his father. Ludwig spent much of his childhood at Hohenschwangau, and it was there he met, as an adult, with his adored Wagner, the themes of whose operas are the inspiration for the decor of Neuschwanstein.

Ideally, one visits both castles in a single day, most conveniently on a commerical bus excursion out of Munich or Garmisch. (Musical note: There are concerts in the Sänger-Saal of Neuschwanstein during September.) The nearest town for rail arrivals is Füssen, just a couple of miles—an easy taxi ride—from the neighboring castles. Neuschwanstein straddles its own crag of a mountain. You may walk up, but it's a half-hour trek. Consider the alternatives: regularly departing buses and amusing, albeit slower, journeys in horse-drawn carriages. The castle is a Ludwigian variation on a Romanesque theme—more vertical than horizontal, affording spectacular views of a pair of Alpine lakes and a cluster of snowy peaks. Interiors, with all the subtlety of a sledgehammer, were the work of designers of theatrical sets, not castle-residences for real-life people. And they look it.

One admires the beautiful workmanship and inventiveness. The galleried, throneless throne room and the imposing Sänger-Saal—both more Byzantine than Romanesque—are the showpieces. Wagner connections are to be found throughout—murals of scenes from *Parsifal* in the Sänger-Saal, *Tannhäuser* in the study, *Lohengrin, Tristan und Isolde,* and *Siegfried* in the living room; more *Parsifal* in the dining room (with its tiny table big enough only for solitary meals for the king himself); and more *Tristan* in the monarch's bedroom. My favorite spot is the throne room's arched balcony—for vistas of two lakes, Alpsee and Schwansee, framing Hohenschwangau, with the Thannheim chain of Alps as a backdrop.

HOHENSCHWANGAU, with its boxy façade and crenellated towers, is more orthodox than any of Ludwig's castles. It goes back to the twelfth century, although by the time Ludwig's papa, Maximilian II, bought it, it had known considerably better days. Restoration was along Victorian Gothic lines, and the best that can be said of the interiors is that they're homey-folksy; you know people lived there, if not in style, certainly in comfort. The room with the most interest—called Hohenstaufen, after an early dynasty—is where Wagner played his works on the piano for host Ludwig. The quarters—salon, bedrooms, and dressing room of Ludwig's anti-intellectual, not very imaginative Prussian mother, Queen Marie—are all to be seen, and the Hall of Heroes comes closest to foretelling the fantasies of Neuschwanstein.

HERRENCHIEMSEE is something else again: It is a testament to Ludwig's reaction to a pilgrimage to Versailles, the home of the French Bourbon monarchs—Louis XIV, XV, and XVI—and the concept of absolute monarchy, to which he was devoted. This castle is in its own formal garden on an island in the lake called Chiemsee. The baroque façade of Versailles is very much in evidence. So are a Hall of Mirrors even more sumptuous than the French original, and an entrance hall with a resplendent stairway. Decoration throughout—in the royal study, reception and dining salons, and state bedroom—is rococo with a vengeance, easily twice as intricate as French rococo or the less restrained

German and Italian variations of the eighteenth century. And by no means without novelty—take, for example, an entire fireplace of Meissen porcelain in the Hall of Mirrors.

LINDERHOF: If Neuschanwanstein is Ludwig's most original castle and Herrenchiemsee his most derivative, Linderhof is the most charming. Its setting is low-key and lovely. Lying between a reflecting pool with a geyser-like fountain and the green slopes of a gentle mountain, this is the smallest by far of the trio, a baroque fantasy from without, rococo—and then some—in a series of opulent chambers within. The ceremonial state bedroom, similar to that of Herrenchiemsee with its canopied, rail-enclosed bed, is a study in dark-blue velvet and gold leaf, with a similar canopy arrangement over the king's desk in his study; tapestried walls in one salon, red-brocade-and-gilt-framed portraits in another: and a set of inventive outbuildings reflecting still other aspects of Ludwig's taste. These include a fantastic simulation of Capri's Blue Grotto with a regal rowboat in the shape of a cockleshell, and a Moorish pavilion with a fanciful—and quite brilliant—peacock throne.

27

Mainz

The Legacy of Gutenberg

BACKGROUND BRIEFING

Little enough known in the New World that its name is often mispronounced (correctly, it comes out *Myntz*), Mainz has a rich, proud, and lengthy past, precious few manifestations of which remain today.

Still, this is a city worth at least a nodding acquaintance. Strategically situated—where the Rhine meets the mouth of the Main—it was an outgrowth of a Roman camp, *Maguntiacum,* which soldiers set up a century before Christ, and from which the German name of the city probably evolved. Exciting things began to happen in the eighth century when Mainz-based St. Boniface became the first German archbishop. His successors, with that famous name behind them, ruled politically as well as spiritually, while acquiring additional domains in the region, which they controlled as princes—and later electors—of the Holy Roman Empire. As time went by, they gained precedence over their fellow electors, and before long it was they who actually crowned the German kings.

And their domain—with considerable help from the city's ancient and honorable Jewish community—became rich both commercially and culturally. (Thanks to native son Johannes

Gutenberg, who invented movable type in the fifteenth century, it was the first seat of the printing industry in Europe.)

The rule of the archbishops ended with the victories of Napoleon in the early nineteenth century, and Mainz became just another German town. Something like 80 percent of the city was destroyed during World War II, after which Mainz became capital of the *Land,* or state, called Rhineland-Palatinate. (Oddly enough, its neighbor city, Wiesbaden, a bridge ride across the Rhine, is capital of still another Land—Hesse.)

The post-war decades have seen considerable rebuilding and restoration, which has not been as aesthetically successful as in so many other German cities. A pity, this. Given its background and location, Mainz should be considerably more attractive and appealing. It is utterly lacking in the sophistication of across-the-river Wiesbaden, and it does not compensate with any substantial cultural or intrinsic historic excitement.

ON SCENE

Lay of the Land: The only interesting quarter is the part of town nearest the Rhine, centering about Marktplatz on one side and the towering cathedral and Liebfrauenplatz on the other. The smaller streets and squares hereabouts—Augustinerstrasse, Korbgasse, Fledergasschen, Höfchen, Gutenbergplatz—are the core of what remains of old Mainz, and agreeable to inspect. Also close by—going toward the Rhine—is a new but attractive district embracing Rheingoldhalle, for conventions and concerts, the adjacent Hotel Hilton International Mainz, and the unusual modern Rathaus.

The hitch is that this region is a considerable hike—through a succession of streets that do not flow into one another as in so many German cities—from the Hauptbahnhof, where many visitors arrive. And, moreover, it is the Hauptbahnhof area where you will find most of the hotels. With the exception of the Hotel Hilton International Mainz—the city's sole slice of sophistication—and its major competitor, the worthy Mainzerhof Hotel, there are no places to stay in Mainz's only interesting quarter. I suggest that visitors who do not put up at the Hilton or the Mainzerhof might want to headquarter across the river in

Wiesbaden. Or, take in Mainz on a one-day excursion from a hotel headquarters in the nearby metropolis, Frankfurt.

The Dom (Marktplatz) or cathedral, except for its cloister, major chapel, and musem, is at its best—by far—from without: a Romanesque (tenth century) and neo-Romanesque-with-baroque (nineteenth century) assortment of spires and turrets and towers that, for all of its brownstone sobriety, makes for a splendid urban exterior. Within, the going is heavy. When one considers this church's age, size, and scattered pieces of art, it leaves at least one visitor more cold than moved. A series of dreadful late-nineteenth century frescoes above the arches on either side of the nave are enough to cancel out much of the ancient architectural appeal of the interior. The twelfth-century Gottard chapel is Romanesque that excites, however; the later Gothic cloister is a joy, too.

The Dom Museum (Marktplatz), approached through the cathedral cloister, keeps its own hours, and charges admission, to which it is well entitled. For it is by far the best show in town: several vaulted floors brimming with extraordinarily beautiful sacred art. There are pages from medieval illuminated manuscripts; groups of thirteenth-century churchgoers immortalized, warmly and humorously, in sculpted stone; tapestries and tombs, Madonnas and crucifixes, vestments and portraits. Do take in the lot.

Rathaus (Rathausplatz): Their old city hall destroyed by World War II bombs, the city fathers acted imaginatively in their plans for a replacement. Ignoring the architects of their own country—of which there are many in the top rank—they crossed their northern frontier to Denmark and engaged that kingdom's preeminent architect-designer, the late Arne Jacobsen, to create a *Rathaus* for them. Critics complain now that, though still quite new, it is already too small, and, moreover, that its grilled windows give it the look of a jail. But the *Rathaus* is, withal, a daring departure from the norm, and refreshingly devoid of the ponderous pretensions that typify so much official architecture. Step inside, ask to see the bright council chamber (you'll recognize Jacobsen's now-classic chairs), and take a ride in the open-shafted copper elevators to the rooftop observation deck.

The Gutenberg Museum (Liebfrauenplatz) should be better than it is, given its location in Gutenberg's own town. It is large and imposing, but it has the air of a classroom, as if the intent were to teach the kids a lesson rather than excite its visitors—adults as well as youngsters—with the wonder of movable type. Still, one wants to see the Gutenberg Bible (1455) in its vault and peer at some of the ravishingly beautiful hand-illuminated Bibles that preceded it. There are, as well, a visual history of the book and its graphic history, and a range of presses and other tools of the printer's art. (Along with the Dom Museum, the Gutenberg is the only other one to bother with; the other museums—Mittelrheinisches and Römisch-Germanisches—are largely bores.)

SETTLING IN

Hotel Hilton International Mainz (Rheinufer Halleplatz) is Mainz at its most enjoyable. Smallish for Hilton International (there are 240 attractive rooms and suites), it straddles the Rhine, with the earlier-described Rheingoldhalle—for congresses and concerts—next door, and the historic district a four- or five-minute stroll away. Aim for a riverview room; it's fun to watch the traffic from your windows. And this is the only hotel in town from which you can do so. Cocktail lounge, kicky disco, pair of restaurants, one of which is commented on in a later paragraph. *Luxury.*

Hotel Mainzer Hof (Kaiserstrasse 98) is smallish—there are 75 pleasant rooms and suites distinguished by oversized baths—but well located near the heart of town, and absolutely full-facility, with bar-lounge and rooftop restaurant worthy of later comment. *First Class.*

Hotel Hammer (Bahnhofplatz 6) is one of several hotels opposite the station and the only one that I can recommend. It's modern, plain, spotless, with comfortable enough rooms (they tend to be small), all 35 of which have private baths. Breakfast only. *Moderate.*

Hotel Grünewald (Frauenlobstrasse 14) is not opposite the station but a short walk from it. It's low-slung modern, with no claim to good looks. But the 45 functional rooms are spanking clean and all have private baths. Breakfast only. *Moderate.*

Hotel Europa (Kaiserstrasse 7) is not opposite the station, but close by. Full-facility and occupying a modern building, it should be infinitely better operated, but all I can recommend is the comfort of the bedrooms and their baths. Of the scores upon scores of hotels in Germany which I have lived in, dined in, drunk in, or thoroughly inspected, this, for me, is one of the most dismal in terms of service. *First Class.*

DAILY BREAD

Rhein Grill (Hotel Hilton International Mainz, Rheinufer Halleplatz) is quite the loveliest dining experience in town. A handsome, high-ceilinged room, with great picture windows looking on to the river, and a decor emulating the dining room of an exceptionally sleek river steamer. The fare is extraordinary—a platter of smoked salmon, trout and eels; cream of leek soup: U.S.-imported sirloin, roast loin of pork with a mustard sauce, or grilled fish, or game; one of Germany's most extravagant dessert wagons. And a wine list that does it all justice. Skilled service, too. *Luxury.*

Panorama Restaurant (Hotel Mainzer Hof, Kaiserstrasse 98): You're way up on the roof, the better for views of town and of the river with its chug-chug traffic. Look is contemporary, menu and service traditional German. Try the shrimp salad, any of the soups, and a house specialty: wild boar sauerbraten, served with light-as-a-feather dumplings. Desserts and wines of quality. *Luxury.*

Stadtparkrestaurant an der Favorite (Karl-Weiser-Strasse 1) straddles the peak of what is now a city park, formerly a royal eighteenth-century estate called Der Favorite. (It's pictured on the menu.) This is a fair taxi ride from town, but the lures are twofold: a smashing vista of Mainz and Wiesbaden and of the Rhine and Main rivers; and dependable fare—foreign as well as native—professionally served in a period setting. There are half a dozen daily full-course lunches or dinners. And an elaborate à la carte. *First Class/Luxury.*

Turin (Schottstrasse) is an Italian restaurant worth knowing about—Italian-operated—with dependable pasta and veal specialties. Nothing fancy. *Moderate.*

Zum Kirchgarten (Kirchgartenplatz) occupies a pleasing baroque house in the shadow of the cathedral, and surprises one with its lively Art Nouveau interior. Go for German specialties at lunch or dinner, or afternoon *Kuchen* and coffee. *Moderate/First Class.*

Dom Café-Konditorei (Marktplatz) has been serving coffee and cake to locals and their guests since 1792. Strategically situated for crowd-watching. *Moderate.*

Haus des Deutschen Weines (Gutenbergplatz 3) is one you may have heard of, as a result of its presumed function—to spur the sale and popularity of German wines. Operated by the wine-producers' promotion board, it has not so much as a flyer or folder, not to mention menu or wine card, in any language save German. And the disagreeable waitresses are reluctant to let you see even these. Still, you may want to take your choice of wines to sample by the glass; meals are nourishing if unmemorable. *Moderate.*

SOUND OF MUSIC

First see *Sound of Music* in the chapter on Wiesbaden, a 15-minute train ride across the Rhine from Mainz's Hauptbahnhof, and with top-rank opera and concerts in sumptuous settings. The *What's On* guide available from hotel concierges is in German only, but lists attractions in both cities. If there's nothing going on in Wiesbaden, consider Mainz's.

Stadttheater (Gutenbergplatz)—a modern setting for the city's own opera and ballet troupes, and its excellent symphony orchestra.

INCIDENTAL INTELLIGENCE

Verkehrsverein Mainz—the city tourist office—is at Bahnhofplatz 2, opposite the station.

28

Marburg

Mini-Medieval Marvel

BACKGROUND BRIEFING

A Zugspitze of a medieval town with modern appendages beyond its center: that's Marburg. The allusion to Germany's highest Alpine peak is not just exaggeration. The core of this smallish west-central city literally climbs a mountain. And its peak is surmounted, in fairy-tale tradition, with a honey of a nine-century-old castle.

What makes Marburg special are the souvenirs of its longevity—all of which are highly visible in an ascending route between the Bahnhof and top-of-town *Schloss*.

The town is as old as the thirteenth-century castle. It began as a Lahn River trading settlement, and as it grew during the late Middle Ages and the Renaissance it gained stature as a seat of the landgraves, or counts, of Hesse. In the sixteenth century the lofty castle saw Reformation figures debate the new Protestantism, with Zwingli on one side, Luther on the other; their unresolved deliberations are known to historians, rather grandly, as the Marburg Colloquy. Pre-Reformation centuries drew Catholic pilgrims to Marburg to pay their respects to Elizabeth, who had been the sainted daughter of a transplanted Hungarian princess who devoted the adult years of her short life to caring for the sick in a hospital adjacent to Marburg's castle.

Today the town is a curious mix of earnest students at its four-century-old university and farm folk from the countryside, in traditional dress. (They're seen in abundance on Saturday and Wednesday, at the market on Marktplatz.)

ON SCENE

Lay of the Land: The Bahnhof is adjacent to the Lahn River at the north end of town. From it, follow Bahnhofstrasse to a pair of landmark churches—Elisabethkirche and St. Michaelkirche—continuing on (always upward) via Pilgrimstein to Marktplatz and the Rathaus. The Schloss, or castle, is even higher up. You may hoof it or, if exhaustion has set in, make the ascent by taxi, allowing time for exploration on foot—en route either up or down—of the streets leading from Marktplatz that are lined with sixteenth-century half-timbered houses.

Elisabethkirche is Marburg's major treasure of art and architecture: a Gothic church—reputedly Germany's first in this style—of extraordinary grace and beauty. Protestant (like the town's university) since the Reformation, twin-spired, thirteenth-century St. Elizabeth's has retained mementos of its Catholic centuries. You'll see a statue and—what is more interesting—the tomb of St. Elizabeth, with a carved likeness of her lying in state with the cripples and beggars to whom she ministered. There is as well an exquisite shrine dedicated to the saint, of gilded copper, embedded with pearls and precious stones, that ranks with the shrines of Charlemagne in Aachen Cathedral and of the Three Magi in Cologne. A whole area is devoted to sarcophagi of the landgraves of Hesse, the earliest dating to the thirteenth century. And the church is the resting place of President Hindenburg, Hitler's predecessor.

Schloss: A symbol—along with St. Elizabeth's—of Marburg, the town's Schloss, or castle, is more attractive for its top-of-town view than for its architecture or interiors. Still, the handsomely vaulted Rittersaal, or Knight's Hall, is considered to be the largest such room in Germany. There is a Gothic chapel with thirteenth-century frescoes, and a mini-museum whose subject—of all things—is comparative religion.

Universitätsmuseum is the university-operated repository of Marburg art and artifacts through the centuries, the lot in a spick-and-span series of galleries whose contents look as if they were dusted hourly. The collection of medieval objects—carved-wood sculptures, stone fragments, paintings, furnishings—are beautiful. There are rooms furnished in the styles of bygone eras. Worth the slight detour from the historic core of town.

Rathaus: The gabled Gothic/Renaissance town hall is still in use after four centuries—and that includes its clock which, hour after hour these hundreds of years, has signaled the time by emulating the crow of the cock. The *Rathaus* is not the only star in the Marktplatz show. Another is a graceful fountain, surmounted by a likeness of St. George and the Dragon. And another is the adjacent Obermarkt, with clusters of half-timbered houses. Two Gothic churches—Marienkirche and Kugelkirche—are a short stroll westward.

Universitätskirche is a quietly handsome Gothic church, ideal for a pause in one's explorations. It's adjacent to a later, mock-Gothic University Hall with striking black-and-white stained-glass windows under lacy carved-wood frames, and murals—lining its four walls—that tell the story of St. Elizabeth's life.

SETTLING IN

Europäischer Hof (Elisabethstrasse 12) is the longtime premier hotel in a town not noted for hotels, primarily because so many of its visitors are day excursionists. It's updated, full-facility, with spacious rooms and baths, a restaurant, smiling service, and an enviable location just opposite Elisabethkirche. *First Class.*

Waldecker Hof (Bahnhofstrasse 23) is closer to the Bahnhof than to the Old Town, smaller and somewhat less elaborate than the Europäischer Hof, but full-facility. *Moderate.*

DAILY BREAD

Bückingsgarten (Landgraf-Phillip-Strasse 6) leads off in this restaurant grouping, not so much because of its fare (which is good, typically German) but because it's just where you may be at lunchtime—way atop the town at the *Schloss,* too tired to want to descend before a lunch pause. The schnitzels are tasty, and the views are sublime, especially from the warm-weather terrace. *First Class.*

Chez Claude (Am Markt 19) is a Marburg surprise: an honest-to-goodness French restaurant (the Gallic owner does the cooking). Setting is an atmospheric and ancient house, on whose red-and-white-checked tablecloths the *patron* serves prix fixe meals that, if not cheap, are delicious. Both French and German wines. *Luxury.*

Santa Lucia (Deutschhausstrasse 35) is the genuine Italian article—nicely sauced pasta, *al dente;* veal specialties, Italian wines. *First Class.*

Zur Sonne (Marktplatz 14): Traditional German fare in a traditional setting (the house is splendid) opposite the Rathaus. *Moderate/First Class.*

Café Vetter (Marktplatz) is for delicious cakes and coffee, snacks, casual lunches. *Moderate.*

INCIDENTAL INTELLIGENCE

A good day's excursion out of Frankfurt. Verkehrsamt Universitätsstadt Marburg—the city tourist office—is at Neue Kasseler Strasse 1, next to the Bahnhof.

29

Meersburg

A Renaissance Romance

BACKGROUND BRIEFING

A find. Meersburg is an enchanting souvenir of past centuries—medieval, Renaissance, baroque—that is almost 100 percent intact, and which has a Lake Constance shoreline setting that is no small bonus.

The beauty of Meersburg is that contemporary technology—electricity, telephones, and the like excepted—has spared its two-tier core. The population, still just a few thousand, has remained small. The ramparts and half-timbered houses, castles old and new, and steep, ancient streets—all remain to beguile visitors who enjoy instant evocation of a romantic past.

ON SCENE

Lay of the Land: Meersburg is an upstairs-downstairs town. Arrive on the car-carrying ferry from the neighboring lakeshore town of Konstanz and you're at the harbor of the Lower Town, whose Seestrasse is an eye-filling waterfront promenade, bordered by hotels, cafés, and restaurants. Oberstadt, the Upper Town, is a steep but short hike, with Marktplatz its handsome core. The gabled Rathaus, or Town Hall, and a skyscraper of a gate, Obertor, are its landmarks.

Take time for an Oberstadt stroll, concentrating on the streets leading from Marktplatz, especially Steigstrasse, with its half-timbered houses, and wending your way to Meersburg's castles, one "old," one "new."

Altes Schloss—the Old Castle—is indeed old: seventh century to be precise. The moated façade is out of a fairy tale, and the interior—more than a score of dusty rooms, none of them with any really outstanding feature—is quite as atmospheric. Take it in, though—walk an easy-to-follow route—and concentrate on the dungeons and an arms collection.

Barockschloss is what the locals call the newer of the two castles, a strikingly situated rococo dazzler, whose grand staircase and great hall you will want to see. Designer was the same Balthasar Neumann who created the Prince-Bishops' Residenz in Würzburg. This castle is used for summer concerts.

SETTLING IN

Hotel 3 Stuben (Winzergasse 1) is Meersburg at its most Old World: a honey of a half-timbered house in the center of the Oberstadt. All rooms—there are only 14 of them—have bath or shower; restaurant-bar. *First Class.*

Hotel Wilder Mann (Kugelwehrplatz 2) is a traditional house, in the heart of the Lower Town. There are a couple of restaurants and a café looking out on the water; summer dancing; many rooms with private baths. *First Class.*

Hotel zum Schiff (Kugelwehrplatz 1) is the across-the-platz neighbor of the Wilder Mann; about the same size and caliber and also with a terrace restaurant. *First Class.*

Hotel Löwen (Marktplatz 2) could not be more romantically sited. This is a small, ancient house, but all of its 15 rooms have bath or shower and the restaurant is cozy. *Moderate.*

Hotel Fischerhaus (Seefelder, a few miles from Meersburg) is a really handsome half-timbered inn, with 15 big rooms, swimming pool in the garden, top-rank restaurant, friendly management. Ideal if you have a car. *First Class.*

DAILY BREAD

Weinstube zum Becher (Höllgasse 4) occupies an aged Oberstadt building, is busy, buzzy, friendly, with run-of-the-mill fare, smilingly served. *Moderate.*

Rosengarten Restaurant (Hotel Wilder Mann, Kugelwehrplatz 2) is for convivial lakefront meals. *First Class.*

Löwen (Hotel Löwen, Marktplatz 2) is the dining room of an earlier-recommended Oberstadt hotel. *Moderate/First Class.*

INCIDENTAL INTELLIGENCE

Take Meersburg in, along with the Lake Constance towns of Konstanz and Lindau, each the subject of a chapter. *Further information:* Kur-und Verkehrsamt—the town tourist office—is at Schlossplatz 4.

30

Mittenwald

Alpine Stage-Set

BACKGROUND BRIEFING

A small-scale, poor-man's Garmisch-Partenkirchen? Not a bit. Though a near-neighbor of Garmisch, Mittenwald is Mittenwald: and that means stage set Bavarian Alps, old-fashioned, schmaltzy, amusing, very beautiful.

And with impressive credentials. It is smack on the site of a north-south trade route that dates to Roman times. A town for fully a thousand years, its golden period embraced the rich Renaissance, when commercial Italian city-states to the south quarreled so much over which would handle the profitable German traffic that Mittenwald won it by default.

With wealth came the splendid houses one still sees today. The baroque centuries witnessed a trade decline but, undaunted, Mittenwald picked up a new and rather unlikely industry—the making of violins. Those instruments, along with others in the string family—cellos, violas, zithers—remain a Mittenwald specialty. So is tourism, in every season.

ON SCENE

Lay of the Land: The beauty of Mittenwald is that it not only enjoys a sumptuous setting in a Shangri-la-like valley, but it's comfortably compact.

Arrive by train and you walk easily from the Bahnhof—just east of the center of town—along Bahnhofstrasse a few blocks west to Obermarktstrasse, the main street, with the principal church and the town museum. Look up as you walk. The snow-capped peaks enclosing the valley of Mittenwald are not to be ignored. Easiest to visit is 7,000-foot Karwendelgebirge, conveniently climbed by a cog railway. Other peaks are even higher: Wettersteingebirge, lower Arnspitze, and the most modest of the immediately neighboring mountains, Hoherkranzerberg—at an altitude of about 4,000 feet. There are lakes nearby; closest is Lautersee, with a respectable elevation of some 3,300 feet, and a hotel whose restaurant is an ideal spot for lunch. But first the town.

Katholische Kirche (Obermarktstrasse): Known to locals as "the church" (although there's another that's Protestant), it's a standout specimen of Bavarian rococo—dating to the eighteenth century—with a fresco-embellished steeple, and an equally rich interior.

Evangelische Kirche (Untermarkt): Mittenwald's Protestant church, an interesting contrast to its ebulliently decorated Catholic counterpart, is somber but eye-filling Gothic.

Geigenbau Museum (Obermarktstrasse) has as its principal display the history of Mittenwald's unique principal industry (after tourism)—violin-making. There's an actual studio reproduced. And there are additional exhibits depicting the town's past. Charming.

Staatliche Geigenbauschule (Partenkirchnerstrasse) is the municipal violin-making school. If what you've learned at the museum whets your appetite for more, inquire within!

House façades are at their handsomest on such streets as Obermarktstrasse, Ballenhausgasse, and Im Gries. Do allow time for a leisurely walk to have a look.

Karwendelgebirge is the easiest to ascend of the peaks fringing town. Go by cable car, at any time of year, for the exciting ride, the views from the restaurant-café at the summit, and—if you're a skier and it's winter—skiing on the slopes.

Lautersee, a close-to-town Alpine lake, is a nice excursion destination; there's regular bus service from town, and a hotel-restaurant on the shore. Make a day or half day of it.

Walking and hiking are the traditional Mittenwald diversions. There are a score of destinations—peaks, lakes, and valleys—for amateur walkers and professional mountaineers. The town tourist office has specifics.

SETTLING IN

Hotel Wiptelder (Reidkopfstrasse) is what might be styled Elaborate Bavarian, with 15 pleasant rooms, and an invariably reliable restaurant. *First Class.*

Hotel Post (Obermarkt 9), if not Mittenwald's most luxurious hotel, is one of its most central, situated in an old house with a gaily painted façade. Most rooms have private baths; atmospheric restaurant-bar. *Moderate/First Class.*

Gästehaus Franziska (Innsbruckerstrasse 24), though not heart-of-town, compensates with a smashing garden setting, smartly low-key lobby-lounge, sauna-gym, terrace for sunning. Breakfast only. *First Class.*

Hotel Wetterstein (Dekan-Karl-Platz 1), a block from Obermarktstrasse in the center, is probably the town's fullest facility hotel, with a superior restaurant-pub, a candlelit cellar bar, pool-sauna-gym facilities, and attractive public spaces. *First Class.*

Hotel Rieger (Dekan-Karl-Platz 28) is central and handsome. Many rooms have baths; restaurant-bar, pool. *Moderate.*

Hotel Mittenwalder Hof (Partenkirchnerstrasse 28) has a cozy chalet look, rooms mostly with private showers, convenient restaurant, and central situation. *Moderate.*

DAILY BREAD

Arnspitze (Innsbruckerstrasse 68) is traditional-style, and, though by no means grand, has a corking good kitchen. Order the veal steak. *First Class/Luxury.*

Bartholomäusstube (Hotel Wetterstein, Dekan-Karl-Platz) is the leading restaurant of a top-rank hotel. Bavarian specialties. *First Class.*

Hotel Post Restaurant (Obermarkt 9) is authentically Bavarian. Alpine ambience. *Moderate/First Class.*

Berggaststätte Karwendel (Karwendelgebirge) is the café-restaurant atop Karwendelgebirge; for a lunch or a snack, after you've taken the cable car up. *Moderate/First Class.*

Hotel Lautersee (Lautersee) is indicated for the midday meal in the course of an excursion to this idyllic lake near town. No charge for the view. *Moderate/First Class.*

INCIDENTAL INTELLIGENCE

Kurverwaltung und Verkehrsamt—the village's tourist office—is at Dammkarstrasse 3.

31

Munich/München

Bavaria's Queen,
Everybody's Favorite

BACKGROUND BRIEFING

It looks it.

Other German cities have known days of glory as royal capitals. None, today, though, comes anywhere near able to carry on as a great dowager. Neither Berlin, which had been capital of the last German Empire, nor Frankfurt, where Holy Roman Emperors were crowned. Smaller cities like Heidelberg, Würzburg and Bayreuth, indicate, through their castles, how their royals lived. The partially rebuilt core of East Germany's Dresden gives one an idea of how grand it must have been.

But Munich puts them all in a back seat. You know, from the moment you stroll its core—with neoclassic squares like Königsplatz, squares from the Middle Ages like Marienplatz, stately streets like Theatinerstrasse—that you are in a city of consequence, style, substance.

No other German city puts it all together quite like this one. No other German city has made quite so spectacular a comeback from the devastation of World War II.

Nor can any other be quite as sophisticated and at the same time as corny as this one. If Germany has an Everybody's Favorite City—leather-panted drinkers in the beer halls through to Wagner at the opera—this is it.

Not that the metropolis at the northern fringe of the German Alps has not had moments of shame as well as glory. But eight centuries had elapsed between its founding and Hitler's abortive Munich *Putsch* and the Munich Pact that preceded World War II.

Munich—München in German—is named for a settlement believed to have been established by medieval Benedictine monks (you'll see a monk in the municipal coat-of-arms) in a region inhabited by a Germanic tribe calling themselves *Baiwarii*—the earliest Bavarians.

The founding date, 1158, is when a Saxon duke razed a thriving village in the Munich neighborhood, and set up another where Munich now stands. Ere long, the founding noble—Heinrich the Lion—was toppled by a warring underling of Holy Roman Emperor Friedrich Barbarossa. His name was Wittelsbach—Otto Wittelsbach—and it's worth remembering. He was the first of a line of Wittelsbachs that extended from 1180 all the way to World War I. A dynasty, in other words, lasting seven centuries.

There were complications as the Wittelsbach clan split into two. The first (or older) group, as dukes of Bavaria, held sway over the Rhenish Palatinate to the west, and the western areas of Bavaria. The other branch—the so-called younger Wittelsbachs—received territory to the east. There was a period—the Wittelsbachs' golden age—when the elder branch ruled a vast realm embracing much of Germany, north and south, as well as the Low Countries.

As the Middle Ages extended into the Renaissance, the two branches made religious allegiances—the Bavarians, Catholic; the Palatinate branch, Protestant. Titles changed, too, as dukes became electors and finally—in the early nineteenth century—kings. The year was 1806 when both branches of the powerful clan were at last reunited with the ascension of King Maximilian I.

His successors also all had strong Munich identification. Ludwig I worked at making Munich a handsome capital and became wise in the ways of the arts, but was forced to abdicate as a result of his liaison with Irish adventuress Lola Montez. Maximilian II was the father of mentally ill Ludwig II, best known of the dynasty as a consequence of his odd adoration of the composer Wagner and his trio of extravagant fantasy-castles in the countryside. (I capsulize his tragic life and death in the chapter entitled "Mad Ludwig's Castles.")

Ludwig II would have been succeeded by a brother Otto, but that young man's insanity made him unfit to reign. So an uncle—Luitpold—who had taken over as regent before Ludwig died, continued in Otto's place, and is rarely given the credit he deserves for building an increasingly grand and culture-rich Munich. (Not only broad Prinzregentstrasse, but the current Rathaus, and the quarters of museums like the Bavarian National and German National, were projects of Prince Regent Luitpold's reign, which coincided with Munich's becoming a magnet for such artists as Klee, Richard Strauss, and Thomas Mann.) The last king was Luitpold's son, Ludwig III, who acceded at the advanced age of sixty-seven, and at the wrong time: 1913. He was ousted as a consequence of Bavaria's post-World War I revolution, first fleeing to Austria, later dying in Hungary.

By the time poor Ludwig III went to his exile in Austria, Austrian-born Adolf Hitler had taken up residence in Munich. The period after World War I was one of complete chaos for the city, a result of which was the 1923 attempt—abortive but not without significance—by Hitler to take over the Bavarian government according to the principles of the Nazi party, that he had proclaimed earlier in a beer hall.

Hitler did not let the 1923 failure stop him. Munich remained his party's seat, and in 1933 he took control of the German government. It is to Munich's credit that it strongly opposed the Nazis; Catholic Archbishop Michael Cardinal Faulhaber spoke out bravely against the new regime from the pulpit of Frauenkirche, Munich's twin-onion-domed cathedral. But in 1938 the city once again figured in world history when—after Hitler announced plans to take over the ethnic German Sudetenland of Czechoslovakia—he was given permission to do so. The infamous Munich Pact was signed by Britain's umbrella-toting Prime Minister Neville Chamberlain, along with France's Daladier and Italy's Mussolini; it became the symbol of the Allies' attitude of appeasement, and paved the way for the commencement, only a year later, of World War II.

Not surprisingly, this of all German cities suffered dreadfully from Allied bombings during World War II. Destruction and mass deaths notwithstanding, no city in Germany has restored itself with more vigor—economically, industrially, commerically, politically (as capital of Germany's biggest *Land,* or state—Bavaria), and artistically. Munich's traditional concern for aesthetics, the fine and performing arts, the good life, all reflect themselves in this vital, inviting, extraordinarily good-looking capital.

ON SCENE

Lay of the Land: Munich is big. Germany's largest city after Berlin and Hamburg, it extends over a considerable area. And there are attractive destinations beyond the center, which is, by and large, walkable. But there are well-designed subway (U-Bahn) and surface-train (S-Bahn) systems. The Hauptbahnhof is central, at the west edge of downtown, facing the square named for it, Bahnhofplatz. Schützenstrasse leads from it to two principal landmark squares, one of which—confusing to newcomers—goes by two names: the real one, Karlsplatz, and the nickname, Stachüs. This square is at once the terminus of most streetcar routes and of the western tip of a beflowered and fountained pedestrians-only thoroughfare—about a mile and a half long—that runs all the way east to the other principal square, Marienplatz. The pedestrians' route is actually two contiguous streets, Neuhauserstrasse, on the western end, and Kaufingerstrasse, on the east.

Marienplatz has a lot going for it. Try and make it there for the daily glockenspiel performance—the time is 11 A.M.—from the tower of the massive and beautifully detailed mock-Gothic Neues Rathaus, the so-called new (since the end of the last century) Town Hall. From Marienplatz, one is close to a pair of additional landmarks, Frauenkirche, the Gothic cathedral, whose matching onion domes are Munich's trademark, and Peterskirche, a millennium old.

The not-to-be-missed open-air food stalls of the Viktualienmarkt are due south of Peterskirche. A palace-church—Munich's greatest rococo place of worship, called Asam after the brother architects—is in this area. Other landmarks are to

Marienplatz's north. Follow Dienerstrasse—which becomes Residenzstrasse after a couple of blocks—north a bit and you've arrived at Max-Joseph-Platz, bordered by the colonnaded neoclassic National Theater (the opera house) and the Residenz (former royal palace, which houses the Cuvilliés Theater within its complex).

Walk west a block from Max-Joseph-Platz to the street running perpendicular, Theatinerstrasse, important because it is a pedestrian-mall with perhaps the smartest shops in town, and also because it leads to a not-to-be-missed church—Theatinerkirche. Nearby streets—Maximilian, Pacelli, Maffei, and Briennerstrasse—are worth noting because of their fine shops. (Follow Maximilanstrasse to its eastern tip and you're at the mock-Tudor Maximilaneum—Bavaria's two-house Parliament.) You will have heard about the Platzl quarter. It lies between Marienplatz and the National Theater, and the Hofbräuhaus beer hall and adjacent Platzl cabaret are its monuments.

The key museums—in one of the world's important museum cities—lie mostly northwest of the center. You might want to consider taking in the Alte Pinakothek and as many of this group as you've time for on the same day: the Lenbachaus, Glyptothek, and Antikensammlungen are right there; these last fringe the neoclassic Propyläen—a monument of Königsplatz. Schwabing, the student quarter, is a subway hop directly north of downtown, to Leopoldstrasse, its café-lined main street. Munich's big city park, Englischergarten, is due east of Schwabing, while the Olympic complex—site of the tragic 1972 games—is to Schwabing's northwest. Schloss Nymphenburg, one of the major European palaces is just beyond.

I've saved for last the site of what is Munich's—if not all Germany's—best-known annual event, *Oktoberfest:* the area locally known as Theresienwiese, which translates as Oktoberfest Grounds, southwest of the Hauptbahnhof, just below Schwanthalerstrasse. Oktoberfest is an every-October binge lasting just over a fortnight, embracing beer (more than one million gallons are consumed); such edibles as ham hocks, barbecued chicken, and grilled sausages; amusements (roller coaster, merry-go-rounds, auto scooters); and oom-pah music. There are special events—parades, folklore demonstrations, and the like—each day.

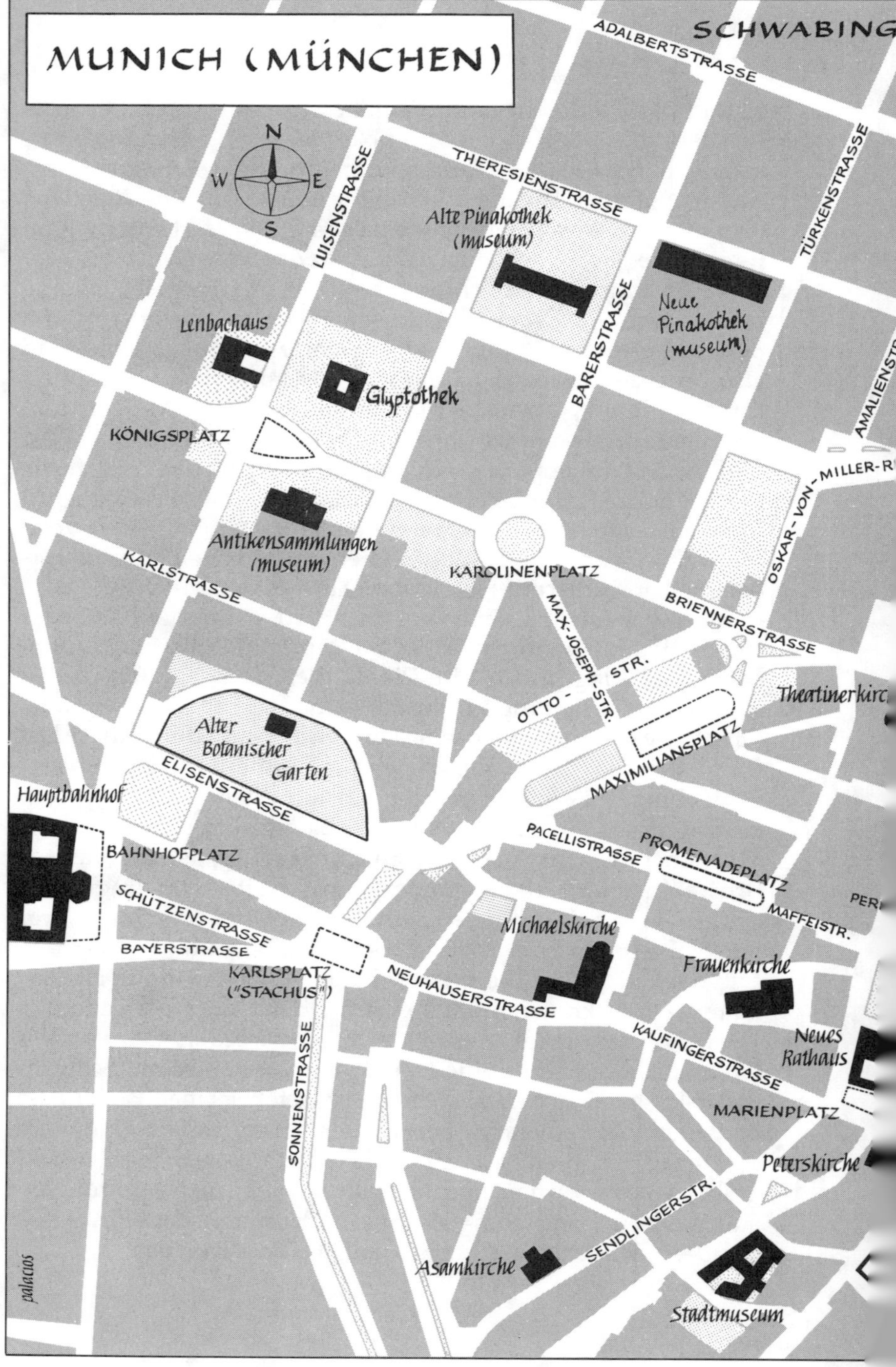
MUNICH (MÜNCHEN)
SCHWABING
N
W
E
S
ADALBERTSTRASSE
THERESIENSTRASSE
LUISENSTRASSE
TÜRKENSTRASSE
Alte Pinakothek (museum)
Neue Pinakothek (museum)
BARERSTRASSE
Lenbachaus
Glyptothek
KÖNIGSPLATZ
AMALIENSTR
OSKAR-VON-MILLER-R
Antikensammlungen (museum)
KARLSTRASSE
KAROLINENPLATZ
MAX-JOSEPH-STR.
BRIENNERSTRASSE
OTTO-STR.
Theatinerkirc
MAXIMILIANSPLATZ
Alter Botanischer Garten
ELISENSTRASSE
Hauptbahnhof
BAHNHOFPLATZ
PACELLISTRASSE
PROMENADEPLATZ
SCHÜTZENSTRASSE
MAFFEISTR.
PER
BAYERSTRASSE
Michaelskirche
KARLSPLATZ ("STACHUS")
NEUHAUSERSTRASSE
Frauenkirche
KAUFINGERSTRASSE
Neues Rathaus
SONNENSTRASSE
MARIENPLATZ
Peterskirche
SENDLINGERSTR.
Asamkirche
Stadtmuseum
palacios

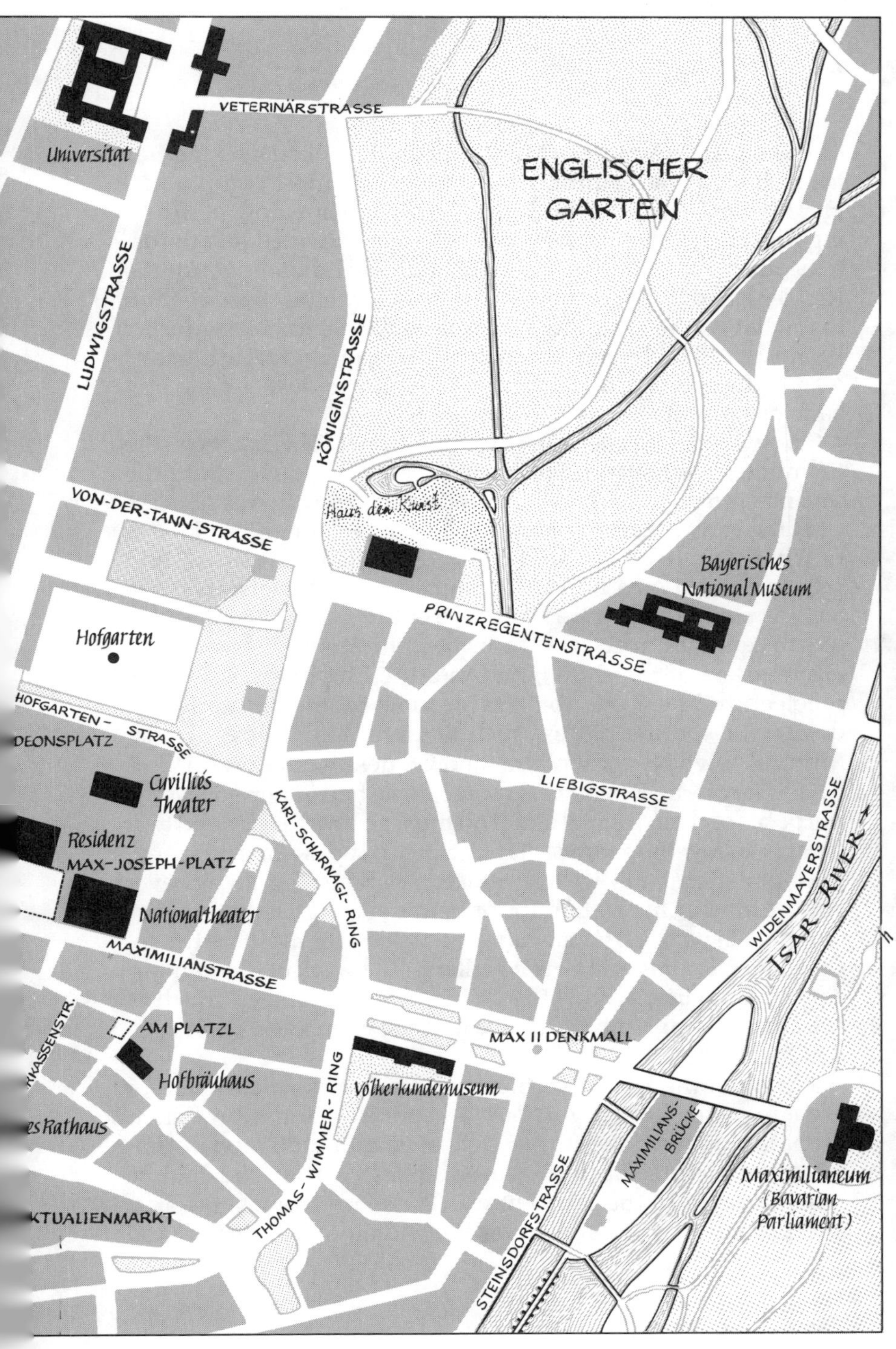

VETERINÄRSTRASSE
Universitat
ENGLISCHER
GARTEN
LUDWIGSTRASSE
KÖNIGINSTRASSE
VON-DER-TANN-STRASSE
Haus der Kunst
Bayerisches
National Museum
PRINZREGENTENSTRASSE
Hofgarten
HOFGARTEN-STRASSE
DEONSPLATZ
Cuvilliés
Theater
LIEBIGSTRASSE
KARL-SCHARNAGL-RING
Residenz
MAX-JOSEPH-PLATZ
Nationaltheater
WIDENMAYERSTRASSE
ISAR RIVER
MAXIMILIANSTRASSE
AM PLATZL
MAX II DENKMALL
Hofbräuhaus
Völkerkundemuseum
es Rathaus
THOMAS-WIMMER-RING
MAXIMILIANS-BRÜCKE
STEINSDORFSTRASSE
Maximilianeum
(Bavarian
Parliament)
KTUALIENMARKT

PALACES

The Residenz Complex (Max-Joseph-Platz) brings together Munich's past at its proudest, richest, and most sumptuous. Here it is: history, architecture, the arts—fine and performing—in one fell swoop. Well, one fell swoop divided into thirds, to be more accurate. You don't just dart in and dart out, for the Residenz and its component parts are heady stuff. Bear in mind that what you're exploring was smashed to smithereens during World War II (although fortunately many individual art objects were hidden away), and I defy you to come up with a more brilliant job of reconstruction.

Start with the Residenz—or palace—proper. This had been the townhouse of Bavaria's ruling Wittelsbachs—dukes until the seventeenth century, prince-electors of the Holy Roman Empire until the early nineteenth, and lastly, kings through World War I. What you'll see are splendidly decorated, furnished, and accessorized rooms of four distinct epochs: Renaissance (fifteenth century and earlier); baroque of the sixteenth and seventeenth centuries; rococo of the eighteenth century (these rooms are the stars of the show); and into the Empire period of the nineteenth. There are, to be sure, some rooms put to use for display of specific pieces, such as porcelain (Sèvres, Paris, Munich's own Nymphenburg, and Chinese work as well). But, by and large, the Residenz is rooms furnished in period, for the purposes of their original use. You must go on a self-guided tour (simply follow the arrows). There are two types—one morning, the other afternoon—with certain duplications. Take whichever you've time or inclination for or better yet, take in both of the tours. Each dazzles. What you want to look for most are the so-called Rich Rooms and Green Gallery—the work of the same architect, Cuvilliés, who is the architect who designed much of suburban Nymphenburg Palace and the court theater, in opulent rococo style.

Second of the Residenz triumvirate is its Schatzkammer—or Treasury—for which you buy a separate admission ticket, preparing as you do so for a goggle-eyed tour of 10 rooms brimming with Wittelsbach treasures, collected from the Middle Ages through to the last century. There are crowns, swords, and crosses of gold embedded with diamonds, rubies, and emeralds; birds carved of crystal; caskets of enamel; beer tankards set with precious stones; mini-sculptures of the saints (George especially) that drip jewels, Madonnas and rosaries, rings and reliquaries. These objects are on a par with a similar collection in Dresden that has been shown in the U.S.

Altes Residenztheater: This third part of the Residenz grouping is last, but not least. Ideally, one visits it for an opera. But, at the very least, go for a daytime look-see at what has to be the ultimate rococo playhouse, the masterwork of the same Cuvilliés responsible for the Rich Rooms of the palace and much of Schloss Nymphenburg. The problem, when you're at a performance here, is one of environmental opulence competing with stage action. Still, Mozart braved the beauty for premiéres of two of his operas: *Idomeneo* and *Gärterin aus Liebe.*

Schloss Nymphenburg (St. Callerstrasse): No self-respecting European ruler spent the entire year in a single palace. Certainly not a Wittelsbach. At least from the seventeenth century onward. That's when Nymphenburg began to rise as the Bavarian rulers' rural retreat. Allow a half day for what is one of the finest royal residences on the Continent. Encircled by a formal park, the main building blends large-scale baroque and intricate rococo with some later-nineteenth-century classic-style rooms. The high ceilinged Steinersaal—or Great Hall—is the main building's stunner, along with chambers lined with portraits of various rulers' female favorites. There are a trio of ancillary pavilions out in the park. Most important—design specialists consider it an even more significant rococo work than the main palace—is smallish *Amalienburg,* originally an electress's hunting lodge. Its Hall of Mirrors and tiled kitchen are special treats. So are the swimming-pool-size bath of Badenburg, the building in which Wittelsbachs took the waters; and the Chinese-motif chambers of the tea pavilion, Pagodenburg.

Schloss Schleissheim (about 18 miles northwest of downtown and easily combined with a trip to Dachau Concentration Camp Memorial Museum, recommended below): Leave it to Munich to have not one but a pair of great suburban castles. Schleissheim, more distant, loses out more often than not to closer-to-town Nymphenburg. If it lacks Nymphenburg's delicate rococo detail, it has other attributes, especially its magnificently scaled rooms that bespeak baroque at its most monumental; with a little-heralded Old Masters art gallery that comes as a surprise to many visitors. A Wittelsbach country house, originally sixteenth century, the Schleissheim one sees today was built at the beginning of the eighteenth century in its own formal park. The central stairway leading from the entrance hall could be reason enough for a Schleissheim visit. But, upon completing its ascent, one is confronted by a room that has to be half a dozen ordinary stories in height, with a glorious fresco spanning its ceiling. This, the Grossersaal, or ballroom, is Schleissheim at its zenith. Still, there are the painting galleries: a quartet of Rubenses, including his *Capture of Samson* and *Martyrdom of St. Lawrence*. Not to mention works by Van Dyck, Jordaens, Brueghel, Teniers, and by Italians including Giordano, Frenchmen including Largillierre. There's an additional gallery of rich tapestries. And at the other end of Schleissheim Park stands little Schloss Lustheim, as visitable for its opulent Grossersaal as for one of Germany's choicest caches of antique porcelain.

MUSEUMS

Alte Pinakothek (Barerstrasse 27): Once again, we are in the Wittelsbachs's debt. This art gallery—one of Europe's choicest—began with a Renaissance duke. Later rulers made significant contributions: King Leopold I had the present building erected; Prince Regent Luitpold bought additional paintings; Ludwig III managed to make contributions before he was overthrown. The consequence of this largesse is overwhelming. There are, to give you an idea, more paintings by Rubens—30 plus—than at either the royal museum in Brussels or even Antwerp, the master's hometown. German works are extraordinary: Dürer (one of his three self-portraits), Altdorfer, Grünewald, Lochner. The Italians shine: Botticelli, Lippi, Fra Angelico, Rafael, Leonardo, Titian (a peerless study of Emperor Charles V), Tintoretto. And much else: Rembrandt to Chardin, El Greco to Hals.

Bayerisches Nationalmuseum (Prinzregentenstrasse 3) is a knockout even from without, a towering mock-Renaissance castle from the turn of the century whose interior disappoints not a whit. Thrusts here are the decorative and plastic arts as they tell Bavaria's story from the Middle Ages onward. Once again, the Wittelsbachs were responsible: in this case, King Maximilian II, who began the museum with a nucleus of royally held objects in 1855. This one is a succession of spectaculars, as much in the dramatic, high-ceilinged settings as in the objects themselves: a whole room of Würzburg sculptor Tilman Riemenschneider's fifteenth-century works in wood, tapestries and stained glass, etched armor and incised ivory, bejeweled daggers and globes of gold, inlaid chests and velvet-cushioned chairs, peasant pottery and delicate Meissen, and beautifully furnished period rooms, every object in each, of surpassing value.

Neue Pinakothek (Barerstrasse 29, but with the entrance on Theresienstrasse) occupies Neue quarters—a warm and gracious structure designed by Alexander von Branca that opened in 1981, when the collection was moved from the Haus der Kunst, which it shared with what is now called the Staatsgalerie Moderner Kunst (below). This museum celebrates the nineteenth century, starting with early greats like David, Turner and Goya, continuing into German Romantics like Friedrich and Schinkel, with stellar Impressionists (Van Gogh, Cézanne, Gauguin among them) representative of later works.

Staatsgalerie Moderner Kunst (Haus der Kunst, Prinzregentenstrasse 1) embodies a collection of international twentieth-century art which is unsurpassed in Germany, and easily among the dozen best such in the world. Its core, logically enough, is German—Kirchner, Beckman, Franz Marc, Paul Klee (sometimes regarded as Swiss because of long Swiss residence). Italians, so often neglected, are present, de Chirico and Marini especially. The Cubist Braques and Picassos are stunners (there are a total of 14 works of Picasso covering several periods of his career). And the New York school—Andy Warhol, George Segal, Robert Motherwell, to name a trio—is on hand, among much else. You'll have a good time.

Städtische Galerie im Lenbachhaus (Luisenstrasse 33) is a charmer of a nineteenth-century mansion that could be a villa with garden in Florence. Now, though, it's a museum mostly of Munich artists' work, starting with earlier centuries—medieval through rococo in small doses, then with representation of the nineteenth century, on into the big draw: our own era. Concentrate on the paintings of the World War I school of the *Blaue Reiter* (Blue Rider) movement, headed by Wassily Kandinsky and named for his painting of a blue-robed horseman, with works by other Munich masters including August Macke, Paul Klee, and Franz Marc—all well known—not to mention a number by less celebrated but no less talented Gabriele Münter.

Glyptothek and Antikensammlungen (Königsplatz) are opposite-each-other museums that are, ideally, taken in tandem, as much for their similar themes as for their neoclassic architecture—on the neoclassic square with its copy of the giant Propylae gate on the Acropolis—that was created in the early nineteenth century by King Ludwig I, as were the pair of museums. The Glyptothek is an exceptionally felicitous setting for an extraordinary collection of ancient Greek and Roman sculptures—heads and torsos and friezes and fragments. Cross the square for the Antikensammlungen. Here, the objects run to pottery, mostly Greek but some Etruscan; and to jewelry, glass, bronzes, and terracotta.

Deutsches Museum (Museum Insel) occupies its own island in the Isar River, in the southeast part of town. The largest museum of its kind on the planet, its massive bulk can scare the hell out of you as you approach. If you let it. Rather, decide how much time you'll allot—a half day should be a minimum—and be selective. This museum puts one in mind of South Kensington's Science Museum in London, with high-ceilinged halls containing entire railway locomotives and airplanes and early cars. There are nearly a dozen rooms devoted to metal-working, a complex mining section, all you ever wanted to know about clocks and telegraphs and astronomy, to indicate but a few departments. Overwhelming.

Stadtmuseum (Sebastiansplatz) is Munich's historical museum, at its most amusing upstairs, thanks to nearly a score of authentically furnished and accessorized rooms. They range from a seventeenth-century parlor, an eighteenth-century kitchen, on into a nineteenth-century *Weinstube,* with an early twentieth-century artist's atelier in Art Nouveau, the most fun of the lot. There's a small museum of brewing in the same building—disappointingly small, when one considers the role beer has always played in Munich life.

Deutsches Jagdmuseum (Neuhauserstrasse 53) is at least as visitable for its setting—a long de-sanctified church/convent—as for its contents. The title translates as Hunting Museum, and exhibits range from exuberant Baroque paintings portraying hunters as well as hunted, through exquisitely crafted spears, swords and daggers from earlier centuries, beyond to silver-handled rifles and sumptuous trophies in gold and crystal. Displays line wide corridors, and strikingly vaulted halls—the *Weisser Saal* most spectacularly. This last is reached by means of a double-pronged ceremonial stairway with almost the grandeur of that in Würzburg's Residenz (Chapter 40)—which is going some. Location—on the heart-of-town pedestrian street—couldn't be more convenient.

Dachau Concentration Camp Memorial Museum (on the outskirts of the town of Dachau, about 20 miles northwest of downtown and well combined with a visit to nearby Schloss Schleissheim, above): Dachau, for those of a certain age, is a word synonymous with the concentration camps of the Nazi era. Indeed, it was the first such; Hitler's police chief, Heinrich Himmler, announced its opening on March 22, 1933, and it remained in operation until American troops liberated its prisoners on April 29, 1945. There were more than 206,000 prisoners, many thousands of whom were killed either by being gassed, burned alive in the now-visitable Krematorium, or through ghoulish medical experimentation. Dachau is a commendable joint operation of the State of Bavaria and the Brussels-based Comité International de Dachau. It is open free every day of the year and it impresses first with gratis brochures describing it, in no less than 10 languages. (I've noted them: Greek, Serbo-Croatian, Polish, Russian, Italian, Hebrew, French, Spanish, English, and German.) The museum itself is full of documentation, both original and photographed, and there is an orientation film. There are mock-ups of cell-block interiors, and other grisly aspects of camp life, even including—for those who have the stomach for it—the Krematorium. On the grounds: Catholic, Jewish, and Protestant chapels, and a sculpture, by Fritz Koelle, called *The Unknown Prisoner.* To understate: a visit to Dachau is a profound experience, moving and memorable.

CHURCHES

Asamkirche (Sendlingerstrasse): If you're going to enter a single church in Munich, this would be my candidate—an excitingly beautiful and intricate specimen of one of the great Bavarian art forms, church rococo. Short of a pilgrimage to what is considered the greatest example of this genre, out-of-town Wieskirche (see below), Asamkirche is as close to the top as you'll get. Actually called St. Johannus Nepomunk, it is best known for the pair of Munich brother-architects—the Asams—whose work it is and, as a matter of fact, of whose richly stuccoed townhouse it is a part. Smallish, with side aisles flanking central pews, its main attractions are a sunburst altar, a ravishing ceiling fresco, and a sculpted crucifixion with St. Peter. Wow!

Frauenkirche (Frauenplatz) is at its best from without, even, for that matter, from a distance, its splendid onion-dome steeples the very symbol of Munich. Within, this handsomely proportioned, originally Gothic church has been almost completely rebuilt since World War II bombing. The giant crucifix suspended from the ceiling is striking, and there are art objects in the side chapels. Below, in the crypt, are tombs of royal Wittelsbachs and of the bravely and articulately anti-Nazi Cardinal Faulhaber—earlier mentioned—who died in 1952.

St. Michaelkirche (Neuhauserstrasse) opened in the sixteenth century as the Jesuits' Munich counterpart of the Gesù church, their headquarters in Rome. It was nearly destroyed during World War II, but unlike Frauenkirche its interior was faithfully reproduced. This is a Renaissance gem of absolutely monumental scale, whose only rival in this respect is:

Theatinerkirche (Theatinerstrasse)—a century newer, baroque rather than Renaissance, and with a classic-style façade embracing a pair of forward towers and a cupola toward the rear, just above the transept within. The entire massive interior is pale gray, even to the elegant stuccowork and sculpture.

Dreifaltigkeitskirche (Pacellistrasse) translates as ''Holy Trinity'' and is rococo, Italian-designed, and intimate, with a trio of gilded altars. A joy.

Wieskirche (some 60 miles southwest of downtown, between Oberammergau and the Castle of Neuschwanstein) is, with reason, considered the finest of the Bavarian rococo churches, and a destination for secular visitors as well as for the religious pilgrims for whom it was built in the mid-eighteenth century, *in der Wies*—in the meadow. The architect-designers, brothers named Zimmerman, created a lilting environment. Behind its somber façade, Wieskirche within embodies rococo at its busiest: ceiling frescoes, a high altar whose gilt frames enclose murals and a sculpture of Christ, a roofed pulpit, gilded Corinthian columns.

OTHER EXCURSIONS FROM MUNICH

See the chapters on Mad Ludwig's Castles (Neuschwanstein, Herrenchiemsee, and Linderhof), Berchtesgaden, Garmisch-Partenkirchen, Mittenwald, Augsburg, and Ulm.

SETTLING IN

Hotel Continental (Max-Joseph-Strasse 5) has the most deceptively simple façade of any German luxury house that I know. Within, though, its designers and architects have used entire Gothic walls with arches, Renaissance ceilings, rococo wall paneling, and accessorized with furniture, tapestries, and fine paintings of the appropriate period. This is Munich's most beautiful hotel, and it's not too big—there are just 160 suites and rooms, no two quite alike, many exceptional. The grill merits further discussion later, and there are additional eateries and a bar. Central. *Luxury.*

Hotel Bayerischer Hof (Promenadeplatz 6) is at once central, traditional, big (400 rooms and suites, with the handsomest in its adjacent Palais Montgelas annex), and full-facility, with amenities ranging from a rooftop pool that's a delight in summer to Germany's only outpost of Trader Vic's restaurants. In between, there are more Teutonic dining facilities, bar, sauna-gym, and a lovely salon for afternoon tea, with a lighted fireplace in winter. Member, Leading Hotels of the World. *Luxury.*

Hotel Hilton International München (Am Tucherpark 7, at the edge of Englischer Garten northeast of downtown) deftly blends the amenities and standards of Hilton International with the flavor of Munich. Rooms are inviting; many have fine views. Facilities? Well, a restaurant worthy of later comment, rooftop boite with entertainment and dancing, a pair of bars, terrace-café that doubles as a coffee shop, swimming pool/sauna, and sprightly service. *Luxury.*

Hotel Vier Jahreszeiten Kempinski (Maximilianstrasse 17) is spacious (there are 365 attractive, traditional-style rooms and suites), with a pair of restaurants, bar, indoor-outdoor pool and sun terrace, fashionably central location (the opera is just down the block, which accounts for this historic hotel's longtime popularity with divas and conductors). The Walterspiel Restaurant (about which I write more on a later page) is an all-Munich ranker. Affiliated with both Inter-Continental Hotels and Leading Hotels of the World. *Luxury.*

Hotel Prinzregent (Ismaninger Strasse 42), though not central, is not inconvenient, with a situation just east of the Bavarian Parliament at the foot of Maximilianstrasse. This recently opened hotel is low-slung, smartly Traditional Bavarian in look, and intimate with but 66 mostly smallish, albeit charming and well-equipped, rooms, many with terraces. There's a congenial cocktail lounge and agreeable breakfast room (lunch and dinner are not served) whose generous buffet is included in the room rate. *First Class.*

Hotel Der Königshof (Karlsplatz 25) is heart-of-the-action, near the station, and on the square where the pedestrians' shopping mall has its western terminus. This is a good-looker of an old house tastefully updated, with innovative-looking rooms that meld traditional and modern decor, a famous restaurant that I counsel on a later page, and a bar-lounge beloved by locals. Likable. *Luxury.*

Hotel Excelsior (Schützenstrasse 11) is medium-sized—just 100 rooms, smart (the look is a modish mix of styles), and comfortable, with a distinguished restaurant (I comment on it later), and bar-lounge. *First Class.*

Eden Hotel Wolff (Arnulfstrasse 4) works very well. Location is opposite the Hauptbahnhof. There are a pair of popular restaurants, cozy bar, astute management, and 225 attractive rooms and suites. *First Class.*

Hotel Drei Löwen (Schillerstrasse 8) is Hauptbahnhof's neighbor; agreeable lobby, restaurant memorably entitled ''Strawberry,'' 160 bright rooms and suites. *First Class.*

Hotel Reinhold (Adolf-Kolping-Strasse 11) is shiny as a pfennig—a medium-sized, no-frills house that's modern, welcoming, and with private baths in most rooms. (Some of the singles have sink and toilet but no shower or bath, please note.) Breakfast only. *Moderate.*

Hotel Alfa (Hirtenstrasse 22) is worth knowing about for its nearly half a hundred functional rooms, many with private baths. Near the Hauptbahnhof. Breakfast only. *Moderate.*

Hotel Schlicker (Tal 74) couldn't be more central with its near-Marienplatz situation. There are 70 neat rooms, a number with private baths. Breakfast only. *Moderate.*

Hotel Daniel (Sonnenstrasse 5) has 80 comfortable rooms, a good number with private baths; near Karlsplatz. Breakfast only. *Moderate.*

Hotel Weinfurtners Garten (Leopoldstrasse 132, in the Schwabing quarter) is relatively recent, with 144 small but functional rooms (the singles have showers but no tubs in their baths), and in all cases, beds are narrow. There's a cozy bar wherein snack lunches are served, and a buffet is featured in the big and handsome breakfast room, but there is no proper restaurant. Friendly. *Moderate.*

Hotel Munich Sheraton (Arabellastrasse 6, in Bogenhausen, east of town) is at the bottom of my group only because of its noncentral situation. This is a big, fully equipped house, with 650 attractive rooms and suites, a variety of places to dine, dance, and have a drink; outdoor pool with sun terrace that's a pleasure in summer. *Luxury.*

DAILY BREAD

Käfer Schänke (Schumannstrasse 1) is at once a mouthwatering charcuterie (on its main floor) and a restaurant occupying a series of connected no-two-alike rooms (upstairs). The look is modish-rustic, the fare is German with Italo-French overtones. There are hearty soups, salads from a bountiful buffet, and a range of meats—pork through poultry. Fresh fish and oysters. Sumptuous sweets. *Luxury.*

Dallmayr (Dienerstrasse 14) is, like Käfer Schänke, at once a food shop (probably Germany's most celebrated—a Teutonic counterpart of Paris's Fauchon and London's Fortnum and Mason) and, more recently, a restaurant. Upstairs you'll find delicious hot dishes, along with the house's own-baked breads, salads, charcuterie, sweets, and coffee. Allow time to explore the incredible array of gourmet foods downstairs. *Luxury.*

Walterspiel (Vier Jahreszeiten Hotel, Maximilianstrasse 17) remains, year in year out, Old Munich at its most proper, and that includes deft service; fare that is essentially German but with appropriate Continental touches—roast pork, for example, or the delicate French veal stew, *blanquette de veau.* Luscious desserts. Finest wines. *Luxury.*

Tantris (Johann Fichte Strasse 7) is a trek from the center—easily a 20-minute drive north, and it takes advance planning; you need to book a day or two ahead, and even longer in advance if there if there are conventions in town. The point of a meal in this smartly contemporary spot is to get an idea of what the food is like in one of Germany's most reputed restaurants. The menu reflects the seasons, mode of preparation is *nouvelle cuisine* albeit with Teutonic accents; venison is a specialty, and so are lovely light mousses, among much else. *Luxury.*

Königshof (Hotel Königshof, Karlsplatz 25) takes the name of the hotel in which it is situated, and is the prototype of the luxurious, old-school restaurant, beautifully Belle Époque, with appetizers from a lavish buffet, or perhaps a crab bisque; entrées with the range filet of Angus beef through, say, grilled fresh trout, on to a trolley of delicious desserts. *Luxury.*

Terrassen, Hotel Königshof, (Karlsplatz 25): Having lunch here, looking through the picture windows to the hubbub of Karlsplatz, is a Munich tradition. Stick-to-the ribs fare mostly, but not exclusively. Consider the daily specials. *Moderate/First Class.*

Maximilian-Stüben (Maximilianstrasse 27) has two menus, one German, the other Italian. I suggest you ask for the latter and have an authentic Italian repast; soups and pastas are delicious, the staff Italian. Smart. *First Class/Luxury.*

Schwarzwälder (Hartmannstrasse 14) is traditional-style, with a tasty international menu—mixed grill or *Wiener schnitzel* or veal steak with sauce béarnaise. And ask to see the wine list, even if you're too hungry to study all 600 entries! Near Frauenkirche. *First Class.*

Hilton Grill (Hotel Hilton International München, Am Tucherpark 7) is high-ceilinged, its walls decorated with eighteenth-century prints, and generous armchairs around its tables. No better Munich source for a T-bone or sirloin steak, lamb chops, or barbecued spareribs as you know them at home. And the roast beef, from England, is carved at your table. Fine service. *Luxury.*

Sankt Hubertus (Hotel Excelsior, Schützenstrasse 11) is what contemporary high style is about. The look is modish, the menu wide-ranging, with German house specialties, French and Italian dishes for flair. Fun. *First Class.*

Zum Bürgerhaus (Pettenkoferstrasse 1) has respectable origins (it dates to 1827), and offers a paneled main room as well as—in warm weather—a pretty patio, for hearty table d'hôte lunches and dinners; you want to sample the venison stew with *spaetzle,* and the unique-to-Germany pudding, *rote grütze. First Class.*

Schneider (Sparkassenstrasse, near the Alte Rathaus) is still another eatery with the emphasis on wines, and a perky turn-of-century look. Daily specials. *Moderate.*

Palais Keller (Bayerischer Hof Hotel, Promenadeplatz 6) is, as the name suggests, in the basement of this luxury hotel. Lively, and the perfect spot for a speedy lunch or dinner. *Moderate/First Class.*

Zum Spöckmeir (Rosenstrasse 9) is big, busy, wine-oriented, two-storied, and serves filling German fare. The *Wiener schnitzel* is commendable. *Moderate.*

Spatenhaus (Residenzstrasse, just opposite the opera) is indicated for a nourishing though not especially festive pre-opera meal. Downstairs is cheaper than up where the *Wiener schnitzel* makes the climb worthwhile. *Moderate.*

Augustinerkeller (Neuhauserstrasse 16) is at once spacious and convenient, handy for a meal or snack. Delicious sausages. Daily plates are good buys. Central. *Moderate.*

Ratskeller (Rathaus, Marientplatz 8): City Hall restaurants are invariably enjoyable and good-value throughout Germany. Munich's is no exception. The pork-chop platter served with vegetables and french fries is tasty. And so is the banana split. *Moderate.*

Haxnbauer (Münzstrasse 2) is for typically Bavarian fare at its most rib-sticking, with pigs' feet and calves' knuckles the specialties. It's as close as some visitors want to get to across-the-way *Platzl,* an eternally tourist jammed restaurant whose lure is a nightly (8 P.M.) performance of ladies in dirndls and gents in leather shorts cavorting and yodeling to beat the band. Haxnbauer's other neighbor of note is *Hofbrauhaus,* an enormous, drab beer hall where people drink beer from enormous steins, and for reasons I will never fathom, fascinate outlanders in the process. If you're hungry, there's a plain albeit decent restaurant up a flight. Tabs at this trio are mostly *Moderate.*

Café-Konditorei Felchernhalle (Theatinerstrasse 23) is a posh place for coffee and cake—or a snack—on a posh shopping street. Everything is delicious. *Moderate.*

Richart's Backhaus (Marienplatz, opposite Rathaus) is a bakery that, happily, has tables so that you can order its scrumptious cakes and pastries with coffee while resting weary bones. *Moderate.*

Hahnhof (Leopoldstrasse 76, Schwabing) is the mother-house of a Munich chain of *Weinstuben,* and as typical a Schwabing spot as any for a glass and a snack, or a simple lunch. All you want of delicious dark bread is on the house. *Moderate.*

SOUND OF MUSIC

Bayerische Staatsoper (National Theater, Max-Joseph-Platz): Happiness in Munich is landing a ticket to the opera. The theater is a masterful rebuilding of an early-nineteenth-century house nearly destroyed by World War II bombs, and one of Europe's most beautiful. The façade is neoclassic, with a lovely colonnade. Within, there are half a dozen tiers, including the orchestra, or *Parkett.* Under a single massive crystal chandelier the red, white, and gold house recreates the early decades of the last century. The state box, the height of two balconies, is supported by caryatids. The red-and-gold curtain blanketing a vast stage is flanked by Corinthian columns, to which are attached five tiers of boxes. The bars and buffets, for champagne, coffee, snacks, are mobbed by ravenous patrons at intermissions.

The company? It goes back four and a half centuries. In the seventeenth it performed the very first German opera (Italian opera had come earlier). Mozart presented two premieres in Munich. Wagner, who exploited pathetic, mad King Ludwig II's worship of him, presented no less than five of his works for the first time here. Richard Strauss, a native Münchener, conducted the opera orchestra for seven years, all told. The repertory is, to understate, catholic. Director Wolfgang Sawallisch's programs include Mozart and Wagner, of course. But also Beethoven's *Fidelio,* Humperdinck's *Hänsel und Gretel,* Janacek's *Jenufa,* Moussorgsky's *Boris Gudonov,* Johann Strauss's *Die Fledermaus,* Richard Strauss's *Salome,* 10 Verdi classics, a quartet by Puccini. And Rossini. The Munich Opera Ballet, directed in recent seasons by Lynn Seymour, out of Britain's Royal Ballet, is one of Europe's best, with a diversified repertory—Adam's *Giselle,* Tschaikowsky's *Swan Lake* and *Nutcracker* among the classics, on into Richard Strauss's *Josephs Legende,* Balanchine's *Symphony in C* by Bizet, and John Cranko's *Romeo and Juliet* to Prokofiev's score. The city's symphony, Bayerischen Staatsorchester, also performs in the National Theater. And note: There are performances of opera—and of plays, as well—in the *Cuvilliés Theater* of the Residenz Complex, next door to the National Theater; no better way to see that rococo gem than in the course of a performance. Other halls are the sites for symphony, chamber music, and classical recitals. (Munich has four symphony orchestras.)

INCIDENTAL INTELLIGENCE

Lufthansa flies transatlantic daily to Munich-Riem International Airport, six miles from town and connected with it by regularly scheduled airport buses. *Further information:* Fremdenverkehrsamt der Landeshauptstadt München, Postfach D 8000 München 1, Germany, is the mail address of the Munich Tourist Office, which has information bureaus in the Hauptbahnhof and at Munich-Riem International Airport.

32

Nuremberg/Nürnberg

In the Tradition of Albrecht Dürer

BACKGROUND BRIEFING

For better or for worse, Nuremberg has not escaped history's attention.

Medieval and Renaissance artisans and artists—native son Albrecht Dürer especially—gave it international fame. Holy Roman Emperors favored residence in its still-standing top-of-town castle. Merchants made it rich as a trade center. Its *Meistersingers* inspired a Wagner opera that gave it musical immortality. Hitler gave it a bad name when his infamous racial laws, decreed at a Nuremberg Nazi rally, took the city's name. Allied bombers made it pay the price during World War II—after which it was the site of war-criminal trials, later flashed across world screens as the subject of a Hollywood film.

If any town knows that fame is fickle, it is Nuremberg. As German cities go, it is not, oddly enough, all that old. Not that a 1,000-year span is anything less than respectable. Nuremberg first appeared in history's records in 1050, was chartered less than two centuries later, after which it was honored by the Holy Roman Empire as a largely self-governing Free Imperial City. With political status came commercial clout. Its Pegnitz River location, in Germany's southwest, put it on lucrative trade routes like Antwerp-Vienna, Hamburg-Venice, Strasbourg-Prague. A concomitant of this Renaissance wealth and power was expertise, not only mercantile but mechanical and artistic. Nuremberg inventors get credit for creating the watch. (It was called the Nuremberg Egg—after its shape.) Nuremberg astronomers set up an observatory. Nuremberg printers built an early press.

Scientists and scholars gave the city éclat. And no less so did artists. This city was the home of sculptors who gained world fame—Veit Stoss, Peter Vischer, Adam Kraft. And painters. Michael Wolgemut, who became celebrated in his own right, set a young native of the city—an apprentice goldsmith named Albrecht Dürer—on the road to immortality by being Dürer's very first teacher.

And, as the town's beauty grew—from the on-high castle to the lower-down churches and merchants' houses—a culture-oriented bourgeoisie evolved. Witness the cobbler Hans Sachs and those of his fellow sixteenth-century artisans who doubled as *Meistersingers* in still-visitable St. Catherine's Church, the first-act setting for the Wagner opera based on their lives and loves.

The Thirty-Years' War put a temporary—though two-century—brake on Nuremberg's development. But in the nineteenth century, after it had been absorbed by the then kingdom of Bavaria, Nuremberg grew with the Industrial Revolution. (Indeed, it was a terminus of the very first German railroad—linking it with the nearby town of Furth.)

The pre-World War II years saw Nuremberg favored by Adolf Hitler, who preferred it to Berlin—perhaps because it was home to Nazi henchman Julius Streicher—for Nazi Party congresses, held annually over a half-decade period, 1933-38. (The Nazis' Reichsparteitag complex, site of the congresses and now a ruined shell, is a grim reminder of the hideous Hitler era.) It was at the 1935 congress that the Nuremberg Laws were announced, under which German citizens of the Jewish faith lost their civil rights and—many, ultimately—their freedom and their lives.

Favored not only for Nazi meetings, Nuremberg became a production center for something like half of the pre-war and wartime production of tanks, submarines, and aircraft. After the war, ironically, Nuremberg found itself the setting for the extensive trials of Nazi war criminals by an international tribunal.

The wonder is, given the merciless Allied bombings that destroyed so much of the city during the war, that Nuremberg has bounced back, gaining not only renewed self-respect, due if only for the rich pre-Hitler centuries, but a center in which major monuments of that past have been meticulously rebuilt, restored, and refurbished.

Of the medium-sized German cities (Nuremberg's population is about a half million), none gives the visitor more pause, none is more worth pondering—or exploring.

ON SCENE

Lay of the Land: If a vote were being cast for Germany's most easily walkable city, Nuremberg would get mine. The old city remains enclosed by bits and pieces of its ancient wall, punctuated by a quartet of gateway towers, and its crowning monument Kaisersburg—the Imperial Castle atop its own hill at the old town's northern fringe.

The Hauptbahnhof, where many visitors arrive, is due south of the castle, at the entrance to the old town, on the capacious Bahnhofplatz. A sturdy walker will enjoy exploration on foot all the way from station to castle. Königstrasse leads from Bahnhofplatz into the core, passing by pedestrians-only shopping streets like Pfannenschmiedsgasse, Breitegasse, and Kaiserstrasse, before it reaches a pair of bridges over the Pegnitz River, which runs right through the heart of the city.

Venerable, handsome Museumbrücke and Fleischbrücke both lead to Hauptmarkt, Nuremberg's main square these many centuries. The lures here are cafés for people-watching, the every-noon performance by the characters—electors of the Holy Roman Empire paying homage to their emperor—of the mechanical clock in Frauenkirche, and an ancient fountain—Schöner Brunnen—aptly called "beautiful," for none that I know in Germany is lovelier.

Continuing north on Winklerstrasse, the route passes the immense Rathaus complex and neighboring St. Sebald's Church. At Albrecht-Dürer-Platz, one bears left to Albrecht-Dürer-Strasse and the painter's house, now a museum. Or one veers a bit right and then north, via Burgstrasse, to the multitowered castle complex. Look sharp as you walk—at the elegant oriel windows of Renaissance houses, the playing waters of sculpted fountains in the squares, the spires of art-embellished churches.

Kaiserburg (Burgstrasse), the core of ancient Nuremberg Castle, which so many Holy Roman Emperors visited and revisited over the centuries, is more a case of great age and ambience than great architecture or stunning interiors. Still, there is no denying the impressiveness of this hilltop cluster of turrets, towers, and bastions. Nor its advanced years. We are dealing here with a tripartite proposition, the castle and the remnants of two earlier castles, and—most visit-worthy of the lot—the Imperial Castle, or Kaiserburg, the name by which the group is called. Kaiserburg's stand-out feature is its chapel, a two-storied Romanesque affair locals often refer to as "Doppelkappelle." The lower, crypt-like part—less elaborate than its upstairs neighbor—was used by minor court functionaries, soldiers, and servants. Above—where the decor is grander, the ceilings higher—the emperor, his family, and his courtiers worshiped. Other interiors—rich Renaissance paneling overshadows generally sparse furnishings—are to be seen: reception room (with coats of arms between the coffers of its smashing ceiling), parlor, living room, knight's hall, guards' room. And from without: the view of the city—with the Pegnitz River bisecting it—immediately below.

Germanisches Nationalmuseum (Kornmarkt): This is one of Germany's most important—and most beautiful—museums, a quite marvelous catchall of great German art and great German artifacts over the centuries (pre-Christian through the nineteenth) with the richest exhibits those of the very same medieval and Renaissance eras that constituted Nuremberg's Golden Age.

The setting itself is extraordinary: a long desanctified Carthusian monastery—gorgeous Gothic church, serene cloister, main and ancillary buildings—that went up in the fourteenth century. A solid morning, with time out for lunch, followed by an equally full afternoon, is not too much time for the German National. You might want to give the prehistoric exhibits once-over-lightly treatment, but the early Christian and Middle Ages work on the main floor, and the second-floor treasures—Dürer onward—are not to be rushed through. No phase of the creative Teutonic spirit has been neglected—a jewel-encrusted cross, a carved ivory plaque, both ninth century; a golden lion and an illuminated manuscript of the thirteenth century; altarpieces and stained glass of the fourteenth century; textiles, caskets, and carved-wood Madonnas of the same era. There are master painters' works—a Konrad Witz *Annunciation,* a Stephan Lochner *Mary Magdalene,* an enthroned *Madonna* by the elder Holbein, a proud burgher as portrayed by Cranach, *The Adoration of the Magi* as Martin Schaffner saw it, Hans Baldung Grien's *Madonna and Child,* a view of *Calvary* by Albrecht Altdorfer. Native son Dürer is represented by such masterworks as his twin paintings of Charlemagne and Kaiser Sigismund, and a sensitive portrait of his teacher, Wolgemut. There is sculpture by Adam Kraft and Tilman Riemenschneider, to name but a pair of immortals. More? I haven't touched upon objects of gold, porcelain, and silver, furniture, folk art, weapons, musical instruments, costumes—with the quality as superb as the quantity.

Albrecht-Dürer-Haus (Albrecht-Dürer-Strasse at Tiergärtnertor) is a near-neighbor to the Kaiserburg—disproportionately high in relation to its girth, multistoried, topped with a dramatic overhanging roof, enclosing a partly half-timbered façade. Dating to the mid-fifteenth century, the house was by no means new when Dürer bought it in 1509, and it was his home until he died in 1528, by which time he had made his mark as Germany's preeminent Renaissance Man. Born of a goldsmith who had immigrated from Hungary (and whose portrait by an admiring son you may remember from the Uffizi Gallery in Florence), Dürer was largely responsible not only for expanding the horizons of painting in Renaissance Germany, but for improving the status of the painter. His travels in Italy and the Low Countries—but especially Italy—influenced him deeply. He innovated at home by going beyond religious motifs in his work. Dürer painted the human body, nude as well as clothed. He pioneered in German civil portraiture (including self-portraits, of which he made a trio—the earliest now at the Louvre, another in the Prado, and the last in Munich's Alte Pinakothek). He drew animals—hares to hippos—and shellfish, plants, and flowers, and he gave his attention as well to landscapes, long before colleagues did so.

At the same time Dürer codified his views on art and artists in a pair of well-articulated theses. And he kept in step with the times, making use of then-infant media like the woodblock and the printing press, so that his work could be reproduced in quantity, allowing ordinary people—for the first time in history—to own art.

His house—to anticipate what may well be your first question—contains no Dürer paintings, only copies. But there are some original prints. The more interesting of the three floors are the second, with an equipment-filled kitchen and a pair of sitting rooms, and the third, where it is believed Dürer worked and where there are reproductions of paintings, and some prints. An annex contains changing exhibitions and a shop.

St. Sebalduskirche (Weinmarkt): Nuremberg, oddly enough, is not the seat of a bishop, and is therefore *sans* cathedral. Which is hardly to say that it is without beautiful churches. St. Sebald's, for one, is a twin-steepled late Romanesque/early Gothic masterwork, with three exquisitely vaulted naves, perfectly splendid scale, and art treasures to make your head spin, including a *Madonna in Glory* by an unknown fifteenth-century master; a relief of the Passion by native son Adam Kraft; still another Kraft, *Christ Bearing the Cross;* a *Crucifixion*—among other work—by Nuremberger Veit Soss; and Peter Vischer's sublime bronze shrine of St. Sebald. Without, note the oriel windows of the church's stone rectory.

St. Lorenzkirche (Pfannenschmiedsgasse) is a twin parish church to St. Sebald. The pair are named for the city's patron saints, and it is a toss-up as to which church's art is more beautiful. St. Lawrence has works by some of the same sons of Renaissance Nuremberg as St. Sebald's—Adam Kraft (who portrayed himself in a memorable sculpture); and Veit Soss, with an *Annunciation* in a delicate wooden medallion hung from the ceiling; and some of the finest stained glass in Germany.

Frauenkirche (Hauptmarkt), with delicate pinnacles surmounting the gables of its façade on Hauptmarkt, began life Catholic in the fourteenth century, became Protestant as an adolescent, and reverted to its original faith as it matured in the nineteenth century. It has a small, squarish, tranquil interior, as if to compensate for the daily performance at noon of a mechanical clock, Männleinlaufen, in which the seven electors of the Holy Roman Empire bow before Emperor Charles IV and the Hauptmarkt passersby. There are frequent evening organ recitals. Exiting the church, take time to inspect *Schöner Brunnen,* the "Beautiful Fountain" on the square. Dating to the fourteenth century, it embraces two score sculpted figures on four levels. The lowest down are philosophers and humanists, and on the upper rows are Old and New Testament figures, electors of the empire, and assorted non-Christian personalities, including Alexander the Great and Julius Caesar. Even more beautiful at night—when illumination brings out the detail of the sculpture.

St. Katharinakirche (Burgstrasse) is the very same church in which the *Meistersingers* held forth during the Renaissance and where Wagner opened his opera of that name. Alas, this church—Gothic, dating to the fourteenth century—was bombed during World War II and has not been restored. Still, because of its *Meistersinger* associations, its ruins are the site of frequent concerts.

Spielzeugmuseum (Karlstrasse 13) is the city of Nuremberg's Toy Museum, in modern quarters hiding behind the façade of a Renaissance townhouse. Nuremberg takes its centuries-long reputation for toy design and manufacture seriously. The museum is a veritable history lesson on toys through the ages—and fascinating. The range is simple wooden playthings through dolls and dollhouses, on into miniature railroads and other mechanical marvels.

Stadtmuseum Fembohaus (Burgstrasse 15) is a magnificent Renaissance house, appropriately enough Nuremberg's historical museum: a score and a half of rooms brimming with bits and pieces of Old Nuremberg—furniture, accessories, documents, engravings, other treats.

Tucherschlösschen (Hirschelgasse 9) is a decorative-arts treasure trove: the longtime home of a leading local family (Dürer's famous portrait of the beautiful Elsbeth Tucher is on view in Kassel, the subject of a chapter in this book). One eye-filling room after another displays antique furniture (foreign as well as German), accessories, tapestries, porcelain, crystal, and paintings by Nurembergers including Dürer's teacher Michael Wolgemut and Dürer's pupils.

Verkehrsmuseum (Lessingstrasse 6): Rail buffs, this one's for you. Nuremberg, you will remember from an earlier page in this chapter, was the point from which the first German train huffed and puffed—back in 1835; a model of it is on display here in the Transport Museum, along with other historic railroad paraphernalia from throughout a very rail-minded nation. There is, as well, a section on the German mail system that rivals the Postal Museum in Frankfurt, and has as its pride and joy a collection of 40,000 postage stamps from all over the globe.

SETTLING IN

Grand Hotel (Bahnhofstrasse 1) is a Nuremberg institution—long on the scene, long esteemed, and with reason. There are 170 comfortable rooms and suites, most with private baths and showers; a large traditional-style lobby, with an excellent restaurant, friendly bar-lounge, and the wood-beamed and walled Walliser Kanne, a Swiss-style *Stube,* for à la carte meals. Location is perfect: just across the street from the station, and a six- or seven-minute walk into the core of town. The Grand has been recently—and tastefully—refurbished by its operators, Penta Hotels. *Luxury.*

Hotel Carlton (Eilgutstrasse 13) runs about neck and neck with the Grand, although it's newer, with not quite the Grand's veneer of age, or its sure sense of style. There are 120 rooms and suites, a top-ranked restaurant on which I comment later, a bar-lounge, warm-weather terrace-café, a near-Hauptbahhof/ near heart-of-town situation. *Luxury.*

Hotel Atrium: (Münchner Strasse 25) is a welcome newcomer—a park-view tower with just over 200 rooms and suites, convenient settings for food and drink, with the Hauptbahnhof as a near-neighbor. *Luxury.*

Hotel Deutscher Hof (Frauentorgraben 29) has the requisite attributes of a desirable hotel: handsome public and guest rooms (all 50 have private baths and are mod-look), inviting lobby, and attractive places to eat and drink—in this case a quartet: *Bierstube* through Theater Eck, as well as a notable salad buffet and its own busy bar. *First Class.*

Hotel am Sterntor (Tafelhofstrasse 8) is well located, between the Hauptbahnhof and opera, and an easy walk to the Hauptmarkt. The look is quiet-modern, rooms are comfortable and most have bath or shower. Drinks and coffee are served in the lounge and there's a restaurant. *First Class.*

Burghotel (Lammsgasse 3) takes its name from the Kaiserburg, a near-neighbor. It's cheery, full of color and atmosphere, with 44 period-style rooms (all with private baths), restaurant-café-bar, even a sauna. *First Class.*

Hotel Merkur (Pillenreutherstrasse 1) is another near-neighbor of the Hauptbahnhof, elderly but recently refurbished, with 100-plus contemporary design rooms, half of which have private baths. Restaurant, bar. *First Class.*

Bayerischer Hof (Gleissbühlstrasse 15) is an across-the-road neighbor of the Grand Hotel, whose owner-management it shares. This one's no-nonsense, graceless but functional modern, with 75 rooms, most of which have private baths. Breakfast only. *Moderate.*

Hotel Kaiserhof (Königstrasse 39) has as its major plus an address on heart-of-the-action Königstrasse. The lobby is small and the rooms simple but clean (by no means all 67 of them have private baths). There's a basement restaurant, Löwenbrau by name, worthy of later comment. *Moderate.*

DAILY BREAD

Goldenes Posthorn (opposite St. Sebalduskirche) immodestly bills itself as "Deutschlands älteste Weinstube seit 1498." Well, not many of us are in a position to check on the accuracy of this bit of history, but the management goes so far as to claim that its clientele included both Dürer and the master *Meistersinger* Hans Sachs. This is, to be sure, an ancient and attractive house, nicely furnished and accessorized—copper pots, peasant pottery, rococo paintings, medieval sculpture, and the like. The menu is rather grand—non-German specialties like tournedos Enrico, native game in season. But you may order local sausages, too. Service can be hoity-toity, but in a restaurant that claims to have served Dürer, well, why not? *Luxury.*

Heilig-Geist-Spital (Spitalgasse, just off the bridge over the Pegnitz called Museumbrücke) is a Nuremberg landmark: It translates as Holy Ghost Hospital, dates, in its present form, to the fifteenth century, and is distinguished by its broad, window-punctuated roof, dramatic oriel window, and the vast supporting arches that separate it from the waters of the river, over which it is built. Though now a home for the aged, it continues to operate a big and always busy public restaurant. Take a table by the windows over the river and order the local Nuremberg sausages. *Moderate/First Class.*

Nassauer Keller (Karolinenstrasse 2) is reputed to be Nuremberg's oldest dwelling house—six splendid stories in stone, with a quartet of oriel windows surrounding its eaves and a history that goes back to the thirteenth century. What you find here, not unexpectedly given an 800-year background, is atmosphere, coupled with good, stick-to-the-ribs food. Central. *First Class.*

Hotel Carlton Restaurant (Eilgutstrasse 13) is ideal for an expense-account lunch, one executive with another. Contemporary decor with four-course set menus, and a delicious à la carte, with such treats as fresh Norwegian lobster and game when it is in season. Fine wines, and the service quite skilled. *Luxury.*

Löwenbrau Restaurant (Hotel Kaiserhof, Königstrasse 39) is not to be overlooked because of its basement location. This is a warm and inviting spot, beloved by Nurembergers, centrally located, and with delicious food. German specialties—sausages, schnitzels, soups—are especially good here, and the full-course lunches and dinners are good buys. *Moderate/First Class.*

Handwerkerhof Nuremberg (Königstor, near Hauptbahnhof) is an unabashedly commercial enterprise—a walled complex of mock-medieval houses within which are an assortment of craftsmen turning out baskets, metalwork, dolls, paintings on glass. And of course there's a baker making *Lebkuchen,* Nuremberg's famous variation on the theme of gingerbread. Nor surprisingly, everything is for sale. And there are places to have a snack, drink, or simple meal, called *Weinparadies* with dry Franconian whites from surrounding vineyards, and *Bratwurst Glöcklein,* platters of Nuremberg sausages, with sauerkraut or potato salad—the specialties. *Moderate.*

Café Kröll (Hauptmarkt) is the main congregating spot on the main square. Go for coffee and *Kuchen,* a snack lunch or a drink, and watch Nuremberg pass in review, with views of the Schöne Brunnen and the façade of Frauenkirche as bonuses. *Moderate.*

City Trattoria (Josephsplatz 9) is, despite its half-Anglo name, authentically Italian, and just the spot for a change from German fare. Central. *First Class.*

Ratsstuben (Altes Rathaus, Rathausplatz 2) is given precious space here only because, if you have read other chapters of this book, you know that I am partial to the restaurants of German city halls. Nuremberg's is an exception: disappointingly unattractive and far simpler than a restaurant in so splendid a building should be, with unprofessional service and only fair fare. *Moderate/First Class.*

Rottner (Winterstrasse 15, in the Grossreuth suburb, just west of town) is a rambling half-timbered house, as atmospheric within as without, and with a worthwhile enough kitchen—snails in wine sauce, expertly sauced asparagus in season, a ranking repertoire of game specialties—to make it worthwhile excursion destination from the city. *Luxury.*

SOUND OF MUSIC

Städtische Bühnen (Richard-Wagner-Platz) is the name for a complex of theaters—Opera House (Nuremberg has a resident troupe), Theatre (plays in German, of course), and Theatre Workshop. Location is west of the Hauptbahnhof.

Meistersingerhalle (Allersbergerstrasse) is the ultra-mod good-looker of a concert hall/convention center, southeast of downtown and the Hauptbahnhof, and a taxi ride from your hotel. But if there's a symphonic or pop concert on during your stay, take it in.

INCIDENTAL INTELLIGENCE

Verkehrsverein Nürnberg, the city tourist office, has information bureaus in the Hauptbahnhof and on the Hauptmarkt. Note, too, that Nuremberg is one of the lucky cities on Lufthansa's domestic network. The airport is four miles north of downtown, with buses running regularly between the airport and the Grand Hotel.

33

Regensburg

Roman and Romanesque

BACKGROUND BRIEFING

It is odd how cities—like clothes—go in and out of fashion. Take Regensburg. Located at the confluence of the Danube and Regen rivers, in Germany's southeast, it was in the very thick of things from the time—some 2,000 years back—that the Romans settled it as Castra Regina.

By the time Charlemagne captured it in the eighth century, it had become powerful as a church center—bishops have been resident since 739—and, thanks to its two-river setting, as a trading town, as much on north-south European routes as east-west traffic all the way to India.

Mercantile and spiritual eminence gained the politicos' respect. In the thirteenth century Regensburg became a Free Imperial City within the Holy Roman Empire, whose Diet used it as a meeting place beginning in the mid-sixteenth century. It was in Regensburg that the monolithic Holy Roman Empire's demise was plotted. Diet delegates, under Napoleon's thumb, met here for a two-year session, 1801-1803. The end of that decade saw long-proud Regensburg absorbed by the kingdom of Bavaria.

And so, as the nineteenth century progressed, Regensburg became a provincial backwater subservient to Munich—and later to Berlin and Bonn—in matters political. World War II blessedly spared the historic core of this historic city, and in the post-war decades it achieved a new vitality with considerable industry and a perky new university.

None of which would be of unusual interest to the visitor from abroad, were it not for the monuments of the past. Together they constitute a façade going back centuries—of which Regensburgers remain almost fiercely proud. The city's once favorable geography is now less of an asset; for most travelers, the southeast location—near the East German frontier—is out of the way. But Regensburg is worth a detour.

ON SCENE

Lay of the Land: The Regensburg of the centuries—Roman, Romanesque, Renaissance—continues to pass in parade. And conveniently. The historic center of town is relatively compact, lying between the rivers—Danube and Regen converge to the north—and the Bahnhof, from which one proceeds into the center via Maximilianstrasse. That artery leads to a square, Alte Kornmarkt, and to adjacent Domplatz, named for the towering cathedral at its fringe. From Domplatz walk south—away from the direction of the Danube—along Plauengasse, which will take you to Neupfarrplatz, named for one of the city's most important churches, and Schwarze-Bären-Strasse, the lively principal pedestrians-only shopping street. The pedestrian zone's eastern termination is at Dachauplatz, site of a onetime monastery that is now the remarkable municipal museum.

All of central Regensburg is walkable. This is a town of formidable tower-like gateways—the better to discourage unwelcome visitors of old—like Baumburgerturm, near the square called Kohlmarkt, and Goldenerturm, on Wahlenstrasse. Scores of houses—the homes of merchants who struck it Renaissance-rich—line streets like Gesandstrasse and Keplerstrasse. There's nothing museum-like about this almost completely old city core; virtually every structure has been deftly converted to contemporary use. Porta Praetoria, a substantial fragment of a gate to the military settlement, Castra Regina, dating to the second century, is not nearly as big or architecturally impressive as the Romans' Porta Negra in Trier (see the chapter on that city), but stands proudly on Schwibbogenstrasse. Steinerenbrücke—-the German for Stone Bridge—spans the Danube, and has been in continuous use since the twelfth century.

Dom (Domplatz): Regensburg's cathedral is one of southern Germany's great Gothic churches, ranking with beauties like the cathedral in Ulm, St. Jacob's in Rothenburg, and St. George's in Dinkelsbühl. For me it is at its loveliest from without, the proud possessor of an intricately lacy façade, surmounted by a pair of slim spires. But do go in, if only to see the sculpted Angel of Regensburg, whose smile has been welcoming the faithful since the thirteenth century. The Dom's own museum of gold work and priests' vestments is off the north aisle. The stained glass is exceptional, no less so than other unusual aspects of the cathedral complex, including a tranquil cloister containing a mini-church—St. Stephen's—and a stunner of an octagonal chapel. Still one more cathedral attraction: its boy choir—Domspatzen, or Cathedral Sparrows—that sings there at 9 A.M. on Sundays when not on tour.

Museum der Stadt Regensburg (Dachauplatz) is the Municipal Museum, and for me, as important a visitor destination as the Dom. Two reasons for this. First, the setting: A Gothic monastery with an extraordinarily beautiful chapel that has been desanctified, and is to be seen today principally as a specimen of the ecclesiastical architecture of eight centuries ago. (Go if you can for a Sunday-morning—or other—concert.) Second, the 100 galleries: Give yourself a good half day or be prepared to pick and choose. A priority might well be the entire room given over to paintings by Renaissance master Albrecht Altdorfer, a native Regensburger whose sixteenth-century works you'll have seen in museums throughout Germany. The most memorable of the lot at the museum is an unusual *Last Supper*. Paintings by artists of other nationalities are to be viewed, along with rooms furnished in the distinctive periods of a span of centuries (early-nineteenth-century Biedermeier stands out), others with tapestries of the Renaissance, sculpture of the Middle Ages, on through the not-to-be-missed marble plaque that—in clearly legible Latin—documents the foundation of the Romans' Castra Regina military camp in A.D. 179.

Altes Rathaus (Rathausplatz) is the Gothic-era Old Town Hall complex. Go inside to see the Reichssaal—(the Imperial Hall) that was in use for four centuries, starting in the fifteenth, for irregularly held meetings of the Parliament of the Holy Roman Empire. From 1630 onward the Reichssaal was the seat of the empire's "Perpetual Diet," and there are historic appurtenances on display that tell the story. In an adjacent room imperial inquisitors used to torture uncooperative prisoners: the gruesome equipment used by them is still to be seen.

St. Emmeramkirche (St. Emmeramsplatz) is a surprise package: a cloistered Romanesque church that goes all the way back to the fifth century but that is, within, joyous Bavarian rococo. Indeed, the church's redesigners, in the eighteenth century, were the same celebrated Asam brothers for whom a church of their creation in Munich is named.

Schloss Thurn und Taxis (Emmeramsplatz) is, to state the case straightaway, a case of more money than taste: a palace for a noble family—who acquired its wealth in Frankfurt, running the German post office—created from the cloistered monastery attached to St. Emmeramkirche. The Thurn und Taxis family, who still live in the Regensburg *Schloss,* opens its state rooms to visitors who are taken through on a more or less hourly basis by a guide. The baroque exterior, including a gracious campanile and a fountain-centerd courtyard, leads one to expect better within than one finds. It's fun to see the family servants in white wigs and livery out of the eighteenth century, and there's a nice rococo-style ballroom. But otherwise, throne room to library through dining and reception rooms, the going is heavy and more devoid of style and taste than any open-to-the-public palace that I know of in Germany. A boring museum of the family's carriages and coaches—in interminable number—adjoins.

Alte Kapelle (Kornmarkt) is still another gay deceiver, sobersided without—it is more than 1,000 years old—but light and lilting rococo within, especially the high altar. This takes the form of a statue of the Virgin Mary, flanked by likenesses of a Holy Roman emperor and his empress, in the center of a triumphal gateway.

Niedermünster (Niedermünstergasse) is a mixed bag architecturally, artistically, and—most important—archaeologically. Descend to its basement to see recently completed digs that reveal significant bits and pieces of the ancient Castra Regina settlement. Upstairs are Romanesque frescoes, Gothic sculpture, and a baroque high altar.

St. Jakobskirche (Jakobstrasse at Bismarckplatz) was founded, visitors are surprised to learn, by Scottish and Irish monks who had wandered far afield of their homelands, in the early twelfth century. Though hardly without surprises inside—the tomb of a priest who was Mary Queen of Scots' confessor, for one—this church is celebrated for its front doorway. When you hear locals talk about the *Schottenportal*—Scottish portal—it's the masterful Romanesque sculpture framing this church's main entrance of which they speak: a complex presentation of the Gateway to Heaven, surmounted by Christ and the Apostles, with the Virgin Mary to the left, as one enters, and temporal authority—as represented by an emperor—at the right. Look to the bottom; the trio of monks are believed to be the church-monastary's Scottish founders.

SETTLING IN

Parkhotel Maximilian (Maximilianstrasse 28) is a deft refurbishing of a venerable structure. Conveniently central, with half a hundred agreeable rooms, bar-lounge, and a pair of restaurants, one of them a U.S.-inspired steakhouse. *Luxury.*

Hotel Karmeliten (Dachauplatz 1) has a convenient historic-core location (on the same square as the monastery that's now the city museum), private baths in half of its 80 pleasant bedrooms, a professional staff who are not afraid to smile, a cozy bar, and one of the best restaurants in town, of which more later. *First Class.*

Hotel Kaiserhof am Dom (Kramgasse 10) should be at least twice as good as it is. But it takes advantage of a sublime situation—front rooms overlook Domplatz and the Gothic façade of the cathedral—and contents itself with a near-tacky lobby, indifferent staff, adequate restaurant, wine-cellar café. The 30 rooms all have private baths, and if you get one in front—with that cathedral view—you're in luck. By Regensburg standards: *First Class.*

Hotel Bischofshof (Krauterermarkt 8) embraces a complex of venerable buildings, and some of its 60 rooms—many of which have baths—are luxurious. There are a couple of restaurants, and an outdoor café in summer. And the location is heart of town. For me, though, this one is heavy-handed, almost depressing. *Moderate.*

Hotel Avia (Frankenstrasse 2): Pity about the Avia's location—across the Danube from downtown. It would otherwise be at the top of my group. The Avia is modern but at the same time small enough to have a nice intimate flavor (there are just 100 rooms); the rooms are attractive (all have baths), as are the public spaces including a bar-lounge, *Bierstube* for casual meals and a crackerjack restaurant. Ideal for business visitors who don't care a fig for getting the flavor of Regensburg, or others with cars. *Luxury.*

DAILY BREAD

Ratskeller (Altes Rathaus, Rathausplatz 1), though with the requisite arched architecture of German town-hall restaurants, is not atmospherically decorated as some. But it is excellent, with its charming service and a wide-ranging menu—super soups, exceptional beef, and rich desserts. You'll like the wines. *First Class.*

Bei Angelo (Drei Mohrenstrasse 11), is known also as Karl IV, occupies a beautifully restored and decorated house of considerable age, and serves—as its name indicates—Italian food. The pastas—including *paglia a fieno* and *capelli d'angelo*—are superb, and so are entrées of fish or veal. Buzzy ambience. Go after the opera, if you like. *First Class/Luxury.*

Hotel Avia Restaurant (Frankenstrasse 2): Beautifully set tables, beautifully served food, including German classics and steaks from a charcoal grill. Save room for dessert, and give the wine card some attention. Terrace in summer, with views across the Danube to the heart of town. *Luxury.*

Regensburger Wurstküche (Steinerenebrücke) has been on the scene for half a millennium, and in the same cramped quarters alongside the Danube in the shadow of Steinerenebrücke—the old stone bridge about which I've written above. You enter in the kitchen, where the ladies who own the place are grilling their trademark sausages. Order a plate, with sauerkraut and a beer, and find yourself a place on a bench at one of the handful of tables. This place is as requisite a destination as the cathedral; no visitor misses it. *Moderate.*

Weinstube Bastei (Fischergasse 32) is posh, ancient, and delicious, with antique bibelots hung from its stucco walls, an open fireplace, and goodies including snails, soups, and schnitzels. *First Class.*

Prinzess Konditorei-Café (Rathausplatz 2) has been baking delicious pastries and making delicious candies for nearly three centuries. Sandwiches, snacks, breakfast too, with goodies in ground-floor counters to be selected before going to the upstairs dining room. *Moderate/First Class.*

SOUND OF MUSIC

Stadttheater (Bismarckplatz) is a honey of a mid-nineteenth-century house, smartly refurbished, with a resident opera troupe, other attractions, including operettas and plays (in German, of course), and a full-service—and most attractive—restaurant-café, where you might want to dine before or after the performance.

Neuhaussaal (Arnufsplatz) is headquarters for the city's symphony—Stadtisches Orchester Regensburg. Still other concerts take place at Regensburg University. Ask your hotel concierge whether or not there will be an evening concert of the cathedral's boy choir, *Domspatzen,* during the course of your stay, in addition to the choir's weekly participation in the cathedral's 9 A.M. mass on those Sundays when it's not touring.

INCIDENTAL INTELLIGENCE

Verkehrsamt Regensburg—the city tourist office—is located in the Altes Rathaus, Rathausplatz.

34

Rothenburg

Period-Piece Enchantment

BACKGROUND BRIEFING

Go back a few centuries and the German terrain was dotted with Rothenburgs. If they were not a Deutschmark a dozen, they were commonplace enough so as not to have aroused any excess of foreign curiosity.

But wars—and not only World War II—take tolls. Rothenburg's miracle is its emergence into our era as a virtually intact specimen of small-town Bavaria, circa the Middle Ages—with a bit of Renaissance as spice.

Like so many German communities, this one sprouted around a nobleman's castle a thousand years ago. With a name out of a fairy tale—Count Conrad the Red—he was a subject of the Holy Roman Emperor, under whom Rothenburg gradually achieved status as a Free Imperial City. Thanks to four-directional trade routes and a river, the Tauber, for ship transport, wealth accumulated, burghers built stately houses—even immodestly naming a principal avenue Herrngasse, or Gentlemen's Lane, after themselves.

One of their number, Heinrich Toppler, became a mayor with clout, and the mid-fourteenth century saw him spur building—a cathedral-size church, formidable fortifications, a remarkable hospital, a still-standing two-tier bridge—to the point where much of the town is a result of his initiative.

Then came pan-European events to which even Rothenburg—by then insulated by a high encircling wall—was not immune: the Reformation (it was successful, as was not always the case in strongly Catholic Bavaria) and the seventeenth-century's Thirty Years' War. It was this event that literally put Rothenburg into a deep sleep. Following an extended period of military occupation that overwhelmed but did not destroy Rothenburg, the town simply succumbed to exhaustion.

In the early eighteenth century this centuries-old Free City had become too somnolent to oppose absorption into the kingdom of Bavaria. Nobody paid much attention to it, as a matter of fact, for half an additional century. In 1865, with the spirit of romanticism in the European air, a writer named Riehl happened through and penned a piece called "A Stroll Through the Tauber Valley" for a Leipzig magazine. That did it. Rothenburg began life anew. Today it is still a magnet for romanticists anxious for an effortless remove to what might be called a medieval time-capsule not 150 miles from Munich.

ON SCENE

Lay of the Land: Rothenburg is a question mark. In shape, that is. Punctuated by a score of gates, towers, and bastions, its wall protects it from without as it has for seven centuries. Arrive by train and you find yourself outside the walls, just a little to the east. Follow Bahnhofstrasse and Ansbacherstrasse toward the walls, and you make contact with the ancient fortifications. Pass through Rödertor, or Red Gate, into the historic core's Rödergasse, an east-west street that becomes Hafengasse just before it hits Marktplatz, the principal square with the landmark Rathaus tower. Then its name changes again to Herrngasse for the final stretch to the remains of Rothenburg Castle and the gate called Burgtor.

The sector of town to the north, mainly between Marktplatz and Judengasse, is filled with monuments. But there are visitable destinations to the south, ending with the hospital complex at the very base of the question-mark-shaped town.

Rathaus (Marktplatz): Rothenburg's former wealth is nowhere better reflected than in the Town Hall that serves also as an effortless lesson in the architecture of two epochs. That half of the building just off the square, with a pencil-slim spire that is an extension of its A-shaped roof, is Gothic. Construction began in the thirteenth century, and it is in this section that one finds the Kaisersaal, or Emperors' Hall—high, wide, handsome, and open to visitors. The part of the Rathaus on Marktplatz, laden with oriel windows, gables, and fine detailing—especially the neoclassic doorways—is Renaissance, completed in the sixteenth century.

Jacobskirche (Geigengasse) ranks with the *Rathaus* as a major monument. This is an immense Gothic beauty. Its dissimilar towers distinguish it from without, the scale and art within cry out for appreciation. The high altar is a gilded, carved-wood Renaissance masterwork whose chief curiosity is a bespectacled St. Peter (eyeglasses were coming into use at this period). Quite as lovely is the west nave's altar, *The Last Supper* by sculptor Tilman Riemenschneider.

Franziskanerkirche (Herrngasse) was put up by the Franciscans at the height of the Gothic period and is distinguished by a choir screen that divides the choir from the nave. Have a look.

The Spital complex, at the southern tip of town, embraces a winning, originally Gothic church (now the main hospital building) and the onetime official residence of its administrator, a charmer known as the *Hegereiterhaus.*

Reichsstadt Museum (Judengasse) could not be more evocative of the Rothenburg past. It occupies a serene, out-of-use Dominican convent, parts of which go back 800 years. Bits and pieces—furniture, maps, paintings, engravings, documents, pottery, metalware, and the kitchen formerly used by the nuns—tell the town's story.

Walking the walls: No other cities, save York, England, and Luca, Italy, have walkable ramparts. Ascend to the walkway via the stairway of the gate called Klingentor. The panoramic views are super and worth the walk.

Doppelbrücke, the Tauber and its valley: You can walk down to the Tauber River and see Doppelbrücke, a remarkable twelve-century-old double-decker of a stone bridge. But there's an easier way to gain a panorama of bridge, river, and the valley—tranquil, green, with a patchwork of isolated farms and tiny stone hamlets. Just walk through the gate called Koboldzellertor, and poof! The valley is before you.

SETTLING IN

Hotel Eisenhut (Herrngasse 3) occupies a quartet of one-of-a-kind medieval houses on the town's poshest street. Three of these mansions are contiguous and constitute the main hotel quarters, with the fourth—an annex just across the *Gasse.* The decor is one of beamed ceilings, brass chandeliers, fresh flowers, dark wood furniture—much of it antique. There are 86 no-two-alike bedrooms, most with charming vistas; a choice of restaurants including one with two levels of galleries above it; inviting cocktail lounge. And in summer, a garden-terrace café. An exceptional hotel. Member, Relais et Châteaux. *Luxury.*

Hotel Goldener Hirsch (Untere Schmiedgasse 16) occupies quarters at once agreeable and ancient. There are fourscore bedrooms, many with private baths and sumptuous views. Public spaces evoke Old Rothenburg, especially the restaurant, which in warm weather occupies a riverview terrace. *First Class.*

Hotel Markusturm (Rödergasse 1) is more intimate than the Big Two above (there are 30 rooms, many with baths, all with charm). Its amenities include a delightful restaurant. *First Class.*

Hotel Tilman Riemenschneider (Georgengasse 11): A hotel named for the Renaissance wood sculptor represented in Rothenburg by his *Last Supper* in Jacobskirche—the only such hotel that I've come across in Germany—has to have something going for it. This house's pluses are a smack-in-the-center situation, half a hundred rooms period-style with bath, and a convenient restaurant. *Moderate.*

DAILY BREAD

Hotel Eisenhut Restaurants (Herrngasse 3): Happiness in Rothenburg is lunch or dinner in one of this unusual hotel's restaurants, preferably the galleried dining room. Veal specialties are delicious, the wines excellent, the pastries memorable. *Luxury.*

Blaue Terrasse Restaurant (Goldener Hirsch Hotel, Untere Schmiedgasse 16) is for warm-weather meals with views of the Tauber River valley. The menu is mostly German but with international favorites. *First Class.*

Hotel Markusturm Restaurant (Rödergasse 1) is pubby and welcoming, traditionally furnished as would befit its setting in a venerable house. Order grilled trout, and pay attention to the wine list; it's exceptional. *First Class.*

Ratsstube (Marktplatz 6): The restaurant of the historic *Rathaus,* or Town Hall, is ideal for lunch in the midst of touring, or for the evening meal. German favorites, and favored tabs. *Moderate.*

INCIDENTAL INTELLIGENCE

Summer sees this little town heavily populated with Romantic Road tourists, on half-day visits. Ideally, one visits at other times of year, and stays overnight, to more fully appreciate it. *Further information:* Kultur-und-Fremdenverkehrsamt—the town tourist office—is located in Marktplatz.

35

Stuttgart

Burghers cum Ballet

BACKGROUND BRIEFING

Stuttgart delights in what it self-deprecatingly professes to be its Swabian—read "regional"—personality. By that it means a no-nonsense, no-frills attitude toward life and living, a shunning of the luxurious, a backing away from the sophisticated, a suspicion of the refined, an apprehension of the innovative.

Yet this almost defiantly unregal onetime royal capital is not without enough attractive aspects to detain the pleasure visitor for a day or two.

It is not the frugal Stuttgarters' fault if their city—in the southwest on the Neckar River—does not look as old as it is. It goes way, way back (as Cannstatt) to the first-century Romans. German tribes, the Alemanni, successfully invaded it in the fourth century.

In the mid-tenth, a son of the Holy Roman Emperor—one Duke Luitpold—started a stud farm from which the present name of the city is believed to derive. It was not until the thirteenth century, though, that Stuttgart was properly chartered, just in time to become the official seat of the counts of Württemberg. They turned the expanding town into their capital in the fifteenth century, at about the time the Holy Roman Emperor decided that they should henceforth be styled dukes.

That title changed again, in the early eighteenth century, as a result of an alliance between the duke of the moment, Frederick II, with Napoleon, who upped him to elector of the Holy Roman Empire. After a few years—in 1806—Elector Frederick became King Frederick, Württemberg's first monarch. His successor, Wilhelm I, not only gave the kingdom a liberal constitution but, more to the point of this chapter, was instrumental in making Stuttgart—through a building and development program—a capital worthy of a royal seat.

By the time of World War II the city had become so heavily industrialized that the Allies were not about to neglect it. They did quite the reverse. More than half a hundred air raids virtually destroyed the historic core. If the restoration of the center has been less than brilliant—at least as regards giving the city its look of yore—it has at least been functional. And there were political developments. Immediately after the war, Stuttgart became capital of a *Land* called *Württemberg-Baden.* In 1953 it became capital of a larger *Land*—three regions merged—with a reverse name: *Baden-Württemberg.*

The hum of industry is again the name of the Stuttgart game, which itself does not a tourist center make. But there are cultural dimensions—a globally reputed ballet troupe and a clutch of orchestras and choruses together with a superb art museum—that are not to be lightly dismissed by the prospective visitor. And vineyards: they descend the hills framing the city almost into the pavements of downtown. A consequence is a Stuttgart penchant for the good Württemberg dry wines.

ON SCENE

Lay of the Land: If its aesthetics are not extraordinary, its compactness is enviable. Central Stuttgart is good walking territory. The coldly monolithic Hauptbahnof a post-World War II rebuilding of what had been a post-World War I landmark, is at the northern edge of the core, with a cluster of major—and minor—hotels in its shadow. The Hauptbahnhof fronts Arnulf-Klett Platz and Schillergasse, off of which Königstrasse, the main drag—with department stores, shops, restaurants, cafés—leads southward into the center. Königstrasse runs parallel to a vast park, Schlossgarten, in which and alongside are a number of destinations, including the Staatstheater, the Staatsgalerie, and the Altes Schloss, which houses the Landesmuseum. The Schloss fronts the main square, Schillerplatz, whose other landmark is the Stiftskirche, an originally Gothic church that must have been beautiful before a post-World War II reconstruction, which left little original save the apse, some stained glass, and sculptures of medieval dukes of Württemberg. Adjacent Schlossplatz is named for a graceful rococo palace, Neues Schloss, last home of the Württemberg kings and now used for government offices. Königstrasse continues south, and at Büchsenstrasse it just misses passing Marktplatz with the Rathaus to the east.

Neue Staatsgalerie Stuttgart (Konrad-Adenauer-Strasse) is one of Germany's sleeper museums, occupying striking modern quarters opened in 1984, adjacent to the still-used, original 1837 building. Its founder was King Wilhelm I, second of the quartet of nineteenth-century Württemberg kings. We're in his debt. He began what has become an extraordinarily rich presentation of great art—from the medieval Germans to today's New York School. There are altars and altar paintings by Swabian and other Germans, including works by the younger Holbein (a head—only a head—of St. Sebastian), Cranach, Baldung Grien, and others unfamiliar to us, like Jerg Ratgab whose four-section Herrenberger Altar out of the fifteenth century is enough to make a visit here memorable. Flemish and Dutch works are brilliant—Memling, Rubens, Hals, van Ruysdael—and a Rembrandt self-portrait. So are those of the Italians—a Carpaccio of St. Mark, a Tiepolo of Jesus and Joseph, a Giordano self-portrait—with this baroque master in black-rimmed spectacles! And a luminous Giovanni Bellini *Madonna and Child.* The French section is extraordinary—works by Bonnard and Vuillard, Gauguin and Pissaro, Cézanne and Signac, Monet and Maillol, Utrillo and Braque, Matisse and Roualt—with maybe a dozen Picassos. I am partial to August Macke among the German Expressionist group, but there are many others.

Württembergisches Landesmuseum (Altes Schloss, Schillerplatz) gets A + for its setting. The Altes Schloss was where the Württemberg rulers lived before nearby Neues Schloss went up in the eighteenth century. The Altes is indeed old, with origins in the tenth century. But it's now mostly a restored Renaissance structure, with a triple-galleried courtyard its principal beauty-point. The museum's thrust is regional culture—the fine and applied arts over the centuries. A golden brooch from the pre-Christian Celts, a cameo of Jupiter from the Roman period, a silver stag out of the Renaissance, richly colored playing cards, medieval stained glass, baroque altarpieces, rococo gowns, and the star of the show: the Royal House of Württemberg's crown jewels, shown off to advantage before portraits of each of the quartet of kings, as well as a painting by Franz Winterhalter—the same artist who immortalized England's Victoria and France's Eugénie—of a Württemberg queen.

Daimler-Benz Museum (Mercedesstrasse in the quarter called Untertürkheim): Should the folks out at the Mercedes-Benz factory change their minds and decide to reopen their museum—it's been closed for security reasons except for visitors who make arrangements well in advance—you might want to have a look. The subject is cars and their beginnings, as reflected in the pioneering achievements of local heroes Gottlieb Daimler and Carl Benz. The former created his automobile engine as far back as 1883; the latter, a complete car not long after. They merged their operation in the decade after World War I, and the museum tells their stories, individually and collectively, with antique species the museum's showpieces.

Schloss Solitude is a good 10 miles west of town, but possibly worth the excursion if you're curious as to how the Württemberg rulers kept house in the country. Not at all badly. Solitude is a palace typical of the rococo era of the eighteenth century in which it was built. People laugh at the extra-large crescent—to accommodate the extra-large stomach of the first king, Frederick I—carved from the surface of the royal writing table. But there are beautiful things to see, including a number of rococo rooms. Allow a half day.

The Weissenhof Colony (Friedrich-Eber Strasse) is for students of modern architecture and city planners. It's an away-from-the-center clutch of model houses out of the nineteen-twenties, with the works of such innovators as Mies van der Rohe, Le Corbusier (with Pierre Jeanneret), and Walter Gropius. The Nazis evacuated the place—it was decreed "degenerate" in 1938—and had planned to have it razed. But they used it for their own purposes, instead. Some houses were bombed during World War II, and then restored, and have come to be recognized as a milestone in the development of mid- and later- twentieth century residential architecture. A half-day, unless you've a car and want to zip through quickly.

SETTLING IN

Hotel am Schlossgarten (Schillerstrasse 23) is a near-neighbor of the station that has the advantage of backing on to Schlossgarten, the inner city's pretty park. This is a likeable modern house with a sense of style. There are 125 attractive, fully equipped rooms and suites, with especially spacious doubles, some with super views. The bar-lounge is warm and inviting, and there are a pair of restaurants with similar bills of fare but different decors—one dressy, the other casual: they're worthy of later comment. *Luxury.*

Hotel Graf Zeppelin (Arnulf-Klett-Passage 7) is post-World War II modern. Bedrooms are formidably severe but offer all comforts. Suites are a bit more relaxed, warmer in look. The lobby has the size—and ambience—of a stadium. A light touch is wanted. Restaurants—a dining room and a grill with very good food—are the hotel at its most cordial. Opposite the station. Part of the Steigenberger chain. *Luxury.*

Intercity Hotel (Hauptbahnhof, Arnulf-Klett-Platz 2) is what train travelers dream of: you literally roll out of bed and you're not only at but in the station for an early-morning departure. Ninety of the 100 mod/functional rooms have private baths; neat bar, convenient restaurant. *First Class.*

Hotel Royal (Sophienstrasse 35): Rather striking in its contemporary decor, with a hundred rooms, 75 of which have full private baths, the remainder sinks and toilets but no showers or tubs. Paneled restaurant, adjacent bar-lounge. Heart of downtown. *First Class.*

Hotel Rieker (Friedrichstrasse 3) is a next-door neighbor to the *Hauptbahnhof*. There are some 60 functional rooms, a good number of which have private baths. Breakfast only. *Moderate.*

Hotel Mack (Kriegerstrasse 7) is a short walk from the Hauptbahnhof, with half a hundred cheery rooms, the majority of them with private baths. Breakfast only. Same kindly management as the Hotel Pflieger, across the street, recommended below. *Moderate.*

Hotel Pflieger (Kriegerstrasse 11) is the across-the-street sister-hotel to the Mack. Twenty-five of its agreeable rooms have baths. This house is older than its partner but has the advantage of an on-premises restaurant. *Moderate.*

DAILY BREAD

Alte Post (Friedrichstrasse 43) has the look of a traditional Stuttgart inn, and the fare of a top-category eating place, which indeed it is. Try some of the Swabian dishes: a beef soup of the region, a veal fillet, or even boiled beef with horseradish sauce—the *Tafelspitz* of Vienna—for a main course. Hot apple fritters—*Apfelkuchel*—with vanilla sauce for dessert. Fine wines, including local ones. *Luxury.*

Alte Kanzlei (Schillerplatz 5) occupies the former kitchens of the Altes Schloss. And very handsome it is: antique prints on its white stucco walls with illumination from shaded chandeliers over each table. The table d'hôte lunches and dinners are good buys; start with noodle soup, go on to roast rabbit, and conclude with a chocolate mousse. I rate it: *First Class/Luxury.*

Zirbelstube (Hotel am Schlossgarten, Schillerstrasse 23): An oak-paneled room for tasty lunches and dinners. Set-course menus might include a schnitzel, or poultry or game entrées. Good cellar. *First Class.*

Mövenpick (Weiner Schlossplatz 11) is one of a Swiss chain that has branches throughout Germany. I like their restaurants wherever I've tried them. Food often has a French touch, but there are local specialties, too. Both table d'hôte and à la carte; snacks. *Moderate/First Class.*

Zeppelin-Stüble (Hotel Graf Zeppelin, Arnulf-Klett-Passage 7) is the hotel's atmospheric grill room chock-a-block with local artifacts on rough-hewn shelves and stone walls. The clientele is as much local as visiting, drawn to the hearty fare, from steaks to schnitzels. *Moderate/First Class.*

König im Königshof (Königstrasse 18): A massive heart-of-town spot popular with locals who want to fill up inexpensively on Swabian specialties, like *Spätzle* (the tiny dumplings that are served with virtually every meat dish in this part of Germany), and the sausage of the region—*Leberwurst* and *Griebenwurst,* not easy to love. There are daily specials with more conventional fare. *Moderate.*

Weinstube Arche (Bärenstrasse 2) is as good a typical wine restaurant as any at which to become acquainted with the Swabian wines, especially the surprisingly good reds—Trollinger, Schwarzriesling, and Lemberger among them. They're dry, with character. Accompany them with specialties like *Zwiebelkuchen*—the Swabian answer to quiche Lorraine; *Maultaschen,* a filled dumpling, ravioli-size; and *Rostbraten,* sautéed beef with onion, served, of course, with *Spätzle. Moderate.*

Café Königsbau (Schlossplatz) is a traditional people-watching spot in the historic Königsbau on Schlossplatz. Order cake or a snack with coffee or a glass of wine, and watch the crowds drift by. *Moderate.*

Café Schlossgarten (Hotel am Schlossgarten, Schillerstrasse 23) is the summer-only outdoor café of this leading hotel, fronting on the park called Schlossgarten—and very appealing. *Moderate.*

Restaurant Fernsehturm Stuttgart (Jahnstrasse): Stuttgarters tend to regard their nearly 500-foot-high television tower as a wonder of the modern world. It is, in fact, no less ugly than its counterparts in cities around the planet. And the view from on high is not so spectacular that the visitor is missing much if he forgoes ascent. Location is south of town, and there are a pair of restaurants on as many levels as well as observation platforms. As with these elevated eateries everywhere, you go more for the view than the viands. *Moderate/First Class.*

SOUND OF MUSIC

Stuttgarter Ballet: Granted that Stuttgart is an unlikely locale for a world-class ballet troupe with an international company and repertory. The fact remains that this company—whose home base is the *Württembergische Staatstheater* (Schlossgarten)—is one of the great ones, right up there with American Ballet Theatre and the New York City Ballet in the U.S.A., Britain's Royal Ballet, the Danish Royal Ballet, Leningrad's Kirov, and Moscow's Bolshoi. South African-born John Cranko—after success at London's Royal Ballet—put the Stuttgart troupe on the map during a tenure that began in 1962, and ended with his death in 1973. His forte was the dramatic full-length ballet with a credible plot line and a contemporary twist but tradition-based choreography. He drew dancers from all over the world. His successors have been American choreographer Glen Tetley, and more recently Brazilian ballerina Marcia Haydée. The company, a majority of whose dancers are American, crosses the Atlantic for an American season every other year, but if they're at the Stuttgart Opera House—its neoclassic façade is far lovelier than its badly restored if spacious interior—while you're in town, you're in luck. The repertory is diverse—Balanchine, Béjart, Kenneth MacMillan, John Neumeier, with younger talents, like New York-born William Forsythe and France's Patrice Montagnon, creating contemporary hits. The Cranko classics—*The Taming of the Shrew, Romeo and Jullet, Eugene Onegin, Carmen*—remain. And the range, otherwise, extends from the traditional *Giselle* to Forsythe's contemporary *Dream of Galilei.*

The Stuttgart Opera, though not as celebrated as the ballet, is a company of quality and imagination, so much so that the Wagner grandsons have used it as a winter venue for avant-garde productions of the summer Wagner Festival in Bayreuth.

Liederhalle (Büchsenstrasse) is among Stuttgart's truly successful post-World War II buildings: a horizontal structure—asymmetric and original—housing a trio of concert halls. Go for the experience of the setting, and for the caliber of the music, including not only the city's symphony and chamber ensembles, but another Stuttgart specialty: choruses, of which there are several.

INCIDENTAL INTELLIGENCE

Stuttgart is a part of Lufthansa's domestic network. Echterdingen Airport is nine miles south of town and connected with the town terminal (near the Hauptbahnhof) by airport buses and taxis. Verkehrsamt der Landeshauptstadt Stuttgart—the city tourist office—is at Luetenschlagerstrasse 3 and in the arcades of the Hauptbahnhof.

36

Travemünde

The Good Life, Baltic-Style

BACKGROUND BRIEFING

You have to be a northern European—accustomed to the frigid waters of the North Atlantic, the North Sea and the Baltic—to want to spend a proper vacation at a northern European seaside resort. Even Americans like me, whose home territory is the northern part of the Atlantic coast, find northern European waters cold and northern European beaches too often sunless.

Withal, these gathering spots for holidaymakers can be fun for short visits—overnight perhaps, or a day's excursion—to take in the crowds, their diversions, and their homes away from home. A good case in point is Travemünde, next-door neighbor to Lübeck (the subject of a chapter) at the very mouth of the Trave River, on the Baltic.

ON SCENE

If you go not expecting Deauville or Torquay, Travemünde can delight. It might be placed on a par with, say Holland's Scheveningen: more substantial than charming.

A onetime fishing village with a respectable history dating back six centuries, Travemünde has known vacationers since the early decades of the last century. But it is mostly contemporary: a wide strand of beach fringed by hotels, with a special attraction—its vast enclosed year-round swimming pool with outdoor pools for adults and children. Diversions run the usual resort gamut—deep-sea fishing and sailing, golf and tennis, casino gambling and disco dancing, walks along Strandpromenade for the sea air, and along the street called Vorderreihe for the shops and cafés. There's a well-equipped health spa. And an added attraction: Look across the water to a distant beach, and you're looking at East Germany.

SETTLING IN

Hotel Kurhaus (Aussenallee 10) is Travemünde at its grandest. This is a lovely old house—it opened in 1913—operated by the owners of the Casino next door. Everything is b-i-g and high-ceilinged—lobbies and lounges, bar, restaurants, and, hardly to be overlooked, 100-plus handsome rooms and suites. There's an indoor pool, and of course the beach, just out front. *Luxury.*

Hotel Maritim (Strandpromenade) is a jumbo of a skyscraper—Travemünde's first—whose graceless bulk adds not a whit of beauty to the pleasant beachfront. There is no denying its convenience, though—functional rooms with terraces and views, restaurants including the inevitable rooftop spot, bars, pool. *Luxury.*

Golf Hotel (Helldahl 12) is seafront, at the golf course, with full facilities, including an exceptional restaurant, of which more below. *First Class.*

Strandhaus Becker (Strandpromenade 7) is a small house with a location on central Strandpromenade; breakfast only. *Moderate.*

DAILY BREAD

Casino Restaurant (Strandpromenade): If you've the opportunity for but one splashy meal, select this seaview terrace restaurant. Menu is international. *Luxury.* (The Casino's *Wein Restaurant* is equally pricey, open only for dinner, and with strolling musicians to compensate for the lack of a sea view.)

Seetempl Restaurant (Golf Hotel, Helldahl 12) is elegant and elevated, with the food as good as the views; cake and coffee in mid-afternoon are equally delicious. *First Class.*

Dietz (Kaisersallee) is agreeable, with a wide-ranging menu and tabs that are mostly *Moderate.*

AFTER DARK

Casino (Strandpromenade): Not strictly after dark, because the Casino is open during the day as well. But more fun at night. Take your choice of roulette (American), blackjack, baccarat, and punto banco. You're never far from the source of drink or food (see *Daily Bread* above). Two caveats: have your passport; and gents, jacket and tie.

INCIDENTAL INTELLIGENCE

Come over for the day or evening from Lübeck (subject of a chapter of its own), which is a quarter-hour's drive; you can even taxi. (Or, conversely, headquarter in Travemünde—its hotels are better—and commute to Lübeck for daytime exploration.) You may arrive or depart by ship; there is scheduled Baltic Sea service on modern passenger liners between Travemünde and four Scandinavian countries: Denmark, Norway, Finland, and Sweden. *Further information:* Verkehrsamt Travemünde—the town tourist office—at the passenger ship terminal in the harbor.

37

Trier

Caesar's Northern Capital

BACKGROUND BRIEFING

Much of Germany is dotted with souvenirs of the ancient Roman presence. But it's a drop in the bucket—or better yet, a marble urn—when a comparison is made with Trier. This way-west West German city was more than a Roman colony. Half a dozen Roman emperors made it their northern headquarters. And even after the Roman Empire fell, Trier did not. Early Christian centuries saw it thrive as an evangelical outpost, and for a second time, albeit in another sense, it was a Second Rome. Trier remained a power through the Middle Ages, the Renaissance, and the baroque. Even today, twenty centuries later, (Trier, as Germany's oldest city, celebrated its 2000th birthday, all year long, in 1984) this small Moselle River Valley port—now a wine-distribution center—is a destination to be reckoned with.

The Romans began reckoning with the Treverians—as they were then called—about the time of Christ when they built a town whose name was a mix of local and Roman terminology: Augusta (for Emperor Augustus) Treverorium. Located at a point where cargoes from the south and west converged with those from due north and east, the settlement could not help but thrive. Shrewd Romans exploited its location for strategic, administrative, and cultural functions. Emperors became partial to the place. They included Julius Caesar, the first to visit it; Augustus, whose name was given to it; Postumus, the first to live in Trier; Diocletian, who made it one of the Empire's four co-capitals; Constantine Chlorus, who was elected head of the Empire's vast western region and embarked on a successful building program to fashion Trier in the image of Rome; and lastly, Constantine Chlorus's son Constantine, who administered all of Rome's colonies from Britain to Spain, through Trier.

Transfer of the principal seat of empire from Rome to Byzantium in the fourth century was the beginning of Trier's fall within the Empire. But about that time, the Christians focused on the city, building a massive church, and later, in Charlemagne's time, creating an archdiocesan seat in its cathedral.

As the Holy Roman Empire came to control Germany's various states, Trier's archbishops became temporal as well as church rulers: prince-electors in the empire that thrived economically, culturally, and politically through the Renaissance and baroque eras, until in the early nineteenth century it allied with much stronger Prussia.

By no means all of ancient Trier that was destroyed in World War II bombings has been reconstructed. But this city has rebuilt a remarkable portion of its core. Add to its monuments preeminence as the major city of the Moselle wine region, and the stimulus of cultural crosscurrents blowing over the frontier from Luxembourg, France, and Belgium, and Trier emerges as eminently visitable.

ON SCENE

Lay of the Land: Trier's center hugs the Moselle, lying mostly between its waters, to the west, and the Hauptbahnhof, to the east. From the station, it's an agreeable walk along Theodor-Heuss-Allee to the premier Trier trademark, the Roman gateway called Porta Nigra. Running perpendicular to Theodor-Heuss-Allee at this junction is pedestrians-only Simeonstrasse. It leads into Square No. 1: Hauptmarkt, whose near-neighbors are adjacent churches—the Dom, or cathedral, and Liebefrauenkirche. Other visitor destinations are nearby.

Simeonstrasse changes its name to Brotstrasse once it crosses Hauptmarkt, going south, eventually taking one to St. Matthias-kirche, the sightseer's southernmost goal. To the west, down at the river, approached directly via Dietrichstrasse are a pair of bridges, one of which—appropriately named Römerbrücke—still has its original Roman foundation posts.

Porta Nigra (Theodor-Heuss-Allee at Simeonstrasse) translates as Black Gate. Its light sandstone façade—dating, believe it or not, to the second century—began to darken with advancing years. It was a name given by medieval Trierians—and it has stuck. But there is more than age and color here. The gate is a substantial double-tower structure, large enough to have housed a pair of medieval churches, and with an inner court to which attacking forces were lured unsuspectingly.

Simeonstift and ***Städtisches Museum*** (Simeonstrasse) are adjacent to Porta Nigra and conveniently visited in conjunction with it. This complex was built as the cloister of St. Simeon Church, and was incorporated into the next-door Porta Nigra. What remains is a galleried Romanesque rectangle that comes through as a Trier charm spot, with a café (there are umbrella-topped tables in the courtyard during warm-weather months) and—not to be missed—the Städisches Museum, the City of Trier's repository of historical momentoes. A range of centuries is represented, including sculpture and painting—Middle Ages (the loveliest, especially as regards the sculpture) to this very month.

Dom and ***Liebfrauenkirche*** (Domfreihof) are the pair of churches just east of Hauptmarkt. The *Dom,* or cathedral, goes back to the fourth century, when Trier replaced its association with the Roman Empire with an allegiance to the Roman Catholic Church. Built on the foundations of what had been Emperor Constantine's Trier palace (and with souvenirs of that era in the *Dom's* treasure-filled Bischöfliche Museum), the cathedral is a felicitous maze of architectural styles—heavily Romanesque on through to baroque. The perspective of mixes is at its most dramatic from the *Kreuzgang,* or cloister: Trier at its most tranquil. Bonus: the so-called Sacred Cloth, in the *Dom's* Treasury; it's reputed to have belonged to Christ. Liebfrauenkirche is something else again—a pure Gothic work, mostly thirteenth century and one of the finest of its period in Germany. The long, vaulted nave, framed by a pair of chapels, is lovely.

Bischöfliches Museum (Banthusstrasse 6), the Bishops' Museum, is a repository of recently found objects of art and artisanship from the fourth century, when the cathedral was first built. Sculpture, fresco fragments, other treasures.

Aula Palatina (Basilika) and ***Kurfürstliches Palais*** (Weberbach) are adjacent monuments. The Aula Palatina, also known as the Basilika—and today a Protestant church, to further complicate its identification—is a somber, mostly Romanesque remnant of the fourth century, when it had been part of the Roman emperor's palace. Adjacent to it is a vastly better-looking building—a graceful baroque work. Long the palace of the Trier archbishop-electors, it remains in service as a government headquarters; pop in to see its breathtaking main staircase.

Kaiserthermen (Weberbach) and ***Amphitheater*** (Olwigerstrasse) are a remarkable pair of near-to-each-other monuments of Roman Trier. The first is what remains of the opulent town baths, including the Caldarium—the spacious pavilion where citizens took their hot dips (distinct from warm dunks taken in the Tepidarium and cold dips in—you guessed it—the Frigidarium). The Amphitheater, in its day—which was 19 centuries ago—seated some 30,000. Even today, it is impressive, with a couple of dozen rows of seats in three tiers enclosing a dozen-plus ground-level rooms, believed to have served as cages for gladiators' lions.

Landesmuseum (Ostallee 44) is a trove of ancient treasures, mostly—but not exclusively—Roman, and including mosaics, pottery, and sculpture in bronze as well as marble. Local medieval artifacts, too.

Karl-Marx-Haus (Brückenstrasse 10): Yes, you are reading correctly. The house in which this son of Trier was born is now a museum of Marxiana; documents, pictures, other memorabilia in what is, to understate, a surprise Trier package.

Paulinkirche (Gobenstrasse) is architectural Trier at its most joyous—an ebullient bit of Bavarian rococo come north. This church wants to be experienced from within—a massive main altar, color-drenched ceiling frescoes.

SETTLING IN

Dorint-Hotel Porta Nigra (Porta-Nigra-Platz 1) says it all in its name: location. A modern house lacking in any special aesthetic distinction, it is to be appreciated for its comfortable rooms, convenient situation, good restaurant-bar, and café with a view. *First Class.*

Dorint-Hotel Europäischer-Hof (Paulinstrasse 1, at Porta-Nigra-Platz) is another perfectly situated house, same management as the Porta Nigra but simpler, with a good proportion of bath-equipped rooms. Breakfast only. *Moderate.*

Central Hotel (Sichelstrasse 32) is indeed central—near Porta Nigra. It's smallish—with 30 rooms, of which some have private baths; restaurant, terrace café. *Moderate.*

Dom Hotel (Hauptmarkt 18) is on the history-laden main square. It's small, just over a score of rooms, some with private baths—and welcoming. Breakfast only. *Moderate.*

Holiday Inn (Am Verteilerring) has the not-to-be-underestimated advantages of all of the links in that chain: comfortable bedrooms (220 all told) and delightfully modern baths with stateside-type showers over the tubs; restaurant and bar-lounge, efficient service. Plus a terrace-café on the roof for panoramas of town and river. Only drawback is location: The inn is riverfront, but it's a fair way upstream from the heart of town. That's why it's at the bottom of my hotels group. *Luxury.*

DAILY BREAD

Ratskeller (Hauptmarkt 14) gets A for Atmosphere. Location is the beautifully arched cellar of a landmark fifteenth-century building on the beautiful main square. This is for German standbys—hearty soups, pork specialties, rich desserts, and of course Moselle wine in abundant variety. *First Class.*

Pfeffermühle (Zurlaubener Ufer 76) is more than the "pepper mill" of its name. This is the town's fanciest eatery, with an extensive menu at once traditional-German and traditional-international, and an exceptional wine list that can double as a primer on the region's own Moselles. Central. *Luxury.*

Zum Domstein (Hauptmarkt 5) is a longtime favorite. Setting is a series of atmospheric rooms in a centuries-old house. The drill—aside from basics like schnitzels and sauerbratens—is the ritual tasting of wines from a cellar that might be likened to a bottomless well. Ask your waiter to lay it on for you. *First Class.*

Brunnenhof (Simeonstift) is an earlier-counseled restaurant-café in the cloister of Simeonstift adjacent to Porta Nigra. There are outdoor tables—in the courtyard—during the warm-weather months. *Moderate/First Class.*

Drehscheibe (Fleischstrasse 40) may not sound like a source of pizza and pasta, but it is. And a touch of Italian fare could hardly be amiss in this onetime co-capital of the Roman Empire. Central. *Moderate/First Class.*

SOUND OF MUSIC

Stadttheater (Am Augustinerhof) is Trier's centrally located multipurpose opera house-theater-concert hall, with concerts by its own symphony, plays, and visiting attractions.

INCIDENTAL INTELLIGENCE

The nearest international airport is at Luxembourg City, Trier being more geographically convenient to the Grand Duchy and Belgium than to most of Germany. While you're in town, book a boat trip on the Moselle; in summer there are overnight cruises to Koblenz (subject of a chapter), at the junction of the Moselle and Rhine, with stops at pretty wine villages en route.

There are, as well, steamer trips into Luxembourg, with tie-ups at its picturesque riverside towns. *Further information:* Trier Tourist Information—a municipally operated office—is at Porta-Nigra-Platz.

38

Ulm

The Danube and a Cathedral

BACKGROUND BRIEFING

A town whose name is spelled out in but three letters has no business being so history-rich. Ulm is a sleeper. Straddling the Danube, on the very frontier between the modern German states of Baden-Württemberg and Bavaria, this ancient city has been a busy river port since the ninth century.

With the advent of the Renaissance, it achieved power, both commercial and political, ruling a considerable realm in the Danube area. At its peak in the fifteenth century, work was well underway on a matchless cathedral.

As trade routes changed and the fortunes of more than one war took their toll, Ulm saw cities to the east and west best it. In the twentieth century it evolved into a double town—old Ulm and its more modern across-the-river partner, Neu Ulm. World War II nearly leveled the historic core, but the cathedral or Münster was mercifully spared, and the medieval quarter surrounding it has been largely rebuilt. Each of the contemporary Ulms is in a different German state—old in Baden-Württemberg, neu in Bavaria. But they share common services, and promote themselves to tourists as a single entity. It should go without saying that old Ulm has the edge.

ON SCENE

Lay of the Land: Arrive by train—from either Stuttgart to the west or Munich to the east—at the Hauptbahnhof, and you're a 10-minute stroll, along Bahnhofstrasse and its continuation, Hirschstrasse, from the ancient core, and the spire of the Münster, the highest point for miles. Neuestrasse, the principal shopping street, is to the south, parallel to Hirschstrasse, with the Rathaus fronting it. The Danube, in its turn, runs parallel with Neuestrasse, a few minutes' walk away. You'll gain a panorama of the old city and Neu Ulm across the river, from a promenade along ramparts at the water's edge.

The Münster (Münsterplatz): Official statistics tell us that it is nothing less than the largest Gothic church in all Germany, save Cologne Cathedral, and that its spire, at 528 feet, is the planet's tallest. But it's not for size alone that one wants to see Ulm *Münster*. Principal reason is beauty, from the lacy façade (part of which, the spire, was completed as recently as 1890) through the consistently Gothic interior. A central nave leads directly (there is no transept) to one of Europe's most remarkable carved-wood choirs. Stalls are the work of a fifteenth-century master named Jörg Syrlin, who surmounted the choristers' seats with two rows of unusual, life-sized carved heads. Even more striking is a series of busts of ancient Greek prophetesses (sibyls) and Greek philosophers that punctuate the stalls' sides. Stained glass in the Besserer Chapel is exceptional, as are the frescoes framing the high altar, and the fan-vaulting throughout. If you have the strength, youth, or both, ascend the spire for a view of Ulm, the Danube, and distant Alps.

Stadtmuseum (Neustrasse): If a second historic Ulm interior is to be explored, make it the municipal museum, which occupies a cluster of mellow houses out of the past. Of special interest are regional furniture, furnishings and crafts, and Ulm's own collection of Renaissance paintings.

Rathaus (Neustrasse): A near-neighbor of the museum, Ulm's City Hall is a gabled treasure dating to the Middle Ages, but with Renaissance additions. You needn't go in to appreciate a façade embracing frescoes, coats of arms, and an astronomical clock.

Fischerviertel is simply the German name for a core-of-town quarter between the cathedral and the Danube. Its streets, lined with ancient houses, lead to the river and the ramparts fringing it, the lot constituting one of the most charming strolls in urban Germany.

Out-of-town treats: *Deutsches Brotmuseum* is precisely what its name indicates: a repository of exhibits and documentation relating to the history of the staff of life; all you wanted to know about bread, in a country that knows how to bake it. Also southwest of the city—but on the opposite side of the Danube (which can be crossed via Adenauer Bridge)—is *Kloster Wiblingen,* worth visiting for two reasons: a rococo chapel with an exuberant fresco covering its ceiling, and a beauty of a library in the same vibrant tradition: golden capitals of its Corinthian pillars support *faux marbre* balconies; shelves bulge with leather-bound eighteenth-century books.

SETTLING IN

Intercity Hotel (Bahnhofplatz) has it made: you walk from your train into the hotel lobby, for this modern hotel is a part of the station complex. It's cheery, with bright rooms (the bulk with private baths or showers), restaurant, bar, *Weinstube. First Class.*

Hotel Neutor (Neuer Graben 23) is smaller than the Intercity, but central and with a restaurant. *First Class.*

Hotel Ulmer Spatz (Münsterplatz 27) is a comfortable house in the shadow of the cathedral. Some rooms with private baths; restaurant. *Moderate.*

DAILY BREAD

Zur Forelle (Fischergasse 25) is an ancient core-of-town house that draws crowds of locals and visitors alike. Order the trout for which the restaurant is named, or one of the day's specials. *First Class.*

Jägerstube (Intercity Hotel) is an inviting *Weinstube,* with antlered deer heads on its walls, Windsor chairs, solid fare. *First Class/Luxury.*

Ratskeller (Marktplatz) is the Town Hall's eatery—reliable as they are, usually, throughout Germany. Try any of the traditional dishes—veal or pork especially—or a daily special. *Moderate/First Class.*

Pflugmerzler (Pfluggasse 6) is traditional-style, and noteworthy not only for its good looks but for the good value of its prix fixe lunches and dinners. *Moderate.*

SOUND OF MUSIC

Ulm Theater: Smallish city though it is, Ulm can surprise with the caliber and range of its presentations—opera, ballet, concerts, plays—in its relatively recent (1969) good-looker of a municipal theater.

INCIDENTAL INTELLIGENCE

Ulm is an ideal one-day-excursion destination, from, say, Stuttgart to the west, or Munich to the east, with excellent rail connections to and from each of these cities. *Further information:* Verkehrsamt Ulm—the city tourist office—is at Münsterplatz 2.

39

Wiesbaden

Kaisers' Playground—Updated

BACKGROUND BRIEFING

The ancient Romans liked their thermal springs and baths and knew how to spot them when they colonized the north of Europe a couple of millennia back. England's Bath was their discovery; so, indeed, was Germany's Wiesbaden. In those days—the first and second centuries after Christ—the name was a Latin one, Aquae Mattiacorum, but the game was not unlike what it has been for most of the ensuing centuries: taking the waters while taking in the scene.

Even at its most fashionable period—in the eighteenth and nineteenth centuries when it was the seat of the duchy of Nassau and later a favorite retreat of the rulers and courtiers of Prussia, by which it was absorbed—it can safely be assumed that Wiesbaden did not have the light touch of Bath. And that still is the case, with Wiesbaden now capital of the modern German Land—or state—that takes the ancient name of the region, Hesse.

Still, all things being relative, there is no question but that this city is a small planet removed, at least in matters like style and ambience, from also-ancient Mainz, its sister city directly across the Rhine River bridges.

Mainz likes to guide its visitors back to the Middle Ages, when its cathedral was built. Wiesbaden, rather sensibly, concentrates on the much more immediate past—the most recent pair of centuries, when it was at its grandest. Its lures appeal to the fit as well as the ailing. For the former, there are opera, ballet, and concerts; a hotel plant that is one of Germany's finest and most convenient (Frankfurt International Airport is less than an hour distant) and an easy-to-negotiate core with an ambience that, if not as lighthearted as that of Bath, comes as close as a north German counterpart possibly can.

ON SCENE

Lay of the Land: Wiesbaden is nothing if not walkable; geography is easily grappled with. Begin where so many visitors do, at the Hauptbahnhof, on Bahnhofplatz. The heart of town is less than a mile away, via the principal thoroughfare, known at the station as Friedrich-Ebert-Allee. Further along it crosses Rheinstrasse and becomes more fashionable—lined with shops and cafés and hotels—and changes name, to Wilhelmstrasse.

Wilhelmstrasse cuts through fashionable Wiesbaden, the area between Rheinstrasse and Sonnenbergerstrasse, with public buildings in parklands to the right as one proceeds from the Hauptbahnhof, and a civic area centering about Marktplatz to the left.

This is a district for leisurely strolls and pauses to watch one's fellow visitors from strategic tables in street cafés. After dark, the look is dressy, for Wiesbaden places great store on its public entertainments.

Kurhaus complex (Kurpark): Architecturally and otherwise, the Kurhaus looks every inch the kind of structure that a turn-of-century German kaiser would officially dedicate—and one did. The emperor was Wilhelm II, the year was 1907. What you see on approaching is a domed neoclassic building lined by long and lovely colonnades that give the Kurhaus what charm it has. Its look, though neoclassic, is the ponderous version of that style popular in the late nineteenth century, modeled after Rome's

Baths of Caracalla, though gussied up with the glossy materials favored by the Edwardians and also approved of by their German cousins.

In World War II the Kurhaus was bombed—and badly. But, like so many German buildings beloved of their communities, it has risen again. What you will want to inspect, or better yet, make use of, is one of the poshest casinos in a nation of posh casinos, with roulette, 21, and a bar; a concert hall ringed by Corinthian columns, with a resident symphony—Staatsorchester Wiesbaden—of deserved repute; the paneled Weinsaal Restaurant and a more formal, luxury restaurant that gives onto a pretty park. Fountains with spa waters to sip are within the wing called Brunnenkolonnade.

Hessiches Staatstheater (Kurpark), a key unit of the Kurhaus park cluster, is Wiesbaden's turn-of-century opera house, beaux arts with a glittering foyer and a four-level auditorium, wherein perform resident opera and ballet troupes; visiting companies, too.

Altes Rathaus (Marktplatz) is the small-scale Renaissance-style city hall of old, still seeing municipal service, and a landmark square.

Schlossplatz, the square adjacent to Marktplatz, is centered by a sixteenth-century well surmounted by a gilded lion framing Wiesbaden's coat of arms. Here, too, is:

Stadtschloss, longtime city residence for the princes of Hesse. Now it is the Legislature of the state of Hesse. Ask if you may have a look at the legislators' chamber.

Wiesbaden Museum (Friedrich-Ebert-Allee near Rheinstrasse) looks, from without, to be a modern-day variation on the theme of an Egyptian temple. Within are a mixed bag of exhibits, including a group of works by the German Expressionist painter Jawlensky, along with some French Impressionists, a scattering of Flemish Old Masters, fine local eighteenth- and nineteenth-century furniture of the region.

Neroberg is Wiesbaden's answer to the Bavarian Alps—a gentle nearby peak ascendable by an amusing cog railway for a visit to a gilded onion-domed chapel (Orthodox) and a restaurant-café with views.

SETTLING IN

Hotel Nassauer Hof (Kaiser-Friedrich-Platz 3) is German hotelkeeping at its zenith—a fine old house transformed into warm and winning mod-look, in beiges and browns, public spaces through guest rooms. The bar-lounge is capacious and cozy. Die Pfanne Restaurant is rustic but not seriously so. The 200-plus rooms and suites are a joy; some even have electric blow-dryers in their opulent baths. And a superbly equipped Executive Fitness Spa opened in 1984. Location: just opposite the Kurpark. Member, Leading Hotels of the World. *Luxury.*

Hotel Schwarzer Bock (Kransplatz 12) is not kidding when it advises that it has been on the scene since 1486. Not, of course, in its present, largely turn-of-century quarters. Still, few hotels have so ancient a pedigree. Warm, inviting, traditional, with no two rooms or suites alike—in contemporary, Empire, baroque, or rococo decor. Antiques-accented corridors, with a cluster of restaurants and bars and an in-house spa with thermal swimming pool. *Luxury.*

Hôtel de France (Taunusstrasse 49) is precisely what its name indicates: a touch of Gaul in Wiesbaden. French-owned and operated, it has comfortable rooms, with bath, welcoming lounge, one of the best restaurants in town, (see *Daily Bread)*, and a location on Wiesbaden's Antiques Row, a few minutes' walk from the Kurpark. *First Class.*

Hotel Blum (Wilhelmstrasse 44) is heart of the action. Indeed, its café is possibly more celebrated than are its sleeping quarters. There are, however, nearly 100 comfortable rooms, and a proper restaurant. *First Class.*

Hotel Fürstenhof Esplanade (Sonnenbergerstrasse 32) is an agreeable, traditional-style old-timer—cozy, central, and with a good restaurant. *First Class.*

Central Hotel (Bahnhofstrasse 65) is closer to the station than the Kurpark; full-facility. *Moderate.*

Hotel Forum (Abraham-Lincoln-Strasse 17) is a good distance from the center of town, boldly color-splashed, ultra-contemporary. Restaurant-bars. *First Class.*

Hotel Aukamm (Aukammallee 31), in the out-of-town Aukamm district, is big, modern, unlovely, and full-facility, next door to the Deutsche Klinik für Diagnostik—a reputed counterpart of the Mayo Clinic in Minnesota. *First Class.*

DAILY BREAD

Die Ente vom Lehel (Hotel Nassauerhof, Kaiser Friedrich Platz 3) is the epitome of dining in the grand manner—eye-filling with respect to ambience, delicious in the case of its *nouvelle*-accented Franco-German cuisine, and with an exceptional wine list. Ideally combined with a gala evening at the opera and/or casino. *Luxury.*

Hôtel de France Restaurant (Taunusstrasse 49) is the genuine French article. The house specialty is seafood—fresh oysters, mussels and lobster. But the repertoire runs a full gamut—pâté de foie gras through escargots, entrées like *carré d'agneau aux flageolets* (roast lamb with beans) and *canard à l'orange* (duck in orange sauce). Delicious desserts. French wines, too. *Luxury.*

Le Capricorne (Hotel Schwarzer Bock, Kranzplatz 12) is the most Old School restaurant in town. One dines in candlelight beneath a coffered, chandelier-hung ceiling. Fare is Franco-German: a delicate shrimp mousse, the chef's own tomato-accented consommé, followed by a tournedos steak or fillet of sole in a champagne sauce. Desserts include Calvados-doused crêpes. *Luxury.*

Die Pfanne (Nassauer Hof Hotel, Kaiser Friedrich-Platz) is for the *plats du jour*—German chicken fricassee, English-style roast beef, Italian veal piccata, fresh raspberries doused with Grand Marnier—in an understatedly handsome environment. *First Class.*

Kurhaus Restaurant is the principal dining room, described earlier, of the Kurhaus complex. Views are agreeable, the crowd dressy in the evening, and the menu standard international. The same building's *Weinhaus Café* is cozier, less costly.

Café Blum (Hotel Blum, Wilhelmstrasse 44) is the see-and-be-seen rendezvous, and has been for a long, long time. Go for coffee, pastry, a snack, or more substantial fare if it's time for a full meal. *Moderate.*

Mutter Engel (Bärenstrasse 5) is a century-old restaurant with a lengthy menu—German, French, and international in scope—and daily specials. *First Class/Luxury.*

Alt Prag (Taunusstrasse 41) is for Czech specialties—the varied appetizers that are the pride of the Bohemian cuisine, and heavier entrées—including the regulation roast pork and dumplings. Imported Pilsen beer. *First Class.*

Mövenpick (Sonnenbergerstrasse 2) is a link in the commendable Swiss-operated chain that operates throughout Germany. *Moderate/First Class.*

Lanterna (Westendstrasse 3), whose owner is also the chef, is one of a number of hearty Italian restaurants, and has well-sauced pastas and veal specialties. *Moderate.*

SOUND OF MUSIC

The Hesse state opera and ballet companies are top-rank, and if either is performing in the Hessisches Staatstheater, be sure to go. Nor should a concert of the city's symphony in the hall of the Kurhaus be missed. Pop fare is to be found in the auditorium of Rhein-Halle, the convention center.

INCIDENTAL INTELLIGENCE

Wiesbaden is less than an hour's drive from Frankfurt International Airport; buses make the run between the airport and Webergasse terminal in Wiesbaden. Base yourself in Wiesbaden to see both that city and Mainz; there is frequent, 20-minute train service over the Rhine, linking the two cities. Or take in Wiesbaden during your stay in Mainz. *Further information:* Kurbetriebe der Landeshauptstadt Wiesbaden—the city tourist bureau—has its main office in the Kurhaus, branches in the Brunnenkolonnade of the Kurhaus, and at the Bahnhof.

40

Würzburg

What the Prince-Bishops Wrought

BACKGROUND BRIEFING

The wonder of Würzburg is its lack of celebrity—celebrity, that is, on the contemporary tourism scene. Oh, pilgrims on the German Romantic Road itinerary make a too-short stop, and there are, of course, other visitors. But today's Würzburg is given shorter shrift than it merits.

It was not always so. In its heyday—the eighteenth century—there was, of course, no international tourism movement if one excepted the aristocratic Englishmen making tediously slow Grand Tours of the Continent in the tow of their private tutors. But Würzburg, in those golden decades, had a constant stream of visitors: artists, artisans, and architects, from points as distant as Vienna, Genoa, and Paris—and the noble and royal patrons whose palaces their work embellished—come to contribute expertise in the construction, decoration, furnishing, and landscaping of a palace that was to become one of the most spectacular on a continent of spectacular palaces.

Despite near-destruction in World War II, that palace—the residence of a succession of Catholic priests who, as prince-bishops, ruled Würzburg—is once again a monument to the rococo genius for synthesizing the fine and applied arts, with grace, wit, and, most of all, especially in Würzberg's case, ebullience.

The participation of clergy in secular as well as spiritual rule, though hardly unique to Würzburg, came about there as a consequence of a much earlier event: the designation, in the eighth century, of this onetime Celtic-settled village as the seat of a bishop. Within a couple of centuries, the Würzburg bishops, replacing the earlier dukes of Franconia, began to wield power as temporal rulers of territory expanded way beyond the confines of the city. They became prince-bishops of the Holy Roman Empire.

The combination of commerce and the cloth proved heady for Würzburg. The city was on a major north-south land route and benefitted from river traffic, as well. Würzburg became rich even before the Renaissance, with still visitable status symbols: a fortress castle atop an eminence at the river's edge, an originally Romanesque cathedral, and a later Gothic church of special beauty.

The baroque era of the Counter Reformation brought building fever to Würzburg as it did to the Continent. Würzburg developed its university and its hospital. But the great leap to fame came in the early eighteenth century as baroque gave way to rococo. A rotund and luxury-loving prince-bishop—Johann Phillip Franz von Schönborn—concluded that the time was ripe for a move downtown from official digs high above the city in the medieval fortress of Marienberg. Prince-Bishop von Schönborn hired a young local architect whose work he had admired to come up with plans. Balthasar Neumann's Residenz—which by the time it was nearly completed in 1774 had become a multinational design project—became an all-Europe showplace. Holy Roman Emperors made it a stop (its sumptuous Kaisersaal was designed for their enjoyment) en route to coronations in Frankfurt. And crowned heads occupied its guest rooms on state visits to the prince-bishops.

Later, as the early decades of the nineteenth century saw Würzburg—like so many of the southern German states—pass to Bavarian control, kings of Bavaria came as temporary residents. The post-World War II years saw an almost miraculous rebuilding on a frame that bombs had only partially damaged. If it is true—to paraphrase the saying about Egypt and the Nile—that Würzburg is the Residenz and the Residenz is Würzburg, it is equally true that the rich cultural heritage of the city extends beyond the palace and its garden. Savor it.

ON SCENE

Lay of the Land: With one major exception—Marienberg Fortress—the visitor's Würzburg embraces that portion of the city on the east bank of the Main, over which there are a trio of bridges, Friedensbrücke, Alte Mainbrücke (an originally Renaissance antique that's still going strong), and Ludwigsbrücke. The Hauptbahnhof is at the northern edge of the core of town. From it, Kaiserstrasse leads due south, crossing Juliuspromenade, to Schönbornstrasse, the lively pedestrians-only main shopping street, and its adjunct, Marktplatz.

Marktplatz is the heart of town. A trio of major churches—Dom, Neumünster, Marienkappelle—are clustered here. By taking Hofstrasse to the east, one comes upon the Residenz and the Hofgarten—its park. The ancient hospital complex, Juliusspital, and the Stadttheater, Würzburg's opera house, are just north of the Residenz on Theaterstrasse. Look up as you walk about; Würzburg façades can be notable—gables and towers of the original university complex, on Neubaustrasse; mixtures of periods that come together in the Rathaus; the stucco decoration of Haus zum Falken, a onetime inn on Schönbornstrasse at Marktplatz; and—on the river side of Marktplatz—the cluster of mellow houses on Carmelitenstrasse.

Residenz (Residenzplatz): First, before you go in, here are a few names you'll want to associate with this eighteenth-century palace of Würzburg's prince-bishops. The prince-bishop whose idea it was, Johann Phillip Franz von Schönborn, was one of a number of von Schönborns to hold the office. He didn't live to see the palace finished, but gets credit for its start and for selecting young Balthasar Neumann as its principal architect. Neumann—a favorite not only of his patron but of the elector of Mainz (whose Residenz, alas, no longer exists)—was forced to collaborate with foreign architects (French, Viennese, Italian) who had powerful clients. And the frescoes—in and of themselves reason for a Würzburg visit—were by the senior of the great Venetian Tiepolos, Gianbattista, with the collaboration of Giandomenico, his older son, and still another son, 14-year-old Lorenzo.

Look sharp, in the Residenz, from the moment you enter. The vaulted vestibule, though but a taste of what is to follow, is not to be ignored, with stuccowork by an Italian, Bossi, and marble busts in their own niches. Then note the gorgeous ceiling fresco in the Gartensaal. You're then partially prepared for what follows: the Treppenhaus, or staircase, a mix of Neumann's architecture coupled with a ravishing Tiepolo ceiling depicting the continents (notice, especially, the portion devoted to America).

The same team did the second-floor Kaisersaal, or Emperor's Chamber, with its splendid Neumann scale, and Bossi stuccowork framing a trio of Tiepolo frescoes. Another chamber, the Weissersaal, or white room—a cool monochrome of Bossi stucco designs—lies between the vivid Tiepolo color of the stairway and the Kaisersaal. But there is more—two wings of smaller, no less lovely rooms—throne room, audience chambers, salons, bedrooms, the lot, with museum-caliber rococo furniture, accessories, paintings, and tapestries.

The Residenz's south wing houses the University of Würzburg's Wagner Museum of classical Greek pottery, paintings, and sculpture. But you're not finished yet. Return to Residenzplatz. Then, before leaving the palace's cobbled courtyard, turn right to the Hofkirche. This is the palace's chapel: ecclesiastical rococo, with still more Tiepolos (the paintings on the side altars), and still more Bossi (stuccowork throughout), all in a gem-like oblong of a room, its walls lined with Corinthian columns that support a multidomed ceiling.

Marienberg Fortress and ***the Main-Franconian Museum:*** Across-the-Main Marienberg is visited for two reasons. First, the fortifications—ramparts, bastions, ruins of bits and pieces of the castle that had been home to the prince-bishops from the thirteenth to the eighteenth century. And second, the views—spectacular vistas of the river and the city from the bastions and from the terrace of a restaurant, which I will mention later. Walking tour completed, head for that building of the complex that had for centuries been its arsenal. It's now the Main-Franconian Museum, one of the very best in Germany, famous as much for the collections as for their evocative setting.

The museum is as good a place as any in town to become acquainted with the work of a late medieval (or early Renaissance, if you prefer) Würzburg sculptor named Tilman Riemenschneider. You see his deeply moving sculpture—mostly of wood and with religious themes—in churches and museums all over Germany. Würzburg, Riemenschneider's home, is especially rich in his work. The museum has an entire gallery devoted to him. Most memorable of the half a hundred pieces is the *Doppelmadonna*—a carved-wood medallion suspended from the ceiling with a likeness of the Madonna on both sides. There are, as well, a striking *St. John the Evangelist,* a luminous *Virgin and Child,* a handsome *Adam and Eve.*

To see, as well: paintings by Cranach and the Tiepolos, père et fils; rooms decorated and furnished in styles of various periods, especially the eighteenth century; a priceless cache of porcelain, rifles, and pistols; folk art that includes clothes, toys, needlework, even a *Weinstube* of centuries past; and a hall of immense antique winepresses used to age Franconia's premium white vintages.

Dom (Domstrasse): Würzburg's cathedral started out Romanesque, in the eleventh century, and ended up baroque-rococo, at least within, where the stuccowork of the ceilings is a highlight. As is a tomb carved by Tilman Riemenschneider. The von Schönborn line of prince-bishops (starting with Johann, who hired Neumann to design the Residenz) are buried in a Neumamn-designed chapel.

Neumünster (Schönbornstrasse) is the *Dom's* next door neighbor, and an originally Romanesque, now mostly baroque beauty, with a Riemenschneider *Crucifixion* and *Madonna and Child,* and a tranquil cloister.

Marienkapelle (Marktplatz) is the special joy of the city's principal square—a pure-Gothic treasure that goes back to the fourteenth century when prosperous merchants chipped in for its construction, to show off to the world the wealth of their town. There is a single slim spire and, within, a Riemenschneider tomb of a local worthy, along with the tomb of Balthasar Neumann.

Rathaus (Marktplatz): What you want to see in this atmospheric complex that goes back to the Middle Ages is the Wenzelsaal, an eight-century-old chamber named for Good King Wenceslas, who stopped for a meal in 1397. And there's a restaurant, which I will describe later.

Juliusspital (Juliuspromenade) is a massive baroque-rococo hospital complex. Ask to see the eighteenth-century dispensary—still quite as it was when it was constructed—the gardens, and the *Weinstube* that features vintages from the vineyards owned by the hospital.

Stift Haug (Juliuspromenade) is the name of an Italian-designed baroque church that suffered heavily in World War II, and is now of interest primarily for its altarpiece of the *Crucifixion* rendered by the sixteenth-century Venetian master, Tintoretto.

Bürgerspital (Theaterstrasse) is still another venerable hospital that is today—after considerable post-World War II rebuilding—a home for the aged. It dates to the fourteenth century and is at its best in the art-filled chapel, charming courtyard, and Weinstube—have a glass!

SETTLING IN

Hotel Rebstock (Neubaustrasse 7) deserves a look from without before one enters. The stuccowork embellishing its windows is eighteenth century, and typical of the rococo beauty of the town. Within, this old house is mostly contemporary and one of the best-operated small hotels (there are 81 rooms and suites) in Germany. Bedrooms, with handsome baths, are mostly capacious and comfortable. There is a top-class restaurant, a cozy *Weinstube* for informal meals, a warm-weather terrace-café, and a bar. *Luxury*.

Hotel Amberger (Ludwigstrasse 17) is somewhat smaller and less luxurious than the Rebstock, but with attractive rooms, all with private baths, and a nice location near the Stadttheater and the Residenz. Breakfast only. *First Class.*

Hotel am Markt (Marktplatz 30) is heart-of-the-action, on the principal plaza, with a restaurant-café, spick-and-span accommodations, not all with their own baths. *Moderate.*

Gasthof Russ (Augustinerstrasse/Wolfhartsgasse 1) is a winner; it's intimate, with fewer than 30 inviting rooms, some with bath; good restaurant and location. *Moderate.*

Würzburger Hof (Barbarossaplatz 2) is central, functionally comfortable with nearly 60 rooms, a number containing private baths. Breakfast only. *Moderate.*

DAILY BREAD

Ratskeller (Rathaus, Langasse 1) is all that a proper German town-hall restaurant should be: atmospheric, attractive, with cheery service and hearty fare. To accompany your meal: a selection from the many wines of surrounding Franconian vineyards. Terrace in summer. *First Class.*

Hotel Rebstock Restaurant (Neubaustrasse 7) is Würzburg dining at its grandest; the view is through picture windows to an atrium-garden. The menu is international: have a steak or a veal specialty. Appetizers and desserts are special. Franconian wines galore. *Luxury.*

Hofkellerei (Residenzplatz) has the Residenz as its closest neighbor, a warm-weather terrace with view of the palace, good things to eat—soups, sausages, schnitzels—and Franconian wines. *First Class.*

Bürgerspital Weinstuben (Theaterstrasse 19) is the café of the Bürgerspital. The setting is ancient, the wines commendable, and the food filling and *Moderate.*

Juliusspital Weinstuben (Juliuspromenade 19) is still another wine restaurant in still another hospital complex of old (see above). *Moderate.*

Da Luigi (Neubaustrasse 10) is an across-the-Strasse neighbor of Hotel Rebstock and worth knowing about if it's an authentic pasta lunch or dinner you fancy. Agreeable service. *Moderate/First Class.*

Hotel am Markt Restaurant-Café (Marktplatz 30) is for a snack, a drink, coffee, or a meal; traditional setting, heart of town. *Moderate/First Class.*

SOUND OF MUSIC

Stadttheater (Theaterstrasse) is Würzburg's post-World War II opera house—too ultra-mod for some Würzburger tastes, but with opera, ballet, and plays. And a central situation.

Hochschule für Musik (Rennweg) is the city's music conservatory and many concerts are given in its auditorium.

Mozart Festival: Ever since 1922—World War II years excluded—the Kaisersaal and Weissersaal of the Residenz have been the site of Würzburg's Mozart Festival in June.

INCIDENTAL INTELLIGENCE

Verkehrsamt Würzburg—the town tourist office—has two locations: in its own building in front of the Hauptbahnhof, and in Haus zum Falken, Marktplatz.

Acknowledgments

To research and write a book about as complex and extraordinary a country as Gemany, you need all the help you can get; I've been lucky in this respect. I am especially indebted to Hedy Wuerz who, as public relations director for North America of the German National Tourist Office, has endeared herself (not to mention her country) to the American travel press; to Hedy's colleague, Hermann Krueger, able director of the German National Tourist Office and manager of the German Federal Railroad's principal U.S. office in New York; to Lufthansa's skilled and congenial North America press relations manager, Lucille Hoshabjian; and to Juergen Arnold, the German Federal Railroad's longtime press man for our continent.

I want also to thank the following, alphabetically, for their personal kindness and professional cooperation: Hans Jörg Anderer, Thomas Axmacher, Mimi Baer, Felix and Rosemarie Baumann, Hans Baumann, Aloys H. Bruns, Mary Carroll, Anne-Marie Dieterici, Max Drechsler, Ulrich Ehrhardt, John Fanelli, William Forsythe, Annmarie Goebel, Alan Gould, Patricia Graves, Erika Greiner, Wolfgang Gutjahr, Horst Handl, Ingrid M. Heil, Mary Homi, Kornelius Kirsch, Herbert Koch, Petra Kokez, Nils Kroesen, Marianne Lambruschini, Margot Liebig, Reinhard Linsel, Bernd H. Lucht, Ruth Maron, Detlev Martensen, Ernest Müller, Rudolf W. Münster, Elfriede Naumer, Fred Peelen, Günter Pieplow, Gert Prantner, Marianne Radner, Hans J. Rathje, Cornelia Rieker, Peter A. Rübartsch, Matthias Rühmkorf, Kurt Schade, Richard Schmitz, Bernd Schütz, Wolfgang Schwehr, Bernd Staupendahl, Anne Sweeney, Barbara Theuerkrauf, Jan Vajnorsky, Hans Von Gösseln, Georg Walter, Michael G. Weber, Rosemarie Weidmann, Herbert Winkler, Traudl Wiesinger, and Vicky Weller.

Last, but hardly least, special appreciation to Mark Pattis, vice president/business manager, of the National Textbook Co., parent corporation of Passport Books; to NTC's president, S. William Pattis; to Executive Vice President/Editorial Director Leonard I. Fiddle; and to my skilled and sympathetic editor, Michael Ross; as well as to my agent, Anita Diamant, and her associates, Al Madocs and Robin Rue.

R.S.K.

Index

O

P

R

S